DATE DUE

SEP 1 2 2011	
SEP 1 0 2011	

BRODART, CO.   Cat. No. 23-221-003

Human Rights in the Arab World

Pennsylvania Studies in Human Rights

Bert B. Lockwood, Jr., Series Editor

A complete list of books in the series is available from the publisher.

Human Rights in the Arab World

Independent Voices

Edited by Anthony Chase
and Amr Hamzawy

PENN

University of Pennsylvania Press

Philadelphia

99567 92

Copyright © 2006 University of Pennsylvania Press
All rights reserved
Printed in the United States of America on acid-free paper

10 9 8 7 6 5 4 3 2 1

Published by
University of Pennsylvania Press
Philadelphia, Pennsylvania 19104-4112

Library of Congress Cataloging-in-Publication Data

Human rights in the Arab world : independent voices / edited by Anthony Chase
and Amr Hamzawy.
    p.   cm.   (Pennsylvania studies in human rights)
  ISBN-13: 978-0-8122-3935-5 (cloth : alk. paper)
  ISBN-10: 0-8122-3935-0 (cloth : alk. paper)
  Includes bibliographical references and index.
  1. Human rights—Arab countries.   I. Chase, Anthony.   II. Hamzawy, Amr.
III. Series.
JC599.A65 H86   2006
323.0917'4927—22   2006044701

"convictions are greater enemies of
truth than lies."
—Nietzsche

Contents

Introduction
Human Rights and Agency in the Arab World

Anthony Chase

Since the events of September 11, 2001 the notion of a clash between
the West and the Muslim world has taken increasing hold, both explicitly in bellicose statements from many sides and implicitly in assumptions in academia and the media. Declarations of jihad[1] have been met
by declarations of war against absolute evil, confirming stereotypes of an
essentialist clash. What has been lost in such mobilizations on the basis
of ideological abstractions is precisely what extremists of various stripes
hope will be lost: the articulation from within the Arab (and, more
broadly, Muslim) world of a politic that directly responds to the particulars of economic, political, civil, social, and cultural rights consistently
denied in the region.

Human Rights in the Arab World draws attention to the status of human
rights as a key barometer of the Arab world's political health. How is
human rights' relevance defined by the Arab world's political, social,
and economic context? What are the theoretical considerations that
must be taken into account regarding human rights' implementation or,
more commonly, lack thereof? This is the first English language text to
collect writings of intellectuals at the forefront of debating these key
issues. It is telling—and regrettable—that until now there has not been
an empirical or theoretical focus on those who work within a human
rights framework, or who struggle to understand the historic and contemporary place of human rights in Arab politics. The Arab world's discourse on human rights cumulatively contradicts the assumption by
many—in both the West and the Arab world—that human rights have
little relevance to the region. This assumption accounts, at least in part,
for the relative lack of attention paid to discourse on this subject and has

limited a robust internal, regional, and transnational dialogue around human rights in the region to a very narrow audience.

In the West the conversation often (too often) starts and ends with a discussion of *whether* human rights are relevant to the Arab world. This book shows *how* human rights have had and can have an impact on the region's politics, both in broad terms and regarding issues of acute concern. Thus, both for those who are conversant with Arab politics and those with a more general interest, *Human Rights in the Arab World* fills a glaring need for an English language text that presents the distinct and varied voices of those who think and work on human rights in this region. The contributors are primarily but not exclusively from within the Arab world. As this discussion is not solely internal (indeed, in a globalized world, it could not be), other contributors are from the Arab diaspora, and still others are Europeans or North Americans who are in close touch with human rights currents in the Arab world.

My concern in this introduction is to cover three points. First is to give an overview of the book's goals and the themes which structure its chapters. Second is to describe the politically and economically repressive realities that are the backdrop to the issues the chapters analyze and to argue for the relevance of human rights to structuring the possibility of alternatives. Third is to make a theoretical argument that supports the book's collective repudiation of cultural relativism and conceptualizes the importance of human rights in sustaining a politics based on the agency of peoples in the region. These three points frame the book's subsequent chapters that address more specific human rights issues.

Overview of Goals and Themes

We will be pleased if *Human Rights in the Arab World* accomplishes three goals. First, and most simply, we want to allow readers unmediated access to important writings by a vanguard of thinkers on the place of human rights in the Arab world. What are the different viewpoints on the relevance or irrelevance of human rights to the Arab world's politics, and what are different ways of conceptualizing how rights interact with the particulars of the region's internally differing political, economic, and social contexts? This will give the reader a sense of the diversity of viewpoints engaged in shaping the contours of the Arab world's human rights debate. This is particularly important in a region whose governments have some of the most dismal human rights records in the world and have made a particular effort to repress this diversity and marginalize dissenters as a means maintaining their power.[2] The argument throughout the book, to be clear, is that human rights are on the intellectual and public agenda, not that they dominate it. In expressing theoretical agreement or disagreement, or in expressing anger at violations or defensiveness about accusations of violations, the human rights debate is part of the Arab world's everyday political conversation. It is featured in newspapers, journals, books, and—where given political space—the flourishing of civil society associations that have organized to pressure governments to address human rights.[3]

Second among these goals is to allow for the expression of a range of opinions on controversial issues of regional and global interest. By placing theoretical debates about the relevance of human rights in the difficult context of Arab politics, the dramatic stakes of this discourse are made clear—they are far from the world of theory for the sake of theory. Academic discourse is often criticized for being disconnected from issues central to public intellectual and policy discourse; placing theoretical issues in the context of dynamic current events is one response to this criticism.[4]

The third goal is to give the reader insight on several theoretical issues, beginning with the much-debated question of whether or not human rights—paired with expanding civil society and democracy—represent a structural alternative to the region's currently authoritarian politics. An underlying theoretical question regards the cultural applicability of human rights standards—is there reason to think the Arab world is uniquely different such that rights' standards are irrelevant to it? A second underlying question regards the domestic and regional impact of a regime of international norms—a central concern of both contemporary international relations and human rights scholarship. One of the indicators of such impact is the invocation of the relevance of such norms at the domestic level, and the chapters in this volume either explicitly or implicitly bear directly on this key issue for those who study global politics.

Though often neglected in Western academic and media commentary, voices discussing and debating human rights in the Arab world have an increasingly prominent niche within the Arab world's intellectual life. The chapters are disparate in context and range across countries and historical periods, but each chapter explicitly addresses the relevance of human rights to the political, social, and economic context of the Arab world and, in so doing, rebuts a notion of the irrelevance of human rights to the region's peoples. Beyond this general connecting tissue, the chapters are marked by the specific themes they address, and are thus divided into four inter-connected sections.

The book's first section treats in a theoretical and practical vein the relationship of human rights to Islam. Anthony Chase begins by deconstructing monolithic conceptualizations of both human rights and

Islam, and the notion that they are in a direct interrelationship. This is an argument against privileging Islam such that human rights must be justified in Islamic terms in order to be deemed relevant. In this sense it is critical of both Islamist assertions of an all-defining Islam and liberal Muslim assertions that human rights can and must be justified in Islamic terms. The relevance or irrelevance of human rights to the Arab world, to the contrary, is determined in shifting political, social, and economic context—not predetermined by a putatively unchanging cultural context. At the level of practice, Bahey el-Din Hassan's "A Question of Human Rights Ethics: Defending the Islamists" begins by relating the interactions of the author—currently chair of the Cairo Institute for Human Rights Studies—in an Egyptian prison with members of Islamist groups. This neatly exposes both the shared consequences of rejecting Egypt's political status quo, but simultaneously the differing implications of an opposition based on political inclusiveness in relation to one that implies an assertion of ideological superiority. It is clear there are no easy choices available to those advancing a human rights agenda, but rather a confusing mixture of ideological and coercive pressures. Hassan goes on to detail the moral and strategic debates that have taken place among Egyptian human rights groups regarding these pressures, debates that get to the heart of the viability of human rights discourse in the region.

If this first pair of chapters give a sense of some of the theoretical and strategic conundrums faced by those advocating rights, the book's second section gives this context by identifying the global context in which the human rights regime has impacted the Arab world. The Universal Declaration of Human Rights (UDHR) affirmation by the members of the United Nations General Assembly (with, notably, the lone abstention of Saudi Arabia among Arab states) in 1948 made rights a global political and legal force. Before that its precedents in all parts of the world were made up of murmurs more than crowning moments. These murmurs, nonetheless, set the stage for the post-World War II impact of the human rights regime. A similar timeline applies in the Arab world, with weak intellectual precedents preceding the UDHR formalization of rights into a discourse with identifiable political impacts in the region.

Amr Hamzawy, author of the first chapter in the globalization section, places this in broad context by examining contemporary intellectual discourse in the Arab world. He does this specifically in regard to globalization and how this has related to the articulation of notions of modernity and authenticity in the Arab world. As Hamzawy argues, this is the fundamental dynamic underlying debates over the place of human rights in the region. Neil Hicks, in a more specific vein, moves into contemporary international relations theory by applying Risse, Ropp, and Sikkink's "spiral model" for explaining the spread of human rights discourse to Egypt. This is useful in that, by putting into global context the status of human rights in a key Arab state, it shows that the strategies used to advance or repress rights are not unique to the region, but rather part of global political processes. Last, Valentine Moghadam's chapter notes how nationalism and Islamism remain the discursive frameworks that most directly contest the idea of human rights. Moghadam remarks on this in regard to equal citizenship rights for women, but it is a framework applicable to virtually all subject areas the book covers and, thus, its theoretical framework is particularly useful.

The book's third section includes three chapters that delve directly into current challenges facing the Arab human rights movement, in both an empirical and a theoretical sense. Empirically, Hanny Megally details a strategy for advancing rights in the Arab world, albeit one that is decidedly pessimistic in that he is fully aware of how deeply embedded are structures of power that resist human rights implementation. Nicola Pratt takes a more explicitly theoretical perspective in regard to the on-the-ground challenges facing human rights in the Arab world, specifically, reasons for the suspicion that often greets human rights discourse. Eyad El Sarraj—head of the Gaza Community Mental Health Programme—articulates, on the other hand, both the hope and the hopelessness of those struggling for rights against the corrupt patriarchs of the Arab world. El Sarraj's surreal experiences when imprisoned by Yasser Arafat (one of several times El Sarraj was imprisoned by Arafat, though Arafat alternated this with offers of high government positions) highlight the absurdities of the patrimonial systems of governance that predominate in the Arab world.

The book's final section focuses on country-specific case studies. These cases are both historical, in regard to Yemen, and contemporary, in regard to Egypt and Morocco. They attempt to move beyond the countries and topics on which there is most commonly a focus in media and academic writing. Sheila Carapico's micro-study identifies in the context of Yemen some of the ideological diversity that characterizes the Arab world, and how monolithic portrayals of its intellectual currents risk being caricatures unless they recognize this diversity, including currents advancing a rights agenda. In the context of twentieth-century intellectual history, Carapico traces Yemen's diversity of ideological expression, projection of political alternatives, human rights confrontations with nationalisms, and the importance of transnational connections. It is from these precedents that one can talk about the development of a distinctly Arab engagement with international human rights, as well as an engagement within the divergent histories of different locales in the Arab world, such as Yemen.

In a more contemporary vein, Tamir Moustafa and Susan Waltz and Lindsay Benstead explore human rights "moments" in Egypt and Morocco, respectively. Both demonstrate the possibilities of human rights. Moustafa details how the Egyptian Supreme Constitutional Court aggressively moved to integrate human rights into its decision-making, and how the Egyptian government has contested this movement once it threatened to seriously constrain its authority. Waltz and Benstead's more optimistic take on Morocco's human rights movement sees its successes as part of a dynamic in which both domestic and transnational pressures—from allies, nongovernmental organizations, and international organizations—played the central role. This contrasts with the Egyptian high court's experience in that, as they say, the "time will be ripe" for human rights only when there is a broader political and social basis for its advancement, rather than the activism of a single actor.

In his concluding discussion of the book's contributions, Amr Hamzawy returns us to contemporary intellectual discourse in the Arab world. He affirms the contested nature of rights discourse in the region, but simultaneously its continued resonance as structuring an alternative to current realities. The vibrancy of this alternative vision is reflected in the book's appendices, which provide the reader with a number of reference documents that have emerged out of the global and Arab human rights movement.

Current Realities and Human Rights Alternatives

Common images of the Arab world coalesce around issues of extraordinary global impact. The most omnipresent image is of terror groups, as currently epitomized by al-Qaida and the events of 9/11. Equally appalling is the documentation of genocide(s) in Iraq and, among the more recent reports out of Saddam's former killing fields, mass graves filled with children buried alive.[5] Of continuing significance are Gulf Wars I, II, and III[6]—the last leaving in place a chaos in which one can find both optimistic and pessimistic portents. And seemingly eternal is the endless Palestinian and Israeli bloodletting, continued Palestinian dispossession, and aborted peace plans.

Behind these headline snapshots lies a drearily authoritarian landscape. The Arab world's regimes give common levels of corruption and repression in other parts of the world a good name. Virtually all independent human rights monitors list the Arab world as among the globe's worst violators of human rights. Over the last thirty years, notes one, "there is only one region of the world where the average level of freedom has declined . . . the Middle East"—with the Arab world having the least freedom within the Middle East.[7] While two-thirds of former communist states have some measure of freedom and democracy, as do most Latin American states, one-half of Asian states, and two-fifths of African states, there are no democracies in the Arab world.

At best, one can hopefully note the region's democratizing experiments in Bahrain and Yemen. Even in countries with irregular elections, however, the lack of institutionalized representative structures and a sustained commitment to the rule of law and human rights substantially depletes such elections of meaning. The region's catalog of rights violations range from the most brutal—including torture, extra-judicial disappearances, and genocide—to the most systemic—including structural discrimination in the political, economic, social, and cultural status of non-Arab ethnic minorities, religious minorities, and women whether of those minorities or not. In short, political and economic rights violations are the regional norm, not the exception.

Scholars and practitioners have linked human rights implementation to equitable economic development.[8] Hence it is not surprising that with a failure to implement such rights the Arab world has simultaneously experienced what can best be termed a proactive process of economic underdevelopment.[9] Human rights relevance is here understood, therefore, as including economic, social, and cultural as well as political and civil rights. It is only when these various categories of rights are understood as mutually constitutive that they can be conceptualized in a manner that recognizes the context for rights violations and the range of issues that must be addressed if rights are to be implemented. The region has lost the comparative advantages it held coming out of the colonial era in measures of human development relative to both Asia and Latin America, a corollary to its relatively low levels of political and economic rights implementation compared to those regions. Instead of economic empowerment, regimes fearful of their own people have used centralization of economic resources as a tool of power—doling out economic favors to buy political support, compromise civil society independence, and punish opponents. There is no commitment to establishing rights to nondiscrimination, education, health, and political liberties as a method of sustaining equitable economic development within the region.[10] Overall economic levels have been stagnant, therefore, as people have not been politically or economically empowered, but rather objects of political repression and economic dependence.

Inattention to political and economic development is counterbalanced by Arab regimes' overdevelopment of external and internal security apparatuses. The region has the world's highest percentage of GDP devoted to military spending, resulting in armies and militias well stocked with arms by which to terrorize local populations. Especially ominous, however, have been the omnipresent *mukhabarat* in the service of so-called *gomalikiyya*, two terms fundamental to contemporary Arab political lexicon. *Mukhabarat* signifies intrusive and often overlapping internal intelligence services. They help maintain in power regimes which Saad Eddin Ibrahim famously dubbed *gomalikiyya*—a neologism combining the Arabic words for "republic" and "monarchy" (as in "repubarchies"). Ibrahim, whose case is examined as part of Tamir Moustafa's chapter on the Egyptian judiciary, aptly summarizes with the term *gomalikiyya* the evolution of the Arab world's post-revolutionary republics into family- and clan-run empires.[11] Whether formal monarchies as in the Gulf, Morocco, and Jordan, or formal republics as in Syria, Egypt, and Yemen, sons are groomed to take power from their fathers, and political structures are a patriarchal, family affair.

Last, completing this picture, there are the Islamist religious nationalist movements. There are variations among and within Islamist movements, and simply making reference to Islam as part of a platform does not make a party Islamic nationalist. Turkey's Justice and Development party, for example, is more akin to a European Christian Democratic party than the Islamist nationalist movement. The true Islamist nationalist movements—i.e., those that believe societies can be ruled via a supposedly "literal" (a contested construct, in practice) application of God's eternal law—also vary in moderation and radicalism, and in any case should not be conflated with Islam as a historical, religious experience. As a generality, Islamist movements both inside and outside the Arab world have served the convenient role of demonstrating that, in fact, things can get even worse than currently dismal realities.[12] Both in opposition (in Algeria, for example) and in power (in Afghanistan or the Sudan, for example), Islamic nationalists have shown zealous enthusiasm for exacerbating already poor human rights situations by an absolutist demonization of their opponents, treating controversial speech and dissent as blasphemous activity to be punished by the state, conceptualizing the Muslim world's historic pluralism and heterogeneity as a threat, and institutionalizing discriminations based on ethnicity and gender.

These are current realities, and they are not easy. Telescoping on these images means ignoring complexities and differentiations within the Arab world's political and cultural life. But while insisting on acknowledging a richer reality behind these images, the fact is that these images are also a fair representation of the contemporary Arab political landscape and cannot be avoided in serious analyses of the region. Too often, however, such avoidance has been the case in intellectual work that has seen political and economic rights violations as a troublesome footnote rather than as an essential issue regarding the region's governance and sustainable political, economic, and cultural life.

The pathologies of the contemporary Arab political system—from al-Qaida and Islamist politics to the corrupt repressiveness of secular Arab nationalist and monarchist regimes—flow out of a lack of political, economic, and cultural freedoms and rights. This flourished in a climate in which systematic violations of human rights became a political norm. This climate was bred, in turn, by the ill-effects of colonial structures of power and autocratic republican and monarchical rule and enabled by the acquiescence of superpower patrons, international and regional organizations, domestic institutions, and intellectual elites. Civil societies have often been coopted into the system via patrimonial handouts or had attention diverted toward external threats. Organizations and individuals that have mobilized in opposition to the region's dominant power structures and ideological formations (in power or in opposition) have, at best, been rhetorically tarnished as political or cultural traitors or, at worst, brutally repressed. The exclusionary power of these structures and ideologies have been and remain a threat to human rights in the Arab world. Focusing on a participatory politics that articulates tangible responses to the rights violations at the heart of these claims is part of a long-term answer to ideological mobilizations that maintain current structures of power.

Both outside powers and transnational intellectual elites have played a particular role in sustaining the region's status quo. Superpowers like the United States, bilateral allies like France, and international and regional organizations have remained committed to a "realist" notion of stability rather than democracy and rights. This has led them to overlook or, at best, only weakly challenge regimes that ideologically demonize and physically marginalize opposition. This investment in stability, as well as regime self-interest in preserving their hold on power by any means necessary, may paradoxically be the ultimate source of the instability that has spilled out of the region. Political repression and gross economic inequalities create the frustration that characterizes popular sentiment. A lack of avenues for meaningful political participation toward internal reform creates the ideological context for valorizing the most extreme forms of opposition as the only viable path toward change. Thus, while the region has indeed been quite stable in a superficial manner, the rights violations that sustained regime stability have been the source of radical opposition to the domestic, regional, and global status quo, making the region's politics a flashpoint for the spread of transnational violence and instability.

Repressive norms are so long-standing and challenges so feeble that many dismiss the idea that human rights are a relevant discourse in the

Arab world and despair of the possibility of an alternative. They believe the political culture of the Arab world is irremediably dictatorial, a sort of pick-your-poison menu of repression. This pessimism is not entirely unfounded, as there is a combination of repressive structures and ideological nihilism at the heart of the region's current political formations. Islamist or secular, monarchical or republican, modes of sustaining power in the Arab world are akin in their patrimonial foundations and repressive results.[13] Similarly, modes of ideologically legitimizing structures of power—from official nationalisms to oppositional Islamism—share a nihilistic foundation no matter their other differences. They have come to be defined by absolutist opposition to an Other (non-Muslim or non-Sunni; Zionist; American; non-Arab such as Kurdish or Persian; etc.). This is sometimes supported, at an extreme, by the totalitarian notion that purified of outside influence a utopia will emerge, and hence domination of governmental authority as well as civil society is a necessity if the Other is to be kept from infiltrating.

This oppositionally defined ideology is bereft of a positive, tangible vision of a political society that can emerge out of the participatory efforts of its citizens and is, therefore, nihilistic. This nihilism is demonstrated in the extremes of violence used to accomplish goals of either the most narrow or most abstract sort. Attempts to atomize societies in favor of personal power or ideological absolutes thrive on incapacitating the possibility of imagining an alternative to current political options. The possibilities become either an acquiescence to a status quo or a flight to utopian fantasies which are as much of an escape from reality as resigned submission.

This leaves the crucial question of whether there are alternatives in the Arab world and, if so, how they might be given the political space to emerge. A search that has been too often overlooked or even derided is one that seeks options that would advance the political and economic rights of peoples within the Arab world and a pluralist political culture accepting of the region's heterogeneity. This search also responds to the geopolitical concern with the radical sectarian violence flowing out of the Arab world. Stability accomplished through maintenance of strong regimes in power is not a viable response to this violence. Rather, change in political and ideological structures that allow alternatives to flower is imperative if the roots of instability are to be addressed and if the energies of the Arab world are to be directed toward genuine economic and political development rather than flow into nihilistic violence.[14]

But what are these alternatives? There are clearly none that are readily available or pre-packaged or can be imposed from the outside. Alternatives must emerge from within, but, as we have seen, political and ideological structures are such that it is difficult for this to occur—and a military imposition from the outside is, obviously, ill-suited for what is fundamentally an internal process. Yet, despite this, as this volume hopes to highlight, there have been voices working from within the region's monolithic authoritarianisms to develop alternatives that respond to the political, social, and economic demands of its populations. And so it must be. The construction of an alternative to the dominant paradigms of the Arab world's politics can only occur indigenously.

"Indigenous," however, should not be understood in a naïve, romantic manner. Amr Hamzawy's conclusion gives some sense of the dynamism of current intellectual debates in the Arab world. Hamzawy both gives intellectual context for other chapters which deal more specifically with human rights issues and makes clear that, despite many obstacles, Arab world intellectual discourse continues to exist in a transnational context. This is not new. As Abdou Filali-Ansary notes by reference to the Middle East, "there has been a great effervescence of thought among Muslim intellectuals since the late nineteenth century. One cannot help but be struck by the breadth, intensity, and sustained character of the debates that have been going on within the Muslim world for over a hundred years."[15] The Arab world's political ideas, from secular and religious nationalisms to human rights-based critiques, have always been elaborated in a transnational context in dialogue with global currents; it is not a parochial backwater. It is important to take note of normative shifts that continue to occur in transnational interchange and to conceptualize the Arab world as open to change—given the political space—in response to the demands of its peoples and evolving normative paradigms.

It is this political space that is fundamental. In human rights terms there is the essential principle of rights as a path toward guaranteeing individual and group agency.[16] This is to give space by which societies can use rights—pushed internationally, transnationally, and domestically—to open up their political space to definition from the bottom up by their peoples, implying protection of rights that guarantee political participation (speech, dissent, nondiscrimination, etc.) and economic participation (health, education, nondiscrimination, etc.). These and other rights, in short, allow peoples to be the *subject* defining their political structures, rather than the *object* of structures imposed upon them from above. In this sense, human rights are not an imposed answer and should not be conflated with an ideology, but rather should be understood to provide a structure through which alternatives can emerge from within societies and out of global dialogue and interchange. This is the fundamental appeal of a human rights framework.

Cultural Relativism and Human Agency

The book's theoretical point of departure is the observation that the pertinence of human rights to the Arab world has too often been slighted in both scholarly and media writing due to cultural relativist assumptions. Of course, it is certainly true that human rights issues in the Arab world, such as Palestinian self-determination or the rights of women, have been subjects of controversy, topical attention, and a body of sustained analysis. What this selective focus of attention misses is a century-long intellectual tradition in the Arab world of seriously grappling with the spectrum of human rights, and the rise since the 1980s of an Arab human rights movement that has had a substantial impact on the region's political discourse, albeit not its practices or dominant ideological paradigms.

While human rights-influenced thought has never been a dominant intellectual discourse in the Arab world, it has been an increasingly important trend deserving of more attention than it has received. This trend has accelerated since the Arab world's crushing defeat in 1967 by Israel and the subsequent ideological decline of Arab nationalism. Putting together this collection was stimulated by dual frustrations: frustration at the lack of writings available in English on this subject, particularly by those most engaged with the topic from within the Arab world, and frustration at the lack of scholarly and media recognition of the relevance of this domain to both topical issues and broader intellectual discourse.

Forces committed to sustaining the status quo have been supported in an odd sort of informal alliance with arbiters of intellectual and cultural life. The result is a deemphasis on attention to political and economic development in favor of a focus on international causes and insular ethnic solidarities—just as the regimes in power would hope. Dissident intellectuals critical of this status quo and hopeful of drawing attention to the ill effects of the region's *gomalikiyya* have been derided for breaking solidarity against external enemies or rhetorically tarred as cultural traitors. This normative status quo has been defended by intellectual elites in the Arab world and, to a degree, a Euro-American academia affected by cultural relativist and Sartrean trends that romanticize developing world nationalisms and stigmatize critical attention to its authoritarianisms. There are many specific examples of this, such as Michel Foucault's famous expressions of solidarity with Khomeini's Islamic Revolution in Iran. One is reminded in this context of Jeffrey Isaac's remark that Hannah Arendt was "traumatized by the arrogance and irresponsibility by so many European intellectuals of the right and left in the face of totalitarianism. In her view this irresponsibility was sometimes due to thoughtlessness, sometimes due to arrogance, and sometimes due to the sheer credulity of intellectual rebels without a cause desperate for some privileged attachment to History, Destiny, or *Volk*."[17] These words still ring true in regard to intellectual discourse on the contemporary Arab world.

The contributions to this book belie stereotypes that human rights thinkers in the Arab world are "inauthentic" appendages to a Western ideology, or that non-Arabs working on human rights in the region are imposing an outside agenda. This stereotype is seen, for example, in Cheryl Rubenberg's noting with approval a characterization by Hisham Nazir of NGOs as "vital and integral parts of the [Western] foreign policy establishment," implying political or cultural (or both) treason by Arabs working to advance human rights.[18] To the contrary, this is not a debate between "the West" and "authentic" Arabs over human rights, but rather a debate within Arab societies that takes place in a global context, and one that has Arab and non-Arab participants on both sides of the debate.

Participants in this debate should not have their agency denied them by simplistic stereotypes that equate advocating notions of rights to food or education or not to be tortured to being a Western fellow traveler of sorts.[19] While even specialists in the region often ignore this debate, its implications are dramatic for the region and for all with an interest in the region's politics or with theoretical questions about the salience of international norms in domestic contexts.[20] The essential underlying issue is agency: allowing people within the region the participatory space to debate the relevance of various rights, not a priori to determine for them their relevance or irrelevance. It is agency that is denied by repressive regimes and, perhaps unwittingly, by cultural relativists who implicitly insist that Arabs cannot legitimately debate these issues.

Of course, as pointed out earlier, some rights issues do receive extensive (though not necessarily sufficient) outside attention, specifically, women's issues and the treatment of Palestinians. These issues are vital. The Palestinian issue is a shadow over almost all discussions of human rights in the Arab world, as it is impossible to ignore the scale of the violations that have taken place under Israeli authority. El Sarraj's contribution eloquently articulates the conundrum Palestinian activists face amid international acquiescence to dispossession and the repressive tactics used by Israel, the Palestinian Authority, and Islamists. Women's issues are equally vital, and we hope the chapter by Moghadam will advance that debate, as well.

Nonetheless, without detracting from the importance of these issues, they are neither more nor less important than other issues, and attention to them does not validate disengagement from the broad spectrum of rights issues. This disengagement takes place on two different levels. On one level is the traditional fear of mixing academia with advocacy and, on a second level, a hesitancy to recognize the relevance of human rights discourse to broader issues of historical importance. In regard to the former, Lisa Anderson comments about academics that they "are often afraid of getting involved in human rights. That's particularly true in the Middle East . . . people [say] you shouldn't get involved because you'll never get a visa to country X again."[21] This silencing of academics—even those from outside the Arab world—is troublesome, and shows itself in the general silence of academics on the relevance of human rights to the politics of the Arab world and of human rights discourse to the Arab world's intellectual discourse. This silence is evidenced in such obvious places as indexes of major textbooks dealing with the Arab world that have no reference to human rights,[22] the bare handful of English-language books that deal with human rights as an issue in the Arab world,[23] the paucity of articles in leading political science and Middle East journals dealing with this subject,[24] and scholarly or media stereotypes of an Arab world inimical to human rights.

This stereotype is encapsulated in Rubenberg's fawning review of Nazir's description of human rights as, in her phrase, "a marketing campaign" to further the West's global colonization and attempt to "universalize Western culture." Human rights in this reductionist caricature is accepted in the developing world only by "the blind, complacent, or co-opted."[25] So much for agency or permitting Arabs (or others in the developing world) to participate in defining their own political future. This sort of blanket demonization of human rights activists in the region has little to distinguish it from the rhetoric used by repressive regimes when threatened by intellectual turmoil and political activism. It is, indeed, ironic to think of intellectual-activists such as Eyad El Sarraj, Bahey el-Din Hassan, Saad Eddin Ibrahim, or others emerging from Palestinian or Egyptian prisons only to be smugly dismissed by Western cultural relativists as "co-opted."

What is also ironic is that this marginalization of the Arab world's rights issues remains common at the same time that human rights have become increasingly mainstream in both broader academic and mainstream discourse.[26] Particular attention has been placed in international relations scholarship on how human rights and other international norms have had a transnational impact via international organizations, nongovernmental organizations, and other forms of transnational interaction.[27] Nonetheless, in the academic literature on the Middle East, characterizations such as those by Rubenberg and Nazir remain a constant, as is a refusal to engage in deeper questions regarding the relevance of human rights that, elsewhere, preoccupy the theoretical literature in political science and international relations theory.

Human rights may not be the Arab world's dominant discourse, but the arrogance of dismissing sectors that focus on rights is striking. This lack of attention is a symptom of the persistent notion that rights do not internally resonate in Arab political societies. This notion is deeply troubling in that it reiterates some of the stereotypes that have long bedeviled an understanding of the Arab world. The ingrained idea of an exotic, "Other" Arab-Muslim world—a world different from an imagined Western "us" and supposedly culturally indifferent to the concept of human rights—justifies ignoring the integration of rights issues into Arab world politics in favor of an assumption of some sort of essentialized cultural incompatibility. Given the debate on human rights in many parts of the Arab world, formal governmental recognition of human rights principles (via treaties or conference documents), and the stubborn on-the-ground presence of local human rights groups, such cynicism about the cultural suitability of human rights to the Arab world is faintly ludicrous, if not surreal—the equivalent of an *Alice in Wonderland* discussion of whether something there is really there.

Whether it be in the social, economic, cultural, civil, or political sphere, the discussion in the Muslim-Arab world of the fundamental, precisely delimited goal of human rights—proscribing state violations of the rights of those under their jurisdiction—evidences itself in diverse forms. To deny this is to deny everyday political reality in favor of an abstract, decontextualized theoretical structure, and to deny agency to those confronting the reality of rights violations on a day-to-day basis. That the human rights thinkers in this volume have so often been ignored is testament to the insistence of many on defining from the outside what is legitimate and authentic to Muslim and non-Muslim Arabs, ignoring what they themselves say.

Conclusion

It may be true, despite the fact that human rights advocates do not fit into the media and academic stereotypes of the Arab world, that they have a very real vision of an alternative to current discourses of power, one that must be taken into account in scholarly analyses of Middle East politics. More important, it may be that they are not renegades at all, but rather represent one trend among others in the region's political diversity and its developing possibilities. A minority? Perhaps, but then the Islamists who have had such a degree of attention focused on them are also, quite clearly, a minoritarian phenomenon.

Ideas and theories have an impact on political and social formations, which is why this is an important debate—indeed, both human rights *and* Islamic norms are examples of the impact of transnational movements on domestic politics. Predetermined notions as to Islam's place in predominantly Muslim societies such as those in the Arab world have too often led to analyses that grant little theoretical space for recognizing how these societies can dynamically generate ideologies in response to their own particular political and social circumstance, and not in a religiously or culturally predetermined manner. But while I would argue that it is political circumstances that make human rights relevant to many predominantly Muslim state-societies, including those in the Arab world, I would not downplay the force and vitality of ideas and theory in structuring ideological forms. In an interconnected world, normative intellectual constructs in Arab and Euro-American media and academia have a part in constructing and reinforcing the ideologies deployed in the Arab world. A predisposition toward seeing authoritarianisms as culturally based leads to a marginalization of other political currents. This one-size-fits-all theoretical construct is simplistic and reductive, distorts perceptions of the Arab world, and robs Arabs of agency in defining their politics.

Among the most interesting intellectual and political phenomena in many parts of the formerly colonized world is a movement to reach beyond nationalist identity politics that have been solely defined by negative opposition to an Other, rather than a positive political agenda. Rejecting simplistic oppositions does not mean abandoning a critical stance toward, for example, the brutalities of an Israel or the double standards of a United States. What it does mean, however, is moving beyond such criticism and not allowing it to be an excuse for internal authoritarianisms. Quite often, human rights advocates have been part of this reconsideration of defensive nationalisms, refusing to use other states' violations or hypocrisy as an excuse to divert attention from domestic rights abuses. Human rights are a regime whose relevance depends on the degree to which it resonates with political, social, and economic concerns of diverse societies, and it should be debated on that basis.

When listing many of the pathologies of the Arab world, one fears understating their horror, as is too often done by apologists. On the other hand, one also fears understating the richness of a region with considerable untapped political, economic, and cultural reserves. Amid the rights violations there have been consistent attempts from within the Arab world to forge alternatives. It is a region with a fertile ideological history and a consistently articulated acknowledgment that, indeed, an alternative to current realities is necessary.

This book is an attempt to bring to greater prominence some of the particular critiques that have been generated and voices from within the Arab world that look to human rights as fundamental to constituting and structuring alternatives. The claim here is not that human rights represent some sort of majoritarian political movement in the Muslim world. Indeed, rights are clearly a controversial topic; in any case, as a limited legal tool they cannot fully inform a political movement, but rather only structure a pluralist and participatory field on which grass-roots movements can engage with the political and economic realities of the Arab world. This book's chapters can be neither comprehensive in their coverage nor entirely up-to-date in their references to current events; they do, however, collectively affirm that a diversity of political possibilities exist in the Muslim world, including those which would undergird their push for alternatives on the basis of a commitment to human rights structures. The marginalization of the voices of this diversity in favor of privileging the Arab world's more reactionary trends must be redressed if analysis is to move from its currently rather static assumptions. This book hopes to be a step toward recognizing this diversity, and therefore aims to present voices from a broad range of disciplines and spheres. There is much to learn from setting aside preconceptions and, simply, listening to such voices.

Part I
Human Rights, Islam, Islamists

Chapter 1
The Tail and the Dog: Constructing Islam and Human Rights in Political Context

Anthony Chase

Looming over discussions of human rights in the Muslim world is the question of Islam: is it inherently contradictory to human rights, or somehow reconcilable? Whether it be in old debates on the Muslim world's emerging postcolonial states, ongoing debates in Iran's Islamic Republic, or fresh debates over Iraq's constitutional future, this question is perceived as fundamental. This chapter's argument is that Islam and human rights can be constructed as oppositional or supportive, but they are not inevitably one or the other, and conceptualizing them as necessarily in a direct relationship to each other is, in fact, an abstract diversion from the real issues defining human rights. In other words, Islam and human rights as a binary relationship must be problematized if debate is to move beyond a simplistic opposition between Islam and human rights or an equally misleading conflation (based on similar assumptions) that sees Islam as inherently supportive of human rights. It is political, social, and economic context that explains the status of human rights, for better or for worse; Islam is neither responsible for rights violations nor the core basis for advancing rights.

Focusing on the context in which Islam and human rights interrelation—or lack thereof—is constructed moves away from essentialized notions of how they inevitably conflict or correspond and toward a historically informed recognition of the variability in Islam's relationship to human rights and, more broadly, the public sphere. Human rights will only be advanced when debate focuses on their political, economic, and social aptness, rather than irrelevant theological justifications that are abstracted from contemporary context. It is, in short, the underlying politics that explain current realities and their alternatives, not an Islamic metanarrative.

Those who see Islam as oppositional or as supportive to human rights are privileging a theoretically distorted metanarrative at the expense of on-the-ground political dynamics. The shared theoretical assumption is that Islam is a defining discourse in the Muslim world and that human rights is a direct challenge to that discourse, therefore, rights either conflict or must be reconciled by being constructed as definable via an Islamic discourse. In terms of the latter, by conceding that human rights have to be justified on Islamic terms, nonreligious arguments for human rights are abandoned—even by those who are rights advocates. This retreat returns us to an assumption that secular norms are irrelevant because Islam is all-defining and all-controlling—the pernicious Orientalist stereotype. Therefore, playing on Islamic turf is not only a transparent, losing strategy, as I will argue, but, more dangerously, it also delegitimizes non-Islamic norms in predominantly Muslim societies and implicitly accepts their marginalization. This is critical at a time when Islamists are, similarly, pushing for this same type of marginalization. This push comes despite the fact that the history of Muslim societies and the contemporary existence of diverse political movements in the Muslim world explicitly contradict this project of marginalizing the importance of non-Islamic norms. It is for this reason that asking if Islam and human rights clash or are reconcilable is the wrong question and leads to a theoretical diversion away from the essential questions regarding the foundations of rights violations in the Arab world and the possibilities for advancing greater respect for individual and group rights.

Islamism

The first distinction to make is between Islam and the political project that goes under the name of, variously, Islamism, fundamentalism, political Islam, and/or integralism. In regard to the former, as a social force Islam inevitably has a political impact, just as do other powerful religions such as Christianity, Buddhism, or Judaism. But Islam's history as a discourse predominantly has kept a certain distance from politics and only rarely advanced the Islamist claim to monopolize the public sphere of law, society, and politics. Whether historically or over just the last century, Islam as an evolving and differentiated set of religious beliefs and social practices has a pattern of coexistence with multiple political structures and ideologies. Islamism, however, does indeed have a history of conflict with human rights, and conflating Islam with Islamism is one reason for the misperception that Islam clashes with human rights. Thus, before directly addressing Islam, it is worth taking a moment to address the Islamist political movement that mobilizes constructs of Islam in apparent opposition to human rights.

The record of Islamists shows how distinct—and modern—their construct of Islam is from what has predominated throughout the Muslim world's history. Islamism is a political project defined by assumptions that have often contradicted the human rights regime's foundation in nondiscrimination, toleration, and human agency (as a generality, Islamism, too, has its variations). Empirically, this contradiction has become apparent when Islamists have taken state authority. The Sudan, for example, has had the Arab world's only Islamist regime and, as with Islamist regimes in Iran and Afghanistan, the results were starkly contrary to democracy and human rights. Power was seized in the Sudan in collaboration with leaders of a military coup and maintained thereafter by nondemocratic means. Repression against non-Arab-Muslim minorities included a bloody, genocidal campaign against African animists and Christians in the south. Dissent has met with retribution, including death or asylum for many—such as, for example, the hanging of liberal Islamic reformer Mahmoud Taha. This repression of democracy, minorities, and dissenters has exact parallels in the practice of Islamist regimes outside the Arab world—Taliban Afghanistan and Iran's Islamic Republic being notable examples of precisely this same pattern of flagrant abuses.

In opposition, as well, Islamists have had a markedly negative effect on human rights in the Muslim world. In particular, in the Arab world they have frightened, intimidated, and physically attacked public figures who dare to critically engage in the civic sphere of culture or politics. In Egypt, for example, a revered literary figure such as Naguib Mahfouz and an imaginative scholar such as Nasr Hamid Abu Zeid have both been subject to physical and legal attacks that have had the broader effect of chilling the general intellectual environment in both the country and the region. This is not to mention, of course, more egregious acts of terror—transnationally by an al-Qaida, or domestically by groups such as Egypt's Islamic Jihad.

This pattern of repressive practice does not flow out of Islam but out of the theoretical foundations of religious nationalist ideologies—be they putatively based in Islam or in the power of some other set of religious symbols. The identification of power with a religious ethnic group and, within that ethnic group, with a privileged elite with access to defining God's law is inherently antidemocratic and impels violations of human rights, including the repression of minorities, dissidents, and democracy.[1] Regimes that ideologically legitimize rule based on exclusivist religious identity cannot tolerate affirmations of equality of other ethnic communities, as evidenced by the status of Muslims in BJP

(Hindu nationalist) India, Palestinians in Israel, or non-Muslim minorities in the Sudan, Iran, and Afghanistan. "Outside" groups may be more or less tolerated but, by definition, if national identity is made coterminous with a particular religious identity, nonmembers are not full citizens. This is the conundrum of nationalist politics in general, one that is exacerbated when the national community is defined in inherently exclusivist and emotively powerful religious terms.

This is even more problematic in cases where the ideological justification for rule moves beyond religious identity to the Islamist project of applying a literalist construction of that religion's sacred texts as temporal law. In this case, rule according to sacred texts means that even within the privileged community dissent is not easily tolerated. Such dissent contradicts not just a political position but a position that constructs itself as representing a transcendental truth. A religious nationalist ideology such as Islamism inherently implies violations of human rights by theoretically defining its hold on power as justified by religious identity and faithfulness to a literalist interpretation of religious texts. It rules according to an elite's construction of eternal truth, not a participatory democratic process; minorities are implicitly disenfranchised as foreign to the dominant cultural community; and dissent is a challenge to religious dogma rather than merely a competing policy preference and is therefore intolerable. This theoretical opposition has been evident in Islamism's practice both in opposition and in power.

Islam, Liberal Islam, and Human Rights

This is not to imply that human rights are incompatible with Islam or Muslim societies. While acknowledging that Islamist religious nationalism is problematic for human rights—both empirically and theoretically—this must be kept distinct from an argument that Islam is incompatible with rights. More broadly, it should be kept distinct from the temptation to conceptualize Islam and human rights as being in a direct relationship.

Scholarly activity starts with posing the right questions. Asking if Islam and human rights either clash or are reconcilable implicitly makes the profound assumption that these two normative systems are jousting opponents. This is, in my view, the wrong question and leads to skewed and unproductive analysis by prompting many observers to conceptualize Islam and human rights in a competitive dichotomy. Islam is often seen as controlling the content of politics and law in the Muslim world—the core Orientalist and Islamist assertion—while human rights tends to be inflated in terms of ambition and impact, and to be seen as blocked or in need of reconciliation because it is contradicted by an all-defining

Islamic monolith. Disentangling Islam and human rights from intellectual conceptions and political ideologies that simplify them into competing dichotomies is essential to understanding their interrelation. Just as a cultural system's dynamism ensures that it does not a priori delineate and define acceptable constructs of law and politics, Islam does not place a box around the political-legal possibilities that exist in Muslim societies. It is imperative not to assume intellectual constructs that superimpose such boxes.

One side of this dichotomous debate is epitomized by Jean Baudrillard's statement that "Islam is the quarters of the centered Absolute, the ultimate face of the anti-modern."[2] Islam is here starkly designated the role of opponent to all that an equally undifferentiated modern "West" supposedly represents, including human rights. The portrayal of Islam as fundamentally opposed to human rights depends on this type of essentialist, ethnocentric view of the Muslim world as alien to modernity, and is at the heart of conceptions such as that in Benjamin Barber's *Jihad vs. McWorld* in which Barber directly counterpoises Islamic and human rights norms and portrays them as mutually exclusive.[3] This conception leaves Muslims—ignoring what they might say themselves—voiceless and alone to suffer the oppressions of their governments. They are theoretically unconcerned with international standards regarding issues such as the right not to be tortured or not to be denied the opportunity to work, or the right to education or self-determination—all issues prominently featured, in fact, by populist and human rights groups in the Arab world that have sought to integrate these international norms into domestic practice. This sort of rhetorical caricature of the relationship of Islam and the international human rights regime as a simple clash sets up a false opposition that is destructive to understanding their political dynamics, which are shaded with far more subtlety and variety than these harsh oppositions allow.

Fuad Zakariya summarizes a common response by those critical of viewing Islam as a clashing monolith by saying, simply, that "Islam is what Muslims make of it."[4] This critical response (cited here in the grossest possible shorthand, of course) emphasizing the constructedness of Islam is undoubtedly more theoretically sophisticated than Baudrillard's or Barber's opposition between Islam and the modern world,[5] and is the bedrock position of many who argue that Islam can be reconciled with human rights norms. What Muslims make of Islam is, indeed, quite changeable, but that does not mean Islam is so malleable that it can always be reconciled to other normative structures. Nor does it mean that Islam *needs* to be malleable in order for Muslim societies to accommodate norms from non-Muslim sources. Islam does not need to be malleable in this manner because it is not necessarily an obstacle directly counterpoised to human rights, thwarting their implementation and surmountable only by remaking Islam in a human rights-friendly manner. This conception of Islam and human rights as direct counterparts is the basic theoretical framework which, despite their different conclusions, a Zakariya shares with a Baudrillard or Barber. This common theoretical premise is troubling in its privileging of a monolithic conception of Islam's political role.

Many liberal Islamic reformers work within this same framework. In terms of human rights, this premise results in arguments that rights can only resonate in the Muslim world by being reconciled with Islam and advanced in religious, culturally appropriate language. For example, perhaps the best known and most sophisticated reformer of Islamic law in the United States is Abdullahi an-Naʿim. Many of An-Naʿim's premises are akin to those of other liberal Islamic reformers, but he works specifically within a human rights framework, attempting to reconcile it to Islam. It is fair to say that An-Naʿim is among those who have most contributed to breaking down stereotypes of Islam and highlighting its historic diversity and textual openness. Nonetheless, there is one element of his early writings that epitomizes a liberal Islam trope that, I would argue, is contradictory to his aims. An-Naʿim argues that human rights will only be applied in the Muslim world if rights are made to coalesce with Islamic public law (his term for a reformed shariʿa), as shariʿa-based law is the only legitimate form of law to Muslims. This seems to implicitly accept a vision of the Muslim world as governed by religion. An-Naim surmises that public law "will have to be Islamized in recognition of the Muslim right to self-determination." An-Naʿim's reform project is entirely informed by and committed to international human rights, but he accepts the axiom of the centrality of Islamic edicts to Muslim political life—that is, that there is no other comparably legitimate form of political or legal discourse in the Muslim world. While An-Naʿim is critical of any notion that Islam and human rights clash, he accepts their juxtaposition and that human rights can only be implemented via an Islamic channel. Thus the necessity that his envisaged "version of public law would be as Islamic as shariʿa has ever been because it will draw on the same basic sources of Islam from which the relevant principles of shariʿa were constructed by the early jurists."[6] This radical reform is done in an Islamic context because, in An-Naʿim's words, "unless such challenges and modifications have religious legitimacy, they are unlikely to change Muslim attitudes and practice."[7]

An-Naʿim does assert the ability to reread Islamic law in terms of historical circumstance and it is, of course, his aim to reform shariʿa. With this privileging of Islam and insisting it must be the basis of all political constructs, however, the question remains whether this does not implicitly reaffirm the same basic paradigm as Islamists and Orientalists: that Islam defines the Muslim world's politics and that Islam and human rights are competing and in need of reconciliation if rights are to be implemented. Islam is a determining monolith in *both* conceptions, albeit a more flexible monolith in the liberal version. Even in the liberal version, however, if Muslims hope to advance human rights, they need to construct an Islam that can be rights' vessel: it is this that is problematic.[8]

One need not deny the importance of Islam in the Muslim world to also point out how this can lead to reductionist conclusions. It is not reductionist because Islam is unimportant; indeed, Islam plays a prominent role in many Muslim societies. It is reductionist because, contrary to an assertion "of the interdependence between [Islam and human rights],"[9] the respect and protection of human rights is not interdependent with Islam. Is Islam stopping Palestinian self-determination, or impelling torture in Egyptian prisons, genocidal campaigns against Iraqi Kurds and Marsh Arabs, or slavery and forced deprivation of food in the Sudan? Of course not. Most rights violations have no plausible basis for even referring to Islam as a justification. To assume as fundamental the interdependence of human rights and Islam and hence the need for their reconciliation diverts attention from the real causes and solutions to the vast majority of rights violations in the Muslim world. Only rarely are these directly connected to Islam. In this sense, the human rights justified via Islam paradigm is a theoretical excursion that avoids facing the central issue: the political structures that explain most human rights violations.

In short, then, Islam has little relation to human rights—human rights being a legal-political discourse that responds to the power of the modern state, not a religious-spiritual discourse. At the same time, most rights violations have little or no relation to Islam. Even rights violations that are justified by an interpretation of Islam need to be understood in the context of the shifting, constructed nature of Islam and how it interacts with human rights and, more broadly, the public sphere.

In regard to the public sphere in the Muslim world, the shari'a has never been as all-defining as is often assumed. The place of religious norms in the Muslim world's public sphere is historically quite ambiguous, opening space—depending on historical context—for references to human rights. For legal and political structures to change, a change in normative context has often been sufficient. In the course of the twentieth century, for example, a variety of non-Islamic-based ideological trends have been dominant in the Arab world, including variants of Marxism, social democracy, monarchism, and nationalism. While human rights is a very specific legal regime, the language of human

rights can be and is invoked by many ideological trends, Islamic and secular. In the Arab world, for example, its language is commonly used by
liberal secularists. It is also adopted, however, by Islamic liberals and,
with no necessary contradiction, more radical religious nationalist
trends which, it is worth remembering, are often most directly faced
with the sort of arbitrary state repression to which human rights is meant
to respond.

Wild swings in Islam's role in the public sphere have been documented by Nathan Brown. Brown notes that the deemphasis on shari'a-
based law during the first part of the twentieth century occurred with
remarkably little opposition or protest.[10] In fact, it is worth reflecting on
the fact that this process went virtually unremarked at the time. This
points to the importance of political context in defining Islam's impact
and contradicts clichés of state and religious institutions being united in
Islam.[11] Indeed, even in those cases where shari'a-based law is currently
applied beyond a very narrow range, this is done with politicized selectiv-
ity.[12] There is such a bewildering diversity of political movements justified by reference to Islam that it is clear that, although political motifs
and imagery may be Islamicized, there is no defined Islamic basis of
politics. Thus, even in cases where there is an intersection between
Islamic and human rights norms, it is up to Muslim political societies
to negotiate this in terms of their internal political dynamics. The sole
requirement from a human rights perspective is that this be done via
participation and with the consent of concerned individuals and groups,
rather than imposed by the state.[13] Despite the protests of Islamists and
Huntingtonian neo-Orientalists, and the demurrals of liberal Muslim
reformers, there is little evidence that this is problematic for most Muslims—in fact it is the historic norm that the state is not the arbiter of
traditionally decentralized Islamic legal structures.

The most important objection to the reformist methodology is that its
use of Islam is not just a diversion but that it actually undermines rather
than legitimizes human rights norms. It is neither theoretically necessary—as discussed above—nor strategically promising to justify human
rights via Islam. The move from a political to a religious justification
(making rights a "theological question," in An-Na'im's appropriate
phrase[14]) is also likely counterproductive—indeed, I would argue that
its privileging of Islam has already been damaging in distorting discourse on this subject.

It is strategically counterproductive to a human rights project because
liberal Muslim reformers change the paradigm for a consideration of
the relevance of rights. Instead of whether the rights regime makes
sense given the political and legal context of Muslim states, the question
becomes whether or not there are convincing doctrinal arguments

regarding the place of human rights in Islamic law. This accepts, in essence, the need for literalist religious justifications for human rights, making an argument for rights a dispute over religious doctrine—a dispute that takes place on an Islamic field of meaning on which reformers have little claim to institutional authority and human rights scant normative power.

Rights arguments made in Islamic language lack institutional authority, and hence do not resonate as legitimate Islamic interpretations; they are sometimes contradicted by explicit Qur'anic verses and hence are not theologically convincing; and they are often delegitimized by appearing to be deployed strategically as a pragmatic ploy rather than being religiously based and hence lack political weight. Attempting to justify rights via Islam has not been successful and will not be for logical reasons. While there are strong political, social, and legal justifications for human rights in the Muslim world, the religious-theological argument is a losing position for those endowed with neither conclusive doctrinal arguments, nor religious authority. Justifying rights in the language of Islam is usually irrelevant to the core causes of rights violations and is not only a theoretical diversion but an unconvincing one. The arguments for human rights are political, legal, economic, social, and cultural and must be justified on their own terms and on the basis of their relevance to the Muslim-Arab world, not on the basis of a "theological" argument.

Islam, Human Rights, and Sociopolitical Praxis

Human rights and Islam can (and do) coexist, but not in a manner that equates culture with legal rights or Islam with political norms and insists that to be justifiable rights must be Islamicized for the Muslim world. This exclusivist conception runs contrary to everyday political realities. We have already noted the irrelevance of Islam to most rights violations and the political basis of both rights violations and arguments regarding the relevance of rights. For a complementary analogy from a different sphere that illustrates how Islam is not all-defining, one notes the preeminence of non-Islamic economic models in the Muslim world. This is not doctrinally justified by detailed, sophisticated reformist theories in which "Western" and "Islamic" economics are reconciled. To the contrary, it simply flows from trends set in place by economic realities that make no pretense of being Islamic. In fact, it is the "Islamic" economic model pushed by some Islamists that still remains peripheral, even in Islamist states themselves. Coexistence (or, more precisely, the irrelevance of a notion of coexistence) has taken place due to economic and political context, not some sort of theoretical reconciliation. Similarly, in the course of the twentieth century, Muslim family law has fluctuated widely depending on historic context, region, country, locality, custom, and political and social pressures.[15]

An even simpler example can again illustrate the manner in which social, political, and economic circumstances can override even norms embedded in Islamic justifications. The Saudi ban on women drivers has attracted a great deal of attention. Leaving aside the question of whether such a ban is valid in Islamic law, the reality is that it was validated—in a country that claims the Qur'an as its constitution—as a stipulation of Islam.[16] Over the last decade, however, there have been repeated whispers that the ban would be overturned. Among the first of these, for example, was a report that noted "a powerful rumour spawning hopes and fears that women in the conservative kingdom may soon be allowed to drive." And why would such a change be made?

Economic concerns make the move—which would end the need for half a million foreign chauffeurs—credible. . . . With weak oil prices slicing some $15 billion off the income of the world's top producer this year and unemployment put near 20 percent. . . . "The average Saudi family finds it pretty hard to afford a driver," a top diplomat said. "Men often leave work to take kids to the doctor or school."[17]

There have been recurrent renewals of this rumor, though no change has yet been made and, currently, much higher oil prices have reversed the economic dynamic that was pushing movement toward change. Nonetheless, both discussion of this point in Saudi Arabia and, simultaneously, the inconceivability in most Muslim countries of laws banning women from driving concisely affirm two key points: the variability of shari'a interpretation and the manner in which political, social, or economic context can quickly affect such interpretation. A change in Saudi Arabia's driving statute, if it ever comes to pass, would undoubtedly be given some sort of shari'a-based justification, just as was the law's original promulgation. The reason for this law's existence, however, lies in Saudi Arabia's tremendously conservative social structure, which is far more severe than that of most Muslim countries (also explaining why these laws do not exist in other Muslim states), and was reinforced by the defensive political position Saudi authorities found themselves in after allowing the presence of U.S. troops during the Gulf War.[18] If this law is overturned, it will be, again, for non-Islamic reasons—this time economic and technological.[19] In other words, for all the invocation of shari'a, the determining factors have little to do on either side with religious arguments and everything to do with historical context.

Be it in driving laws, economics, family law, or human rights, political, economic, and social context is the primary variable. In regard to human rights, if they are perceived as relevant and necessary, they will consequently become contestants in public debate—indeed, they already have. Arguments to be made regarding rights should be waged around their relevance and aptness. It is this, not elaborate Islamic justifications, that will or will not lead to greater integration of human rights norms into the Arab world's politics. As Reza Afshari elegantly states, "one may argue that the ways of the future will appear through the exigencies of sociopolitical praxis and not necessarily by means of persuasive theory."[20] To focus on theoretical justifications as though they will impel change is to focus on the tail wagging the dog. The place of human rights will not be established by reforming or transforming Islam but by opening state-societies to political changes that reflect sociological realities within those states and participatory demands of Muslim populations. Such openings as one has seen in the Muslim Middle East reflect political, social, economic, and cultural demands, not a movement for a rereading of Islamic theology.

This is not to argue that placing rights concepts in culturally diverse language is unhelpful to gaining greater currency for human rights. Rights are not an autonomous legal system, imperially above culture and society. There does need to be societal legitimacy for rights, as they are not simply an abstract, apolitical legal concept. While rights neither flow from nor attack culture (though they do provide specific protections of certain cultural rights, including language, religion, and traditional practices of indigenous peoples), opportunities for their expansion are certainly greater if they can be justified in a manner that coalesces with both local political concerns and cultural language.

The challenge for those who discuss the place of human rights in the Muslim world, however, is to show how human rights respond to the political situations and structures of its diverse and particular locales, not to dress human rights up in a false Islamic suit of armor. Islam is neither the source of human rights nor (usually) the cause of rights violations. The variability of shari'a does not mean that lonely reformist interpretations are likely to overturn established norms; rather, it means that as social and political contexts change, so too can the manner in which shari'a is (or is not) applied and human rights is (or is not) integrated into politics and law. The important point is making clear the relevance of rights to issues of day-to-day concern (the right to work to Palestinians denied that right; the right to food to Sudanese facing forced starvation; the right to education for minorities and women systematically denied that right; the right to political participation for those not permitted to engage politically in so many Arab states, and so forth), as well as broader issues of peace and security, rather than the focus one too often finds on abstractions such as rights' cultural DNA.

Conclusion

Three points must be kept in mind which, in summary, underscore the Islam versus human rights paradigm's underlying misconceptions and dangerously misleading implications, and point to a more appropriate conception of their interrelationship. The first of these points is the paradigm's tacit overemphasis on Islam's centrality in Muslim societies, reflecting a common tendency in neo-Orientalist commentary on the politics and law of the Arab world. Islam is the subject of almost obsessive academic and media focus which affirms its place—despite the caveats sometimes made—as *the* defining aspect of predominantly Muslim states.[21] This has its roots in the much criticized Orientalist model, but it continues even among many critics of Orientalism. This sort of stereotype has led to a degree of attention to Islam that has largely drowned out discussion of other political and social currents in a diverse region that extends from Morocco in the west to Iraq in the east, and whose majority is in non-Arab states such as China and Nigeria. It is important to place political Islam in perspective by remembering that it is a minority phenomenon—often a rather small one—in most parts of the Muslim world, including theArab region.[22] The danger is that a discourse of a "resurgent" political Islam and of a totalist Muslim political culture will reinforce and legitimize trends that share these traits and delegitimize other trends. The political impact of an Islamic heritage is quite diverse, often indefinable and fluctuating in its impact on both internal politics and international relations. Islam—like other normative systems—is neither necessarily an obstacle nor a foundation of rights; in fact it is essentially indifferent as a factor in comparatively analyzing state records of human rights abuse.[23]

Without dismissing the presence of an Islamic metanarrative, it is equally important to bear witness to the evident historic and contemporary diversity—cultural and political—in the Muslim world which makes clear that there is no singular cultural construct decisively determining political-social outcomes. Simply put, within any state (including "Western" states, which have mixed human rights records and regularly face the same culturally justified opposition to rights) is a plurality of cultures and subcultures and diversity of political belief and ideology within these cultures. Identifying a single culture with a particular form of discourse is historically untenable, theoretically implausible, and empirically unsustainable. This is particularly true in the face of the contemporary world's increasingly fluid, interconnected political and cultural realities. Culture is not a unified "thing"; it is a field of meaning that defines and redefines particular world views in social, political, and economic context. It is never static or fixed.

Accepting at face value the claims of Islamists and cultural relativists that Islam represents the sum total of the values of these societies is to uncritically accept a corporatist conception of Muslim societies that insists on a monolithic construct of culture. A critical perspective on Islamist movements must cast a wary eye on stereotyping their members as "fanatics." It must also, however, be equally wary of a corporatist, communitarian perspective that reifies them as the only culturally authentic representatives of Muslim political society and, therefore, stereotypes those who might dare disagree as inauthentic or unrepresentative. If the repetitive invocation of Islam versus human rights is a distraction from insightful dialogue on key intellectual and political issues, and if this distraction is also a practical impediment to intellectual thought on forms that better reflect contemporary social realities, then it is an urgent task to critique this paradigm.

The second point regarding this paradigm is that human rights is also often exaggerated in ambition and impact. Critics of international human rights law, for example, sometimes portray it as an enormous instrument designed to impose uniform cultural and political practice on the world, attacking indigenous normative systems such as Islam to which it is unsuited. An example of this is Winin Pereira's misinformed caricature of human rights as a "huge and gargantuan structure [that is part of] a universal culture proposed during the past fifty years [that] was nothing more than an elaborate Westernisation proposal."[24]

There is no doubt that invoking solidarity with anti-Western politics has an understandable political resonance in regions that have suffered under colonialism and the continued imbalance of global power, and thus have felt the need for ideological unity against the West. Unfortunately, this all too easily flows into intellectually reductionist assumptions about human rights as a Western projection. This helps sustain the nationalist claim that there is an absolute opposition between a particular cultural tradition—such as Islam—and international norms, caricatured as alien and invasive. Not only is this reductionism objectionable on purely scholarly grounds, but it also has the political effect of justifying insular, xenophobic political practices and ideologies that thrive on notions of a cultural clash.

The flip side is invoking human rights on behalf of all manner of causes that have little or no relation to the texts of human rights instruments. In reality, human rights are a relatively circumscribed band of international law with a specific scope and restricted implementation and enforcement procedures—far from the fantasies of both uninformed opponents and exponents. Human rights instruments provide increasingly important fora for monitoring actions that arbitrarily violate restrictions on the use of state power, are a legal-political authority that can be invoked to supersede state-defined legal norms, and are—in short—a powerful tool that can inject protection of individual and group rights into international law and international relations.[25] As such, they can play a positive role in protecting individuals and groups that are confronting the reality of the powerful, intrusive modern state, and for this reason local, regional, and transnational groups expend considerable energy seeking to have rights implemented at the domestic level. They are, in essence, a legal regime that reacts to the political structures and needs of postcolonial modernity, far from a project for a "universal culture," as opponents claim.[26] In the Arab world, they can play a role in establishing structures that permit the sort of participatory politics and economics which can facilitate the emergence of alternatives to the status quo.

A reductionist perspective on "Western" human rights appears in both the Muslim world and Europe and the United States, but in conflating rights with a history of Western imperialism the harm falls predominantly on the Muslim world. A focus on the Western "Other" can be all-defining, risking constructing the Muslim self as a mere echo of the West. One of Mohammed Arkoun's central themes is that colonialism brought supposedly Western values to the Muslim world in the context of aggression.[27] The dilemma of the Muslim world is how to get beyond this negative association of "Western" human rights and "Western" imperialism, which risks a form of entrapment in a never-ending colonial discourse. This negative association is intensified when it is identified with countries such as the United States and France which have the habit of not allowing human rights rhetoric to interfere with support for states that are noted for their rights violations. Accepting or rejecting a rights discourse because of its cultural pedigree or because of the hypocrisy of that pedigree, however, is to simply play the echo to another's tune.

The fundamental question is not whether the genesis of human rights is the Magna Carta, Declaration of Independence, Declaration of the Rights of Man, the UN General Assembly Universal Declaration of Human Rights, or the expanding body of hard law treaties acceded to by a broad range of states. Nor is the fundamental question whether the United Kingdom, the United States, and France have double standards. They do, as do all states. The question that may be more productive is of what utility human rights as an international legal regime may be to the states of the Arab-Muslim world and to the individuals and groups who live under the political rule of these states.

The third point, consequent to these misconceived exaggerations of both Islam and the human rights regime, is that the Islam versus human rights paradigm's evocation of a clash (or a need for reconciliation) between Islam and human rights is vastly overstated, as previously out-lined. Just as often—if not more often—Islam and human rights func-tion on fundamentally distinct religious-cultural and political-legal planes that make talk of clash or reconciliation an irrelevant diversion from the true issues of importance. One way to ameliorate the self-perpetuating perception of such a clash is to place discussion of their relationship on a theoretical basis—as described above—that avoids overly monolithic conceptions of both Islam and human rights and includes the practice of politics in the Arab world. It is this practice that puts the empirical lie to theories that privilege a clash between Islam and human rights.

The motor of change in the Muslim world is an ever-shifting political and social context—in driving laws as in family law, in economics as in human rights. A dynamic, cross-cultural justificatory strategy that brings states and peoples to rights out of a sense of self-interest and normative appropriateness is what has allowed the global consensus on rights to form. It may also allow it to take on deeper roots in areas where the rights regime has been more controversial, as in some parts of the Mus-lim world. Strong internal voices finding political space to articulate sup-port for human rights is the most effective manner of advancing a rights agenda, but until now such political space has been rare in many parts of the Arab world.

The importance of both transnational Islamic and human rights norms in contemporary Muslim societies is real, as are some particular complications of their interrelationship in discrete, contested areas. What is also clear, however, is that these complications do not signify a direct clash between two monoliths. What they do indicate are vary-ing areas of friction in diverse ideological environments in a relation-ship which, overall, is characterized by distinct fields of concern. An uncritical juxtaposition of Islam and human rights is dangerous. Its propagation in popular and academic discourse feeds into a reduc-tionist pigeonholing of Islam and human rights both inside and out-side the Muslim world. Islam is not a discrete entity that must dominate, be reconciled, or be excluded from the political world. It is entangled in social and political structures in a complex, differenti-ated manner. It is at times of paramount importance, at times of no importance, and most often somewhere between the two extremes. It is primarily a religious discourse, but its impact on politics and society is indeterminate—defined in historical context rather than by eternal essence.

Exploration of these practical imbrications is crucial if the debate around topics that implicate human rights and Islamic law is to escape their current stalemate. More important, dialogue on these issues can open up points of view on alternative models that more realistically reflect the complex, interwoven ideological fabrics of the Muslim world and more properly appreciate the scope and limits of both Islam and human rights and their status within varying political, economic, and social contexts.

Chapter 2
A Question of Human Rights Ethics: Defending the Islamists

Bahey el-Din Hassan

The incidents that took place in March 1987 at Mazra'et Tora prison in a Cairo suburb provide a symbolic framework to illustrate the relations between political Islamists and human rights activists on the one hand, and the dynamics of the formation of the human rights movement in Egypt and the Third World on the other. The prison housed two groups of political prisoners, one Islamist, accused of committing acts of violence, and the other Nasserist, accused of planning to commit acts of violence against foreign establishments to protest the settlement of the Arab-Israeli conflict. The prison administration treated the Islamists more brutally than it did the Nasserists, both because of the difference in the two groups' politics and objectives and because the Islamists had a long record of violence. This violence had reached its apex in 1981 with the assassination of president Anwar Sadat and the attack on the Security Directorate in Upper Egypt that claimed the lives of dozens of enlisted men and officers and involved the attempted assassination of a number of government officials.

In prison, the Nasserists tried to integrate with the Islamists, holding joint social activities such as prayers and discussion groups and sharing some of the privileges the Nasserists enjoyed—for example, meals that were brought from outside the prison and the "broadcast" service they established in the prison. The Nasserists also negotiated some demands on the Islamists' behalf with the prison administration. This created a good atmosphere in that dismal place. Late in March, the authorities released a number of Nasserists, which greatly increased the percentage of Islamist detainees. The morning after the release, the Islamists, armed with whatever they could lay their hands on, savagely attacked the remaining Nasserists, causing severe injuries.

Most of the members of the Nasserist group were released the following month. The court subsequently found them all innocent, including
their leader who had made detailed confessions. The court established,
however, that the confessions had been extorted under torture. Before
their release, none of the group had encountered the concept of human
rights, the Universal Declaration of Human Rights, or the Egyptian
Organization for Human Rights (EOHR), which had been established
two years earlier (April 1985). During the years following this incident,
some of the members of the Nasserist group joined the EOHR as volunteers or salaried lawyers, and later came to hold leadership posts in the
EOHR as well as in new human rights NGOs they helped establish. No
one from the Islamic group at the prison became active in human rights.
At the time of the Nasserists' release, the EOHR board was engaged in
an ongoing conflict concerning its working strategies, including what
position to take on defending the human rights of Islamists who violate
the rights of others. The conflict was settled in July 1988 when the
author was elected to the post of secretary-general, and the EOHR established a policy of opposition to human rights violations regardless of victims' political or ideological background or the nature of the charges.
This position was further consolidated with the election in May 1989 of
a new board of trustees.

The members of the Nasserist group who joined the EOHR joined the
rest of the staff and officers in applying this policy without hesitation
and without being prejudiced by what the Islamists had done to them in
1987.[1] The incident in Mazra'et Tora prison is emblematic of the relation between the human rights movement in Egypt and the political
Islam movement. The former has committed itself to an overriding
moral principle, whereas factions of the latter embrace acts that are in
direct opposition to both Islam and morality.[2]

The Rise of the Human Rights Movement

The official date of the founding of the human rights movement in
Egypt is April 1985, when the EOHR was established as a branch of the
Arab Organization for Human Rights (AOHR).[3] Yet the roots of the rise
of the Egyptian movement date back to the 1960s. A wave of rebellion
against the iron cage of the Nasserist regime rose in February 1968, nine
months after the lightning defeat of the Egyptian and other Arab armies
at the hands of Israel. The defeat resulted in the occupation of Sinai in
Egypt, the Golan Heights in Syria, and the remains of Palestine—the
West Bank and Gaza—and it profoundly shook the soul of the Arab peoples in general. Its impact on the Egyptians was much deeper, however.
The most populous Arab country (currently around sixty million), with

the most advanced industry, best-known culture, dialect, and art in the Arab world, and the largest and best-equipped army, Egypt was a prime candidate to be the Arab world's regional power. Indeed, in the mid-1950s President Nasser (1952–70) had started to introduce a scheme for a greater Arab state unified under his leadership. The greater the hopes, the deeper the shock.

The defeat inflamed national demands for reprisals and the reclamation of the occupied territories, but it also provided an impetus for radical revision of the political, social, and cultural factors that had ushered in the defeat. The amount of scrutiny to which the national disaster was subjected was proportional to its size. Were the sacrifices that had been made justified, even in defeat? Or were the types of sacrifices that had been made—including limits on human rights—part of the defeat? Egyptians had sacrificed their very freedom in the name of the pan-Arab nationalist project and for having confronted Israel. Had it been worth it?

The choice had seemed simple—democracy versus a greater Arab state—and was based on the model of the "just despot" that is deeply rooted in Egyptian/Arab/Islamic politics and history. Democracy, for which Egyptians had struggled for decades until gaining a constitutional monarchy in 1923, was to be sacrificed. To this end, democracy was depicted as synonymous with the "disintegration and division" that would facilitate foreign (Western/Israeli) infiltration and thus undermine the establishment of a greater Arab state that would enjoy social justice inspired by the Soviet socialist model.

Egyptians woke up on June 5, 1967, to discover that, in addition to having already sacrificed democracy, they had now lost national independence, land, dignity, and the dream of might and justice. On June 9 and 10, Egyptians took to the streets to protest the defeat and voice their support for the despotic patriarch who was their president. They found it unthinkable that any other ruler could reclaim national soil, let alone that achieving this would demand both another ruler and a different system of government.

Nine months later, Egyptians again took to the streets, this time to protest the light sentences given to a number of military leaders tried as scapegoats for a regime that refused to hold itself accountable. Not only did they consider the sentences too light given the magnitude of the defeat, they were also convinced that the causes of the defeat were as much political as military. Therefore their slogans demanded democracy and freedom of the press in addition to calling for the retrial of the military leaders.

Thus it can be argued that the demonstrations of February 1968 marked the beginning of an arduous, long, and as yet uncompleted journey to rediscovering the correlation among national independence, social justice, democracy, and human rights. An appreciation of this correlation first appeared early in the twentieth century, but certain factors—most of which are not of concern here—helped disaggregate these elements. One of the most prominent of these factors was the Arab-Israeli conflict, which started with the usurpation of half of Palestine in 1948 in order to establish Israel with the support of the Western superpowers, and had its most crushing effect on Egypt with the defeat of 1967. This conflict is also the crucial factor that prevented the completion of the journey to return democracy to its previous status in Egyptians' consciousness. The shock of defeat caused the remolding in the 1980s and 1990s of several political trends that had previously been either coopted or marginalized by Nasser's regime, and it gave shape to a new political map in Egypt.

The first and primary trend, which has been dominant in Egypt since Nasser's death in 1970, is a reorganized Nasserism that included (1) restructuring the economy to allow for a gradually increased role for the private sector and foreign capital at the expense of the public sector; (2) restructuring international relations to accommodate Israel (now considered a fact of life) and the West so that confrontation is excluded but the possibility of retaining tense surface relations is not; (3) restructuring the local political landscape to allow restricted pluralism to exist alongside a single, immutable ruling party; and (4) keeping the military off the main stage of political life while retaining its role in determining the course of major strategic issues.

The second trend is another sort of modified Nasserism, one that maintains a leading role for the public sector, does not recognize Israel, and views the Arab-Israeli conflict as the central issue determining all other internal and external policies, including relations with the West. This trend also accords the military a crucial role, not only in Egypt but also in the Arab world as a whole, viewing it as a vanguard of pan-Arab unionism. The role of the military is also seen as decisive in confronting Israel and in holding Arab countries together to face intimidation from the colonialist West. Regarding democracy, this trend espouses much the same kind of restricted pluralism as do the proponents of the first trend, though the political discourse of the second group may give the impression of a greater acceptance of pluralism. The most prominent representative of this perspective is the officially recognized Nasserist opposition party, though several small groups, made up mostly of students, also represent it.

The third trend is leftist with Marxist roots. It differs from the second trend in that it does not advocate that the military should have a leading role. And, despite its hostility toward the West, some of its sectors are willing to accommodate Israel so long as it is within the framework of a new map and a new balance of power. This group is also distinguished by its willingness to accept political pluralism. This trend is represented by several small groups, the largest of which is the officially recognized Nationalist Progressivist Unionist Coalition.

Fourth is the liberal trend. It supports privatization, restriction of the role of the military, a genuinely democratic parliamentary system, and complete openness to the West. However, the stalled peace negotiations and the West's complicity with Israel force the liberal perspective on this issue to differ little from that of the first three trends. The liberal trend's progress has also been seriously hampered by the fact that its roots, having been severed in July 1952 when the army took power, are still weak, and it gives priority to the confrontation with the outside world (Israel and the West) at the expense of internal issues. These factors often drive the party representing this trend to swing between an alliance, whether covert or overt, with the Muslim Brothers or the ruling party.

Finally, there is the Islamic trend. It is second only to the first variant of a restructured modified Nasserism in influence and impact on political life. Its main focus is the application of shari'a (Islamic law) and the establishment of an Islamic state, and this determines its strategy on the other key issues. It accepts political pluralism, but only on condition of acceptance of, or at least nonopposition to, the rule of shari'a. It espouses a central role for the military, which is to be Islamicized. The Islamist movement also advocates a capitalist economic system tinted with the hues of Islamic economic principles. Their great animosity toward Israel and the West serves the Islamists well as a tactical tool for mobilization. It argues that in such a polarized atmosphere, and after the devastating failures that afflicted the pan-Arabists, Nasserists, and Marxists, there is no alternative to political Islam as an umbrella for the Arabs (including Christians).

The political organization most representative of the Islamist movement is the Muslim Brotherhood. It is also the most influential and the most engaged in political life. Although there are some well-known Islamist moderates who are less rigid than the Muslim Brotherhood, in the final analysis their efforts benefit the Brotherhood and the Islamist movement as a whole. At the other extreme are the more intransigent armed groups. However, their influence has increasingly receded since the early 1990s, and their remnants support the Islamic political umbrella of the Muslim Brothers.

It was against this backdrop of forces that, in April 1985, a number of Egyptian figures from various political backgrounds founded the Egyptian branch of the AOHR, which three years later became the EOHR.

Five years after its founding, the EOHR had become a powerful political player in Egypt and soon gave rise to a number of specialized human rights NGOs that infused additional vitality into Egyptian civil society and the political community. The AOHR came out of an Arab regional conference on democracy, and—like later Arab human rights NGOs— its rise, growth, and the shaping of its agenda were closely associated with the Arab-Israeli conflict. After the Israeli invasion of Lebanon in June 1982 and the first occupation of an Arab capital (Beirut) since the establishment of Israel, some of the Arab world's most prominent political and intellectual figures convened the AOHR conference. The central concept was the same as that underlying the 1968 demonstrations in Egypt: both the 1967 defeat and the Arab world's inability to save Lebanon and Beirut in 1982 could be explained by the prevalence of despotic regimes in the Arab world, the suppression of freedom of opinion and expression and the right of participation in decision making, and the trampling of the dignity of the Arab citizen—all of which have led to enervated political societies.

The incentives for establishing the EOHR, however, were more closely linked to the Egyptian political environment, which the Islamists had been playing a vital role in shaping for a decade. In the mid-1970s, the Islamists made a comeback onto the political stage after a long absence behind bars or in voluntary exile to escape persecution by Nasser. President Sadat, who succeeded Nasser in 1970, initiated a process of political reconciliation with the Islamists that grew into an outright alliance because he so feared the leading role the Nasserists and Marxist left were taking in the student movements and, consequently, in society. Sadat gave the Islamists an influential say in designing education curricula and mass media programs (especially for radio and television). Their alliance was further consolidated by an amendment to the constitution stating that the principles of shari'a shall serve as a primary source for legislation. In return, the Islamists supported Sadat's regime and engaged in daily bloody battles to undermine—and eventually completely marginalize—the Nasserists and Marxists, especially on university campuses. This alliance stood until Sadat was assassinated by the armed wing of the Islamic movement in 1981.

This assassination, and the horrendous acts of violence that accompanied and followed it, paved the way for the human rights conditions that persist today, and thus catalyzed the foundation of the EOHR. The human rights situation in 1985 was characterized by the following:

• The escalation of bloody violence between the security apparatus and nonstate entities (largely Islamist at this point). The scope of violence was eventually extended to include secular intellectuals, Copts, and tourists, as well as hapless bystanders.

- The return of torture as an officially condoned practice. In cases of torture of politicians or those suspected of proselytism, the perpetrators were protected from judicial pursuit. Torture was widespread and permitted under Nasser, but under Sadat it stopped being used officially and routinely against politicians and was restricted to isolated cases against criminal suspects in police stations. After Sadat's assassination, however, it resurfaced as a routine practice.

- The escalation of pressure against the freedoms of thought, belief, and opinion. This was a result of the growth of the Islamist movement (in both its armed and unarmed wings) and the state's gradual but growing submission to pressure in the name of religion.

- The declaration of the state of emergency in 1981, which has remained in force ever since. This gave the security forces exceptional powers of detention and the ability to expand a circle of suspects. It also granted impunity for arbitrary practices such as collective punishment of entire neighborhoods or villages, pressuring subjects to turn themselves in by holding members of their families hostage, and circumventing the law—including the Emergency Law itself.

The Loaded Question: Which Is More Dangerous?

The overwhelming majority of the founding members of the EOHR (the author among them) had secular backgrounds, and this was reflected in the makeup of its first board of trustees (1985–86). At first, its main work involved confronting the Islamists' violations of human rights. Also, in cooperation with a women's group, the EOHR moved to form a new group for the defense of national unity (between Muslims and Christians)—a group that would defend the freedoms of thought, belief, and religion against the formidable pressures of Islamic fundamentalism. This venture required considerable effort and time on the part of the fledgling organization.

The issue of defending Islamists' human rights was not an easy one to address for people who had spent a good part of their lives in intellectual or political battle against the Islamists. In addition, with the onset of widespread bloody violence, the would-be defenders started to realize that they themselves might become targets—if not immediately, then definitely if the Islamists took power. Could they ignore what the Islamists did to intellectuals and politicians and their lawyers upon taking power in Iran six years earlier and, in the name of human rights, stand at the side of their potential executioners? The question, in short, was,

"Which danger is imminent, which is more remote, and of the two which is more dangerous to human rights?" This dilemma was not confined to the Egyptian human rights movement. When it was faced in Algeria the result was the founding of two human rights organizations, each focused on a separate pattern of human rights violations— violations by the Islamists for one organization and by the government security apparatuses for the other.

Posed again eight years later in the Tunisian League for Human Rights, the question led to bitter struggles, and the decision the Tunisians reached in 1994 was the opposite of that of the EOHR. It was a victory for the wing that rejected defending the Islamists' human rights under the misapprehension that the Tunisian authorities would support the human rights movement against the party "more dangerous" to human rights. This perspective eventually greatly weakened the Tunisian league and made it easier for the authorities to marginalize and manipulate it and then to assault its leaders. Today, the Tunisian government brutally suppresses both Islamists and secular human rights defenders.

A human rights organization would undermine its own principles and integrity if it refused to defend Islamists' human rights. Refusal would mean that political—not human rights—considerations were determining human rights strategies. Further, it would imply an unprincipled political alliance with a government capable of flagrant human rights violations. Lastly, it could require human rights NGOs to relinquish one of their most important roles, namely to strive to make political practice more ethical by making it more consistent with human rights principles—or at least not in opposition to them. In short, a human rights organization making this sort of unholy alliance would be stripped of credibility and more easily marginalized, as has been seen in countries such as Tunisia.

"No" would not have been the wise answer to the question of whether or not to defend the human rights of Islamists. The very form of the question implied that governments cannot confront the violence of armed political groups without flagrantly violating human rights. Doubtless, such violent confrontations necessitate elaborate precautions and preventive security measures, and any human rights organization should take this into consideration. But this does not mean that these organizations should overlook practices that almost routinely breach the law and violate human rights on a wide scale.

This was the most serious concern raised in debating the question, for it implied granting prior approval to human rights violations. Considering such a question politicizes the everyday work of human rights defenders by preoccupying them with the question, "To what extent does this or that position weaken the greater danger (the Islamists) or the imminent danger (the government)?" And this question would not be raised only when Islamists were assaulted but also when the EOHR was called on to take a position on the suppression of non-Islamist forces—striking workers, for example. Such political "calculation" is far removed from the defense of human rights, as well as from principles and morals.

Adopting any strategy based on selective application would have meant excluding some categories of victims from the EOHR agenda, depending on the victims' political or religious backgrounds or, to put it more bluntly, for political reasons stemming from the political orientation of those in charge of the EOHR. This would have been tantamount to discrimination against a category of people, even complicity in the violation of their human rights. Moreover, it would automatically have undermined the EOHR's credibility and its ability to defend and protect other victims, for human rights organizations possess nothing if not their capacity to mobilize local and international public opinion to pressure governments to stop or curb rights violations. If credibility is undermined in the eyes of the public, the organization in question loses its capacity to act and its influence.

Thus the kernel of the dispute was not the particulars of the EOHR's position on Islamists but rather what its fundamental strategy would be. Was the EOHR to follow its conscience and act according to internationally recognized principles and mechanisms to defend victims without hesitating at their political, ideological, and religious backgrounds or the charges against them, even if those charges were violations of human rights? Or was it to take the road leading away from the organization's ethos and principles toward its ultimate self-destruction? This latter was the fate of all human rights institutions established by Islamists in Egypt, and it resulted from their strategy to defend victims from only one political tendency or, more accurately, one political organization—the Muslim Brothers. Within the EOHR the main issue of controversy was the opinion held by one wing—eventually defeated—that criticism of the Egyptian government's human rights practices and record would undermine its political strength to the benefit of the more dangerous enemy (the Islamists). This led them to argue that the organization should exclude human rights defense activities such as observing, monitoring, and reporting rights violations and restrict its role to cultural activities propagating human rights principles.

Another controversial issue emerged when, about two years after the EOHR was founded, the Egyptian government refused to recognize or deal with it. This development challenged the EOHR to choose between two responses. The wing in favor of limiting the EOHR's scope of activity suggested dissolving the organization or freezing its activities in order to avoid a clash with the authorities. The other wing argued that the EOHR should stand up to the government, stressing that a human rights organization that cannot defend its own right to exist cannot successfully defend the rights of others. Without delving into the details of that intellectual conflict, suffice it to say that the latter wing prevailed, though it was supported only by a tiny minority on the board of trustees (two of eleven). However, the board made the democratic motion to meet in consultation with the membership, and those attending the general meeting unanimously accepted the minority view. In August 1989, one year after laying out the new plan of action, which included both defense of Islamists and continued work despite governmental pressure, the EOHR paid the price for its new strategy: two of the new board members were arrested and tortured during a wave of detentions that swept up about sixty persons on the contrived charge of "founding a communist organization."

A Consistent Strategy

During the new board of trustees' first year in office, several times the EOHR implemented its new policy of intervening in some of the prominent cases concerning Islamists. It intervened successfully to stop the flagellation of the leader of the Islamic Jihad movement, Aboud el-Zommur, and his colleagues who were in prison for their part in Sadat's assassination. It was interesting that a prominent leader of one of the two most prominent armed Islamic groups would present a complaint to a human rights organization, especially since it requested stopping flagellation, which a great many shari'a interpreters consider a legitimate penalty. The EOHR argued that flagellation is a cruel and degrading punishment prohibited by the International Convention against Torture ratified by Egypt three year earlier.

The EOHR also intervened in the case of Tal'at Fou'ad Qassem, a principal military leader of the second most prominent armed Islamic group. In September 1988 he had completed the seven-year prison term to which he had been sentenced for his role in Sadat's assassination, but he was not released. He had been subjected to monstrous kinds of torture the year before the EOHR intervention.[4] Another intervention was on behalf of members of an alleged Shia organization arrested in 1989 and subjected to the worst kinds of torture. For the first time, the EOHR reports contained graphic depictions of some of the sadistic means employed in their torture. They were all subsequently released. Yet another example was the case of a group suspected of belonging to the Muslim Brothers. They were detained along with eighty children between six and ten years of age who had been attending a summer camp that the security authorities accused the adults of administering for the purpose of inculcating religious extremism. The children stayed for two nights in the police station, where they were subjected to various forms of mistreatment, including beatings. The adults remained for several weeks, during which they were subjected to various types of torture until they were released without trial. As a final example, on September 11, 1990, the EOHR brought a serious charge against the state security apparatuses: the assassination of the spokesperson of the armed jamaʿa islamiyya, who had been shot dead in the street nine days earlier. The EOHR accusation was based on a unique investigation it had undertaken. The following month, the jamaʿa islamiyya assassinated the Speaker of the Parliament in retaliation. These are the most prominent among the many cases the EOHR adopted during this period that concerned members of the Islamist movement.

The EOHR campaigns were not restricted to cases of Islamists. During the same time span as the Islamist cases cited above, it also intervened in many cases involving victims considered members of the left. These included the suppression of the workers' strike at Egypt's central iron and steel factory, crackdowns on the Communist Workers Party and the Egyptian Communist Party, and a number of individual cases of trade unionists. It also adopted cases of individual citizens and even members of security forces who were arrested and tortured in return for their demanding some improvements in work conditions. In January 1990 the EOHR started issuing what might be called "theme" reports on human rights violations. These comprehensive reports tracked victims from various political and trade union backgrounds who had all been subjected to the same type of violation. In January 1990, as a result of EOHR campaigns, among other factors, the fiercest and most violent minister of the interior since the time of Nasser was discharged. He had made a practice of challenging the EOHR and publicly attacked it with violent language on several occasions.

The EOHR also sharply criticized the practices of the Islamic groups that violate human rights—whether directly or indirectly—by instigating violence, promoting religious and sectarian bigotry, or urging that freedoms of opinion, expression, and belief be curtailed. The EOHR issued a number of reports verifying and documenting Islamists' acts of violence (just as it had done with the government's human rights violations) and calling on the armed groups to lay down their arms. This practice was unprecedented among international and local human rights NGOs, which generally restricted their work to addressing governmental violations and considered anything outside that domain to fall within the purview of international humanitarian (not human rights) law.[5]

Among these sensitive issues was the censorship by Al-Azhar University of freedom of opinion, thought, and artistic creativity. The censorship role the state granted to Al-Azhar has been enlarging with the growth of the Islamist movement and the state's succumbing to it in the intellectual and cultural realms. The EOHR adopted cases involving the freedoms of opinion, thought, and belief, including the cases of writers accused of "deriding religions." It also adopted the cases of people subjected to persecution for converting from Islam to Christianity. All news media, it should be noted, have refrained from mentioning the EOHR reports on this subject. Moreover, when some Islamic scholars with considerable status as spiritual leaders justified acts of violence, the EOHR publicly and severely criticized their positions.

The most telling expression of the depth of the EOHR commitment to nonideological human rights principles was the position it took after the assassination of one of its founding members—the secular intellectual Farag Fouda, a member of the board of trustees from 1986 to 1989. Fouda was assassinated in June 1992 at the hands of members of the armed jama'a islamiyya on the pretext that he was "hostile to Islam." A statement issued by a number of Al-Azhar scholars had described him as such. The EOHR issued a statement severely attacking these positions. When the EOHR learned that those suspected of the assassination had been tortured, it intervened with the prosecutor general to urge it be stopped and the perpetrators prosecuted.

Conclusion

This chapter characterizes the strategies of the Egyptian human rights movement, with a focus on the EOHR's struggle to define its human rights principles and its eventual insistence on maintaining a separation between the victims of rights violations and their political, ideological, or religious affiliations. This strategy endowed the EOHR with moral power and freed it from indebtedness to any faction. Indeed, most political factions in Egypt have found cause to be grateful to the EOHR or, in the case of the Islamists and the government, at least to express an ironic combination of appreciation and hatred. This strategy has also given the EOHR the ability to take audacious human rights stands on very sensitive issues, which it could not have done had it been working on only one front—focusing on violations by the Islamists.

Part II
Globalization and the
Impact of Human Rights

Chapter 3
Globalization and Human Rights: On a Current Debate Among Arab Intellectuals

Amr Hamzawy

The concept of globalization has been ubiquitous in intellectual debates in Europe and North America over the last decade. A wide range of technological, economic, and social transformations have been explained through the discovery of this magical concept, and it quickly displaced modernity/postmodernity as the dominant explanatory paradigm in contemporary intellectual discourse. The information revolution, the decline of the nation-state, mobility, hybridity, risk society, and the compression of time and space represent just some of the evolving concepts discussed under the edgeless umbrella of globalization. European and North American discussions on globalization inspired intellectuals worldwide, including those in the Arab world. The Arab debate, however, pursued a rather different path, one that focused in particular on globalization's impact on attitudes toward human rights.

There were a number of precursors to the Arab world's globalization and human rights debate. Although conducted under the guise of a variety of terms, in the early 1990s an intensive discussion took place on phenomena and processes that are now subsumed under the concept of globalization. Included in these discussions were issues of the universal spread of Western political and social models, the information revolution, the Americanization of everyday life, the Westernization of Arab elites, the threat to local identities, the crisis of the national state, the liberalization of international trade, and the role of transnational companies.[1] Within these debates there was often an underlying skepticism toward currents perceived as carriers of Western ideology. And since this dialogue was taking place around the time of military action by the

United States and its allies against an Arab "renegade" state (Iraq), it was preprogrammed that the majority of Arab authors would primarily perceive the threat as American hegemony and would to a large extent overlook other aspects of transitions taking place during the early 1990s. The American-Israeli vision of a "New Middle East" in the mid-1990s strengthened the feeling among many in the Arab intellectual community that Arabs would be the ones victimized by global change.[2] This resulted in an increased resonance for cultural relativist arguments against human rights, with many intellectuals embracing a particularistic notion of culture in the Arab world. Although this attitude has receded, it continues to characterize some contemporary contributions on human rights and globalization.[3] In addition, in times of crisis in the Arab world—such as the outbreak of the second *intifada* in the Palestinian-occupied areas in autumn 2000 or after the terror attacks of September 11—cultural particularism's ideological resonance is given new impetus.

Although globalization covers a wide range of topics, closer inspection of the literature suggests that the majority of Arab intellectuals are primarily addressing the cultural challenges of globalization and the ways in which local identities are affected.[4] The Egyptian economist Jalal Amin, for example, sharply criticizes globalization's harmful influence on the Arab cultural heritage and the Arabic language. This criticism is derived from an understanding of cultural globalization as founded equally on Westernization and Americanization. While Amin accepts the importance of global standards and global discourse with regard to the democratic formation of the political sphere and the recognition of human rights, he insists that they will only be effective if they are transferred to the local context and articulated there authentically.[5]

To arrive at an understanding of the globalization debate, the following questions are relevant:

1. Which views of cultural globalization and local culture can be derived from recent Arab publications? Is globalization mainly equated with the hegemony of Western standards and forms of life, and to this extent interpreted as another attempt to push through Western-style cultural homogeneity, or can other patterns of perception also be identified? Subsequently, is the push for adherence to universal human rights in the region regarded as a threat to the "authentic," or do some thinkers, for example, those engaged in the Western globalization debate,[6] argue that the globalization processes leads to an intensification of cultural plurality as well as greater enjoyment of human rights?
2. What is the relationship among globalization, human rights, and

the concepts of culture and identity? In other words, is a negative continuum constructed that suggests "globalization implies threat to local culture implies loss of authentic identity," or do some of those taking part in the debate break with this static view of culture and identity and address, instead, globalization's dynamic elements?

3. To what extent can the attitudes of cultural pessimism and cultural optimism behind the positions outlined above be assigned to different positions in the human rights debate and central currents of thought in Arab societies? More specifically, do only Islamist thinkers criticize processes of cultural globalization, whereas other-minded intellectuals emphasize its positive effects, or are both views represented across all camps and tendencies?

4. To what extent does the controversy that has existed since the 1970s in the Arab public sphere about modernity (*hadatha*) and authenticity (*asala*) represent the intellectual frame of reference for the globalization debate? The human rights debate? Is the duality "global-local" replacing the dichotomy "modern-authentic"?

5. Are we seeing a new version of older debates, in which new terminology may be permitted but the debate continues to be dominated by rigid structures of thought—specifically, secular, Islamist, and reformist discourse on the relationship between modern and authentic, and on the relationship of identity and cultural heritage? Or is it possible to identify other new developments in addition to terminological changes?

6. Subsequent to the above points, does the intellectual debate on globalization, and more specifically human rights, represent a structuring issue in the Arab public sphere similar to controversies about democracy and the future role of the nation-state? Are there layers of normative and political consensus that have been generated in the debate that are of potential relevance to major societal actors? Or does globalization face the same fate as discussions on the implementation of the shari'a which, though intensively contested in the 1980s and the 1990s, did not lead to any substantial closing of the gap between secular and religious currents as far as the normative underpinnings of contemporary Arab polities and societies are concerned?

To begin, the origin of the human rights debate in the Arab world will be considered, laying a framework for the later discussion of various intellectual reference points in the globalization debate.

The Discovery of Human Rights in Arab Debates

The Crisis of the Nation-State

In the 1950s, 1960s, and 1970s, the nation-state received praise in both traditional and modern political projects in the Arab world either as the agent for securing stability for society or as the impetus for change. It was hoped that the nation-state would either consolidate the existing state or humanize, liberalize, democratize, or Islamize it. In the political discourse of the postindependence era the centrality of the nation-state was sacralized, especially under the dual influence of the modernization paradigm and Marxist ideology. Thus the rather violent implementation and expansion of state power in many Arab countries was often unquestioned. In the first half of the 1980s, the severe social and economic problems exacerbated the state's apparent inability to fulfill its normative agenda regarding development and the preservation of national independence. The acknowledgment of such problems led a number of Arab intellectuals to criticize the politics of existing governments and predict their ultimate loss of legitimacy.

These criticisms, however, did not lead to a discourse that questioned the role of the state but resulted in further enthusiasm for the nation-state, which was reflected in the articulation of alternative state models. The reformed nation-state, the Islamic state, the pan-Arab state, the secular state, the democratic state, the socialist state, and the modern state—such terms dominated the language of politics at the time. Hidden behind these catchphrases, however, were a range of societal conflicts concerning the foundations of the political organization of society and the place of religion in modern Arab societies. The goal, once again, was to use the state to introduce change and reform. Given that the majority of Arab countries remained unaffected by this wave of criticism—with the exceptions of a few minor liberal concessions in Egypt, Algeria, Yemen, Jordan, Kuwait, Morocco, and Tunisia—liberal elites and other opposition forces started in the second half of the 1980s to shift the discursive nexus of their discussions to democracy. By moving to underpin this through concepts such as human rights and civil society, these groups distanced themselves from their reliance on the state.

The Rise of Islamism

The second political change that drew more attention to human rights was the rise of radical and moderate Islamist movements and political parties. The 1979 Iranian Revolution and the assassination of Egyptian president Anwar Sadat in 1981 marked the emergence of a new understanding of the relationship between religion and politics in the Arab world. The political dimension of Islam, which the secular principle of the separation between religion and state had negated, increasingly gained a more central social relevance. This shift was preceded by an extensive religiously oriented social critique of both liberal and socialist modernist ideologies. The new religious discourse(s) dismissed modern ideas of secular democracy as both culturally foreign and harmful to society. The introduction of the principles of shari'a (Islamic law) and the establishment of an Islamic state were strongly advocated in order to re-Islamicize Arab societies. In light of political Islam's rise, some liberal and leftist groups aimed to utilize the emerging notion of human rights—defined by them as inherently secular—as a means of banning and excluding Islamist movements from the public sphere and articulating an anti-Islamist understanding of democracy. On the other hand, state-imposed restrictions on the participation of Islamist groups and their leaders' fear of political marginalization led moderate Islamist groups (for example, the Muslim Brothers in Egypt and Jordan) to attempt to appropriate and redefine human rights in an "authentically" Islamic manner. Hence the notion of rights was integrated into moderate Islamist discourses and equated with the classical term *maslahat ar-ra'aya* (citizens' interests) in order to religiously legitimize its usage and defend religious movements' position in the public sphere.

Approaches to Globalization and Human Rights

The current Arab discourse on modernity, authenticity, and human rights has its origins in the intellectual repercussions of the Six Day War of June 1967. The *naksa* (setback) meant the political end of the nation-state-led pan-Arab project and was followed by a process of questioning and rethinking the normative and political foundations of modern Arab societies. From this, three main currents of Arab thought crystallized: secular, religious, and reformist discourse.[7] From this point onward talk was either of the dangerous revival of Islamically based, retrogressive ideologies or of the crisis (or failure) of the transfer of Western modernity to the Arab world and the necessary search for authenticity.[8] With the growing polarization of the intellectual community between these secular and religious positions, the reformist tendency has been marginalized, but some of its representatives have considered the possibilities of a theoretical compromise between secular and religious approaches.[9]

In order to cast some light on the common features and differences within and among these currents of thought, we will examine whether they are clearly distinctive or if there are ways in which they coincide. If the latter, does this pave the way toward new forms of normative and political consensus?

Secular Approach

In terms of ideal types, secular thinkers emphasize that global processes of modernization and secularization lead to the inevitable destruction of common traditions and styles of life and to an erosion in religious worldviews. Religious institutions and discourses are everywhere losing social relevance as a result of the acceleration of processes of change. From a secular point of view, Arab culture is not an exception. The religious body of thought is referred to as intellectually primitive and socially reactionary, and its current upsurge is regarded as an irrational expression of deep existential crises in modern Arab societies.[10]

Typical of the secular approach are the writings of the Syrian historian ʿAziz al-ʿAzma. He understands modernity as a worldwide, all-encompassing reality that has put an end to Islamically dominated medieval continuity in the Arab world, and has initiated a process of secularization in all areas of society. Consideration of concepts of cultural heritage and authenticity are at the center of his analysis. Thus he refers to all forms of intellectual or political expression that deny the realities of global modernity and secularization as a pathological rejection of the present. The contemporary variants of this "irrational thought," in particular the Islamist discourse on *turath* (cultural heritage) and *asala*, are for him a "reactionary flight from the here-and-now" in the name of an imaginary continuity and a newly found religious identity.[11]

In his secular approach, al-ʿAzma stylizes modernity as a model for historical developments worldwide, unaffected by time and space, and defines it mainly by negative associations with its counterpart, tradition. Whereas the modern is generally understood to be future oriented and constantly subject to change, traditions are typified as exclusively backward looking and static obstructions to progress or change. The central importance attached to the secularization process explains why for al-ʿAzma the concept of modernity is enriched by its normative undermining of tradition and, at times, religion. In this way the terms "modern" and "tradition" are constructed as opposites just as many in this debate associate human rights with the term "modern" and therefore see the implementation of these rights as oppositional to Arab culture's values and traditions. Largely because of these types of positions, the ongoing authenticity discourse is intellectually discredited, from this perspective, as an irrational remnant of a primitive religious worldview.

Proponents of secular thought—with the exception of the Marxists who have some doubts as to whether the concept of globalization is a carrier of imperialism—embrace the notion of the universality of human rights and further trust that the historical and contemporary influence of the West both politically and culturally on the Arab countries enables its applicability.

Islamist Approach

In contrast, religious intellectuals dispute the universality of Western modernity and human rights and emphasize the historical and socio-cultural particularities of their own Arab-Islamic societies. From this they derive the necessity for an authentic form of social thought. In their views and discourses the concept of tradition is of major importance. Tradition is understood as a cultural corpus handed down from generation to generation with a uniform content of ideas, and which gains its legitimacy from the depths of time. It allows each traditional collective, in this case the Islamic *umma*, to preserve a continuous identity through spatial and temporal changes.[12] This is not to say that the religious approach is always in opposition to human rights. Although some religious intellectuals may argue that there is an opposition, others suggest that human rights-based reform must simply be based on both global and local society to ensure that it is sensitive to the Arab world's particularities.

In contrast to secularists, the Egyptian Islamist thinker ʿAbd al-Wahhab al-Misiri embeds his understanding of modernity and authenticity in the context of a fundamental criticism of the Enlightenment and its guiding principle of secularization. He reduces the tradition of the Enlightenment in Western thought to a supposedly all-encompassing materialism, which he views as the "key paradigm of modernity."[13] Al-Misiri makes the assumption that the materialism of Western modernity is based on the total negation of the religious and the spiritual in people's lives. He distinguishes between partial and total secularization. Whereas partial secularization (*al-ʿilmaniya al-juziya*) represents primarily the separation of state and religion, which he views as a historical process accompanying the growing differentiation of human societies, total secularization (*al-ʿilmaniya ash-shamila*) involves a conscious desacralization of the world in the name of supposed universal progress. On the basis of this total secularization, al-Misiri produces a portrait of a humanity stripped of its enchantment: without any religious standards, values, or ideas, it is unprotected against the brutal laws of materialism.[14]

Universal phenomena accompanying modernity may be accepted as historical fact, but Islamist thinkers emphasize the foreignness and cultural immanence of the philosophical discourse that accompanies these phenomena, and which they completely reject. According to al-Misiri, the Enlightenment concept of progress, for example, only became universalised as a result of scientific and technical developments in the nineteenth century. The underlying credo lay in the unity of all people on the basis of an "unstoppable evolution." The crimes of the twentieth century and the nonlinear development of modern societies have, in his opinion, not been able to put an end to the belief in progress in Western thought.[15] For a better appreciation of historical processes, he therefore proposes a religious interpretation of history that draws on the "righteous" and "decadent" elements of humanity in order to free "our history from the nihilistic illusion of evolution."

In his rejection of Western modernity, al-Misiri takes recourse in the past and in local traditions. The claim is that only by searching for authentic origins can a way be found to a creative expression of the present and the future.[16] The key for him lies both in the rejection of a preoccupation with the West (*tahayyuz*) and a strengthening of cultural and religious identity (*huwiya*). While he uses the first term—*tahayyuz*—as an accusation against secular thinkers and thus denies Arab understandings of modernity any form of intellectual credibility and originality, he uses *huwiya* to raise the historical experience of the *umma* to a coherent expression of an unchangeable religious logic. The latter task is fulfilled, in his opinion, by the Islamist discourse of authenticity, which he refers to as "dynamic, aware of its past and also directed to the future."[17] Many Islamists perceive the Western origin and tradition of human rights to be culturally and ideologically dependent on the Western historical experience. They therefore question the relevance of Western understanding(s) of society and politics to the Arab world, negating rights or embracing them only under particular conditions.

Reformist Approach

The proponents of reformist discourse attempt to resolve dichotomies between rational thought and belief, philosophy and religion, citizenship and Islam, modern science and revelation. This is done by selecting and syncretizing components of secular and religious worldviews. They take, for example, the opposition of secularism and religion as a constructed paradigm anchored in a modernistic interpretation of history and social change that dates to the Enlightenment. They do recognize rational thought as universal but localize its beginnings in the Arab Middle Ages rather than solely in the West. In order to revive the Arab-Islamic *turath* in an era predominantly influenced by Western culture it is necessary, in the view of reformist thinkers, to critically review both the existing concept of *turath* as well as philosophical production from the West. Only in a hybrid structure, based on *muᶜasara* (contemporality) and *asala*, will it be possible to end the Arab world's stagnation.[18]

The aim of the Moroccan philosopher Muhammad ʿAbid al-Jabiri, for example, is to investigate the interaction and dynamics between current Arab thinkers and Western modernity, whose core questions he views as universal. He wishes to free the "essence" of this interaction from the numerous conceptual and ideological accretions that have grown over it in recent decades, and in this way to move to the center the key question of the relationship between Arabs and modernity.[19] The concept of authenticity, according to him, embodies on the one hand reference to the past as a constant foundation of Arab thought, and on the other hand the contemporary search for the conditions of a return to a true understanding of cultural heritage—which he sees as a "re-presentation of the past"—with the goal of ending the Arab world's stagnation.[20] The *turath* concept is defined by al-Jabiri as "the sum of all elements both from our past and also from the past of other cultures which accompany us in the present."[21] He distinguishes between historical-ideological content that reflects Arab-Islamic civilization's social and political reality in its various epochs,[22] and the universal truth of *turath*'s content that takes shape in the Islamic worldview or in normative ideas and philosophical concepts based on it.[23] In essence, this distinction resembles the separation anchored in Islamic thought between the constant and the changeable—that is, between Islam's sacral and profane elements. However, al-Jabiri extends its applicability to differentiate cultural heritage from historically bound and universally valid elements. His primary goal is to "emancipate" the universal value of the *turath* from retrogressive, idealized past moments.

After having highlighted Arab culture as a *thaqafa turathiya* (*turath*-oriented culture), al-Jabiri turns to the historical particularity of modernity and its effects on contemporary Arab thought. In doing this he denies the claim of modernity for universal validity (al-ʿAzma), but distances himself at the same time from the one-sided Islamist rejection of it and its reduction to a materialist approach (al-Misiri). For example, al-Jabiri differentiates in his conceptualization of human rights' relevance. He sees the rights regime as having general political relevance, despite its particular origin; on the other hand, as a philosophical discourse it can only be understood in the context of the European historical experience.

For al-Jabiri the efforts for rationalism and democracy in the West involve three aspects: critical thought, the necessity for a more just formation of the political sphere, and the protection of minorities on the basis of civil and human rights.[24] These three components, in his view, are also of enormous importance for Arab societies. On the basis of the ongoing confrontation over secularization and the view of modernity as "a decision for or against Islam," however, this had lost its relevance in Arab thought. In contrast, al-Jabiri emphasizes that neither rationalism nor democracy necessarily excludes Islam; the particular importance of each could be based on the authentic foundations of Islam's heritage.[25] But the precondition for this is the deconstruction of the dominant, retrogressive understanding of *turath* in order to modernize the body of thought contained in it (*tahdith at-turath*). Reform-minded intellectuals, therefore, can embrace rights and stress cultural heritage in giving local substance and meaning to those rights.

Common Features and Differences in Secular, Islamist, and Reformist Approaches

Secular thinkers were among the first to explore the Western literature on globalization. Their forums for discussion, especially the Center for Arab Unity Studies[26] and the Ahram Center for Political and Strategic Studies in Cairo, have organized numerous discussions and conferences over the past few years, and their results have been presented in a series of introductory monographs and anthologies. The strategically favorable starting position of having introduced this conceptual frame allowed secular thinkers, almost unhindered, to determine the parameters of the globalization and human rights debate in its initial phase.[27] The contributions of secular intellectuals clearly demonstrate the relevance of existing views of modernity and authenticity to understanding the cultural effects of globalization and universal human rights in Arab-Muslim societies. On the one hand, liberal thinkers tend to stylize emerging global culture as the normative completion of secular modernity and to evaluate local traditions either as an expression of irrational constructions of authenticity or outdated values in need of reform. In contrast, Marxist authors, in their condemnation of both the capitalist culture of globalization and its apologists, use a local discourse with traces of authenticity to defend enlightened modernity and a differentiated *turath* concept, distinguishing between backward-looking and forward-looking elements. Further differences can be identified within the secular approach with respect to its understanding of identity. Whereas cultural optimists supporting liberal attitudes see in globalization a chance for rationalization of local identities in Arab societies or for bringing them into the present, culturally pessimistic Marxists emphasize the instrumentalization of reactionary ideas of identity in the context of global culture's hegemonic discourse. Both variants, however, share a common underlying conviction that the deficits of local culture can be overcome by incorporating universally valid norms such as tolerance, pluralism, and humanism into the repertoire of contemporary Arab thought. In other words, in the secular camp, regardless of criticism of the political dominance of the West or the rejection of its capitalist ideology, there is a predominantly positive assessment of interactions with the cultural "Other" for its innovative effects on one's own culture.

The flood of secular contributions to the globalization and human rights debates confronted Islamist thinkers with views and interpretations that called into question the credibility of their own attitudes toward the dichotomy of modernity and authenticity. This forced them to take the new public debate seriously.[28] In the Islamist camp there is clearly a majority that rejects globalization and, at its extreme, this leads to the concept of global culture being replaced by categories such as "civilizational invasion" or "cultural penetration." The first impression can be that this is just another rehash of the wave of religious criticism of ideas originating in the West and the threat to identity that can result from transferring them to Arab-Muslim societies. In that case, a systematic review of the Islamist contributions to the globalization debate would be relatively unproductive, since they would tend to be repetitive.[29] A closer inspection of the literature, however, shows that there are also Islamist voices which, like some Arab Marxists in the previous section, go beyond rejection to an alternative view of globalization. In this context, analogies to secular views of Western and Arab origins serve to widen the frame of reference for some Islamists and, consequently, lead to a process of partial renewal in the religious camp. Do the contents of the Islamist contributions to the globalization debate merely reflect the repetition of older, backward-looking patterns of thought? That would be putting things too simply. Condemnation of Western secular thought's importation to Arab societies does not stop some Islamist intellectuals from taking positive connotations from certain Western approaches, albeit prefaced with evident skepticism. In part, this is the result of the search for inspiration, a desire for intellectual contacts outside the familiar frame of reference and, in the end, for recognition by the cultural "Other." As a result, a new form of interaction emerges, a sphere of acceptance in Islamist thought regarding Western ideas and concepts beyond the West's obvious scientific and technological achievements. The reference to non-Islamic historical experience in connection with the search for authenticity can be bedded in the same context. The intention is to position authenticity discourse as the expression of a universal strategy in the struggle against secular modernity and one-sided globalization, and thus in the end to justify these against the superior West—following the slogan "that is not the only way."

Finally, the position of reformists in these regards can be outlined relatively briefly because in content they differ little from the moderate

Islamists already considered. They, too, emphasize the fundamental difference between the negative features of globalization and the positive essences of universalism. They operate with an almost identical repertoire of concepts and metaphors. Reform-oriented thinkers such as al-Jabiri or Muhammad Mahfuz[30] also draw on categories like "cultural penetration," "cultural conquest," "civilizational interaction," and "civilizational project," and they are used with similar meanings. Nevertheless—and this justifies in part the separate consideration of their discourse—the reform proponents differ from Islamists in their response to the question, "What is to be done?" As already noted, they go a big step further in their method and apply their critical approach above all to their understanding of cultural heritage. This begins by attenuating negative perceptions of the Other and emphasizing shared features between the "self" and the "foreign." It continues with a call for the energetic modernization of local cultures in Arab societies by means of their liberation from backward-looking views on cultural heritage. Al-Jabiri and Mahfuz use the discursive bridges put down by some secular and moderate Islamist intellectuals. In addition, they try to place the values of democracy, human rights, and rationalism at the forefront of this debate. In consequence, weighting of topics and fields of discourse is reversed from that of other approaches: reformists begin with a critical view of one's own heritage and the identity constructions based on it and only then is this followed by a consideration of the influence of the more powerful cultural Other. This revaluation represents an important shift, because it brings with it a further opening up of the debate. The starting point is the articulation of a contemporary understanding of *turath* that allows Arab thinkers to interact with the cultural Other.

Conclusion

In contemporary debates on human rights and democracy, the historical experience of Arab countries regarding state formation and the political organization of society is interpreted in a contradictory manner. One side blames Islam for historically legitimizing the despotic state, whereas the other side finds the liberal tendency of Islam suppressed by modern worldly authority. Following the first interpretation results in the exclusion of religion from the secular public sphere overseen by the modern nation-state. Advocates of the second approach, however, make an argument for redefining politics by reference to so-called liberal institutions of the *umma* that guarantee human rights. The Arab world has come to yet another intellectual crossroads.

The variety of the contributions to the globalization debate demonstrates the intensity of contemporary intellectual confrontations in the Arab public sphere when new concepts are introduced. The question raised in the introduction about the evaluation of the cultural consequences of globalization and human rights discourse can be answered as follows: views about cultural globalization range from the hope of the secular thinkers that with the help of new phenomena it will be possible to complete modernity, through to the fears of Islamists concerning a renewed Western cultural hegemony. Within this broad spectrum, some participants in the debate balance globalization's positive and negative aspects and distinguish between political forms that can be advanced under the guise of globalization and other normative elements that are, indeed, universally valid. It is, thus, possible to place views on local culture between two poles: representatives of the secular current of thought view these as outdated traditions to be modernized or replaced by rational ideas and universal norms, whereas Islamist thinkers see in the defense of local culture a foundation for the preservation of authentic identity. A minority of moderates in both camps and reform-oriented intellectuals see the need to emphasize the relevance of local cultures but that these should open up gradually and appropriately to accept positive global changes, including universally accepted human rights standards.

Views about cultural globalization and local culture reflect, in part, conceptualizations that were articulated in the debates about modernity and authenticity in the 1970s and 1980s. At times it seems as if the pairing of global-local was only a fashionable replacement for the previous modernity-authenticity paradigm. The relevant connotations for the articulation of political and social models remain almost unchanged, despite being enriched with new lines of argumentation and new metaphors, including the current debate on the implementation of human rights. For some secular thinkers the increased emphasis on globalization's political core brings with it noticeably increasing caution. Furthermore, there has been a revaluation of Arab authenticity discourses, which are now regarded as potentially effective strategies in the struggle against Western superiority. Moderate Islamists and reform intellectuals are expressing more clearly their acceptance of normative ideas such as human rights, democracy, and rationalism, which are characteristic of Western modernity. Not least because of the credibility of these intellectuals, these concepts are gaining a central position in Islamist and reform-oriented discourses. In this context the distinction between the constant and the changeable elements of cultural heritage has moved to center stage. This may allow space where the preservation of culture and tradition can coexist with positive global advances, such as the desire to ensure that the human rights of individuals in all regions are realized.

Chapter 4
Transnational Human Rights Networks and Human Rights in Egypt

Neil Hicks

The "Spiral Model" of Human Rights Socialization

In 1999 three political scientists, Thomas Risse, Stephen Ropp, and Kathryn Sikkink, published a book that sets out a theory of how human rights change occurs within particular states and that demonstrates how international human rights norms and the activities of transnational human rights advocacy networks impact human rights conditions.[1] The book contains eleven case studies that apply the theory to human rights developments in diverse countries from different geographical regions.[2] The authors conclude, "our case-study evidence strongly suggests that the spiral model has applicability in strikingly diverse domestic circumstances."[3] All of the countries in their sample showed substantial progress along the spiral toward improved respect for human rights, apart from Tunisia.

The theory developed by Risse, Ropp, and Sikkink is of great importance to human rights advocates, who form the component parts of transnational human rights advocacy networks. If we can understand the factors that contribute to or cause positive human rights change, then we can be more effective in accomplishing our goals of promoting and protecting human rights. The utility of the theory is that it sets out in a systematic manner the often unstated assumptions on which much of the work of what might be referred to as the human rights establishment is based.

The case of Egypt is a difficult one for any theory of positive human rights change because there has been so little of it. In this chapter I will apply the spiral model to the Egyptian case, thereby illuminating the points among the interactions between different actors involved in the process of implementatiing international standards where the process appears to have stalled. In this way, I will seek to provide an explanation of the failure of transnational human rights networks to bring about substantial human rights improvement despite decades of effort by diverse local and international actors.

The spiral model takes into account four levels of interactions in the "socialization process by which domestic actors increasingly internalize international human rights norms."[4] These are

- interactions between norm-violating governments and their domestic society;
- interactions between the domestic opposition and transnational human rights networks;
- interactions among transnational advocacy networks, international organizations, and Western powers;
- interactions between transnational networks, international organizations, Western powers, on the one hand, and norm-violating governments on the other.

The theory further identifies three modes of social interaction that operate during the "phased socialization process": strategic bargaining and instrumental rationality; arguing and persuasion; and institutionalization and habitualization.[5]

Five phases of development are put forward as being part of the spiral model of human rights change. In a time of repression, the first phase, the norm-violating government tends to respond to criticism by denying the validity of human rights norms. Thus, the second phase is denial. Under sustained governmental and nongovernmental pressure the norm-violating government makes tactical concessions to human rights—the third phase of the spiral. As a result, the margin of maneuver for the norm-violating government is limited and pressure builds for either a regime change or a controlled liberalization. The fourth phase of the spiral comes when human rights norms achieve prescriptive status—when states ratify international human rights treaties and make them applicable in domestic law. The fifth and final phase comes when the government demonstrates rule-consistent behavior—when human rights are applied in practice.

The book makes a persuasive case for the application of this theory to case histories where positive human rights change has taken place, that is, in ten out of the eleven countries examined. It shows the inadequacy of alternative theories of why human rights change occurs to account for the developments in these countries. The theory strongly suggests that positive human rights change is likely to occur because denial of the validity of international human rights norms has become an increasingly untenable position for norm-violating states to hold, and once tactical concessions are made, by, for example, ratifying international instruments, then the pressure for change only increases. The authors view "a fully mobilized domestic opposition with transnational links" as a virtually irresistible force for change. Moreover, they suggest that the power of international norms is only increasing with time. Overall, the theory provides a generally optimistic outlook for human rights implementation throughout the world.

Applying the Theory to Egypt

Which factors impact human rights conditions in Egypt? Any analysis of human rights conditions in Egypt should begin with the authoritarian nature of the state and its centralizing, patronage-based form of governing. The state discourages and suffocates autonomous political or social forces, such as opposition political parties, local government, the press, professional associations, and private voluntary organizations. The government may be characterized as non-ideological, primarily concerned with sustaining itself—a pursuit at which it has excelled.

Egypt appears to fit the model for a state that has been subjected to the various types of interactions that have been observed to contribute to human rights progress elsewhere. Egypt has a long history of interaction between the state and domestic political and civil forces pressing for greater popular participation in government, and for respect for civil liberties and human rights. It has, for example, one of the longest parliamentary traditions in the region, dating back to the late nineteenth century. Its bar association, labor unions, professional associations, women's movement, and student movement have at different times made substantial contributions to human rights progress. The long anticolonial struggle, culminating in the Free Officers seizing power in 1952, mobilized many different elements of political and civil society over decades of struggle against British occupation and domination.

In recent decades, in line with global trends, interactions between domestic human rights advocates and international human rights networks have increased. Nongovernmental organizations established with the specific purpose of promoting respect for international human rights standards developed in Egypt in the early 1980s. The movement grew in the late 1980s and early 1990s, and organizations proliferated from the mid-1990s. The movement grew initially as a domestic branch of a regional international organization, the Arab Organization for Human Rights (AOHR), founded in 1982. Cooperative ties with

Western-based, international human rights organizations grew with the development of the movement.

Egypt has a tradition of granting access to international human rights research missions. As a relatively open country, it has been the subject of much reporting and monitoring over the last two decades. Transnational human rights networks came to the aid of Egyptian human rights advocates when they were the targets of government persecution. For example, in 1989, when Egyptian Organization for Human Rights (EOHR) executive board members Amir Salem and Muhammad al-Sayyed Sa'id were imprisoned, the work of Egyptian human rights NGOs rose to international and domestic prominence. The international campaign on their behalf was successful in that the two activists were released promptly.

Transnational advocacy networks have tried to apply pressure through Western governments and available international human rights mechanisms for many years. Egypt has submitted reports to the UN Human Rights Committee on its compliance with its treaty obligations, and has from time to time replied to inquiries from UN special rapporteurs on various human rights issues.

As the second largest recipient of U.S. foreign aid (after Israel), the potential for the aid relationship to be used to promote human rights exists. In addition, Egypt is also involved in complex trade and aid relationships with the European Union and its member states. Human rights conditions are increasingly part of the bilateral relationship between Egypt and the United States, and Egypt and Europe. Western powers and international organizations have supported training programs and other events designed to promote human rights and democratization in Egypt.

Thus we can see that Egypt has been fully exposed to the four levels of interactions by which human rights norms have been internalized elsewhere. In seeking to persuade the Egyptian government to reform its human rights practices, different modes of social interaction have been employed. Sticks and carrots through threatening to condition aid have been employed, as well as arguments that have appealed to Egypt's sense of itself as a distinguished member of the world community, a regional leader with a strong liberal tradition. And yet Egypt appears to have made precious little progress along the spiral of positive human rights change.

Egypt has had its share of repression throughout its modern history, although this has ebbed and flowed with the prevailing political conditions. Repression has usually remained within limits, allowing most people to feel somewhat free most of the time, and single devastating incidents of human rights abuse, such as have occurred in many neighboring countries, have largely been avoided. Thus the government has been able to maintain a relatively benign international image, despite persistently failing to live up to international human rights norms. Egypt's international reputation is important to its leaders, not only because Egypt relies so heavily on revenue from Western tourists who might be less willing to visit if they thought it was a wild, lawless place, but also because Egypt is proud of its image as a cradle of civilization.

This sense that human rights conditions are not so bad in Egypt has enabled the government to engage in a kind of soft denial when faced with human rights criticism. Egypt has never engaged internationally in public denial of the validity of international human rights norms. It participated in the drafting of the Universal Declaration of Human Rights and ratified the International Covenant on Civil and Political Rights, and the International Covenant on Economic Social and Cultural Rights in 1982.[6] While international standards have been largely free of official criticism, nongovernmental human rights advocates and organizations have been regularly upbraided for defaming Egypt, engaging in double standards, giving aid and comfort to terrorists, and even acting as agents of hostile foreign powers. This is certainly a form of denial because for the most part local and international human rights NGOs have done none of these things.

The Egyptian government has been under sustained international and local pressure to improve its human rights performance for many years. Much of this pressure, which arguably increased throughout the 1990s, was the kind of concerted (if not always coordinated) internal and external pressure, involving a diverse mixture of local and international actors, that has brought about change elsewhere. Despite this pressure, the government has made few tactical concessions to the demands of the international human rights movement. Although it has ratified a raft of international human rights treaties, many of the rights and freedoms they contain are not applied in practice. In fact, the Egyptian government appears immune to the phenomenon of self-entrapment and limiting of its own margin of maneuver, which has been a precursor of change elsewhere. As international and local activism for human rights reform increased through the mid- and late 1990s, the government set about systematically dismantling domestic sources of criticism while ignoring international objections. Throughout this period it never let slip the pretense that Egypt was a firm supporter of the international human rights regime.

Thus we can observe that human rights in Egypt have not attained the fourth stage of the spiral. For the most part, they cannot be said to have a prescriptive status in law and practice. It is questionable whether the third phase has been reached, that of tactical concession, because the "concession" of ratifying international instruments has had so nugatory an effect on practice. Although the Egyptian government has paid lip service to international human rights norms, it has not engaged in vain-glorious claims for its human rights achievements or sought to make protecting human rights a basis of its political legitimacy, as the Ben Ali regime has done in Tunisia, for example.[7] It is worth noting that the government has made some apparent tactical concessions in 2004 and 2005 with President Mubarak's formal acceptance of the political reform agenda and such measures as the formation of the national Human Rights Council and the agreement to hold contested presidential elec-tions in 2005. Such concessions carry risks that eventually the interna-tional community and the local population will begin to take the government at its word and begin to expect the human rights the gov-ernment so freely promises and boasts of being implemented. Egypt had until the early years of the new century eschewed such risks. As noted above, the denial phase in Egypt has focused on the messenger and not the message, and an all-out confrontation with global forces for con-formity with human rights norms has thus been averted. So Egypt remained becalmed in phase one of the spiral, practicing repression at a level that to date has not elicited an effective response from transna-tional human rights networks.

This is a remarkable state of affairs. How can a state that appears as susceptible to the transnational power of international human rights norms in fact remain so resistant to it? Is Egypt a greater exception to the spiral theory than Tunisia, where now, belatedly, the combined forces of international concern and a resilient domestic human rights movement seem to be putting some pressure on the government to change? At least until 2004, pressure for human rights change in Egypt over the prior decade seemed to recede rather than increase.

The rest of this chapter presents a brief typology of the human rights violations from which Egypt suffers. It will then review the development of the local human rights movement, its integration into transnational human rights networks, and the ensuing problems and difficulties. The government's deliberalization policies and the extent to which they may be seen as a response to human rights criticism will be assessed. The chapter concludes with some reflections on the Egyptian case and its implications for theories of human rights change, as well as for the prac-tice of domestic and international human rights advocates.

Human Rights Violations in Egypt

Human rights encompass a broad area of human activity in the civil, political, economic, social, and cultural spheres. While the corpus of international human rights standards is designed to be interdependent and indivisible,[8] it is possible to focus on particular basic rights as indicators of overall human rights conditions. The rights to life, liberty, and security of person, which include basic rights to be free from arbitrary killing and arbitrary detention and torture, as well as the right to fair trial and equal treatment under the law, may be considered core rights. Another subset of rights, having to do with basic freedoms of expression, association, and conscience, as well as the right to take part in the government of one's country, will be considered in the context of the government's deliberalization policies.

Governments bear the primary responsibility for upholding and protecting human rights. They agree to be bound by the treaties they ratify, and generally speaking they are the grantors and guarantors of rights and freedoms to their citizens and others falling under their jurisdiction, the grantees. There are nongovernmental entities, like opposition groups and multinational corporations, which have taken on sufficient governmental characteristics in some circumstances to be considered accountable to international human rights standards.[9] In Egypt, where extremist Islamic opposition groups have engaged in numerous acts of political violence in which members of the security forces and civilians have been killed and seriously wounded, the government has sometimes argued that the real perpetrators of human rights violations have been the extremist groups, usually referred to as terrorists by the government. The violent actions of terrorist groups are indefensible and the government is fully empowered to take all necessary measures to apprehend perpetrators and protect society from the scourge of terrorism. However, it is misleading to refer to criminal acts by armed opposition groups in Egypt as violations of human rights. They are criminal acts, violations of the law. The government has the right and obligation to hold perpetrators of such acts accountable in accordance with the law.

For these reasons, this review of human rights violations will concentrate on government actions. Egyptian law and the Egyptian Constitution uphold the basic freedoms provided in international human rights instruments. However, exceptional laws have facilitated the wholesale disregard of basic rights and freedoms, especially with regard to protection from arbitrary detention and torture, and the right to a fair trial.

The Emergency Law[10] has been maintained throughout the presidency of Hosni Mubarak, who came to power after the assassination of President Anwar Sadat in 1981. This law cedes to the president, or his designated agent, broad powers to detain without charge or trial individuals suspected of involvement in activities deemed harmful to national security. It provides for the trial of those suspected of crimes against national security by emergency state security courts from which there is no appeal, and whose verdicts must be ratified by the president.[11] Tens of thousands of Egyptians have been detained without charge or trial under the emergency legislation since 1981.

It is often stated that the government's resort to repressive tactics came in response to an upsurge in political violence by Islamist opposition groups. While this is certainly part of the explanation, it does not tell the whole story. The emergency legislation predates the escalation in Islamist violence in the early 1990s. Such legislation has in fact been in force in Egypt, with only a short break in 1980–81, since 1967. Egypt's near permanent state of emergency, like other elements of the state's repressive apparatus, is a holdover from the one-party rule of the Nasser era—a legacy that the ostensibly democratic Mubarak regime has been in no hurry to shake off.

The government did intensify its repressive powers in response to political violence. Law 97 of 1992, the Anti-Terrorism Law, increased the number of offenses punishable by death, introduced a broad catchall definition of terrorism, and made it possible for the president of the republic, or his representative, to refer civilians accused of terrorism for trial before military courts.[12] Trials before military courts fall far short of minimum internationally agreed upon fair trial standards.[13] Unlike Egypt's civilian judges, who are appointed for life by the Higher Judicial Council, military judges are appointed for renewable two-year periods by the minister of defense. Military judges are not independent. Since 1992 military courts have been used to try defendants accused of violent crimes and, since 1995, to try defendants from among the government's ostensibly peaceful political opponents.

The state also sought to close off the political space in which the Islamic opposition to the government was organizing. For example, the November 1992 executive order for the closure or nationalization of private mosques was aimed directly at diminishing the influence of the political Islamic movement. A succession of other restrictive measures certainly had the Islamists in its sights, but resulted in damaging a much broader range of targets among independent political and civil society groupings. These included laws designed to strengthen governmental control over such bodies as professional syndicates, rural local government, and university faculties.[14]

If these restrictive measures may be seen as primarily targeted against the Islamists, others such as Law 93 of 1995,[15] which imposed new restrictions on the press designed to silence journalists engaging in strident criticism of government policies as well as exposing corrupt practices by senior government officials and their family members, had other purposes. For example, on February 24, 1998, a Cairo court sentenced two journalists for the opposition *Al-Sha'b* newspaper, Magdi Ahmad Hussein and Muhammad Hilal, to one year's imprisonment for publishing articles suggesting that Ala al-Alfi, son of the minister of the interior, Hassan al-Alfi, had profited corruptly from his father's position. With the passage of the new press law, even in its revised form, the number of libel suits filed against journalists increased dramatically.[16]

The sustained official hostility toward independent nongovernmental human rights organizations gathered pace during 1995 and culminated in the now suspended Law on Associations, Law 153 of 1999, and was similarly indicative of a growing official intolerance for independent criticism of all kinds. In May 2000, the U.N. Committee for Economic, Social, and Cultural Rights, reviewing Egypt's compliance with the International Covenant on Economic, Social, and Cultural Rights, stated that the law "gives the government control over the rights of NGOs to manage their own activities, including seeking external funding."[17] In 1998, the government had signaled its hostile intent toward Egyptian nongovernmental human rights organizations by bringing charges against the secretary general of the EOHR, Hafez Abu Sa'da, for "receiving foreign funds without permission," using Decree Law 4 of 1992, an emergency measure introduced in the aftermath of the devastating Cairo earthquake designed to cut off funding for independent Islamic relief agencies, which were outperforming the state's relief efforts. This draconian measure was used again in the prosecution of Saad Eddin Ibrahim and staff members of his Ibn Khaldun Center for Development Studies in 2001. Dr. Ibrahim is one of Egypt's foremost campaigners for democratic reform and one of the founders of the contemporary human rights movement.

The evolution of Decree Law 4 of 1992 from an exceptional measure with a specific purpose to a tool of more general repressive application serves as a good model for how restrictions of basic freedoms are facilitated in Egypt. The government is in the habit of passing exceptional laws, which bypass constitutional and internationally guaranteed human rights safeguards available in Egyptian law, in order to meet particular needs of the moment. Rather than rescinding these exceptional powers when the particular circumstance for which they were designed is past, the laws remain on the books in perpetuity. Thus the executive branch of government has a wide array of exceptional powers available to it, dating back to the Nasser period and beyond, which in practice remove any notion of legal consistency from the protection of human rights and basic freedoms for its citizens. In the language of the spiral model theory, despite their presence in Egyptian laws and statutes, human rights standards have no prescriptive force when the government chooses to apply an alternative set of laws, stripped of human rights protections.

The Development of the Local Human Rights Movement

The local human rights movement in Egypt has been shaped by the adverse legal and political circumstances in which it has developed. It is important to note at the outset, given the complications that have attended the local movement's relations with its international partners and supporters, that the Egyptian human rights movement has domestic origins. Certain political and intellectual elites became dissatisfied with the slow pace of political, social, and economic development in Egypt and began to search for alternative forms of political and social engagement with the state and society.

The calamity of the humiliating Arab defeat in the 1967 war with Israel dealt a serious blow to the prestige of postindependence republican regimes in a number of Arab states, and to the Nasser regime in Egypt in particular, that was only partially repaired by the Arab successes in the early days of the October 1973 war. The Nasserist ideology of nationalism, single-party rule, and state control of the economy began to lose its gloss as Egyptians realized that the country was not striding forward in its national development. Egypt began to experiment with multiparty politics under President Sadat in 1976, and began a gradual process of economic liberalization. The 1979 Camp David peace treaty with Israel secured the return of the Sinai Peninsula, territory lost to Israel in 1967, but left Egypt isolated from the Arab world for more than a decade and put to rest the myth of Arab unity.

The political, economic, and social malaise of the 1970s created the conditions in which human rights ideas took hold in parts of Egyptian society. As one commentator has noted,

By the 1970s, the developmentalist state had begun to tire. This fatigue created an opportunity to rethink the assumption that had dominated pre and early postwar politics: that collective rights, first political (independence), then economic (development) must naturally take precedence over individual rights.[18]

The future leaders of the human rights movement, which developed in the 1980s, came from distinct groups. Some were former senior state officials who had either fallen afoul of the repressive apparatus, developed under Nasser, or had become disillusioned with both the direction of policy and the autocratic manner of rule under President Sadat.

Other leaders from an older generation included independent leftist figures who had chafed under the single-party orthodoxy of the Nasser years and suffered persecution accordingly. Fathi Radwan, a hero of the independence movement, gave the new movement strong nationalist credibility until his death in 1988.

Younger leaders came to the human rights movement after growing frustrated with the factionalism and blocked avenues of radical left-wing student politics. Sadat's Egypt with its controlled democracy left no space for the development of independent opposition political parties. Negad al-Borai, secretary-general of the EOHR between 1993 and 1995, describes their motivation:

Most of us had come to human rights as a way of saving ourselves. Most of us had been active in politics but had become disillusioned with it. In fact we were all from a political background. Human rights looked brand new. It was not narrow and sectarian like party politics had become in Egypt. It was like an adventure and through it we found ourselves.[19]

Some on the left saw the human rights movement as a way of continuing their political project through other means. One such leader, Amir Salem, describes it thus:

The theoretical basis of what we were trying to do had its roots in the Marxist student movement. We were interested in forming intermediate organizations between the intellectuals and the people.[20]

As the way was blocked for forming a mass political party, some activists hoped to use the new structures of nongovernmental organizations to mobilize new constituencies for change.

In 1981, in the months prior to his assassination by Muslim extremists, President Sadat had ordered the imprisonment of more than 1,500 independent and opposition figures from across the political spectrum. The detainees included Coptic priests, Muslim Brothers, leftists, nationalists, and liberals. Sadat's increasingly erratic and arbitrary rule further persuaded activists and independent figures in Egypt that something ought to be done to rein in the power of the state.

While internal factors were paramount in the minds of the founders of the Egyptian human rights movement, international factors cannot be completely discounted. Egypt was not unaware of movements toward democratization, the so-called third wave, that started with transitions away from authoritarianism in southern Europe in the mid-1970s and continued through much of Latin America, culminating with the collapse of communism in Eastern Europe in the late 1980s.[21] Developments in Eastern Europe and the dissolution of the Soviet Union had a particular impact on leftists who had looked to these countries for a model. Several leaders of the Egyptian human rights movement readily admit that they have moved away from their Marxist origins to a more liberal orientation.[22] By definition, in associating themselves with the human rights movement former Marxists were dissociating themselves from the traditional Marxist view of human rights as bourgeois and individualistic.

Voluntary associations in Egypt have a long history, including in the field of political advocacy around such objectives as women's suffrage. However, traditionally most voluntary associations have been linked to religious organizations and have been primarily focused in the area of social welfare, providing services to the poor and disadvantaged. The idea of creating associations independent of the government and, indeed, designed with the intention of placing pressure on the government to change its policies was something new.

From the outset, the state has given the local human rights movement, especially in its more militant, adversarial forms, a cold reception. The EOHR, formed as a local chapter of the Cairo-based AOHR in 1985, saw its application to register as an association under Law 32 of 1964, the Law on Associations, rejected by the Ministry of Social Affairs. The AOHR, with its leadership drawn from Egypt's ruling elite, recommended a low-key approach from its Egyptian chapter until the legal recognition question could be resolved. Young activists, who had received their political education in the more confrontational traditions of the left-wing student movement, were unwilling to be quiescent in the face of official violations of human rights.

The case that made the EOHR's national reputation involved the government's suppression of a strike by iron and steel workers at the giant state-owned Helwan factory. Struggling to apply stringent economic structural adjustment criteria imposed by international lending institutions, the government was plagued by unrest among public sector workers and the millions of Egyptians who received public subsidies who saw that their standard of living was under threat. The government used force to break up a sit-in at the Helwan factory and accused the workers of being part of a left-wing conspiracy to overthrow the government. The EOHR objected to the government's rough treatment of the protesters, its violation of their right to freedom of assembly, its arbitrary detention of hundreds of workers, and other violations of human rights. Two members of the EOHR's executive board, Amir Salem and Muhammad al-Sayyed Sa'id, were chosen to write the organization's statement. That same night, in August 1989, they were taken into detention and beaten by interrogators from the state security intelligence police.

The detention of the two young activists, one a lawyer, the other a leading social scientist, had an electrifying impact on the EOHR. A member of the executive board at that time described it:

We began to feel our importance in the society. Suddenly, we started to receive hundreds of membership applications, and people started coming to us with complaints about violations. It opened our relations with other opposition political factions. We started to be approached by supporters of the Muslim Brotherhood and the *Gama'at Islamiya* (Islamic Groups).[23]

The detention of the two young activists also brought the new organization global attention. The release of the two activists after a relatively short period of imprisonment and without further criminal prosecution was seen as a great victory for international pressure. "For the first time in my life I spent only fourteen days in prison,"[24] commented one of the detainees, reflecting on the impact of combined local and international pressure on the government. This apparent victory over the government stood in stark contrast to the directionless impotence of the traditional political opposition.[25]

The period 1989–93 was one of rapid growth and high achievement for the EOHR. Two basic problems bedeviled the development of the EOHR and the Egyptian human rights movement more broadly: relations between the human rights movement and preexisting domestic political forces; and relations between the movement and the international community, particularly with respect to the question of foreign funding. Both of these problems may be traced back to the authoritarian character of the state apparatus in which the movement was developing.

In what was effectively a one-party system, competition between divergent ideological trends found expression in other, nonparliamentary venues. The EOHR became a new venue for political competition. Islamists, Communists, and Nasserists came to view the organization as something they had to control.

The EOHR leadership soon realized that politicization of the organization was a threat to its identity as an impartial human rights organization.[26] The EOHR was established as an open membership organization, but as the organization grew in national prominence, so did the threat of domination by one or another organized political faction. A pattern of controlled open membership was established, an uneasy compromise that left the leadership open to accusations that it was engaging in political favoritism and excluding individuals it disagreed with.

For the Fourth General Assembly in May 1991 the leadership tried to contain political tensions by putting forward a list for the executive board with a quota of candidates from each political faction. This was not wholly successful because political factions worked behind the scenes to defeat nominees from other tendencies.[27] Moreover, long-term activists excluded from the executive board's list of candidates because of the need to accommodate the different factions became alienated from the organization.[28]

There were competing views about how the organization should move forward. The idea of turning the EOHR into a closed organization was considered. The two real options available were to greatly increase the membership of the organization or to continue with a controlled gradual expansion of the membership. The leadership increasingly favored the latter course because experience had taught them to be mistrustful of the depth of the adherence to human rights principles of some members in comparison to their commitment to political ideologies.[29]

These different views, which were debated at a special meeting of the organization in August 1993, became identified with competing factions within the organization. The left was identified with the mass mobilization concept, whereas the Nasserists and liberals supported limiting the organization's expansion. Interfactional conflict continued until the climactic and notorious Fifth General Assembly in January 1994 at which the Nasserist faction secured a controlling majority on the executive board, but at the expense of alienating many longstanding members from other factions.

The EOHR's early leaders had envisioned a human rights movement in which activists from across the political spectrum could participate but would not itself be a forum for political competition. Purposeful depoliticization, whereby activists would leave their partisan affiliation at the door when they came to an EOHR event, was the aspiration, perhaps even grounded in a charter of cooperation for human rights between the different factions. None of this was achievable in practice. The human rights movement in Egypt fragmented after 1993, and many former EOHR leaders either left human rights activity completely or formed their own private organizations. When the government stepped up its repression of the human rights movement in the late 1990s, the movement's failure to develop strong roots in the society was exposed. The authorities faced little opposition to their characterization of the movement as an inauthentic, alien implant working against the interests of the nation. Former members of the EOHR joined in the barrage of criticism against the movement in the media. The failure to build a broad local base for human rights through effective collaboration with existing political forces was a major impediment to human rights implementation in Egypt.

The domestic political isolation of the human rights movement has broadened the body of domestic opinion willing to engage in damaging public criticism of the movement. At the same time, Western material support for the movement, and Western criticism of the Egyptian government's human rights record, however justified, has provoked a defensive reaction from political factions with a traditional antipathy toward Western policies, including leftists, nationalists, and Islamists. This combination of circumstances has left the movement with few friends.

The controversial decision to accept foreign funding was attributable to several factors. On the one hand, the EOHR was starved of resources, constrained by its position of seemingly interminable legal limbo from establishing the organization with the size and reach it aspired to. Another pertinent factor was that funding was available for human rights organizations in Egypt. Moreover, there was a demand from Western-based human rights organizations, Western governments, and the international media for news about human rights conditions in Egypt. Egyptian human rights activists could best equip themselves to meet that demand by accepting the readily available foreign funds.

The presence of foreign funding changed the nature of the Egyptian human rights movement. What started out as a choice quickly became a dependency. Professionals staffed what had once been voluntary institutions. Repeatedly professional staff at the EOHR left the organization after a few years of experience for the richer prospect of being director of their own human rights organization. Most of these new organizations made no effort to create a base of local support through developing a membership core; instead they relied almost completely on foreign funding.

With the benefit of hindsight, it is easy to say that the decision to base the local movement in Egypt on foreign funding was a mistake, and that certainly the dependency on foreign funding that has developed is evidence of that wrong turn. But the leaders of the Egyptian human rights movement in the early 1990s faced few choices. They could do nothing and allow the movement for which they had already sacrificed a good deal to wither from inattention and want of resources, or they could seize hold of the promised lifeline from the international donors.

The EOHR decided to accept foreign funding at a board meeting in November 1992. In the words of one board member, accepting foreign funding "prevented the organization from perishing under mounting financial difficulties."[30] However, "in the political and intellectual climate prevalent in Egypt, agitation based on foreign funding was the easiest weapon for character assassination and the defamation of individuals and the organization itself."[31] In 1993, three members of the executive board announced their resignations over the decision to accept foreign funding and became vociferous public critics of the human rights movement.

It was not the issue of foreign funding alone that raised objections within Egypt; the whole issue of international networking went against the grain of nationalist sensibilities. The EOHR leadership faced criticism for giving too much attention to international relations at the expense of domestic initiatives. Muhammad al-Sayyed Sa'id argued persuasively that this line of criticism was unfounded: "EOHR did not overlook any real opportunity for action within Egypt." But he observed astutely:

What gave the impression of overriding emphasis on international networking was fundamentally the existence of greater room and potential for development in the external environment than what is factually possible in Egypt itself.[32]

There was a disequilibrium between the high receptivity of international bodies to various types of advocacy, campaigning, and promotion of human rights in Egypt on the one hand, and the low capacity of domestic structures in Egypt to channel this energy into constructive pressure for human rights change on the other. As a result, too often foreign pressure became counterproductive and was used to discredit the domestic human rights movement.

The Destruction of the Local Human Rights Movement

In recent years official pressure on the human rights movement has increased to the extent that it is appropriate to speak of a policy to systematically destroy the independent nongovernmental human rights movement, at least in the form in which it had developed by 2000.

A change in the government's attitude toward local human rights organizations became discernible in early 1995. On January 22, 1995, the legislative department of the Ministry of Justice issued a ruling on the status of so-called civil companies, saying that if they failed to register under the Law on Associations then they would be liable to prosecution.

From then on government officials habitually referred to local human rights groups as illegal organizations and began to discourage international human rights organizations from cooperating with local groups. The government informed international donors that they should not provide grants to organizations not registered under Law 32 of 1964. Almost all human rights organizations were not so registered. For a time no measures were taken to enforce this tougher official line, and international support of Egypt's growing human rights community continued. Nevertheless, the authorities succeeded in undermining popular support for the human rights movement by attacking human rights activists and organizations through the state-controlled media.

The attack was carried out primarily on two fronts. Human rights organizations were criticized for objecting to human rights violations against alleged supporters of militant Islamic groups. Government officials accused human rights groups of giving aid and comfort to terrorists. The second line of attack focused on the foreign connections of local human rights organizations, especially their reliance on foreign funding. Such attacks played on fears of foreign interference in Egypt's affairs and on memories of the injustices of the not so distant colonial past.

While this concerted and orchestrated campaign of defamation against the local and international human rights movements may certainly be characterized as a self-serving attempt by the government to distract attention from its poor human rights record, the tactic was effective because it drew on genuine concerns and grievances felt by many Egyptians. The country was unsettled by political violence from militant Islamic groups that had targeted tourists—thus damaging the economy—and state officials. Even within the human rights movement itself, the issues of foreign funding and reliance on the mobilization of foreign pressure were highly controversial. It is not surprising that many Egyptians, who were unfamiliar with international human rights in both theory and practice, would be deeply suspicious of the purposes of these foreign organizations and governments in criticizing Egypt.

It is worth considering the government's motivation in going on the offensive against its human rights critics since 1995. What has been called the deliberalization of Egypt during the 1990s (some contradictory trends have appeared since 2000) appears to be a response to several factors.[33] The repression of the local human rights movement, and a stolid resistance to international human rights pressure, should certainly be seen as part of this process of deliberalization. Between 1991 and 1994 the government faced a dangerous escalation in political violence that reached the level of an insurrection in parts of Upper Egypt, and targeted for assassination senior government leaders, including President Mubarak. At the same time Islamic groups were gaining popular support and demonstrating their electoral appeal by winning control of powerful professional associations, including the Medical Syndicate, the Engineers Syndicate, and, in 1993, the bar association. The government felt that it was losing control of the situation and was alarmed when Western press reports began to speak of official U.S. government security assessments predicting that "Islamic fundamentalist terrorists will continue to make gains across Egypt, leading to the eventual collapse of the Mubarak government."[34]

Eberhard Kienle argues that political deliberalization should also be seen as a corollary of economic structural adjustment, as well as a policy designed to stifle discontent from the millions of Egyptians whose livelihoods have been negatively affected by economic liberalization and to head off social conflict arising from increased income inequality. Since the 1977 bread riots (widespread riots followed President Sadat's attempt to cut government subsidies on bread prices), Egyptian governments have been cautious in their approach to reducing state subsidies and entitlements.

Other factors were also at work. The rapid growth of nongovernmental advocacy groups in Egypt was a new phenomenon. The state was obliged to take notice of this new dynamic sector of society through a series of major international conferences on social and economic issues during the mid-1990s, including the UN Conference on Population and Development in Cairo itself. Large, vociferous delegations of Egyptian NGOs attended each of these conferences, stripping the state of its accustomed role as the sole representative of Egypt on the international stage. Some of these NGOs were critical of government policies. They were also well connected internationally and supported financially by foreign governments and donor organizations. These organizations commanded a respectful international audience, not least in the human rights field, and the government found itself on the defensive in international fora, like the UN Human Rights Committee, coming under criticism on the basis of information collected by local NGOs. The government may well have decided that it did not have to tolerate this kind of international embarrassment and resolved to bring unruly NGOs more firmly into the official orbit.

The government's response to human rights pressure also appears to fit into a domestic political strategy of responding to the threat of political Islam with a mixture of accommodation and repression. While the state did not hesitate to use repressive force against its Islamist opponents, both violent and nonviolent, it also went along with and even encouraged greater Islamization in society in the social and cultural spheres. In doing this, the government tried to portray itself as the defender of traditional Islamic values in an attempt to siphon off support for Islamist opposition groups. The critique of human rights as an alien Western concept and of human rights activists as agents of foreign powers had the dual benefit of supporting the government's brand of nativist Islamism while undermining its human rights critics. Moreover, the government was aware of its vulnerability to domestic criticism because of its close association with U.S. policy in the region. Engaging in harsh rhetoric against its human rights critics enabled the government to place some welcome distance between it and the U.S. government, which was seen as employing human rights ideas to serve its own interests. The government calculated correctly that dissonance at the rhetorical and practical levels on human rights would not threaten the bilateral U.S.-Egyptian relationship.

Finally, in considering the government's response to the merited criticism of its human rights record, it must be noted that the Egyptian government was aware of its strategic importance to the West and that this provided considerable leeway in what its allies would tolerate in its treatment of its own citizens. Egypt was the first Arab state to sign a peace treaty with Israel and has continued to play a role, in accordance with U.S. policy, in promoting peace between Israel and its neighbors. Egypt was pivotal in the creation of the Desert Storm coalition that drove Saddam Hussein's Iraq out of Kuwait. Like many Arab states allied with the West, the Egyptian government has been adept at trading on Western fears of militant Islam, thereby gaining a degree of international indulgence with respect to what it may do in order to quell internal dissent. Taking these together, the Egyptian government remains highly insulated from international human rights pressure. Part of its reasoning in pursuing a hard line against domestic human rights advocates must surely be that it knows it can get away with it. The cost in terms of international penalties has been negligible, whereas the benefit of a tamed, quiescent local human rights movement is readily apparent.

The destruction of the local human rights movement that developed between 1985 and 1995 started in the mid-1990s, but it has accelerated. In December 1998, Hafez Abu Sa'ada, secretary-general of the EOHR, was detained in connection with a controversial report issued by the EOHR about human rights violations in the predominantly Christian village of Al-Kosheh in Upper Egypt. The government accused the EOHR of receiving money from foreign sources in order to defame the reputation of the country.

Despite the state's demonstrating its readiness to use the tools at its disposal to penalize local NGOs for receiving foreign funding, local human rights organizations continued to receive grants and carry on with business as usual. There were, however, clouds on the horizon.

The government was moving forward with its plans to replace the much criticized Law on Associations, Law 32 of 1964. At first, most human rights activists thought that this might be an opportunity to do away with the obstacle to legal normalization for many groups that had been a major hindrance to their development and acceptance in Egyptian society. Some cautioned that they had learned how to work around the old law, whereas the government could be expected to be more insistent on enforcing a new one. The human rights NGOs were divided as to how to approach the government on the issue. While there was broad agreement that any new law should simplify the registration process and protect the independence of NGOs from governmental interference in accordance with developing international standards regarding the work of human rights defenders,[35] there was little accord on how this could best be achieved. The government offered to consult with NGOs as part of the process of drafting the new law. Some regarded this as worthwhile; others thought that it would bind the NGOs into a governmental process that would not work to their advantage. As it turned out, NGO activists who did participate in the drafting process found their work disregarded when the government pushed its own version of the law through Parliament, Law 153 of 1999, in May 1999.

The law failed to meet the expectations of human rights activists and fell short of international standards upholding the rights of human rights defenders. For example, Article 11 of the new law outlawed "political" activities by NGOs, a loosely defined restriction that could be used to penalize legitimate activities by human rights defenders. Article 75 of the law banned the receipt of money from abroad or domestic fund-raising without prior permission from the authorities. In June 2000 the Constitutional Court suspended the new law on technical grounds. However, the government declared its intention to apply the new law without substantive changes as soon as procedural hurdles could be overcome. It also announced that all organizations would have to apply for registration under the new law, including those currently registered as not-for-profit civil companies. Organizations that continued to work without registration would be subject to prosecution.

The government's imposition of a new law maintaining its control over NGO activities, despite the temporary uncertainty created by the Constitutional Court's intervention, was a major blow to the human rights movement. Activists had hoped that the government would be sensitive to pressure from international donors, who spend millions of dollars in Egypt each year on a range of social welfare and development projects, to liberalize the Law on Associations. But when the crunch came:

Donors just disappeared in the fight with the government. They had taken strong positions saying that the government should enact a new law compatible with international standards protecting the rights of independent NGOs. But, when the government ignored these demands they did nothing. They said they wanted to protect their broader programs.[36]

All donors are not the same. By far the largest donor to the nongovernmental sector in Egypt is the United States Agency for International Development (USAID). It has long emphasized funding in the areas of economic and social development. It has not funded advocacy groups or professional associations. This is an important distinction. The government's hostility has been directed primarily at advocacy groups, especially those, like human rights organizations, that have developed strong international connections, capable of embarrassing the government on the global stage. Advocacy groups, and in the early 1990s professional associations, have been anomalous in the Egyptian context as channels for the expression of dissident opinion, which state authorities have refused to tolerate. The government has welcomed international support for a wide range of economic and social development projects that do not challenge government policies or provide political space for the government's opponents. Mustapha Kamel al-Sayyid has noted that

"U.S. officials value the friendship of the Egyptian government more than the strength of civil society organizations."[37] In 1999, USAID signaled its agreement with government efforts to centralize control over NGO activities by announcing its support for the NGO Service Center that appeared designed to channel international support to officially approved NGOs and, in time, could be used to exclude nonapproved NGOs from any place at the funding table. Only NGOs registered under the Law on Associations are eligible to receive funds from the NGO Service Center, which is run in collaboration with the Ministry of Social Affairs.

Other smaller donors, including other governmental donors, have been willing in the past to make grants to NGOs not registered under the Law on Associations. It is not hard to imagine a near future in Egypt in which the only nonregistered NGOs will be human rights groups unwilling to be sufficiently quiescent to earn governmental approval. When that time comes, it is unlikely that any substantial funding agency will be prepared to endanger its other programs—with perfectly legitimate, independent NGOs lucky enough to be working in less controversial areas than human rights—by offering funds to nonregistered human rights groups.

However, the full impact of the new law did not need to be felt for human rights groups to suffer a near devastating blow to their ability to receive the foreign funding on which they depend. On June 30, 2000, the police arrested Saad Eddin Ibrahim, director of the Ibn Khaldun Center for Development Studies. He was held until his release on bail on August 10, 2000. His trial on various charges, including accepting foreign funding without permission under Decree Law 4 of 1992, began on November 18, 2000, and ended with the conviction of Saad Eddin Ibrahim and three of his staff members on May 21, 2001, on three charges: the receipt of foreign funding without permission; dissemination of false information abroad; and appropriating money by fraudulent means. He received a seven-year prison sentence.

Saad Eddin Ibrahim is no ordinary prisoner, and his prosecution and conviction, regardless of what may happen at any subsequent appeal stage of the trial, or in any appeal for clemency to the president, has already sent a clear message to human rights activists that the government is willing and able to enforce the law to cut off flows of foreign financial support that it does not supervise. Heeding that message, most human rights groups have been forced to radically curtail their programs as their funding sources have dried up. For example, the EOHR first closed its regional offices, then laid off all but three of its staff members in its Cairo headquarters. Its output has slowed to a trickle. The local human rights groups focused on Egypt are now a collection of individuals with no institutional foundation for their activities.[38]

Saad Eddin Ibrahim is an internationally renowned sociologist who was somewhat resented in NGO circles in Egypt for his close ties to government officials, including the president. Ibrahim, despite his proximity to government leaders, was also a persistent government critic. In recent years his work had focused on promoting free elections as well as the expansion of civil society and the welfare of Egypt's religious minorities. Professor Ibrahim was a founding member of the EOHR, and over the years he had collaborated with the human rights community on many issues of common concern, including the new law. When he was arrested, Egyptian human rights advocates recognized Ibrahim as one of their own. The sobering conclusion they were forced to draw was that if it could happen to Dr. Saad, who was thought to lead a charmed life because of his influential friends, it could happen to any one of them. Other sectors of Egyptian society were less supportive of Ibrahim. The government and the press found him a suitable target for criticism as someone in the pay of foreigners to damage the good name of Egypt. In a way, he came to epitomize the government's animus against the independent human rights community in general.

By arresting Ibrahim the Egyptian government again demonstrated its majestic indifference to what the world thinks about its human rights practices. It could hardly have picked a target more well-known in the worlds of academia, the media, and international development, and, indeed, by government officials from many countries, including Egypt's closest allies—precisely the people most likely to be active and influential in mounting an international campaign for his release.

To return to the spiral model, denial is too strong a word for the Egyptian government's response to transnational pressures to improve its human rights record. Indifference better captures the passivity that has been the hallmark of its reactions. The question now arises, of course, whether the persecution of Professor Ibrahim is a step too far and whether Egypt's allies may begin to take seriously the human rights conditions attached to the various trade and aid relationships by which they are bound to Cairo. Writing in the immediate aftermath of the trial, there is a marked increase in interest in human rights issues in Egypt in Washington, D.C., but that may pass, and the Egyptian government has already shown its ability to absorb and deflect foreign criticism of human rights violations to its own advantage.

Egypt and Human Rights Change

Egypt has clearly failed to develop "a fully mobilized domestic opposition with transnational links" that is the irresistible force for human rights change envisaged by the authors of the spiral model theory. In doing so, it stands as a caution to the optimistic implications of the spiral model theory, that the power of international human rights norms are increasing, and that international and domestic factors will, given time, combine toward the implementation of human rights in practice. Egypt demonstrates that a government can engage in a substantive manner over a long period of time with international human rights instruments and be little changed by them in practice. In Egypt's case, ratifying international human rights treaties and participating in the international human rights system cannot be equated with having made tactical concessions that have weakened its resistance to human rights implementation.

What is especially disquieting about Egypt is the extent to which its government appears to have been successful in turning international pressure from foreign governments and international human rights organizations into a negative factor for human rights implementation. In effect, they have turned international pressure against local human rights activists and appear to have had some success in discrediting both the activists themselves and the concept of human rights. One could argue that the domestic pressure for human rights implementation was stronger in Egypt in 1989 than it is today, after more than a decade of effort, investment, and personal sacrifice from local activists.

The authors of the spiral model theory emphasize correctly that "Sustainable change in the human rights area can only be expected, once pressure is exerted on norm-violating governments 'from above' [externally] *and* 'from below' [internally]."[39] But the example of Egypt would appear to cast doubt on one of their conclusions:

Our findings also suggest that the *indirect* effects of external pressure placed upon norm violating government can play just as important a role in strengthening the domestic opposition. Pushing governments toward making tactical concessions almost always opens up political and discursive space in the society of the "target state" during early phases of the change process.[40]

In Egypt precisely the opposite seems to have occurred. Pushing the government on human rights has closed the discursive space and weakened the domestic opposition.

In fact, the development of the Egyptian human rights movement indicates that at a relatively early stage leading local activists came to realize the limitations of the conventional technique of exposing violations and bringing pressure to bear on the government to change. Bahey el-Din Hassan founded the Cairo Institute for Human Rights Studies in 1993, recognizing the need to "focus on the question of culture" and the need for research and education.[41] Amir Salem, who founded the Legal Research and Resource Center for Human Rights in 1991, came to focus on public education and awareness-raising projects. Hisham Mubarak's Center for Human Rights Legal Aid, founded in 1994, focused on using the courts and legal system to make human rights gains through litigation. Negad al-Borai headed the Group for Democratic Development, a project aimed at enhancing the effectiveness of the Egyptian legislature, after serving as secretary-general of the EOHR for two years. None of these initiatives relied on direct international pressure on the government as a major part of their strategies for bringing about human rights change. They did depend on foreign funding, but as most of their work was not seen as instrumental in generating international criticism against the government, it was less provocative to the authorities. The EOHR remained engaged in conventional monitoring and campaigning work, but by the late 1990s, even before the detention of Hafez Abu Sa'da in 1998, the center of gravity of the movement had moved elsewhere.

Another element of the spiral model theory argument does appear to be borne out in the Egyptian example: the phenomenon of the increasing prevalence of international human rights norms. The Egyptian government has in no sense turned its back on the international human rights regime. Even as it has taken to steps to systematically eliminate an independent local human rights movement that it found to be an irritant, it has been moving forward with programs that create a formal place for international human rights norms within governmental activities. In 2000, the AOHR signed the formal Headquarters' Agreement with the Egyptian government after eighteen years of negotiation. Muhammad Fayik, secretary-general of the AOHR, commented that this means "the Egyptian government has opened the human rights file in Egypt."[42] At first this appears to be an odd statement. Surely the human rights file was opened by the Egyptian government almost twenty years previously when it ratified the two covenants, if not before.

On further reflection, Muhammad Fayik's statement is insightful. For the first time the Egyptian government voluntarily formally recognized an independent nongovernmental human rights organization active in Egypt. The still incomplete process of implementing a new law on associations may be seen in the same light. Even though Law 153 of 1999, as it was presented, did not comply with international standards or meet the expectations of local activists, it did indicate interest on the part of the government in formally recognizing the existence of the independent local human rights advocacy community. The willingness of certain parts of the government to negotiate with NGOs in the drafting process of this law and the discussion of the establishment of a national council on human rights incorporating state officials and NGO figures are also signs of the state's willingness to acknowledge and cooperate with local NGOs, as long as such cooperation takes place on the state's terms. Furthermore, the government has entered into agreements with UNDP and with the office of the UN High Commissioner for Human Rights to implement human rights promotion programs, which have already included training for senior police officials in human rights. Perhaps these measures are the "tactical concession" that may begin a process of human rights implementation in Egypt.

It is ironic to think that in some ways the contemporary debate among Egyptian human rights activists about how to respond to the state's highly contingent willingness to come to terms with it harks back to the discussions after the EOHR was initially refused permission to register as an association under Law 32 of 1964, in 1987. Then the activists chose a path completely independent of the government and in time found ample international support to sustain them. But the state remained unmoved, and human rights implementation has not progressed. The state has made clear that it will engage in a domestic debate on human rights on its own terms, or not at all. Moreover, the state has learned— and most NGO activists have also realized—that human rights concerns will never trump the overriding strategic interests of Egypt's key Western allies. Therefore the only option that appears open to local and international human rights activists who wish to bring about positive human rights change in Egypt is to make the best of the limited opening for cooperation with the government in the human rights sphere.

State sponsorship of the domestic human rights debate, while not ideal, may well be better than a conscious policy of state obstruction and official defamation of human rights ideas. International human rights organizations and donor organizations face new challenges of how to support local activists as they tread a narrow path, balancing their independence and their obligations to comply with conditions imposed by the state. These challenges have only been made more acute as the pace of change, or at least the potential for change, has increased since 2004.

Chapter 5
Women, Citizenship, and Civil Society in the Arab World

Valentine M. Moghadam

In the late twentieth century, the worldwide social movement of women disrupted traditional notions of the public-private divide and the distinction between human rights and family matters by advancing slogans such as "the personal is political," "women's rights are human rights," and "for gender justice and economic justice." Women challenged their marginal role in the public sphere of politics and markets, their position as minors and dependents in the private sphere of the family, and the exclusion of women's issues and perspectives from debates on politics, economics, culture, and human rights. Today, women's rights and women's participation are on the global agenda and on national agendas everywhere.[1]

This is as true of the Arab world as it is anywhere. Women have formed their own organizations, and they have joined forces with human rights and transnational women's organizations in a broad regional movement to define and extend the rights of citizens, to expand women's rights, and to build a functioning civil society. This chapter focuses on citizenship in the Arab world, especially women's contributions to its definition and expansion. Conceptually and politically, citizenship and human rights overlap, and both are linked to the state, inasmuch as rights are defined in contradistinction to the power of the state, while the state is also expected to be the guarantor of the civil, political, and social rights (or human rights) of citizens. Like human rights, citizenship refers to a legal status as well as to a practice. In this chapter I examine how feminists are challenging their second-class citizenship—largely institutionalized in patriarchal family laws—and are calling for an extension of their civil, political, and social rights.

Theoretical and Comparative Overview

As issues of citizenship and civil society have taken center stage in recent years—partly as a result of the challenges of globalization, and partly as a result of democratic struggles in various parts of the world—the question of women's citizenship has assumed prominence. Feminists sympathetic to existing concepts of citizenship have pointed out that citizenship has been central to many women's struggles, from suffrage to welfare rights to political quotas.[2] Others argue that the autonomous, rights-bearing citizen is a Western construct, and that citizenship and civil society are patriarchal and capitalistic constructs.[3] Nevertheless, rights, citizenship, and civil society are increasingly in demand in developing countries. Citizenship, certainly for women, concerns social standing, political participation, and national membership. Empirically, women's citizenship is reflected in their legal status, in access to education, employment, and income, in the extent of their participation in formal politics, and in the formation of women's organizations.

In T. H. Marshall's famous formulation, the eighteenth century was the century of civil rights, the nineteenth century that of political rights, and the twentieth century the era of social rights.[4] As several scholars have pointed out, the evolution of rights has been different for women and for members of excluded racial and ethnic groups. Historically and currently, concepts and processes of national identity formation and citizenship have been infused with gender (i.e., understandings of femininity and masculinity); they have included some and excluded others (whether by sex, class, religion, race, ethnicity, or national origin); and they have led to the organization of public and private spheres in ways that privilege men and subordinate women. The relationship between national identity politics and women's rights has been unpredictable and uneasy.[5] In some cases, especially in the early part of the twentieth century, nationalism and women's rights were equated, while in other cases, especially in the second half of the twentieth century, national identity politics sought to recuperate traditional norms, including the public-private division. In nearly all cases, the state, citizen, and public sphere have been cast as male; and although the family is the province of women, its "headship" is legally male.

In developing and postcolonial countries, the trajectory of citizenship has not been the same as in Marshall's formulation. Much of the struggle over citizenship unfolded in the twentieth century, and it continues. Revolutions and liberation movements certainly have contributed to concepts of rights, but in most cases calls for civil, political, and social rights are part of more recent demands for democratization and civil society. This is true also of the Middle East and North Africa, where non-

TABLE 5.1. Types of Citizenship Regimes

Liberalism	*Communitarianism*	*Social/expansive democracy*
Rights > Obligations	Rights < Obligations	Rights = Obligations
Legal and civil rights emphasized	Social rights more developed; obligations emphasized	Legal, civil, social, and participation rights and obligations equally emphasized

Source: Janoski, *Citizenship and Civil Society*, 19.

governmental organizations and human rights organizations spread during the 1990s.[6] In particular, women's rights organizations have placed women's rights—and, by implication, citizen rights and human rights—high on the national agenda. Indeed, in Algeria, Morocco, Tunisia, Palestine, and Jordan, women have been at the center of struggles to define and extend democracy, citizenship, and civil society. By bringing the question of women's rights to the fore, and by insisting that the state amend existing laws and guarantee rights for women, feminists and women's organizations are challenging the role of the state and the status of the citizen.

On Citizenship and Civil Society

T. H. Marshall's definition of citizenship as "full membership in the national community" encompasses civil, political, and social rights and obligations. As such, it is a legal status as well as a practice and a process. Bryan Turner points out that citizenship refers to both passive and active membership in a community.[7] It is about universalistic rights enacted into law and implemented for all citizens, not informal, unenacted, or particularistic rights. Rights are not citizenship rights unless they are universally applied within the country and backed by the state. In the same way that Gøsta Esping-Anderson has identified three distinct "welfare regimes,"[8] Thomas Janoski has identified three distinct "citizenship regimes"[9]—liberal, traditional/communitarian, and social-democratic—with different combinations and levels of legal, political, social, and participation rights and obligations. These definitions and understandings are relevant to the Arab world, where rights are particularistic by gender and religion; where universalistic rights embodied in constitutions are not uniformly implemented and enforced; and where communitarianism in its most traditional and patriarchal form holds sway (see Tables 5.1 and 5.2).

Citizenship is intimately linked to civil society and the state. In liberal theory, the state is the guarantor of citizen rights, while also extracting obligations from citizens (such as payment of taxes, military duty, voting,

TABLE 5.2. Types of Women's Citizenship Rights

Legal/civil rights	Political rights	Social rights
1. Contract	1. Vote	1. Health services
2. Equal treatment under the law	2. Run and hold office	2. Family allowances
3. Freedom of expression	3. Form or join a political party	3. Schooling until at least tenth grade
4. Freedom of religion	4. Engage in fundraising	4. Higher eduction
5. Privacy	5. Naturalization on residency	5. Vocational education
6. Control over body	6. Refugee and contract worker rights	6. Social insurance, including paid maternity leave and childcare.
7. Choice of residence	7. Minority rights	
8. Choice of occupation	8. Dissident rights	

Source: Adapted from Janoski, *Citizenship and Civil Society.*

obedience to laws, and so on). In some interpretations, the state is seen as protecting citizens from the vagaries of the market. Thus the public sphere of the state provides a counterweight to the private sphere of the market. Civil society—the realm of associational life, civility in public discourse, and state-society relations—is the crucial mediator between state and citizen. Civil society organizations balance the strength and influence of the state; they are supposed to protect citizens from abuses of state power; they play the role of monitor and watchdog; they embody the rights of citizens to freedom of expression and association; and they are channels of popular participation in governance.

Debates revolve around the precise nature of the relationship between the state and civil society. The Marxist view is that civil society is never independent of the state; in liberal capitalist societies, the state needs and uses civil society to ensure that consensual hegemony is maintained. Others point out that civil society, left to itself, generates radically unequal power relationships, which only state power can challenge. As one scholar asserts, "Only a democratic state can create a democratic civil society; only a democratic civil society can sustain a democratic state."[10] Yet others argue that civil society is analytically separate from the state, an arena where there is autonomy from the state. This privileging of civil society is the understanding that emerged from the democratic struggles in Eastern Europe and that informs discussions of democratization in the Middle East and North Africa.

The notion of global civil society extends this argument to the international sphere. In this view, international NGOs seek to pressure states and institutions of the global market—such as the World Bank, the International Monetary Fund, and the World Trade Organization—to make them more responsible.[11] The relevance of global civil society to the Middle East and North Africa lies in the discursive space, legitimacy, and sometimes resources that global civil society offers to women's rights and human rights organizations seeking to achieve their objectives in the region's politically restrictive and culturally conservative environment. International NGOs such as Oxfam, intergovernmental agencies of global governance such as the United Nations, bilateral agencies such as the Canadian International Development Agency (CIDA) and the United States Agency for International Development (USAID), and the major foundations such as Ford and MacArthur have designed "civil society institution-building" projects to promote think-tanks, human rights organizations, women's organizations, chambers of commerce, purchasing and marketing cooperatives, environmentalist societies, community centers, and so on.[12]

Civil society is a modern construct that allows citizens to maintain solidarities through associational life. It consists of voluntary associations, professional societies, and all manner of nongovernmental organizations, some of which may be at philosophical and political odds with each other. Civil society also encompasses social movements and popular struggles, which often are in conflict with the state. How these competing interests and conflicts are handled and resolved depends on the strength of democratic institutions, the nature of the state, and the balance of social power. At present, the Middle East and North African (MENA) countries have strong states and weak democratic institutions. In the sphere of civil society, much of the social power is still wielded by religious institutions and Islamic forces; the family is another strong institution, and it is protected by Islamic family laws. Both the state and the Islamic forces are at odds with certain demands that are emerging from what I argue is an incipient civil society—especially those pertaining to the human rights of citizens, freedom of expression and association, and the rights and equality of women. Thus citizenship rights—as they are being defined by human rights organizations and women's rights organizations in the region—are highly contested terrain.

General Characteristics of the Movement for Women's Citizenship

Much has been written about the problematic nature of women's rights in Arab societies. But from what does it result? The sources of women's second-class citizenship are complex: the persistence of patriarchal gender relations, the political economy, family laws that are based on patriarchal interpretations of Islamic law or the shari'a, and the state.

Patriarchal gender relations are maintained by precapitalist forms of economic and social arrangements—such as petty commodity production, kinship-ordered agrarian systems, and the preeminence of the social institutions of the family and religion—and by the power of "the father." In such a context, property, residence, and descent proceed through the male line; women's principal roles are in marriage and childbearing; the senior man has authority over everyone else in the family, including younger men; and women are subject to distinct forms of control and subordination. Such patriarchal social and gender arrangements, which were once common throughout Europe, persist in parts of Asia and North Africa and are evidenced by early marriage, high fertility, and the importance of female virginity to the family's honor.

All societies are stratified by gender—and by class and ethnicity or race—but many of the Arab countries exhibit extreme forms of gender stratification and discrimination, as manifested in the differential legal rights of women and men, women's underrepresentation in political structures, and their limited access to paid employment. Although a common cultural view is that gender norms and roles are reciprocal and complementary with respect to the spheres of production and reproduction, it is more accurate to posit the existence of a "patriarchal gender contract" that codifies women's (dependent) family roles and thereby limits women's choices, opportunities, and participation.[13] Premised on the male breadwinner and female homemaker ideal, the patriarchal gender contract finds expression in family laws, marriage contracts, and cultural discourses, and is a determinant of women's limited access to paid employment. Of course, women's limited participation in formal employment and access to earned income also is explained by the region's predominantly oil-based economy. The highly capital-intensive and masculine nature of oil production and export impeded the massive incorporation of Arab women into the labor force throughout the twentieth century. UN data show that women's average economic activity rate for the Arab states was about 20 percent in 1999, half of the average for developing countries as a whole.

Patriarchal gender relations are codified in the legal frameworks, especially in the family laws—or the personal status codes/laws, as they are known in North Africa, Egypt, and Lebanon—that prevail throughout the region. What distinguishes the Arab world from other regions is the preeminence of laws derived from religious texts, particularly in the area of family law.[14] In almost all countries, religious law is elevated to civil status, and religious affiliation is a requirement of citizenship. Although Islamic law gives women the right to own and dispose of property, they inherit less property than men do. Furthermore, inasmuch as religious/civil laws require that women obtain permission of a father, husband, or other male guardian to marry, seek employment, start a business, or travel, this means that women are seen as incapable of enter-

ing into contracts on their own. The highly formal Islamic marriage contract does require the consent of the wife, and in some countries women
may insert stipulations into the contract, such as the condition that she
be the only wife. Marriage, however, remains largely an agreement
between two families rather than two individuals with equal rights and
obligations. Moreover, marriage gives the husband the right of access to
his wife's body, and marital rape is not recognized.[15] Children acquire
citizenship and religious status through their fathers, not their mothers.
Muslim women may not marry non-Muslim men.

In countries with such constitutions, there is a discrepancy between
constitutional clauses stipulating equality of citizens and the family laws
that undermine this equality. Moreover, the distinction between the
public sphere of markets and governance and the private sphere of the
family is reinforced by Muslim family law, especially through the concept
of male guardianship over female kin and spouses. By casting wives and
daughters as dependents in need of male guardians, the family laws
reproduce women's economic dependence and the patriarchal gender
contract. In extreme cases, family laws implicitly encourage male violence against female kin who may be dishonoring the family through
real or perceived transgressive behavior.

Legal constraints on women's rights are backed by the state, which is
best defined as "neopatriarchal."[16] Although there is some tension
between the state and communal entities such as tribes and extended
families, the neopatriarchal state upholds the traditional order in a
modernizing context. Thus it is the state that has reinforced family laws
and family and social control over women. Selma Botman shows, for
example, that Nasser-sponsored state feminism allowed women unprecedented access to education and employment, but the regime would not
address the family law; this served to reinforce patriarchal gender relations and the distinction between the public and private spheres.[17] Mervat Hatem has described the demise of Nasser-era state feminism and
the deterioration of women's rights in Egypt in terms of the adoption
of the privatization model by the Sadat and Mubarak regimes.[18] Nemat
Guenena and Nadia Wassef argue "that recent political discourse in
Egypt is dominated by the conservative polemics of the Islamists and that
the state, in its attempt to contain the Islamists, has subordinated wom-
en's issues to its own concerns for security and legitimacy."[19]

Related to this is the absence or underdevelopment of democratic
institutions in the region. The neopatriarchal state is authoritarian,
hence the limited nature of civil society and political participation. Male
citizens have few political rights, and women have even fewer. In several
Arab Gulf countries women have yet to receive basic political rights.[20]
Even in countries where women do have the right to stand as candidates,

TABLE 5.3. Women and Political Participation, Arab Countries

Country	Year women received right to vote or stand for election	Year first women elected (E) or appointed (A) to Parliament	Parliamentary seats occupied by women (%)		Women in government: ministerial levels (%)	
			1995	2004	1996	2001
Algeria	1962	1962 (A)	7	6	0	0
Bahrain	1973+		0	0	0	n.a.
Egypt	1956	1957 (E)	2	2	3.1	6.1
Iraq	1980	1980 (E)	11	n.a.	0	n.l.
Jordan	1974	1989 (A)	1	6	6.1	0
Kuwait	*	*	0	0	0	0
Lebanon	1952	1991 (A)	2	2	0	0
Libya	1964	+	0	n.l.	4.5	12.5
Morocco	1963	1993 (E)	1	11	0	4.9
Oman	*	*	0	n.l.	0	n.a.
Qatar	*	*	0	n.l.	0	0
Saudi Arabia	*	*	0	0	0	n.a.
Syria	1953	1973 (E)	10	12	6.8	11.1
Tunisia	1959	1959 (E)	7	23	2.9	10.0
UAE	1997+	*	0	0	0	n.a.
Yemen	1967**	1990 (E+)	1	0	0	n.a.

Sources: UN, The World's Women 2000, Table 6A and its updated on-line version as of 28 June 2005; UNDP, *Human Development Report 2001*, Table 25; *Human Development Report 2004*, Table 29.
n.a. indicates data not available; n.l. indicates country not listed.
+ No information or confirmation available
* Women's right to vote and to stand for election not yet recognized.
** Refers to the former People's Democratic Republic of Yemen
According to the *Human Development Report 2004*, Oman and Qatar have never had a parliament.

few make it to national office. In 1996 five of the region's fourteen countries had women in their cabinets. Jordan, Syria, Egypt, and Algeria each had two female ministers. There was one female member of the Palestinian Authority. In 1998, two women were appointed to cabinet posts in Morocco when a socialist was appointed prime minister—both developments highly unprecedented in this conservative monarchy. No Arab woman has ever been prime minister of her country. Until recently, the percentage of women representatives in the National Assembly has been tiny: between 1 and 10 percent. And Arab women's rate of economic participation has been far lower than that of men's, and far lower than that of women in other regions in the world economy (see Tables 5.3 and 5.4). It is precisely this state of affairs that the women's organizations have been seeking to change.

The movement for women's citizenship and for the establishment of civil society has had to contend with patriarchal Islamist movements,

TABLE 5.4. Arab Women's Economic Participation in Comparative Perspective: Female Economic Activity Rate (age 15 +)

Region	Rate (%)		Index (1985 = 100)		As % of male rate	
	1997	2004	1997	2004	1997	2004
All developing countries	39.3	55.8	111.3	101	68.0	67.0
Least developed countries	41.1	64.2	99.7	99.0	76.5	74.0
Sub-Saharan Africa	37.8	62.1	97.7	99.0	73.9	73.0
East Asia*	55.1	68.8	114.2	99.0	86.6	82.0
South Asia	29.1	43.7	99.4	107.0	51.7	52.0
Latin America and Caribbean	28.8	42.5	140.0	110.0	51.3	52.0
Arab states	*19.2*	*33.0*	*123.7*	*118.0*	*38.6*	*42.0*
Eastern Europe and CIS	45.6	57.4	97.3	99.0	82.4	81.0
OECD countries	41.9	51.5	119.4	106.0	72.6	71.0
World	40.2	55.3	111.3	102.0	69.8	69.0

Source: UNDP, *Human Development Report 1999*, 236; *Human Development Report 2004*, 232.
*In the *Human Development Report 1999*, the Asia region was disaggregated into East Asia, East Asia (excluding China), South-East Asia and the Pacific, South Asia, South Asia (excluding India). In this table, we have retained only the category East Asia (1997).

neopatriachal states, and religious-based family laws—a rather formidable combination of forces. It is all the more remarkable, therefore, that women's institutionalized second-class citizenship is being challenged by women's organizations throughout the region. These organizations are made up of highly educated women with employment experience and international connections who use a variety of legal and discursive strategies. Some use a secular discourse and take a confrontational stance while others frame their demands in Islamic discourse or engage in consensus building. The fact that these organizations exist at all is a sign of important demographic changes, of women's increasing access to the public sphere, and of the gradual process of democratization (or liberalization) in the region. What is noteworthy is that the women's organizations are working to change the nature of that public sphere, to enhance the rights of women in the private sphere, to advance democratization, and to build civil society.

In general, feminists and the women's organizations are challenging women's location in the private domain and men's control of the public domain. In particular, they are calling for: (1) the modernization of family laws; (2) the criminalization of domestic violence and other forms of violence against women; (3) women's right to retain their own nationality and to pass it on to their children; and (4) greater access to employment and participation in political decision making. They are also pointing out that existing family laws are at odds with universal standards of equality and nondiscrimination embodied in international instruments such as the Convention on the Elimination of All Forms of Discrimination against Women, and the Beijing Declaration and Platform for Action.

Organizing Women

The 1990s have been described as part of the "third wave of democratization," and this process has seen the proliferation of civil society organizations. Much has been written about the expansion of human rights, environmental, development, and various political organizations that are said to make up civil society. Less has been written about women's organizations and their relationship to civil society, the state, and democratization.

During the 1990s, the Arab world experienced the proliferation of women's organizations—some explicitly feminist—in the region. In previous work I have identified seven types of women's organizations: service organizations, worker-based organizations, professional associations, women-in-development (WID) NGOs, research centers and women's studies institutes, women's auxiliaries of political parties, and women's rights or feminist organizations (see Table 5.5). The WID NGOs play an important role in fulfilling the development objectives of civil society: decentralized, participatory, and grassroots use of resources. In countries such as Bahrain, "women's voluntary associations have come to form an integral part of civil society," which is responsible for "initiating all organizations for the handicapped as well as institutions for modern education."[21]

It is the women's rights or feminist organizations, however, that are the most significant contributors to citizenship and civil society. Such organizations are most numerous in North Africa, where they formed the Collectif 95 Maghreb Egalité, which was the major organizer behind the Muslim Women's Parliament at the NGO forum that preceded the Beijing conference in September 1995. The Collectif (later 2000) formulated an alternative "egalitarian family code" while also pushing for enhanced social rights for working women. In Tunisia, feminist-oriented WID NGOs seek improvements in the quality of women's working conditions, and the respected Centre for Research, Documentation, and Information on Women (CREDIF) conducts studies on women's socioeconomic conditions and rights. In Morocco in 1995, a roundtable on the rights of workers was organized by the Democratic League of Women's Rights, and a committee structure was subsequently formed, consisting of twelve participating organizations. The objective was the revision of the labor code to take into account women's conditions, to include domestic workers in the definition of wage workers and the

TABLE 5.5. Women's Organizations, by Type, Selected Arab Countries, 1990s

Type/country	Algeria	Egypt	Jordan	Morocco	Palestine	Tunisia
Service organization	SOS Femmes en Détresse	Red Crescent Society	Noor al-Hussein Foundation	Association for Protection of the Family	Women's Health Program	Tunisian Mothers Association
Professional association	SEVE (women in business)	Women's Committee of the Chamber of Commerce; Medical Women's Association	Professional and Business Women's Association	Moroccan Association for the Promotion of Rural Women	Palestinian Business-women's Association	National Chamber of Women Heads of Businesses
Development research center or women's studies institute		New Woman Research & Study Center; Ibn Khaldun Center for Development Studies	Princess Basma Women's Resource Center	Center for Studies and Research on Women (Fez)	Women's Studies Program of Birzeit University	Center of Research, Document. & Information on Women (CREDIF)
Women's rights organization (or women's press)	Egalité; Triomphe; Emancipation; Rassemblement des Femmes Démocratiques	New Civic Forum; New Woman Society; Women's Rights Committee, EOHR	Jordanian Women's Union SIGI/Jordan	Moroccan Women's Democratic Association	Al-Haq; Women's Center for Legal Aid & Counseling	Assoc. of Democratic Tunisian Women
Women-in-development NGO		Association for Development & Enhancement of Women		Committee of Moroccan Women for Development	Women's Unit, Bisan Research & Development Center	General Association for Vocational Training and Prod. Families
Worker-based and grassroots women's organization		ETUF Women Workers Department			Palestinian Working Women Society	National Commission on Working Women
Official Women's Organization	Union Nationale des Femmes Algériennes	National Council for Childhood and Motherhood	General Federation of Jordanian Women	Women's section of USFP	Women's Affairs Technical Committee	Union National des Femmes Tunisiennes

delineation of rights and benefits, to set the minimum work age at fifteen, and to provide workers on maternity leave with a full salary and a job-back guarantee. Indeed, more so than in Middle Eastern countries, North African feminists have developed a kind of social feminism, one that emphasizes not only the modernization of family laws but also the rights of women workers. This may be due to the different history and political culture of North Africa, which includes a stronger tradition of trade unionism and socialist and social-democratic parties.

Demographic, political, and economic changes are the internal factors behind the growth of women's organizations, but global effects—including the UN and its world conferences—have been important as well. Women's organizations from the Arab countries first met at a regional meeting in Amman, Jordan, in early November 1994. Sponsored by the UN's regional commission for West Asia (ESCWA), as part of UN preparations for the 1995 Beijing conference, the two-week deliberations resulted in a document titled "Work Program for the Non-Government Organizations in the Arab Region."[22] That document summarized women's conditions in Arab countries as follows: (1) women suffer a lack of employment rights and undue burdens caused by economic crisis and structural adjustment policies; (2) the absence of democracy and civil rights harms women especially; (3) there is inequality between men and women in authority and decision making; and (4) women suffer from violence, including "honor crimes." The solutions offered were comprehensive. The document called for the immediate ratification and implementation of the Convention on the Elimination of All Forms of Discrimination against Women, and a revision of all national laws that discriminate against women. It demanded "revision and modernization of the legislation related to women's status in the family," the insertion of the rights of the wife in the marriage contract, and "the amendment of nationality laws so that children can join their mothers and enjoy their nationalities."[23] The document stressed the importance of legal literacy and free legal services for women, as well as the promotion of women judges.[24]

The cooperation of women's rights and human rights organizations—especially in Egypt, Tunisia, Morocco, Algeria, and Palestine—has been fruitful for the expansion of both civil society and citizenship rights. Two examples will illustrate this point. In Egypt, women's organizations, human rights organizations, and some professional organizations collaborated to protest the imminent passage of a controversial NGO law. The women's groups included the Center for Egyptian Women's Legal Assistance, the Egyptian Center for Women's Rights, and the New Woman Research Center. A hunger strike and a sit-in were organized, mainly by women activists. They included two women psychiatrists associated with the El-Nadim Centre for the Rehabilitation of Victims of Violence, a women lawyer with the Center for Trade Union and Workers Services, and a writer associated with the Forum for Women's Development.[25] In the second example of collaboration between human rights and women's rights organizations, the First International Conference of the Arab Human Rights Movement took place in Casablanca, Morocco, on April 23–25. 1999. It issued a declaration that called for an end to the practice of torture; the need to respect freedoms of expression, assembly, and association; the realization of economic and social rights; securing citizens' rights to participation, including guaranteeing public oversight of the public revenues of the state; and the recognition of women's rights as an integral part of the human rights system. The declaration asserted that women's enjoyment of human rights is an integrated and comprehensive process that should encompass all facets of life within and outside the family. It is worth quoting from the declaration in some detail, as it shows the promise of such cooperation, as well as the influence that the feminist groups seem to have had within the human rights community:

Real equality between women and men goes beyond legal equality to encompass changing the conceptions and confronting the stereotypes about women. Thus, it requires not only a comprehensive review of laws, foremost of which are personal status codes, but also the review and upgrading of educational curricula as well as the critical monitoring of the media discourse.

In this respect, the conference stressed the necessity of engaging women's and human rights NGOs in the process of reviewing current legislations and in upgrading civil and criminal laws, with a view to resolutely confronting all forms of violence and discrimination against women. The conference also called upon the Arab governments that did not ratify (the women's convention) to do so expeditiously, and those that ratified it to lift their reservations.

It also called upon women's and human rights NGOs to work to refute these reservations, to challenge the culture of discrimination, and to adopt courageous stances in exposing the practice of hiding behind religion to legitimize the subordination of women. These NGOs were also charged with giving special attention to the continued monitoring of the compliance by Arab governments to their international commitments concerning women's enjoyment of their rights.

The necessity of considering the possibility of allocating a quota for women in parliaments, representative institutions, and public bodies is a temporary measure. This should stand until appropriate frameworks for women's voluntary activity take shape and until the awareness of the necessity of equality and the elimination of all forms of discrimination increase.[26]

Building support for women's rights within their countries and the favorable international climate have enabled Arab women's organizations to register some legal and social gains. In Jordan, the criminalization of honor killings of daughters and sisters became a major social issue, a preoccupation for feminist lawyer Asma Khader (named minister of culture in 2005), journalist Rana Husseini, and other activists, as well as some concerned members of the Jordanian royal family. Initially, the state was timid in the face of a tribe- and kin-based social structure, but women's groups and the Royal Commission for Human Rights pushed for legal reforms. In December 2001 the Jordanian cabinet approved several amendments to the Civil Status Law. The legal age for marriage was raised from fifteen for women and sixteen for men to eighteen for both, and Jordanian women were given legal recourse to divorce. New restrictions on polygamy require a man to inform his first wife of plans to marry again and to submit evidence of his financial ability to support more than one wife. As a result of an amendment to the penal code, perpetrators of honor crimes are no longer exempt from the death penalty (though judges are still allowed to commute the sentences of the convicted).

In Yemen, a woman was appointed state minister for human rights in 2001, and a successful campaign was launched against the "house of obedience" law, or the forced return of a woman to the matrimonial home. Yet much remains to be done. Feminists and human rights activists seek to insert an equality clause into the constitution (it was removed four years after the 1990 unification of the progressive South and the conservative North), to criminalize honor killings (the penal code currently exonerates a husband's killing of his adulterous wife), to decriminalize sexual misconduct by women (90 percent of women prisoners are charged with adultery or similar sexual misconduct), and to change the electoral laws to allow for quotas for women candidates. Activist Amal Basha has explained that the strategy is to encourage "a progressive, enlightened reading of the Shari'a, one that hopefully is acceptable to religious leaders."[27]

Neopatriarchal states in the Arab region remain ambivalent about women's rights, but circumstances, along with women's collective action, can lead to policy changes. Algerian feminists have shown a most audacious opposition to Islamism—and to state autocracy as well—in a manner that cost a number of women activists their lives during the wave of Islamist terror in the 1990s.[28] For this they were rewarded with government positions. Khalida Messaoudi, one of the leaders of the antistate women's campaign in the early 1980s and the antifundamentalist women's campaign in the late 1980s and early 1990s, was appointed advisor to President Bouteflika after he assumed office in summer 1999. In sum-

mer 2002 she became one of five women cabinet ministers—the largest
number in MENA. When Bouteflika issued an amnesty to several thousands who had been jailed for terrorism, he initially acquiesced to feminist demands that Islamists guilty of rape be exempt from the pardon.[29]
Algerian women's involvement in the judiciary has increased as well. In
2001, they constituted about 25 percent of judges, and President Bouteflika increased the number of courts headed by women.[30] He also agreed
"to the long and persistent demand of Algerian women's organizations
for the need to amend the Family Status code issued in 1984."[31] Some
reforms were adopted, though the Code still does not establish full
equality within the family.

In Morocco, a quota to increase women's political participation was
adopted (mainly by the progressive parties), raising the number and
percentage of women parliamentarians in the 2002 elections. What is
more, the twelve-year struggle by the Moroccan women's organizations
bore fruit when a landmark reform bill to enhance the status of women
in the family and society through changes in the Personal Status Code
(Mudawwana) was passed by Parliament in early 2004.

Some Concluding Remarks

Arab women's struggles confirm T. H. Marshall's thesis regarding the
historical process of the expansion of the rights of citizens. The incorporation of new groups into the body politic—such as the European working class in the early twentieth century and Middle Eastern women in
the late twentieth and early twenty-first centuries—heralds the expansion of rights and the enlargement of civil society. Arab women's struggles also confirm the salience of international factors—the global
women's human rights agenda has given Arab women the additional discursive and moral legitimacy needed to advance their movements for
full citizenship.

A reading of the literature produced by women's organizations and
women's rights activists suggests that some gaps remain in the conceptualization of rights and obligations, and some tensions need to be
resolved. Among them are class issues (including the social rights of
working men and women, and of the poor), the status and rights of
immigrants and contract workers, and the rights of religious and ethnic
minorities. This latter issue is important, given the systematic discrimination that non-Muslims experience. More emphasis on women's social citizenship rights is important, as this can alter gender stratification and
the patriarchal gender contract. The relationship between the state and
citizens, and their respective rights and obligations, also requires elaboration. It is true, as many feminists argue,[32] that the empowerment or

full citizenship of women is an inseparable part of the formation of civil society.[33] But it is also true that the emergence of civil society is contingent on the existence of a state that enforces universal legal norms and guarantees protection of civil, political, and social rights regardless of gender, race, ethnicity, class, and religion. Through their insistence on the rights of women as individuals, women and the feminist organizations are forcing a reconsideration of the role of the state vis-à-vis its citizens. But this role and relationship need to be elaborated and more explicitly addressed.

A major difficulty facing women's rights and human rights activists lies in the tension between a national identity based on Islamic civilization and culture, and the call for civil and political rights that may be construed as unduly inspired by Western traditions. In Lebanon, where communal traditions hold sway and the state is weak, changing the legal framework would be difficult, even though many feminists are in favor of civil codes that supersede sectarian authority. In Syria, where the state is strong, legal changes may be more feasible, but there is still a powerful official ideology that invalidates "Western" concepts and practices and relies on the politics of "authenticity." Thus, nationalism and Islam remain the major discursive frameworks, although this seems to be changing. Among the countries of the region, Tunisia seems to have crafted a national identity and legal framework that reflect its own Arab-Islamic heritage as well as social and gender rights as understood internationally. Elsewhere, women's organizations need to develop a framework for recognizing identities and elaborating equal rights for all in a way that draws on history, cultural understandings, and global standards.

Citizenship and civil society are contested concepts and conditions, reflecting historical processes and social relations, culture and political economy. They are products of internal processes as well as external pressures. It is unlikely that the Arab countries will ever develop citizenship regimes that resemble either the liberal model or the social-democratic model. However, several countries could well develop a citizenship regime that is still communitarian, but less patriarchal and more consistent in its implementation and enforcement of civil, political, social, and participation rights and obligations.

In the meantime, the "modernizing women" of the Middle East are challenging popular understandings and legal codes regarding the public sphere and the private sphere; they are demanding more access to the public sphere, full and equal participation in the national community, and full and equal rights in the family. These gender-based demands for civil, political, and social rights would not only extend existing rights to women but also, and more profoundly, broaden the political agenda and redefine citizenship in the Arab world.

Part III
Problems of Human Rights
NGOs and Activism

Chapter 6
Human Rights in the Arab World: Reflections on the Challenges Facing Human Rights Activism

Hanny Megally

As we enter the twenty-first century, human rights activists in the Arab world are looking back at more than twenty-five years of activity and reflecting on their achievements and their failures. Successes have been few and far between, progress—when it has come—has been painstakingly slow, and human rights violations remain widespread across the region. During the same period human rights organizations have grown, diversified, and mushroomed across the region. These developments have led some activists to question the overall effectiveness and impact of their work. The future is full of challenges, ranging from the nondemocratic nature of the ruling regimes to the lack of legislative safeguards protecting rights, the preponderance of restrictive laws hindering free expression and association, and the need to develop new and more effective techniques. Yet the greatest challenge they face has to do with the perception that human rights is a foreign concept and that their activism lacks support and legitimacy in the region. If activists and their organizations have any chance of improving the human rights situation in the region they must urgently address these perceptions as they raise fundamental questions about the nature and effectiveness of their work.

Historically, human rights groups in the Arab world have developed in a seemingly hostile environment in which they have lacked political, legal, religious, cultural, or social legitimacy. In the 1970s and early 1980s the organizations' founders—many of them leftist political activists—turned to human rights activism after becoming disillusioned with the limited space for active political participation, with the one-party systems and rigged elections, and with the rigidity of the existing opposition parties, which themselves lacked legitimacy or popular support. The founders had begun to see human rights as a tool to critique the policies of the existing regimes and a way of mobilizing local and international pressure to defend themselves and their colleagues against arbitrary reprisals by governments. Though some human rights activists were quick to shed the vestiges of their political past—and as the organizations developed they were joined by activists from other walks of life—governments nonetheless saw them as political opponents and not as independent, impartial advocates of universally held values and principles. They were also viewed with suspicion by many Islamists who, among other things, saw in the message of free expression, tolerance, and equality a threat to their own rigid interpretations of Islamic laws, customs, and practices. Even their erstwhile colleagues in the secular opposition viewed them as potential competition—an alternative movement and message—and cold-shouldered them.

Human rights organizations in the Arab world are under attack from all sides, while at the same time their discourse has been seized upon and used opportunistically by political parties, religious groups, and governments. The irony seems to be that the strengths of the movement are also its weaknesses. Islamist groups are resorting to human rights concepts and terminology in seeking to defend and protect their supporters in detention, at risk of unfair trial, torture, or execution. Yet these very Islamists appear to pose the biggest threat to the spread of human rights values and the growth of an activist rights movement in the region. Secular political opponents are raising the banner of human rights and the principles enshrined in the Universal Declaration of Human Rights. Yet they have undermined those very principles by using human rights discourse as a tool for political gain in an environment where outright political opposition has not been tolerated. It is politics by proxy. Governments have also learned to pay lip service to human rights principles by constantly referring to such values in their public manifestations and by establishing human rights commissions, advisors, ministers, or departments in ministries.[1]

Hostility from the political establishment—governments and opponents alike—is not an insurmountable obstacle if counterbalanced by support among the masses. Yet there is little evidence of popular support in the region for human rights activism or for the principles and values that the activists espouse. Equally there is much information to suggest that human rights groups are still relatively unknown, their principles and motivations are widely misunderstood, and their activities continue to be viewed with suspicion. Admittedly, given the overall lack of freedom of expression and association across the region, it is difficult to support this perception with empirical evidence. There have been no opinion polls, no mass rallies or demonstrations, and no membership bases to help measure the level of support for human rights activism.[2] Nonetheless, in reviewing the historical development of the human rights movement in the Arab world there are some interesting clues that may shed light on its ability to muster support and legitimacy in the region.

The first lies in the character of the relationship between local and international human rights groups and how this has impacted the growth of the national or regional movement. Over the past four decades international human rights groups such as Amnesty International and Human Rights Watch have developed specific techniques and strategies for monitoring, reporting, and carrying out protection work. These have included campaigns involving global solidarity with the victims and direct international pressure on the violating governments; reliance on international fora, such as the United Nations, for putting violating governments in the dock; utilization of the international media as a way of giving international public opinion a voice to mount external pressure; and emphasis on the principle of the universality of human rights as a way of preventing governments from reneging on their obligations by dishonestly pleading cultural or religious reasons. In the Arab world these tried and tested techniques were initially replicated by the local or national human rights organizations—often at the prompting and with the active encouragement of activists in international organizations—with spectacular effect. For example, in a region where governments appear immune to any internal pressures, many Arab governments showed themselves to be highly sensitive to international pressure. In a region where the media are tightly controlled by the state and often declines to publish the tracts and appeals of the local human rights groups, reliance on the international media and the support of the international human rights movement enabled them to broadcast their message. Often such publicity gave the domestic organizations international recognition and prestige, which they may have lacked at home, and afforded them some protection from arbitrary retaliation by governments.

However, by totally or overwhelmingly focusing on the international arena many domestic human rights groups neglected the process of developing their domestic constituency. In appreciating the relative success of the techniques used at the international level local groups sought to emulate them. However, the reliance on mobilizing outside pressure has proved to be a double-edged sword in the hands of activists in the Arab world. While this technique has often been used to good effect—especially by regional or international groups—when employed by local groups it brought into question their own patriotism and their loyalty to the state and to national causes. Governments in the region were quick to recognize this Achilles heel and depicted human rights activists at best as unwitting tools in the hands of outside powers, or at worst as traitors to the national cause. These accusations have been repeated over the years by critics of the movement from all sides of the political spectrum and have found resonance in both the popular and the state-controlled Arab media. Although local activists endeavored to counter this deliberately misleading propaganda, they did not put the necessary resources into developing grassroots support or a human rights movement at home. Without a groundswell of domestic support activists were too easily portrayed by governments and other critics as puppets being manipulated by external forces.

By seeking to emulate the relative success of the international movement, the local human rights movement was also drawn more and more into activities at the international level. This necessitated attending annual meetings at the United Nations in Geneva, New York, or Vienna; participating in other international fora to ensure that local agendas were being heard; espousing international declarations, treaties, and conventions; and lobbying foreign governments. Such activities, legitimate as they are, did not exactly endear these organizations to their constituents back home, many of whom viewed the governments of Europe and the United States, if not the United Nations itself, as having shown time and time again that national self-interest, which ultimately defines their foreign relations, always comes first even at the price of turning a blind eye to human rights violations.[3] Arab intellectuals were quick to point out that Iraq's appalling human rights record—including the genocidal Anfal campaign against the Kurds—was ignored by most governments while Iraq was an ally of the West and a bastion against the threat posed by Khomeini's Iran. Once Saddam Hussein began asserting his independence by invading Kuwait and threatening Saudi Arabia's oil fields, human rights violations that had previously been ignored or carefully shielded from public debate were suddenly highlighted and used to justify military action against Iraq. Double standards of this kind were and are recited all over the Middle East and North Africa with the overall effect of calling into question the motivations of the governments and institutions with whom the activists communicated and undermining the values contained in the human rights message.

The perception that the movement is too concerned with the international arena or that it is too influenced by agendas set abroad, and less with developing mass support or with responding to local needs, was further exacerbated by the near total dependence of a growing number of organizations on foreign funding. The acceptance or not of foreign funding has been a highly divisive issue within the human rights movement in the Arab world. Some avoided the risks associated with accepting such funding—risks that are often ones of perception rather than reality—and took clear-cut positions in refusing it. Others recognized that the benefits outweighed the risks and sought to ensure that their own plans or agendas were not compromised. Whatever the merits of the two positions, the reality has been that groups who accepted such funding grew spectacularly fast and were able to establish and expand their programs, often to great effect. Those who did not clearly struggled. This should come as no surprise in an environment where fundraising at the local level remains a difficult task and where human rights work has attained neither the popularity nor the respectability to make it a safe place for individuals or corporations to make donations. However, by accepting foreign funding groups provided further ammunition to those who sought to attack them, to question their integrity and loyalty, or to raise suspicions about who really controlled their agendas.

The availability of foreign funding may also have had an indirect but fundamental impact on the institutional development of human rights groups. In an era when such funds were not easily available, and in countries where this remains the case today, organizations have relied more heavily on a voluntary workforce and have focused more on local projects. Those who accepted such funds were less dependent on voluntary workers and placed more emphasis on national or international projects. The debate in the region about the strengths and weaknesses of what has been termed the "professionalization of human rights work" has not ended. Some lament the loss of the spirit of volunteerism while others point to the greater opportunities for effective work that have come with trained professional staff and greater resources. It is certainly clear from the reaction of those in power in Egypt and in the Palestinian Authority—two examples of areas where human rights groups have mushroomed in recent years and where many of them are dependent on foreign funding—that they feel threatened by the impact of such funding and will do everything to ensure that they can control the availability of such funds in the future.

A final key in understanding how human rights groups are perceived locally relates to how successful they have been in two areas—in adapting the message of universal human rights and making it relevant to their own communities, and in overcoming the seemingly widespread belief that human rights is a foreign, Western concept that has no roots in Arab/Islamic culture. The human rights movement at large has long debated issues surrounding the universality and cultural relativism of rights. This debate was fully played out in Vienna in June 1993 at the World Conference on Human Rights, when some governments tried to use arguments of cultural differences to undermine the universal application of human rights standards. Fortunately, they did not succeed.

The discussion, however, was also about the different methods used by international and local groups to explain the message and to elicit support. While international organizations have tended to focus on commonality and standard setting, they have relied on their local and national counterparts to make the connections with their own communities. Human rights are universal; of that there is no doubt. It is, however, important to show how this links with the culture and history of a given nation or people in order to make these universal standards relevant for them and to be able to elicit their support in ensuring their local application. That task cannot be carried out by international organizations; it has to be initiated from within a given community. The global human rights movement has a responsibility to assist in the process but not to initiate or organize it. In the context of the Arab world one cannot discuss human rights without being confronted with everyday issues of religion and culture.

Initially, local human rights groups in the Arab world avoided tackling such sensitive issues and focused on the internationalist line of universality. Tactically this was necessary since they were relying on international standards in reporting on their own governments' human rights records. Furthermore, it enabled them to establish their own credentials within the global movement. It also appeared to be the safer option in a no-win situation. With the rise of political Islam there was little or no room for publicly debating interpretations of Islamic law or codes of conduct. Individuals who sought to do so risked the wrath of unforgiving violent Islamists or the ire of regimes seeking to legitimize their own positions by taking on the mantle of defenders of the faith.

For a while this approach seemed to work as local groups set about establishing themselves, refining their techniques, and gaining some recognition for their work. However, it meant that for a long time opponents and critics of the human rights movement were allowed to argue with near impunity that human rights standards were not compatible with the precepts of Islam or with Arab culture and customs. The result was that many human rights groups failed to penetrate more deeply into their own communities and found themselves isolated and lacking essential local support when they fell victim to government repression. In recent years Arab activists have come to the conclusion that they can no longer cede this ground to a few extremists or a dominant minority, particularly if they are aspiring to build grassroots support. They have come to recognize that by looking into their own culture and religion for the same values enshrined in the Universal Declaration of Human Rights they are not undermining but strengthening the principle of universality. They have also realized that in order to succeed in raising awareness about rights issues they need to adapt the message so that it is understood within their own societies.

This brief review seeks to suggest that in addressing the challenges lying ahead, human rights groups in the Arab world need to give primary consideration to the development of a strong local constituency. This need is not new and has been identified in previous discussions and meetings, including the momentous April 1999 First Arab Human Rights Conference in Casablanca conference, which brought together over one hundred activists from around the region to address the challenges facing the movement. Yet this need is almost always overshadowed by other needs, such as the need for greater solidarity and coordination among the groups, for developing more effective techniques of interventions, for strengthening institutional capacities, for expanding outreach, and so forth. The past quarter of a century of activism has been a time of trial and error and of learning from successes and failures alike. Human rights activists have come to understand that real long-term change can only come through pressure from within and through the existence of a strong and supportive constituency on the ground. If they grasp the moment, they can transform themselves from a collection of dedicated and committed individuals and organizations into an irreversible movement for change.

Chapter 7
Human Rights NGOs and the "Foreign Funding Debate" in Egypt

Nicola Pratt

The "foreign funding debate" refers to a set of debates within Egyptian civil society over the advantages and disadvantages of Egyptian NGOs accepting funds from non-Egyptian, particularly Western, organizations (nongovernmental and governmental). These debates have become particularly heated with regard to human rights NGOs because of the more politicized nature of their work and the political activist origins of many human rights advocates.[1] Debates over foreign funding take part among and between NGO activists, members of political parties, journalists, and intellectuals in seminars, in informal gatherings, and via the media. In addition, the government adds to the debate by determining the legality of accepting funds from abroad.[2] The topic of foreign funding has become so ubiquitous that it is currently impossible to discuss the subject of human rights NGOs in Egypt without someone mentioning the "F" word (funding).

The foreign funding debate is not about NGO financial matters but about the identity of those who provide funds (that is, organizations located in the West) and Egypt's relationship with them.[3] The foreign funding debate constitutes a discourse largely promoted by Egyptian civil society for controlling Egyptian human rights NGOs and regulating their relations with the West. In this sense, the foreign funding debate does not reflect an objective reality about NGOs and foreign funding. It is not based on rigorous, empirical observation of the impact of foreign funding on NGO operations. Rather, it represents a dominant way of thinking about or interpreting Egypt's relations with the West. Nevertheless, this discourse not only operates in the realm of ideas about Egypt and the West but also shapes the real practices of the state and civil society toward Egyptian NGOs, thereby illustrating the link between discourse and power.[4]

Representations of and attitudes toward Egypt's relations with the West have been shaped by more than two hundred years of encounters between the Occident and Orient, particularly by the experience of the French and British occupation of Egypt. Anticolonial resistance in Egypt (and other colonies) was constructed around an identity that celebrated the supposedly inherent cultural and moral differences between the colonized and the colonizers.[5] While the construction of essentialized difference was a tool of empowerment during the struggle against colonialism, today it has become a mechanism of authoritarian politics. The continued desire to maintain the boundaries between "us" and "them" and to perceive everything Western as a threat leads to a situation in which civil society condemns those who transgress the boundaries in the name of protecting the nation-state. Human rights NGOs that have forged links with organizations in the West have become a target of such condemnation, and the foreign funding debate represents a means of disciplining them.

This chapter identifies the principal trends within the foreign funding debate in Egypt. I will demonstrate how, despite the apparent variety of positions, they all adhere to the internal logic of the binary division separating Egypt from the West and the role of Egyptian civil society in maintaining this division in order to resist "dangerous" Western influences. Even those who seek to defend foreign funding, frame their arguments within this logic. In light of the dangers of reproducing essentialized differences between Egypt and the West, in the final section I argue for a deconstruction of the binary oppositions that give meaning to the foreign funding debate.

The Arguments Against Foreign Funding

There are two principal arguments against foreign funding that can be traced back to the deliberations within the Egyptian Organization for Human Rights (EOHR) in 1991 over whether the organization should accept funds from abroad. At that time, the organization was facing a financial crisis that threatened to severely limit its ability to work.[6] The first argument against foreign funding, which has been the predominant argument used by former members of the EOHR and some NGO activists, is based on the paradigm of dependency that rejects foreign funding because the West is economically stronger and, therefore, can employ funding to exploit Egyptian NGOs for its own purposes.[7] The second argument, which has been employed principally, although not exclusively, by members of civil society outside the EOHR, is based on a paradigm that rejects foreign funding on the basis of essential moral characteristics of the West, that is, the West is not Egyptian and, therefore, must necessarily be morally dangerous to Egyptian national interests. In practice, these two arguments are often combined and used simultaneously.

The dependency paradigm was originally developed by Latin American scholars to explain the continuing difference between rates of economic development in the West and those in previously colonized countries.[8] This paradigm asserts that due to the structure of the (global) capitalist economy, the West or the core countries develop at the expense of the periphery (that is, the Third World or developing world). This relationship of dependent development, which leads to underdevelopment for the periphery and a global division of labor, is reproduced through the economic transactions between the core and the periphery. Some of the effects of the dependent relationship include the exacerbation of income inequalities in periphery countries; the creation of an elite strata, or "comprador bourgeoisie," which is linked to the core through business interests; the establishment of branches of multinational corporations in periphery countries, which expatriate profits and destroy local entrepreneurship; the export of inappropriate technology from the core to the periphery at the expense of self-sustaining development based on domestic technology and local entrepreneurship; the distortion of the local labor market by foreign and multinational companies paying higher wages; and the reliance of national governments on foreign capital, which encourages the maintenance of political stability for the sake of foreign investment at the expense of democracy.

The funding of Egyptian NGOs by Western agencies, it is argued, mirrors the dependent economic relationships between the core and the periphery. Many opponents of foreign funding incorporate the above themes into their arguments. One activist, a member of an NGO working on women's rights who prefers *not* to call herself an NGO activist because of its association with foreign funding, described to me the funding system, in terms of its prevention of the emergence of a strong democratic movement and its distortion of the existing movement toward the interests of Western donors:

I am against accepting any foreign funds because to accept foreign funds is to accept the funding system, which is part of the New World Order. Funding, at its best, builds weak and dependent NGOs and mostly it creates organizations that are not controlled by the people who are supposed to receive the support. . . . When you are part of a strong movement, you have the power to define your conditions. But we are weak and I do not believe that we can set conditions outside of the agenda of the donors except by being dependent on yourself. Funding does not allow people to become self-reliant. You can only build a strong movement through experience and your own efforts. Funding allows you to bypass experience and to set up your project without any effort. . . . Funding is a whole system that is corrupt and it is not true that you can accept funds without accepting the whole system. There are questions of who controls the funding, and how it is spent.[9]

In a similar vein, a former member of the EOHR who resigned in 1993 argues that foreign funding boosts the external forces (of globalization) at the expense of building a domestic democratic movement. This is achieved through incorporating Egyptian human rights NGOs into a globalized elite (not unlike a "comprador bourgeoisie") that is divorced from the rest of society:

public work "paid for" from outside does not activate the democratic movement in any way, rather this trend only activates the movement of "globalization" of NGOs, separating the local membership from the issues of society in an age in which control is imposed through this "globalization."[10]

Rather than constructing a model based on structural economic inequalities, the second argument constructs a binary division between Egypt and the West based on essential moral differences. The supporters of this argument consider anything national to be necessarily good, while anything Western, including funding agencies located in the geographic West, is necessarily bad and a threat to national interests. The existence of these essential moral differences is demonstrated by the history of violations suffered by Egypt and other Arab countries at the hands of Western governments. The West is also extended to include Israel and Zionism—an association that further demonizes the West. This argument assumes a continuity of interests of the West over time and a homogeneity of interests within the West. The ultranationalist weekly newspaper *Al-Usbu'a* has been at the forefront of promoting this type of argument against foreign funding.

Finally, I say, have some of our brother activists in the human rights field who have been supplied with dollars, forgotten that they [the Western donors] are an indivisible part of the British occupation that suffocated Egyptians for 72 years; of the tripartite aggression against Egypt in 1956; of those [i.e., Israel] that bombed the Bahr Baqr School and the Abu Za'bal factory workers in 1967; of the supporters of Zionism [i.e., the United States] who provided equipment and arms to attack the Egyptian people in 1973; and that these are the people who have put sanctions on the people of Iraq and Libya for eight years? Where are the human rights here?![11]

In addition to the binary division of "Egypt/the West: Good/Bad," the proponents of this argument create a binary division between the

state and civil society. They argue that the state is solely capable of representing and protecting national interests in interactions with the West,
since the state is the expression of public interests. On the other hand,
any civil society interactions with the West are dangerous to the national
interests of Egypt since civil society is an expression of private interests
that are much easier to corrupt. This makes civil society a potential entry
point for Western influence.

The easiest way to get rich is to open a center defending human rights or animal
rights and equate female circumcision with the slaughtering of sheep. It doesn't
matter who or what is persecuted. The important thing is who hunts for the
information and gives it to the funding bodies . . . to exploit it to harm the
nation or weaken its institutions.
    . . . funding bodies, which are controlled by intelligence agencies, have
pounced upon Egypt and opened their coffers to the weak of mind [i.e., NGO
activists].[12]

Both arguments (the dependency paradigm and moral essentialism)
rely on a set of three assumptions for their self-validation: first, that the
West is a homogeneous bloc of interests represented by the actions of
Western governments (who are, principally, the United States, Britain,
and France); second, that Egypt is a homogeneous bloc of interests; and
third, that the interests of the West are diametrically opposed to the
interests of Egypt. Based on these three assumptions, it is argued that
civil society links with the West in any form, particularly through foreign
funding, provide an opportunity for the West to pursue interests inside
Egypt, which, necessarily, weaken the nation.

These arguments have been regularly employed by the government to
discredit human rights activists and their work since 1991. The foreign
funding debate has been extensively employed to justify amending the
law governing NGOs to render it more restrictive and to harass NGOs
and their activists for writing reports on human rights violations in Egypt
that are circulated abroad.[13] Most recently, the foreign funding issue was
the linchpin in the case against civil society activist Saad Eddin Ibrahim
and his colleagues at the Ibn Khaldun Center, who were found guilty of
accepting funds from abroad without official permission and using these
funds to write reports that "tarnish Egypt's reputation." They were sentenced to varying prison terms, including seven years for Ibrahim, on
May 21, 2001.[14]

The Arguments in Defense of Foreign Funding

The arguments in defense of foreign funding are made not only by activists who are members of NGOs that accept external financial support

but also by other members of civil society, including writers, journalists, and members of political parties. However, those countering the anti–foreign funding trend continue to remain in an unenviable minority. This helps explain the defensiveness of some of the arguments put forward in justification of foreign funding. Nevertheless, even those who defend foreign funding on the basis of a critique of the anti–foreign funding arguments remain within the boundaries of the orthodoxy regarding relations between the Orient and the Occident and the existence of national interests.

At the most defensive end of the continuum, we find a pragmatic approach to funding. This position was found among a significant number of NGO activists with whom I spoke. They see foreign funding as an unfortunate necessity in light of the lack of domestic sources of funding. For example, one individual with a history of involvement in leftist politics and now a member of an NGO working with torture victims told me the following:

In Europe, they allocate a part of the state budget for NGOs and that is better. Also, in Europe, businesspeople contribute more to NGOs. However, that does not happen here because capitalists here all have shared interests with the ruling authorities. If they funded an organization that is opposing the government and its policies, then they would be deprived of all the benefits that they currently get. As for ordinary people, their income is small and, anyway, it is difficult to collect donations because of the legal restrictions. Therefore, you only have one choice and that is external funding. There are suspicious funding organizations but there are also organizations that are not suspicious.[15]

The categorization of funding organizations into "suspicious" and "not suspicious" refers to their perceived political objectives. This is usually determined by the national location of the organization and the foreign policies of its government, but can also be established by the status of the organization, that is, governmental or nongovernmental. Based on these categorizations, NGOs lay down conditions for accepting or rejecting external funding. For example, many NGOs refuse funding from any organization, whether governmental or nongovernmental, whose national government policies are regarded as harmful to the "Arab people," particularly, the Palestinians. Therefore, a large number of NGOs do not accept funding from any U.S. organizations but do accept funding from Danish, Dutch, and Swedish organizations. Other NGOs differentiate between governmental and nongovernmental donors; they reject funding from the United States Agency for International Development but accept funds from the Ford Foundation. Finally, a few NGO activists do not accept funding from any organization located in the geographic West but do accept funds from international organizations, namely the UN, or from Arab sources, such as businesspeople from Arab countries.

Although some argue that there is a large degree of hypocrisy in these positions—"After all, foreign funding is foreign funding, whatever you try to call it"—the different approaches by different activists demonstrate the significance of negotiating foreign funding for negotiating one's own identity and credibility. These identities range among Egyptian, Arab, non-Western, and nongovernmental. In most cases, activists try to bridge these different identities, for example, accepting support from NGOs on the condition that their country's foreign policies toward the Arab world are not perceived as harmful.

One human rights activist who has been at the forefront of constructing a critique of the anti-foreign funding argument is Mohammad al-Sayyed Sa'id. He counters what he regards as three major fallacies concerning the call for restrictions on foreign funding: that individual Egyptians are susceptible to becoming agents of external forces; that it is possible to isolate civil society from the outside world; and that the defense of national identity can be achieved through closing oneself to the outside world.[16] Al-Sayyed Sa'id argues in favor of international interactions on both nonofficial/nongovernmental and official/governmental levels as the only way for Egyptian society to thrive. He criticizes the argument that all interactions between Egyptian individuals/nongovernmental associations and non-Egyptian entities should be carefully monitored and even restricted as a direct threat to public freedoms.

In Egypt, and in any society, some individuals are predisposed to treason or penetration. They need not work in NGOs or engage in public action to become agents. We cannot circumvent NGOs or shrink their margin of free action at the local and international levels because of this exceptional minority. Moreover, we cannot devise a special law to punish this minority because laws are not made for exceptional cases. We have enough laws to protect the security of our nation without any need to restrict private non-governmental activities.[17]

Al-Sayyad Sa'id identifies the faulty logic of argumentation and illiberal consequences of the anti-foreign funding position. He demonstrates that Egyptian national interests are not harmed by interactions with the West but that society avoids "stagnation, erosion, and degradation" through its openness.[18] Yet, in the rest of his article, he neglects to undermine one of the assumptions identified in the previous section that underpins the anti-foreign funding position, that is, that Egypt and the West each represent distinct and indivisible blocs of interests. Below, I will explain why such an omission is dangerous.

Other defenses of foreign funding have attempted to address further the issue of what constitutes national interests in relation to NGO work.

One of the most prominent examples of such a defense has been *Al-Ahram* newspaper daily columnist Salama Ahmad Salama. He has attacked the anti-foreign funding argument on the grounds that many organizations that accept foreign funding are playing a vital role in "renewing the political system," thereby bringing Egypt into the twenty-first century.[19] In other words, Salama and other writers reframe national interests in terms of a vibrant civil society and respect for human rights.[20] However, Salama does make a distinction between the patriotic activities of certain NGOs and other NGOs who are engaged in "suspicious" activities.

The final arbiter and the first judge [of the acceptability of foreign funding] is the national conscience, which is able to separate between suspicious objectives and patriotic objectives. In an organization such as the EOHR, which includes on its board the finest men in Egypt, it is not possible to target them with accusations of treason or working to tarnish the reputation of Egypt and turning their sons into a group of mercenaries.[21]

His suggestion for ensuring that NGOs accepting foreign funding do not engage in "suspicious objectives" is to give "various parties," that is, governmental and nongovernmental, a watchdog role in a joint body. This body would be responsible for monitoring foreign funding and dealing with any complaints against organizations accepting foreign funding.[22]

Writers such as Salama oppose one of the principal elements in the argument against foreign funding, that is, that private individuals or organizations do not necessarily risk corruption by the West. Yet, they do accept the proposition that some individuals and organizations are susceptible to this risk and must, therefore, be subject to public scrutiny. The criteria for judging whether organizations that accept funding are suspicious or not is whether their activities serve the national interests. Salama and others define these interests as the promotion of civil society and respect for human rights. This is a more progressive position than that of the foreign funding opponents, who see Egyptian interests as protecting Egyptian civil society from "foreign penetration." Yet this argument, like the anti-foreign funding argument, maintains that there is something out there that we can objectively define as national interests and that civil society and human rights activities should be subordinated to them. In order to ensure this, foreign funding should be subject to public scrutiny.

Deconstructing the Foreign Funding Debate

This section will attempt to deconstruct the arguments on all sides of the foreign funding debate in order to demonstrate the dangers that the current parameters of the debate pose to the future of human rights activism in Egypt and also to clear a space in which a counterdiscourse may emerge. As we noted above, there are three principle assumptions underpinning the anti-foreign funding position. These three assumptions are constructed on the basis of two binary divisions: first, that of the Orient/Occident or Egypt/the West, and second, the state/civil society. Each part of the binary division is constructed as a homogeneous unit. Historical references are often used to establish the unchanging essence of each of these homogeneous units. Each part of the binary opposition is represented as a mirror image of the other part, thereby demonstrating their absolute dichotomy.

These binary divisions are historically rooted within Egypt's encounters with the West, particularly its experience of colonialism. The colonizers constructed the colonized as the opposite of everything they, the colonizers, purported to be. The colonized were ahistorical, irrational, morally inferior, lazy, cunning, weak, feminine, sexually degenerate, traditional, and passive.[23] This "Manicheanism" was constructed as the justification for colonialism and it was at the core of the violence perpetrated against the colonized.[24] As a means of reclaiming their agency to resist the colonizers, nationalist leaders and intellectuals reversed these binary divisions. It was not they who were morally inferior but the colonizers. The "traditional" was not a negative feature of their culture but a positive thing. They were not feminine and passive but displayed the traits of masculinity by fighting for their nation.[25]

The debate over foreign funding demonstrates the extent to which these binary oppositions continue to operate within Egyptian civil society. In both the dependency and moral essentialist paradigms, the West (as a homogeneous bloc of interests) is represented as a danger to the Egyptian nation. Within the dependency paradigm, the West seeks to exploit Egypt through the economic structures of the (global) capitalist system. Within the moral essentialist paradigm, the West necessarily seeks to dominate Egypt (and the Arab world) because it is morally corrupt and has no respect for the rights of Arab people. Consequently, it is in Egyptian national interests to rid the country of foreign economic exploitation and/or political domination. Those that have linkages with the West, such as businesspeople or NGOs that accept funds from abroad, are considered to be aiding the economic exploitation or domination of Egypt by the West and, therefore, pose a danger to the Egyptian nation.

The dependency and moral essentialist paradigms, on the surface, appear to differ in their interpretations of the role of Egyptian civil society. Those who adhere to the dependency paradigm argue that it is the role of civil society to resist exploitation by the West by resisting all interactions with it.[26] Meanwhile, those who adhere to the moral essentialist paradigm believe that civil society represents the nation's weak spot that must be closely monitored and guarded by the state. However, if one analyzes the two different representations of civil society in terms of a gendered discourse about the Egyptian nation and its relationship with the West, we find that both representations constitute two sides of the same coin.

In the dependency paradigm, the representation of civil society as the last line of defense against the West can be seen as similar to the representations, during anticolonial struggles in many countries, of the private sphere (of culture, religion, and family life) as the last line of defense against colonialism. Partha Chatterjee has described how nationalist leaders in India portrayed the private sphere as the "inner domain of national life" over which they could proclaim their sovereignty.[27] Women, who have historically been associated with the private sphere in the majority of countries of the world, were represented in Indian nationalist discourse as the guardians of the national culture.[28] Since women, as guardians of the "inner domain," represent an essential foundation of the nation, the argument follows that they must be protected from Western corruption.

The representation of civil society as a weak spot in Egypt's resistance against the West is the other side of the coin of the dependency paradigm's representation of civil society as the last line of defense. Civil society's strength and weakness lie in the fact that it represents the inner essence of the nation. This inner essence is a weapon against the moral corruption of the West. However, because the West is morally corrupt, the inner essence of the nation also becomes a target for Western influence. Therefore, civil society also represents a potential danger to the integrity of the nation. The logic of both sets of arguments is that civil society must resist any links with the West and that the Egyptian nation (state and society) must take measures to protect civil society from the West in order to protect the nation.

As argued above, the construction of a binary opposition between Egypt and the West is rooted in Egypt's experience of colonialism. This binary opposition continues to operate in discourses about Egypt's relations with the West because of the continuing injustices that occur today at the hands of the United States, Britain, France, and other Western nations. These injustices range from glaring economic inequalities to Western governments' continued support for Israel's oppression of the Palestinians and the invasion and occupation of Iraq. In other words, representations of the West as morally corrupt and dangerous to Egyptian/Arab interests resonate with many people in Egypt because of how they see international political and economic realities. This explains why defenders of foreign funding find it so difficult to put forward their case.[29]

While the reversal of the binary oppositions constructed during the colonial encounter acted as a way of resisting colonialism, it is important that human rights activists and all those seeking to promote democracy stress that the continued existence of these binary oppositions is implicated in the creation and reproduction of domestic mechanisms of authoritarianism that oppress ordinary Egyptian people. The construction of a homogeneous bloc of Western interests seeking to dominate Egypt creates a "siege mentality" where the violation of human rights may be justified in light of protecting Egyptian national interests. A distressingly large number of members of Egyptian civil society believe that Saad Eddin Ibrahim and other human rights activists represent a real danger to Egypt through their insistence on publicizing Egypt's human rights record internationally and thereby providing a pretext for Western intervention in Egyptian affairs. However, depriving human rights activists of fundamental political and civil rights sets a precedent and empowers the government to further limit the public sphere. Indeed, the government has already substantially reduced the public sphere over the last decade on the pretext of protecting Egypt from Islamist terrorism, ranging from the sequestration of the bar association in 1994 to the closure of *Al-Sha'b* newspaper in 2000.

As Frantz Fanon has argued, it is not sufficient to merely replace the colonizers by the colonized once independence comes. The colonial system must be destroyed.[30] If the continued basis for authoritarian politics in the postcolonial era is the reproduction of binary oppositions, then in order to undermine authoritarianism and clear the way for democracy it is necessary to destroy, and not merely reverse, the binary oppositions. In order to overturn the binary oppositions it is necessary to directly address the three assumptions underpinning the anti–foreign funding arguments and many of the defenses of foreign funding.

First, the West is not a homogeneous bloc of interests. To begin with, there are differences between national governments and their civil societies. While it is true that the U.S., British, and other Western governments are implicated in many human rights tragedies, not only in the Arab region but throughout the world, including in their own countries, it is even truer that some of the most fervent opposition to their policies has come from their own civil societies. On the other hand, Arab governments have often been the last to act to oppose human rights atrocities against the Iraqi and Palestinian people. For example, Egypt was one of the last countries to break the sanctions on Iraq—four years after Voices in the Wilderness mobilized their first sanctions-busting mission.[31]

Second, Egypt is not a homogeneous bloc of interests. It is important to stress that Egypt is constituted of a plurality of people with different interests and opinions that cannot be determined on the basis of their nationality. These interests and opinions may be influenced by their class, geographical location, educational background, gender, age, or religion. Therefore, it is impossible to define objectively what constitutes national interests. Any attempt to do so involves the imposition of the interests and opinions of the dominant group in society on the less powerful, usually to the detriment of the latter. Rather, it is more democratic to eschew the terminology of national interests and to create criteria for evaluating NGO work centered on the dignity of the Egyptian citizen and the standards of human rights. Only in this way can we avoid the practices of exclusion and harassment that befall individuals who accept funding from abroad for NGO work.

Third, the process of globalization provides new challenges, such as multinational corporations, environmental degradation, and human trafficking, that do not subscribe to the paradigm of Western domination over Third World or periphery countries. On the contrary, individuals and organizations in the Occident and the Orient are affected by or implicated in these problems. The cross-border nature of these challenges makes it necessary to build a resistance movement that is also transnational. Such a movement empowers ordinary people everywhere, rather than subjecting one section of people to foreign domination. The universality of human rights provides a framework for creating new solidarities across borders that override the exclusiveness of nationalist paradigms while recognizing that individuals need protection against the excesses of global capital markets and other dangers associated with the processes of globalization.

In personal interviews, almost all the human rights activists I spoke with criticized the assumptions underpinning the foreign funding argument. Yet many have also simultaneously subscribed to some definition of national interests in justifying their actions. Moreover, in their public writings and conversations, the overwhelming majority of human rights activists fail to deconstruct the dominant representations of the West and Egyptian national interests, stressing instead the contribution of their work to Egyptian national interests. It is important that human rights activists attempt to overturn the binary oppositions that give meaning to the foreign funding debate, rather than reframe these oppositions or avoid them. These binary oppositions are at the heart of the discrediting of human rights work and the harassment of activists by the authorities.

Conclusion

The foreign funding debate represents Egypt and the West as two diametrically opposed and essentially different entities. The notion of difference and opposition renders the West an enemy that threatens the very existence of the Egyptian nation. This discourse also represents Egyptian civil society as a target for the West in seeking to undermine the Egyptian nation. Based on these assumptions, the existence of Western links with Egyptian civil society in the shape of donations by organizations located in the geographical West to Egyptian human rights NGOs is constructed as a problem that must be dealt with by state/public control and regulation. By advocating for the control of human rights NGOs, participants in the debate contribute to the justification of state harassment of human rights activists and, more significantly, the tightening of the already limited public sphere available to Egyptian civil society actors.

Different positions within the foreign funding debate (both those against and in defense of it) share the same logic of argument and, in that sense, may be considered as being part of the same internally coherent discourse about Egypt's relations with the West. Therefore, even arguments in defense of foreign funding contribute to the reproduction of the assumptions about the West that form the basis for the arguments against foreign funding. In order to go beyond the foreign funding debate, it is necessary to deconstruct the current discourse concerning Egypt/the West by stressing the heterogeneity of both. Within the current juncture, where a significant number of human rights activists feel embattled, such a task may seem secondary to the primary task of survival. However, without a systematic and public discrediting of the assumptions underpinning the foreign funding debate, the future of not only human rights NGOs but also public freedoms in Egypt is endangered.

Chapter 8
Justice in Heaven

Eyad El Sarraj

It was a night to remember. I had come home around midnight after spending the evening at Haidar Abdul Shafi's in a stimulating discussion of the politics of peace with a group of Israeli leftists. I was so pleased when I entered my house to see that Federico Allodi had arrived. Of Spanish origin, a scholar and a philosopher and a professor of psychiatry in Toronto, Federico is a rare friend of Palestine and dear one to me. Busy and active in Canada for the cause of a just world, throughout the time of the *intifada* he has not missed a visit to Palestine every year.

We were drinking and talking with a group of friends when the bell was rung at the gate. It was them, the police. The young officer, from a good Gaza family—how clever a choice—told me that I was to accompany him to the police station for a cup of coffee, at the invitation of the attorney general. Having learned my lesson from previous such occurrences, I politely declined the invitation as long as there was no warrant to arrest me. Ten minutes later the officer returned with it.

My brother and Federico were visibly shocked and angered. It was a strange situation. Even as I was being rushed by the police officer, I was trying to calm my friends and family by making assurances that no harm would be done to me. No such luck. Within an hour of being in police custody I had been severely beaten and thrown into a small cell. It still makes me tense to think about it. It is a simple, albeit sickening memory. The sharpest image is of a green hulk brutally beating me with fists and boots. The image is not of the hulk, but of what I saw from my angle on the floor as he beat me: another policeman cocking his rifle. For a split second I knew he was going to murder me. The faces of my children flashed in front of my eyes as my life spun madly through my head. That he did not in the end shoot made me feel strangely relieved even as my body continued to absorb bruises and injuries.

Four days into the solitary confinement and I was going mad. The officers had clear instructions not to allow me out of the cell or to mix with other prisoners. The first hours were the worst as I was suffocated in that small iron box in the heat of June. But something fortuitous occurred that was to change things for me. I was called by the police chief who very angrily asked me, "How did you manage to tell the world about the beating?" He suspected that I had a cellular phone with me! The result was that I was moved into the maximum security prison where Hamas and jihad "terrorists" were locked up. I still do not know if Mr. Jabali realized that his decision was really a blessing. I was warmly welcomed and looked after by the other prisoners for the rest of my incarceration and, for that, I will be grateful for the rest of my life.

I knew all along that the reason behind my arrest was a letter I had addressed to Mr. Arafat. It was very critical of the Palestinian Authority's repeated violations of human rights and urged Arafat to take action against them. I was told later of the outrage in Arafat's office when the letter was handed over to him and how some people urged Arafat to "discipline" me, resulting in the trumped-up charges I was now facing. The attorney general made the farcical claim that "Dr. Sarraj was arrested for possessing illicit material"—hashish. When the other prisoners heard the accusation on the radio, they were not surprised but rather quite amused. One told me, "It reminds us of Egyptian comedies." But that lie would not be the only comic scene in this movie. There would later be the military court trial, which lasted ten minutes and found me guilty of beating a policeman, although in a Kafkaesque manner the judge told me he did, in fact, believe that it was I who was the victim of a beating. There would be the civil court when it was disclosed that the police had no search warrant when they found the hashish in a "drawer" in my desk at the Gaza Community Mental Health Programme—a desk which, in fact, was merely a flat board without any drawers. Absurd and farcical? Yes. But I remained in jail.

After my first four days in detention and before my theater of the absurd court appearances, I was on edge. I could only wonder when they would release me. Certainly they must be under intense pressure. Surely Hanan Ashrawi or Haidar Abdul Shafi had exerted some pressure on Arafat. What about the Palestinian Legislative Council members? They must have approached him. This episode is undoubtedly costing the authority dearly. Perhaps the Swedish government, or the Norwegians, or the Danes, or maybe the British have contacted Arafat. That man cannot simply imprison me without someone telling him that a scandal will erupt. But again, Arafat wants to prove to everyone that he is master of the game. By my example, he wants to show everyone the consequences of criticism or denunciation. Arafat was never able to tolerate dissent.

He dealt with opponents either by co-opting them or by punishing them. Some of his closest aides had warned me of this repeatedly and some told me that a killing could be arranged, and at the funeral my killers would be among the first line of mourners. One of Arafat's security men had once told me that a car accident was never hard to arrange! This perhaps explains why my murder was the first thing that came to my mind when Arafat's incredible hulk began to slam into my back with his boots and the policeman trained his gun on me. That's it, I thought.

Four days of June heat. The best thing that could happen was a breeze. The detention center was stifling. I spent most of my time there, in that small cell without a window. But for the kindness of the other prisoners, I wouldn't have managed to survive. Many of them went out of their way to be supportive. They gave me soap, underwear, pajamas, and sandals. When their families visited, they insisted I partake in the food delivered to them. I was invited to pray with them, and some would play chess with me. I was supposed to be confined to my cell, not to communicate with the outside world, but some sympathetic guards would occasionally let me out, would give me newspapers, and together we listened to the radio. These guards, who were supposed to be my captors, treated me humanely. I was allowed to go outside my cell and returned to it only when a senior officer was arriving.

Not that my imprisonment was pleasant, of course. That first night, after being severely beaten and then thrown into my stifling cell, I banged on the door and pleaded with the guard.

"What do you want?" he asked.

"I want to get out," I said.

"That's not allowed."

"I am suffocating, please. Let me out."

"I'm sorry," he said. "I have my orders. But you can go to the bathroom."

"I want to go to the bathroom."

Imagine my surprise when he opened that enormous black door. I was overjoyed to be outside that horrible cell. I stayed in the bathroom for nearly half an hour.

When I came out, ten prisoners had gathered. They'd been awakened by the noise I had made, it being 3 A.M. Again, I was surprised when they greeted me and told the guard I was a good man. The guard, bewildered and shy, later apologized for the way I was treated. An officer had told him to be careful with me because I was an Israeli spy!

The prisoners were wonderful, however. They protected me and looked after me. Some even smuggled my notes to the outside world. By these actions they expressed solidarity with a man whom they believed was imprisoned for defending their rights. In fact, they were proud that

I was now among them, though frightened that I was an example of what would happen if someone spoke up against the Palestinian Authority.

After these four days in that tiny detention cell in the company of these good people, I was ordered to dress up, as they wanted me upstairs. My Egyptian film scenario was to continue. This is it, was my first thought. They will release me. But within fifteen minutes I was before a military officer who sat behind a small desk. There was also another man who appeared to be a visitor. I walked toward the officer to shake his hand, but he politely stopped me, saying, "Stay standing, please."

I didn't know what to think. This is a military court, the officer said.

Well then, I said, can I have a lawyer? The officer, apparently also the judge, said that there was no need for a lawyer. The whole thing would be over in ten minutes. I grasped at a hope: this might be a formal way for Arafat to release me and avoid being further embarrassed by the episode.

The officer asked his assistant to read the charges. The assistant stated that I was charged with beating a policeman. My aggression, he continued, was unprovoked, and according to the medical report I had broken the policeman's arm. Absurdly, even though I had been refused a medical report by the doctor who examined me, my torturer managed to send a report to the military court claiming that he had a broken arm as a result of my attack on him. For the crime of suffering a brutal beating, I was to be held criminally liable! The officer-judge asked me to respond. My disgust was apparent, as was my amazement at how low they were willing to stoop. The charge, I said, was ridiculous, and that I need only rely on common sense to respond: Did he really think someone my age and of my physique could possibly beat a policeman and break his arm? My life history was my best evidence, I continued, and I challenged him to bring anyone in Gaza who would say that it was in me to beat another man.

The officer listened impatiently and looked around him, as if for an escape route. He looked down and said, "Doctor, I extend your detention for a further fifteen days."

"But I thought you understood," I said.

"Yes, I do, doctor," he said. "I'm sorry."

"But where, Your Honor, is justice?"

He replied, "Justice, Doctor El Sarraj, is in heaven. We all are helpless, and God is our last hope."

I was immediately escorted to the civil court to face the other charge of possessing hashish. It was heartbreaking to see my sisters there. The judge was a courageous man. He cut the prosecutor into pieces when he asked him why did they not search my house, as it would be only logical if they were looking for hashish. Then he asked, "Where was the defendant when you found the hashish?" The prosecutor replied that he was already in prison. The judge then looked him in the eye and said, "Do you arrest people before you find the relevant evidence? Was it not logical to have the accused in his office when you claim to have found hashish?" Then the devastating question, "Did you have a search warrant?" and the answer, "No."

After the circus of two courts, one military and the second civilian, I was taken back to prison, to my good friends. Many of them had had some experience with Israeli military and courts, and now the Palestinian side. So we were comparing. I related how the Israeli military were not very happy about my work with Gazan youth. They accused me of using the children for political propaganda by exposing their emotional trauma as a result of the violence of Israel's occupation. They refused to register my Gaza Community Mental Health Programme, and I was called in for questioning several times. Rohama Marton, head of Physicians for Human Rights in Israel, related to me how Dr. Nimrod (the chief of Israel's medical staff in Gaza) went to her house in Tel Aviv to warn her that I was a PLO mole. Eli Lasch, Nimrod's predecessor, told me once that he was warned by the military commander in Gaza about me because "this man talks about peace and corrupts Israeli minds. He works for the PLO." I was dismissed from my work in Shifa Hospital in 1971, six months after assuming my position in the children's department. The official letter, which was signed by Dr. Khairy Abu Ramadan, said that he was to order my dismissal for "security reasons." I was virtually fired from my work a second time in May 1988. Why? "Because, simply, we do not like you just as you don't like us and we want you to go to see your family in England and not come back," in the words of the Israeli Arab Affairs officer as he was giving me my travel document after weeks of refusal.

One of the Islamic Jihad members told me that although he was tortured severely by Israelis, being tortured by Palestinians was much more painful. Torture by the enemy was a kind of medal of recognition, but to be tortured by your own people . . . that is intolerable. For him, the only way to escape the pain was to consider the Palestinian officers as infidels who function against God.

It is easier after years have passed to write about it all and see it in perspective. One can reach a conclusion that the Palestinian Authority (PA) suffers from a fundamental lack of democracy and poor professional and ethical standards. While this state of affairs conforms to the prevailing Arab political culture, it was shocking to us in Palestine, which was supposedly on the path to liberation from the brutal Israeli occupation and to attaining our fundamental human rights. People in the West

Bank and Gaza were horrified by stories of torture by PA officials that led to the death of many, their shooting and killing in Gaza of fourteen people outside a mosque, the frightening lawlessness, and the sudden creation of an elite monopolizing wealth and behaving outside the law.

The irony is that it is the same Palestinians who revolted against the tyranny of the Israeli military establishment who are terrified today of their own liberating authority. It is understandable that the PLO forces are not familiar with democratic principles, given their exposure to non-democratic means of governance in the countries that hosted them. Indeed, it was clear from the early moments of the PLO entry into Palestine that there would be both a political and cultural confrontation between the PLO and local communities with their indigenous politics that had been established during the years of the *intifada.*

Many believed, however, that the special Palestinian experience under occupation should have better equipped them for a democratic system of governance. Nonetheless, the voices of Palestinian intellectuals have been muted since Oslo, as have those of many local leaders. At one level, Palestinians today are in a state of paralysis, as they are torn between being acutely aware of the continued Israeli occupation and having to confront an emerging Palestinian authority. It is certainly the Israeli occupation that they should resist and not their own regime. But how can they accept that their rights are violated now by their own brethren? Helplessly, they have resigned fatalistically to the notion that they are no different than other Arabs and as such not entitled to a better regime.

On another level, one could argue that Palestinians have also lost their identification with the just cause. For generations, individually and collectively, they have found themselves through identification with the question of Palestine. The struggle, *al-nidal,* was their way to self-actualization. They excelled in education, joined the liberation movement, and launched the *intifada* and fueled it for six long years. All that energy, the days and years of suffering and sacrifice, seemed to mean nothing when the Oslo agreement was signed. Oslo compromised Palestinian dreams of a just peace and meant the acceptance of a status quo that had been rejected for so long. Is that what we were fighting for? Or was this a surrender?

I was struck by that thought when I was being interviewed at the Gaza beach refugee camp for an ABC newsclip. That was the usual place to show-and-tell the story of uprooted refugee life and the resulting poverty, deprivation, illness, and other Israeli crimes against humanity. But on that day a new and spreading building fever seemed to have infected the camp. The shanty town was so transformed that my American host wondered what was going on. I thought then that the dream was lost and people were waking up to the reality of Oslo and its aftermath.

There was joy and hope, but also sadness, almost guilt. As we sat on the roof of his three-story unfinished building, I asked the municipality driver if he would prefer to go back to Jaffa. He politely dismissed my "hypothetical" question and said, in a matter-of-fact tone, "This is my home." A dream deferred had become a dream denied. Refugees who for generations had refused to accept their lot had now submitted.

Some describe it as sickness, others say it is immoral materialism, but all agree that dramatic changes are taking shape in Palestinian society. The same people who were the struggle's leaders now only strive to make a living. Some time ago, when the PA prevented laborers from working in Israeli settlements in Gaza, they protested and demanded jobs. It is they, of course, who were stoning the Israeli army only a few years ago. The truth is that people have been thrown into "normal" living after decades of war. Ill prepared, almost dazed with the sudden light of reality, they must find their way and their fate. Life is simply a struggle to find a job, find shelter, educate children, take them to the hospital, and make money.

It is no wonder that as many as 47 percent of young people would immigrate if given the chance. There is a prevailing sense of apprehension, sometimes panic, even among the old but particularly among the newly rich. One member of this group told me that his suitcase is ready because he will leave immediately when things change. This man is representative of the new class of high officials who surround Arafat and exploit their bond with him unashamedly. This same man told me, "If you really want to work for human rights, then come and see me. I can release prisoners and arrange for trials. I can help you become rich and I can find jobs for anyone you would recommend."

Another member of the group asked me, "Why are you so concerned about human rights and willing to risk your life for them?" It occurred to me that the man was emerging from the dark ages, where human rights were not an issue. Maybe the idea of human rights was used only as propaganda directed against the Soviet Union, or against the Israelis, the Syrians, and the Iraqis, but was not a serious matter when it came to ourselves. The usual line is that human rights are Western and used in particular by the United States to control Palestinians and Arabs. A human rights activist is, therefore, suspect. A police general told me once that when I was detained in June 1996, it was circulated in the highest circles that I was a Canadian spy. The genius who thought that up was disturbed by Federico Allodi and his unstoppable campaign to have me freed. A second common excuse for the flagrant disrespect of the law is to blame, with a distinct twist, the American connection. They claim that the U.S. administration continues to exert pressure on the Palestinians to show their commitment to the peace process by respecting Israeli demands for arresting members of the opposition groups and particularly the Islamic groups. Therefore, it is the United States that pushes the PA to violate human rights.

The Palestinian Authority, however, is bluntly honest. It continues to send clear though alarming messages about the irrelevance of human rights in its agenda. Is it because the PLO forces have lived for so long outside the law and on the margins of the communities that they are not prepared to subscribe to the rule of law? And yet, how could a freedom fighter who was tortured by Israeli interrogators turn into a torturer of his own people?

One day during my last detention I overheard a Palestinian officer interrogating a Palestinian man. He was calmly asking questions, but there were no answers. Gradually, the interrogator was raising his voice, and then was shouting. Suddenly, he was screaming, but in Hebrew. I was stunned. That was a graphic illustration of the powerful psychological process of identification with the aggressor. In simple terms, the Palestinian officer who was once a helpless victim in an Israeli prison was now assuming the position of power, which in his mind was symbolized by the Israeli officer.

Torture is endemic in this part of the world and it runs from generation to generation and from nation to nation. The Palestinian psyche has grown to mirror the Israelis, who themselves are victims of the horrible past. The peace process should not stop at the political settlement, but it should continue to touch and heal the souls of the traumatized communities. Palestinians have great potential for making peace and building a country out of decades of accumulated rubble. During the last years of self-rule, there have been a few positive changes in the areas of government, human rights, and democratization, but these are far from what we hope to achieve. The road, however, is still wide open and hopeful.

Part IV
Country-Specific Case Studies

Chapter 9
Some Yemeni Ideas About Human Rights

Sheila Carapico

Yemeni intellectuals voiced human rights concerns throughout the twentieth century. Of course, as elsewhere, the early incarnations of a human rights movement in this most populous corner of Arabia did not use the term *huquq al-insan* (human rights), popularized only in the 1990s. Moreover, the emphasis was consistently on limiting arbitrary governance and justice. Still, Yemenis tackled issues such as social equality, popular participation, judicial autonomy, due process, prison conditions, and intellectual freedom, among others. This chapter explores how a fragmented yet tenacious intellectual movement grounded in indigenous political culture produced writings intended to breach authoritarianism for over half a century. Contemporary Yemeni human rights activism draws on Arab and/or Islamic precedents and texts to articulate many of the principles expressed in international covenants. Concepts of human rights surfaced as intellectuals, jurists, and other political elites challenged tyranny and oppression, often in ways affected by Yemen's geographic position at the crossroads of Africa, Asia, and the Arab world, but always with reference to indigenous religious and societal values. Far from being some sort of alien Western construct superimposed on a Muslim Arab context, values now referred to collectively as human rights are deeply woven into Yemeni political culture and scholarship.

Rights are claims individuals or groups make on states. It is useful to distinguish positive from negative rights, as in "freedom to" and "protection against." Political and civil rights, also known as citizen rights, first-generation rights, or bourgeois liberties, are often distinguished from the so-called second-generation or social and economic rights. The evolution of rights in Europe began when an emerging bourgeoisie asserted privileges previously enjoyed only by the aristocracy. Eventually citizen rights became a cornerstone of the "social contract" between governments and the people they ruled, and complex codes evolved to guarantee freedoms of expression, participation, association, and the like, as well as protections against arbitrary justice or cruel treatment. These rights, then, are firmly entrenched in Euro-American political philosophy, and were the basis of the Universal Declaration of Human Rights issued after World War II and the covenants affirming socioeconomic and collective rights of workers, women, and other social groups brought before the world in the 1960s and 1970s by socialist and Third World governments. These themes found their way into Yemeni writing and activism about the same time.

Even before the infamous Abu Ghraib prison torture scandal, many Arabs rightly pointed to a double standard applied by Westerners to human rights abuses in the Middle East. European colonial sermons about human dignity and nonviolence masked sometimes ruthless practices. During the cold war era, officials, media, and independent groups in the United States and other NATO countries lambasted human rights abuses in the Soviet Union, the People's Republic of China, the People's Republic of (South) Yemen, and other states of socialist orientation, often simultaneously overlooking egregious offenses committed by friends and allies of the West. Yet all the while intellectuals and activists in Africa, Asia, Central Europe, and Latin America clamored for legal protections, political freedoms, and other rights. Apparent victories by rights activists from Moscow to Manila and from Berlin to Buenos Aires in the late 1980s and early 1990s emboldened journalists, attorneys, teachers, and others around the world. In the last decade of the twentieth century, there was a deepening and widening of the international consensus on the universality of moral claims to basic protections and freedoms even as neoconservatives in the Arab world triumphed over a discredited Arab socialism. As we will see, in vociferous debates on good governance, Yemenis teased anticolonial, socialist, and liberal internationalist messages from the Arabic classics in which they were trained even as their own national history—British colonialism followed by Marxist revolution in the South and very gradual modernization in the North, culminating in unification in 1990—echoed world politics.

Perhaps the most salient fin-de-siècle challenge to the universalization of human rights came from some Islamic leaders and thinkers who rejected international norms as another form of Occidental political and cultural interference.[1] Variously known as *jihadi* or *salafi*, these Muslim scholars that claimed human rights as understood in the West is antithetical to Islam. Such "rejectionists," as a prominent Yemeni human rights advocate calls them,[2] falsely claim to speak for all Muslims. Both

Western cultural essentialists and Islamist rejectionists typically frame the disjuncture in terms of a sort of universal Islamic law discerned from selected passages in the Qur'an, the Hadith, and various fatwa on shari'a, with such particular emphasis on dissonant matters of corporal punishment and family law that larger commonalities in ideas of justice and fairness are obscured. Less attention is given to Arab Muslim scholars, jurists, journalists, and others whose works have defined, debated, and asserted legal and moral rights throughout the twentieth century. Some observers both in the Arab world and abroad automatically assume that human rights considerations are a product of Western influence. This chapter traces some of the high points in the development of a human rights consciousness in a corner of the Arabian Peninsula relatively insulated from Western influence since the British left Aden. My focus is on the exposition of human rights concepts and reasoning in some well-known Arabic documents and manuscripts by prominent Yemeni scholars, jurists, and politicians. The articulation of human rights concepts does not translate automatically into implementation, of course, but is nonetheless probably an important prerequisite.

Although the Ottomans established a few schools in North Yemen and the British trained some Adenis (of Indian or Somali as well as Yemeni parentage) for colonial administration, European educational influence was minimal in southwest Arabia. There were no Christian or colonial colleges, universities, or schools, so the intellectual elite were trained in classical Arabic and Islamic law, literature, and sciences. Even late in the twentieth century, only a fraction of professors, jurists, and writers were Western educated, others having studied in Cairo, Baghdad, Khartoum, Moscow, Prague, Bombay, or Singapore. At Sana'a and Aden Universities and in Yemeni schools, Egyptian, Iraqi, Saudi, Kuwaiti, and Sudanese influences were far more salient in most fields than European or American models. Overall, then, the intellectual conversations were framed in Arabic, with reference to Yemeni, Muslim, Arab legal traditions, informed by perspectives that were international without being Western. These conversations were grounded in the two main Yemeni sectarian traditions, Zaydi Shi'ism (technically, the Hadawi school), based in the large high plateau region around Sana'a, and the Shafi'i (Sunni) sect predominant along the Red Sea and Arabian Sea/Indian Ocean coasts. Many writers referred explicitly or implicitly to the great seventeenth century Yemeni jurist Muhammad 'Ali al-Shawkani, whose political writings sought the common jurisprudential ground between Shafa'i and Zaydi precepts.[3] I take up this conversation in the early twentieth century as Yemeni writers and activists criticized many traditional practices and advanced a series of proposals for "sacred" or "national" charters guaranteeing citizen rights and limiting the powers of governments. Although writings and even constitutional declarations were not translated into actual practice, there is evidence of widening and deepening popular support for such a social contract to protect people from government.

Reform Within Tradition

The Arabian Peninsula, of course, was the cradle of Islam. At the dawn of the twentieth century, several different forms of Islamic law were in effect in different parts of the peninsula. The austere doctrine of Wahhabism that formed the ideological basis of the emergent Saudi kingdom was quite distinct from the Sunni Ottoman laws introduced in Yemen from Istanbul. The Zaydi Shi'ism of North Yemen's imams differed from the Ibadi Shi'ism of Omani imams, and the Shafi'i sultans of South Yemen's coastal region and Shafa'i scholars in North Yemen interpreted Sunni Islam in ways different from all of the above. These various schools of Islamic law held different positions on matters such as governance, taxation, education, and descent from the Prophet. (Systems of customary tribal law were also in effect in rural southern and central Arabia.) Each sect and polity trained jurists and legal scholars in its particular judicial and scholarly traditions. These were not stagnant but constantly developing interpretations and precedents. And within each polity, rulers attempted to impose central interpretations on academic training and judicial practice.

The cliché that "in Islam there is no separation of church and state" obscures the potential and sometimes real independence of religious institutions including *zakat* (a tithe), *waqf* (endowment), religious education, and judicial appointments and interpretations. Historically, various imams and sultans asserted their prerogative to collect and expend the religious tithe on wealth and production, but Shafi'i and even Zaydi communities often resisted its centralization. Eventually tax farming, surcharges, and other abuses had distorted a pious obligation beyond recognition. Regimes further attempted to control the considerable wealth of *waqf* funds as well as the intellectual content of the institutes, libraries, and mosques they supported. In the mid-1920s, North Yemen's Imam Yahya redirected the resources of Shafa'i schools into pro-imamic Zaydi institutions that trained jurists and teachers in an effort to mold legal and scholarly opinions. In South Yemen, too, at least one of the Hadrami sultans transferred administration of a school funded from an endowment in Singapore out of the hands of local religious scholars who protested that their academic standards were compromised.[4] In short, state control of religious institutions and interpretations was always controversial.

A new generation of the educated elite that came of age in the 1920s and 1930s criticized the status quo[5] and pressed for reforms that touched directly on what would later be considered human rights concerns. Influenced by trends in Egyptian, Sudanese, and even Indonesian education, North Yemeni liberals founded a couple of modern model schools, and an early Islamist reform movement in the Hadramawt defied the elite monopoly on reading and writing by educating the sons of ordinary tribesmen. Such schools became sites for the performance of ironic morality plays and the reading of political poetry. A range of Yemeni and foreign books and essays, many of them officially banned, circulated among the slowly expanding reading public. Themes of liberty and justice echoed in literary production and reverberated the punishment for dissent. The al-Akwa' brothers in Ibb, the elder of whom was a jurist, teacher, and playwright, were arrested for participation in a Reform (Islah) Society and sent to the infamous Hajjah prison with other intellectuals.[6] Detainees wrote pleas for leniency, conciliatory compositions to the imams, eulogies for slain colleagues, tributes to other scholars, poetry, history and works of protest or parody, and even issued two hand-written newspapers.[7] The famous Zaydi poet and jurist Muhammad al-Zubayri was exiled to Cairo for advocating a consultative imamate, and imprisoned on his return. Zubayri's writings, especially a 1952 pamphlet entitled "The Demands of the People" and another called "The Imamate and Its Menace to Yemeni Unity," developed the ideas of popular sovereignty and individual rights and freedoms as an alternative to personalized rule. It was a wide-ranging polemic, denouncing status differentiation, abuse of the religious tithe, and other injustices.[8] Muhsin al-'Ayni, another prominent republican, wrote a review of the Qur'anic account of the ancient Yemeni Queen Bilqis (the Queen of Sheba) to make the case that the original, Islamic, and true form of government was and ought to be a republic.[9] Some other young scholars accused by the administration of altering the Qur'an were acquitted by a Sana'a appeals court judge—who, with colleagues, subsequently issued a legal brief challenging forced payment of *zakat*, uncanonical taxes, tax farming, and trade monopolies, and demanding the pardon of political exiles.[10]

One of the most important public documents of the prerevolutionary period was a Sacred National Charter published in February 1948, wherein a group of mostly Zaydi religious scholars, some of whom had contacts in the Egyptian Muslim Brethren, called for modern constitutional rule. The charter began by saying that "to safeguard the True Religion and Our Independence, the representatives of the Yemeni nation of the different classes have convened in the form of a Congress to discuss the matter of establishing a good and legal regime." It called for the immediate establishment of a constitutional Council to design a monarchy along the lines of those then in power in Egypt and Iraq, with a legislature elected via universal adult suffrage and including representatives of towns, tribes and provinces, and émigrés. In the meantime, a seventy-person Consultative Council and a Council of Ministers should run things alongside an elected imam.

Although the precise shape of government was left to be determined, Articles 27 through 32 called for certain kinds of rights: "Injustice and oppression of the subjects must be quickly abolished"; "Life and property of all shall be assured"; "All the Yemen people shall be of the same level in respect of absolute equality"; "They shall be ruled according to true Moslem law, which shall be applied to all without any distinction." Moreover, "Freedom of opinion, speech, sufficiency (sic) and meeting" and freedom from "ignorance, poverty, and disease" were to be guaranteed.[11] There was also a call for "connections with the civilized world." Issued ten months before the Universal Declaration of Human Rights adopted by the General Assembly of the United Nations at the end of 1948, the document unsurprisingly does not echo all its provisions, and it does have a couple of disconcerting phrases about punishment of traitors. But it offers evidence that Yemeni intellectuals were conversant with contemporary pan-Arab and international discussions of rights and freedoms.

In 1955, Yemeni exiles in Cairo and Aden continued their constitutional campaign, according to another republican writer, emphasizing "a bill of rights as a basis for the government. In a pamphlet they drew up a new proposed national pact based on the [universal] declaration of human rights."[12] In South Yemen, where Great Britain had colonized the port city and signed protectorate treaties with rural sultans, the issues were different. Inside Aden Colony, a bustling commercial hub and naval base, a full-fledged anticolonial struggle developed. Newspapers representing a wide range of conservative, liberal, Arab nationalist, and socialist viewpoints stimulated political awareness and debate, perhaps especially when colonial authorities shut them down. The concerns of disenfranchised Yemeni immigrants to the city were best represented by the trades unions. From the beginning, white-collar leaders of the Aden Trades Union Conference set out to draft a "constitution" and publish a newspaper.[13] In 1958 the union newspaper was banned and its leaders arrested. Nevertheless an expanding syndical movement expanded and organized hundreds of strikes over the next decade to protest the absence of voting rights, inflation, and British actions elsewhere in the Middle East. In response to these pressures, limited elections for a newly created Aden Legislative Council occurred in October 1964 amid widespread political detentions and a ban on public meetings. Once elected, otherwise pro-British parliamentarians insisted on repeal of martial law, institution of universal adult suffrage, UN supervision of new elections, and respect for ordinary freedoms.

Colonial officers blamed widespread popular opposition to their administration on either cultural traditions (Islam and tribalism) or outside influences (Ottomans, and later Nasirites or Yemeni republicans). To stem the rising tide of dissent, authorities resorted to raiding meetings, rounding up activists, torturing some of them in prison, and blocking the International Red Cross and Amnesty International from visiting Adeni prisons.[14] In other respects, too, the United Kingdom established an unfortunate precedent for violating fundamental rights. Even before the onset of the armed struggle, nonviolent partisan leaders were jailed. Repeatedly, protests turned into riots when police and soldiers aimed their weapons into crowds. Suspected rabble-rousers were rounded up, sometimes by the dozen and sometimes by the hundreds, and then variously released, tried, or deported.[15]

In those days there were evidently no human rights or legal aid societies, but there were scattershot efforts to defend legal and civil liberties. Detentions and deportations were the proximate cause of many work stoppages. Resorting to a technique used in India, 15 of 107 jailed unionists staged a hunger strike in 1963. Students marched, and political detainees penned letters, poems, memoranda, satire, and petitions. Adeni authorities protested martial law. Essayists, theorists, and journalists broadcast defied censors with broadcasts and pamphlets. Yemeni intellectuals were in touch with the United Nations, Red Cross, and Amnesty International. Under the umbrella of the call for the right to self-determination were a number of specific demands for due process and intellectual license.

The constitutional movement gained momentum in the 1960s. Anticipating a future quite different from the past, intellectuals in both North and South Yemen put forth new constitutional proposals at popular conferences. In ʿAmran, north of Sanaʾa, a group of republicans and tribal leaders drew up a list of demands calling on the Egyptian-dominated North Yemeni military regime to create an executive council and a consultative council including tribal leaders. Rebuffed, they called a second meeting, chaired by the nationalist al-Zubairi and attended by sheikhs of both royalist and republican leanings. The ʿAmran resolutions reiterated earlier proposals and called for committees to resolve tribal disputes.[16] In a somewhat parallel development in one South Yemeni Protectorate, a tribally organized group called the Yafaʿ Reform Front that mediated local conflicts by employing common law mechanisms such as collecting rifles from each party to a dispute also advanced a "free Yafaʿ constitution."[17]

In 1965, a larger, more inclusive conference brought traditional and modern scholars from throughout North Yemen to Khamir, north of 'Amran, in the tribal heartland. Whereas previously the civilian liberal-republican literature had articulated mainly urban intellectual perspectives, now the concerns of ranchers, farmers, and villagers were reflected. The "provisional constitution," sometimes called the Khamir constitution, issued by this conference drew upon the 'Amran document, the earlier Sacred National Pact, common law notions of local self-governance, and some liberal language in an explicit effort to cast a wide net. One clause stated that "All Yemenis are equal in rights and responsibilities," and named among the rights justice, education, and association.[18]

During this same time period, South Yemeni partisans held their own conferences, once in Beirut and later (after 1962) inside North Yemen. The most historic of these was the first conference of the National Liberation Front (NLF) in Taiz in 1965, where a national charter was presented. In formulating its ideological positions, the NLF intellectual leaders drew on the populist egalitarianism of the early Islamist reformers and the Aden trade union movement, as well as on Nasserism, the Arab Nationalist Movement, and international socialism. Its program was radical by any standards, calling for "complete economic liberation from foreign exploiting capitalism" and elimination of the rule of "agent reactionary sultans." The charter further proposed "to restore their natural rights to women, and their equality with men . . . thus providing the basis for human justice and giving women the position in life to which they are entitled as full participants."[19]

Human Rights Promises and Abuses

To this point, then, alternative political elites developed some of the language, concepts, and principles of political rights and liberties. This discourse was idealist rather than realist: the power of the pen, not the power of the gun. New regimes promised these ideals would become governing principles. In the 1960s and early 1970s, when Free Officers and the National Liberation Front respectively came to power, constitutions were issued acknowledging many rights. The North Yemen (the Yemen Arab Republic, YAR) 1963 provisional constitution, the first of several documents reflecting Egyptian models, specified equality before the law, due process, and property and labor rights. Revisions in 1964 added freedom of opinion, press freedom, and the right to unionize. The 1970 "permanent" constitution (suspended in a 1974 military coup) further emphasized scholarly and press freedoms. Article 42 called for policies recognizing "human [or perhaps humane] rights common to all humanity on an equal basis" ["al-huquq al-insaniyya l'al-bashar jami'yan b-safa mutasawiyya"], with specific mention of the rights of women, children, the aged, the infirm, prisoners, and exiles; and of nondiscrimination on the basis of religion, color, or gender.[20] The 1978 Southern constitution, drawing on Socialist as well as Arab models, explicitly mentioned the International Declaration, and further specified a rather long list of social and economic rights for all citizens.[21] The People's Democratic Republic of Yemen (PDRY) also practiced "state feminism," promoting women's education, employment, and political representation, issuing a progressive family law, and eventually signing the Convention to Eliminate Discrimination against Women.[22] Although the two Yemeni governments advertised different kinds of rights, it can be inferred from their pronouncements that successive regimes in both Sana'a and Aden believed that the enunciation of basic rights would bolster their domestic and/or international legitimacy.

Unfortunately, the regimes in the PDRY and the YAR, were (to put it bluntly) both unstable Third World dictatorships that did not live up to these proclamations. Post-imamic and postcolonial policies did eliminate the status differentiation of old, suspend hated tax practices, expel royal families from power, and recognize Yemeni citizenship. But progress toward the full realization of basic rights and liberties called for by reformists and revolutionaries was negligible. Notwithstanding the contrasts between socialist "law and order" in the PDRY and the North's "chaotic capitalism," national security forces operated beyond constitutional or judicial constraints in both systems. Grave atrocities were committed during and after the Southern revolution, and inside Aden, especially, the group that evolved from the NLF into the Yemeni Socialist Party controlled political activity tightly. Because every new regime issued a new list of state criminals, security prisons remained full even after the periodic amnesties. Fifteen hundred people were detained after Aden's intraparty bloodbath in 1986, and much was made of the political trials of a hundred traitors. Whereas the YAR permitted the Red Cross to inspect its admittedly medieval and rat-infested jails, the Aden regime, like its colonial predecessor, denied reporters access to its detention centers.

Sana'a's military regimes and an increasingly pervasive security apparatus also suppressed dissent, open political organizing, and flow of information. Moreover, by the mid-1980s a new, right-wing sort of Islamism was spreading in North Yemen and among émigrés to the Gulf. This movement had its intellectual legacy in puritanical Wahhabism as taught in Saudi-financed religious schools established throughout the Muslim world at the height of the oil boom. Its militancy was cultivated for the Afghan anti-Soviet jihad. As instructed to Yemeni immigrants by Saudi preachers, to Yemeni students by fundamentalist Egyptian and Sudanese teachers, and to volunteer mujahideen training in Pakistan, this "born-again" fundamentalism put greatest emphasis on the elements of shariʿa that seem most antithetical to international conceptions of human rights, such as hyperseclusion of women, corporal punishment, and hatred of infidels. With Gulf funding and government support, the intellectual wing of this movement gained a slew of influential positions at Sanaʾa University, where a sociology professor was branded an apostate for "blasphemous" writings, a bare-headed woman was assaulted, and self-appointed zealots policed male-female encounters. By the late 1980s, a reformist movement was taking shape in Aden. Show trials following the shootout in 1986 became a forum for legal defense of political dissent. Constraints on speech, press, association, and movement were loosened. The impetus for this tentative but unmistakable liberalization evidently came from within and beyond the party. Leading socialist intellectual, Jar Allah ʿUmar began urging the ruling Yemeni Socialist Party toward pluralism (taʿaddudiyya), human rights (huquq al-insan), citizen rights, freedom of intellectual pursuits, and other liberties. As a first step, intellectuals, businessmen, and popular organizations should be engaged in the ongoing constitutional and unity negotiations. In view of perestroika in the USSR, the events of January 1986 in the PDRY, and religious currents in the YAR, he argued, it was time for tolerance of opposition parties and relaxation of restrictions on the press. A new elections law relaxed nomination and polling supervision and redrew constituency lines.[23] To one American diplomat, there seemed to be a "tacit agreement" within the ruling party to allow "freer journalistic expression" as well as "the first stirrings of political demonstrations and strikes."[24]

Contemporary Discourses

The language of human rights began to permeate national political discourses in many languages and settings around 1990. Yemeni unification in 1990 ushered in a new era of unprecedented, if still hardly unfettered, freedom of association, expression, publication, and movement. For the first time, political parties campaigned in contested elections. A constitution drafted (nearly a decade earlier) by a committee of the nation's best jurists, adopted in popular referendum in 1991, offered a significant bill of rights and promised a democratic form of government. In addition to universal adult suffrage, the constitution guaranteed "freedom of thought and expression by speech, writing, or pictures within the law," "equal treatment" without discrimination due to "sex, color, racial origin, language, occupation, social status, or religious beliefs," and the presumption of "innocent until proven guilty." Political rights including freedom of association "inasmuch as it was not contrary to the constitution" were also affirmed. There were fewer military checkpoints, a number of political detainees were released, and many exiles returned home. All the political tendencies from the previous generation of activism surfaced, from the socialist left through various brands of Arab nationalism to liberal globalism to different sorts of Islamism. In one way or another, each and every significant political tendency adopted the discourse—perhaps one should say the rhetoric—of human rights.

Several socialist and independent progressive intellectuals, especially those involved with the Yemeni Writers Union, had introduced the term "human rights" into political debate even before 1990 as part of a plea for tolerance. Northern and Southern educators, journalists, and attorneys from the liberal-left were well represented among the first group to meet to found what later came to be called the Yemeni Organization for the Defense of Human Rights and Democratic Liberties (ODHRDL) in the early 1990s.[25] Professors introduced human rights curricula at Sana'a University and penned editorials on the subject. From the intellectual elite, there was some trickle-down as students and others formed branches of Amnesty International. Indeed, rather quickly, the language of rights spread across the full political spectrum. The platform of the party organization that had ruled North Yemen and was still rightly called the ruling party, the General People's Congress (GPC), made "citizen rights in freedom, equality, and justice" a leading principle.[26] A second association called the Yemeni Organization for Human Rights (YOHR) was founded by members of the two major parties on the right, the GPC and the Reform Party.[27] Although this group sacrificed some credibility to a blatant security presence in their midst, it nonetheless signified a widening of the discourse of human rights, in recognition of the wide popular appeal of notions of liberty, justice, and nonviolence. The YOHR leadership included at least one prominent traditionally educated judge, Hamud al-Hitar, who familiarized himself with and encouraged others to read international covenants. YOHR's first aim was to "promote greater respect for human rights and liberties as outlined in shariʿa, current legislation, the International Statement on Human Rights in Islam, the International Declaration on Human Rights, and in Arab, Islamic, and international charters, conventions and agreements."[28] Other stated objectives were equality; the pursuit of liberty; protections against violence and surveillance; judicial and penal reform; and attention to the rights of women and children under shariʿa. Like ODHRDL, YOHR published investigations of prison conditions in the many weekly newspapers then widely available.

Notions of political liberties and legal protections were widely discussed among the political elite. Although exercising unprecedented editorial leeway with the suspension of prior censorship, newspapers were sued by the Ministry of Information in Sana'a for a range of alleged misdemeanors. Journalists and attorneys, enjoying newfound possibilities for non-civil service careers, animated their syndicates to defend the reporters and editors from various charges. Publicity for these cases, some of which have attracted the attention of international organizations to protect freedom of the press,[29] was another occasion for the articulation of legal principles. So much did the discussion of protection of human rights catch on, in fact, that in the months leading up to the 1994 civil war an experienced foreign human rights investigator worried privately that "human rights has become a stick both sides [GPC and socialists] beat each other with." Some citizens, perhaps a majority, doubted the sincerity of political leaders' rhetorical commitment to basic protections and freedoms. By the same token, there is no doubt that the term "human rights" was bandied about in ruling circles as well as by popular organizations because of its widespread appeal.

On the far right, the most puritanical wing of the Islamist tendency[30] has tailored a notion of "Islamic human rights" to a particular political agenda.[31] Most conspicuously, neo-Islamists advanced a separate notion of "women's rights": women and girls have rights to separate education and work spaces, to be supported by their male kinfolk, to travel with an escort, and so on. Thus restrictions are portrayed as rights. Inequalities under legislation introduced in the mid-1990s assert women's inferior capacity to serve as witnesses in court, mandate lower inheritance for sisters than for brothers, insist on spousal obedience, and tolerate polygamy and unilateral divorce by husbands but not wives. But even at the extreme fringe of the post-Afghanistan, radically antisocialist fundamentalist movement, Yemeni neo-Islamists were not questioning whether women have citizen rights. They recognized that women must be free from family or state violence and forced marriage and are entitled to participate in parliamentary elections, hold public office, and press contractual obligations in court.[32] In the lead-up to the 1993 parliamentary elections, the Reform Party organized the first ever nationwide campaign to register women voters. Feminine voluntarism, for instance, concerning human rights violations in Bosnia, Kosovo, Chechnya, and Kashmir is encouraged.[33] The neofundamentalists—among them some fully veiled spokeswomen—insisted that women and men should all be educated in their rights under shari'a and that female illiteracy is a major barrier to protection of women's legal rights. At the center and left of the political spectrum, many authors writing within Islamic or civil law frameworks contradicted the rejectionists. A number of authors deduced rights principles from an Islamic, Arab notion of what it is to be human, citing both moral principles and legal doctrine. Only a few of these can be cited here. Muhammad ʿAbd al-Malik al-Mutawakkil refuted the "rejectionist" perspective by quoting from Qurʾanic, scholarly, and Saudi sources on the major issues on which Islam is sometimes said to conflict with the Universal Declaration: freedom of belief, gender equality, inheritance, polygamy, and female legal competence. In an essay for the Sanaʾa official daily newspaper, Ahmad al-Marwani traced the idea of human rights to the ancient Yemeni kingdom of Maʾen, the ancient Greeks, and the Qurʾan.[34] Zayd al-Wazir philosophically reconciled Zaydi political theory with internationally-recognized precepts of democracy and human rights.[35] A prominent politician and benefactor of a scholarly foundation, Ahmad Jabir ʿAfif, published a long essay on women's rights using both civil and religious law precedents to demonstrate governmental obligations to equal treatment before the law,[36] and legal scholar Ahmad al-Wadaʾi's controversial analysis of North Yemeni constitutional and legal documents emphasized the legal obligation to protections consistent with international standards.[37] Several other legal histories and countless editorials expounded on these notions.

The many pleas of human rights activists seemed to fall on deaf ears as Northern and Southern armies squared off in the winter and spring of 1994. As in earlier national moments of crisis, political elites joined together to try to write a social contract. The National Dialogue of Political Forces was a committee of three members from each of the leading parties, one from each of a half-dozen prominent lesser parties and the opposition coalition, and several independents, a total of twenty-seven men, all with national reputations, selected to represent every major region and social group from within the body politic. University faculty, legal scholars, journalists, and others seized the opportunity to present their research in the many seminars arranged to discuss subjects like the line between censorship and libel, women's rights, and shariʿa. Excerpts and full transcripts of these symposia appeared in the popular press, thus influencing wider discourse and ordinary conversation. At the popular level, a score of regional conferences involved tens of thousands of people, mostly but not all men, in the national dialogue. Protection of human rights was among the resolutions of mass meetings in cities and towns across the country. The most common themes overall were public safety, removal of the military from population centers, elections for local administration, judicial independence, a serious plan to limit government corruption, and the building of modern state institutions. These issues in turn were incorporated into the accords issued by the Dialogue Committee on January 18, 1994.[38]

The document opened with a set of proposals to curtail the roles of security forces and the interior and defense ministries in politics and policing. These immediate "law and order" concerns were to be followed up through provisions for the independence of the judiciary, for separation of armed forces from criminal prosecution, and for ministerial, parliamentary, and civilian control of the security establishment. In the remainder of the accords, three major modifications of the current constitutional order were called for: a bicameral legislature, a limited executive, and decentralization. Support for these constitutional principles was widespread. Amid gathering war clouds, more conferences affirmed the work of the Dialogue Committee and their proposals. Urban scholars, attorneys, and other professionals held weekly seminars to examine each section of the document. In meetings from Sa'adah in the far north to Lahij and Hadramawt in the south there were calls for prompt, full implementation of the Accords. Members of the Dialogue Committee now met in Sana'a, Aden, Taiz, and elsewhere to plan a strategy of regular, peaceful, sit-in protests in cities and towns throughout the country, Ample coverage of these events in the partisan press showed how the GPC, Socialists, Reform Party, and other parties each tried to associate themselves with a movement that clearly represented majority public sentiment.[39]

War erupted between the two former armies, however, and human rights suffered as a consequence. A security crackdown accompanied the three-month state of emergency,[40] and subsequently the victorious Sana'a government (a wartime alliance of the GPC and the conservative Reform Party) sponsored constitutional amendments and legislation that threatened human rights by strengthening executive authority, retracting women's legal competence, eroding judicial autonomy, and constraining other rights and guarantees of rights. As a number of intellectuals were interred or beaten up and honest judges found themselves in obscure rural courts, the challenges to the weakened nascent human rights movement were formidable indeed.[41] Members of the Dialogue Committee outside the ruling coalition, including Abu Bakr al-Saqqaf, Anis Hassan Yahya, and Omar al-Jawi, charged the regime with disregard for human rights.[42] Even six years after the civil war, facing no significant domestic security threat, the administration persisted in harassment of independent newspapers, judges, associations, and opinion leaders. While the political security organization seemed ever-vigilant, ordinary crimes often escaped prosecutors' attention.

Still, as Naguib A. R. Shamiry of the Supreme Judicial Council observed, Yemen was bound by its signature to thirteen international human rights covenants and instruments. In principle, the courts were constitutionally charged with upholding human rights in a number of ways, including presumption of innocence, protections against unwarranted search, right to legal defense, prohibition of torture and forced confessions, and punishment commensurate with the crime.[43] There were at least some indications that the regime was conscious of these obligations. After the war the victors said they had fought for unity and the values of "democracy, political pluralism, freedom of the press and respect of human rights."[44] In 1998, the National High Committee for Human Rights in Yemen, established some years earlier, declared 10 December National Human Rights Day.[45] The president of the republic himself, in the opening address at a human rights day conference in December 1999, reiterated the national commitment to guarantee citizens their rights.[46] His GPC party's Web page contains a strong statement of the goal to "protect and preserve human rights and public freedoms."[47]

Official statements may well be purely rhetorical pronouncements for foreign public relations purposes, since it is clear that practice does not live up to rhetoric.[48] But politicians across the political spectrum seemed to recognize the popular appeal of this discourse as well. Awareness was higher than ever at the end of the twentieth century, especially within the growing legal community. Just as civil society institutions may protect political pluralism, wrote Ahmad al-Wada'i, the courts were the guarantors of human rights and liberties; both zones are highly politicized, and the protection of rights proceeds both through individual cases and in larger efforts to secure judicial autonomy.[49] In terms of Yemeni culture, argued attorney Muhammad Naji 'Alaw, there is both a philosophical tradition of judicial independence and a history of political attempts to bend legal practice to the imperatives of governing authorities.[50] Research showed that, despite many obstacles, members of the judiciary did attempt to exercise their constitutional function in the protection of the law.[51] Under a program conceptualized by an Egyptian teacher with help from the British Council, there was even a project called Children Painting Their Rights, involving students from thirty-six schools in five provinces in publicity for the rights of children.[52] In the mid-2000s, a traditionally trained jurist, Judge Hamud al-Hitar, earned international attention by training jailed neo-Islamist militants in a learned reading of the Islamic rules of war that prohibits targeting of civilians.[53]

In conclusion, then, "human rights" was not an alien concept introduced into southwestern Arabia by Euro-American influences, but an ideal that has evolved endogenously and continues to develop as Yemenis reconsider the nature of law and its implementation. This conversation, reflected in essays, constitutional proposals, legal briefs, and the press, has been influenced by international movements, ideologies, and declarations. It has also involved a fair number of citizens, over the years, in constitutional conventions and popular conferences. Although I have by no means reviewed all the literature or explored specific legislative developments, in ongoing constitutional debates ideas of "freedom to" and "protection from" were steadily refined and expanded. It is simply wrong, or a wrongful simplification, to represent this as a polarization between traditionalists and modernists or Islamic versus Western values, for we have seen a range of political perspectives weigh in on human rights issues. Moreover, there is nothing traditional about the neo-Islamist rejection of "human rights;" many Yemenis searched their own intellectual heritage for legal, moral, and logical support for international conceptions of human rights. If rights are not respected, it is not because traditions and values stand in the way but because actual practices do not stand up to stated, widely held ideals.

Chapter 10
Got Rights? Public Interest Litigation and the Egyptian Human Rights Movement

Tamir Moustafa

When human rights activist Saad Eddin Ibrahim and his twenty-seven colleagues were ushered into an Egyptian Emergency State Security Court on February 26, 2001, it was effectively the entire Egyptian human rights movement that stood trial. Despite a campaign by international human rights groups, a vigorous legal defense, and testimony from some of Egypt's most respected figures, Ibrahim was found guilty and sentenced to seven years in prison for "propagating false information and vicious rumors abroad . . . which would weaken the state's prestige and integrity."[1] Although Ibrahim and his colleagues were eventually acquitted by the Court of Cassation and released in March 2003, there was little to celebrate. The two-year ordeal was the final assault on a movement that had endured years of government harassment, crippling new legislation regulating NGO activity, and financial strangulation through the closing of foreign funding sources. By the time of Ibrahim's release, little remained of a human rights movement that just a few years earlier had promised to be the most effective force for political reform in the Arab world.

Why did the Egyptian government act so forcefully to shut down the country's fledgling human rights organizations? One clear motive was to derail a movement that had brought international attention to the regime's unsavory methods of political control. But more importantly, political retrenchment was the reaction to a productive synergy that had emerged among Egyptian human rights organizations, opposition parties, and progressive judicial activists in the state's own court system.

In this chapter, I examine how opposition and human rights activists mobilized through Egypt's relatively independent judicial institutions to challenge the regime in ways that were never possible in other formal political arenas.[2] I explore how the Egyptian Supreme Constitutional Court, in particular, enabled political activists to credibly challenge the regime for the first time since the 1952 military coup by simply initiating constitutional litigation, a process that required few financial resources and allowed activists to circumvent the state's highly restrictive, corporatist political framework. I find that constitutional litigation provided institutional openings for political activists to challenge the state in ways that fundamentally transformed patterns of interaction between the state and society by enabling activists to challenge the regime without having to initiate a broad social movement, a task that is all but impossible in Egypt's highly restrictive political environment.[3] Ironically, however, I also find that the advantages of legal mobilization eventually impaired the ability of human rights organizations to effectively defend themselves against increasingly aggressive legal and extralegal assaults without broad-based societal support.

The Judicialization of Egyptian Politics

Egyptian judicial institutions and the Egyptian legal profession have a long and rich history of progressive political activism.[4] Although independent judicial power was impaired through much of the Nasser and Sadat eras, courts reemerged as prominent political institutions with the establishment of the independent Supreme Constitutional Court (SCC) in 1979, and with judicial reforms to the civil and administrative courts in 1984.[5] Almost immediately, opposition activists mobilized through the courts to achieve important victories.[6] In one of its earliest rulings, the SCC enabled hundreds of prominent opposition activists, such as Wafd Party leader Fuad Serag Eddin, to return to political life.[7] Another ruling in 1988 forced the legalization of the Nasserist Party against government objections.[8] The SCC even ruled national election laws unconstitutional in 1987 and 1990, forcing the dissolution of the People's Assembly, a new electoral system, and early elections.[9] Similar rulings forced comparable reforms to the system of elections for both the Upper House (Maglis al-Shura) and local council elections nationwide.[10] Although rulings on election laws hardly undermined the regime's grip on power, they did significantly undermine the regime's corporatist system of opposition control.[11]

Even when the regime reversed course and initiated a campaign of political retrenchment throughout the 1990s, judicial institutions became the main avenue of political resistance.[12] Opposition activists continued to score victories in the SCC throughout the decade, most

TABLE 10.1. EGYPTIAN POLITICAL PARTIES IN 1995

Party	Date of establishment	Avenue for attaining legal status
NDP (ruling party)	1976	presidential decree
Tagemmu Party	1976	presidential decree
Liberal Party (Ahrar)	1976	presidential decree
Socialist Labor Party	1977	approved by Political Parties Committee
Wafd Party	1978	administrative court ruling
Umma Party	1983	administrative court ruling
Green Party	1990	administrative court ruling
Misr al-Fatah Party	1990	administrative court ruling
Union Democratic Party	1990	administrative court ruling
Nasserist Party	1992	SCC ruling
Populist Democratic Party	1992	administrative court ruling
Egypt Arab Socialist Party	1992	administrative court ruling
Social Justice Party	1993	administrative court ruling
Al-Takaful	1995	administrative court ruling

notably in the area of press liberties. In February 1993, the SCC struck down a provision in the code of criminal procedures that required defendants in libel cases to present proof validating their published statements within a five-day period of notification by the prosecutor.[13] On the heels of this legal victory, the Labor Party successfully challenged a provision of Law 40/1977 concerning the opposition press and vicarious criminal liability in front of the SCC.[14] The court initially took a cautious approach in its 1995 decision by limiting the ruling of unconstitutionality to the president of political parties. However, just two years later, the SCC extended its ruling to ban the application of vicarious criminal liability to libel cases involving the editors in chief of newspapers.[15]

Judicial activism in the administrative courts and the SCC also enabled opposition activists to successfully challenge decisions of the regime-dominated Political Parties Committee and to gain formal opposition-party status. By 1995, ten of Egypt's thirteen opposition parties owed their very existence to court rulings (see Table 10.1).

Opposition parties and human rights organizations, once at odds with one another, also began to understand that they were fighting the same struggle for political reform. In the mid-1990s they started to work with one another, and cooperative efforts began to bear fruit almost immediately. This is perhaps best exemplified by their effort to monitor the 1995 People's Assembly elections. Six months prior to the elections, leading human rights organizations in conjunction with the major opposition parties announced their plans to establish the Egyptian National

Commission for Monitoring Parliamentary Elections. The idea of a citizen-based electoral monitoring commission was a historic first for Egypt, but the campaign picked up considerable momentum in a short period of time. In just a few months, the commission had grown to involve over 100 academics, over 600 human rights activists, many prominent journalists, and the five most important opposition parties.[16] Dr. Saad Eddin Ibrahim, professor at the American University in Cairo and head of the Ibn Khaldun Center for Development Studies, was appointed secretary-general.[17] The goal of the commission was to monitor the election from start to finish and to systematically document electoral corruption in Egypt for the first time in order to induce pressure for political reform and to generate documentation that would facilitate litigation in the courts.

The findings of the commission were startling. In the months leading up to the elections, the commission documented hundreds of irregularities in voting lists and harassment by government officials.[18] Human rights groups also recorded the regime's crackdown on opposition candidates. Two months before the election, the unofficial headquarters of the Muslim Brotherhood was closed by the government, and eighty-five leading Islamists, including four former members of the People's Assembly, were tried before a military court. In the month leading up to the election, 1,392 more Islamists and opposition party members were detained so that opposition candidates would be unable to place representatives at the polling stations to prevent government-orchestrated election fraud.[19] Additionally, election campaign materials for opposition figures were seized, dozens of election workshops were derailed, and opposition marches were prevented or suppressed. Human rights organizations documented thousands more irregularities during the election itself including physical assaults on voters and candidates, ballot box stuffing, vote buying, and other forms of electoral fraud, as well as the extensive use of state resources for regime-friendly candidates.[20] By all accounts, the 1995 People's Assembly elections were the most corrupt and violent on record, with 60 people killed and up to 820 seriously injured.

The cooperation between opposition parties and human rights groups through the national commission produced immediate results. In the months following the elections, 914 petitions challenging election results across the country proceeded on to the Court of Cassation. The detailed reports and extensive documentation provided by human rights organizations were the most important pieces of evidence in these cases. Judges concluded that electoral fraud was rampant, ruling that 226 seats in the People's Assembly (over half of the total 444 seats) should be disqualified. Opposition parties lauded the Egyptian judiciary for its role in exposing the corruption of the regime with headline banners such as, "Judges Confirm the Collapse of Governmental Legitimacy."[21] Opposition newspapers continued to publicize the irregularities and gave a prominent voice to the findings of human rights groups. *Al-Sha'b* described the elections as "a massacre," *Al-Wafd* described them as "the worst elections in Egypt's history," and even articles printed in the government-run newspaper, *Al-Akhbar,* could not deny that "The names of living persons disappeared and those of the dead reappeared."[22]

Despite impressive success in the courts, however, not a single seat was turned over to opposition candidates and no new elections were held for seats ruled invalid by the administrative courts. As in previous elections, the regime-dominated People's Assembly invoked Article 93 of the constitution, which explicitly states that "the People's Assembly shall be competent to decide upon the validity of the membership of its members. . . . Membership shall not be deemed invalid except by a decision taken by a majority of two-thirds of the Assembly members." Fathi Sarour used this article to justify the refusal of court rulings and instead claimed that the People's Assembly would initiate its own hearings into allegations of election fraud.[23] Moreover, the High Administrative Court issued a ruling on November 17, 1996, that gave the People's Assembly, rather than the administrative courts, the final word on election challenges. The ruling dismayed opposition activists, and judges were disturbed by their inability to have rulings implemented. However, in this circumstance, the explicit wording of the constitution itself prevented the judiciary from playing a more assertive role.[24]

Following the 1995 People's Assembly elections, Egyptian opposition parties again turned to the SCC in an attempt to break the regime's control of elections. Lawyers representing the main Egyptian opposition parties worked together to challenge the constitutionality of the election law, and their focus turned to Article 88 of the Egyptian Constitution, which states that "the law shall determine the conditions which members of the Assembly must fulfill as well as the rules of election and referendum, *while the ballot shall be conducted under the supervision of the members of a judicial organ*" (emphasis added). Using this article, opposition activists filed court cases challenging the legal framework governing elections, which allowed for state employees to supervise election substations where the majority of electoral forgery occurred. As we will see, these efforts paid off handsomely five years later when the SCC ruled in favor of full judicial supervision of elections.

Got Rights? The New Battleground of Public Interest Litigation

The 1990s also saw a new breed of Egyptian human rights organizations that went beyond simply documenting human rights abuses to confronting the government in the courts. The most aggressive group engaged in public interest litigation was the Center for Human Rights Legal Aid (CHRLA), established by the young and forceful human rights activist Hisham Mubarak in 1994. CHRLA quickly became the most dynamic human rights organization, initiating 500 cases in its first full year of operation, 1,323 cases in 1996, and 1,616 by 1997.[25] CHRLA's central mission was to provide free legal representation to those who had experienced human rights violations at the hands of the government. Additionally, CHRLA documented human rights abuses and used the cases that it sponsored to publicize the human rights situation. As with every other human rights group in Egypt, CHRLA depended almost completely on foreign funding, but throughout the mid-1990s foreign funding sources proved plentiful and CHRLA quickly expanded its operations, opening two regional offices in Alexandria and Aswan.

In hopes of emulating the model provided by CHRLA, human rights activists launched additional legal aid organizations with different missions. The Center for Women's Legal Aid was established in 1995 to provide free legal aid to women dealing with a range of issues including divorce, child custody, and various forms of discrimination. The center initiated 71 cases in its first year, 142 in 1996, and 146 in 1997 in addition to providing legal advice to 1,400 women in its first three years of activity. The Land Center for Human Rights joined the ranks of legal aid organizations in 1996 and dedicated its energies to providing free legal aid to peasants. With the land reform law (Law 96 of 1992) coming into full effect in October 1997, hundreds of thousands of peasants faced potential eviction in the late 1990s and lawsuits between landlords and tenants began to enter into the courts by the thousands. Between 1996 and 2000 the Land Center for Human Rights represented peasants in over 4,000 cases and provided legal advice to thousands more.[26] The Human Rights Center for the Assistance of Prisoners (HRCAP) similarly provided legal aid to prisoners and their families by investigating allegations of torture, monitoring prison conditions, and fighting the phenomenon of recurrent detention and other abuses through litigation. In its first five years of operation, HRCAP launched over 200 court cases per year and gave free assistance (legal and otherwise) to 7,000–8,000 victims per year.[27] Opposition parties began to offer free legal aid as well, with the Wafd Party's Committee for Legal Aid providing free legal representation in over 400 cases per year beginning in 1997.[28] Similarly, the

Lawyers Syndicate was active in providing legal aid, and it greatly expanded its legal aid department until the regime froze its functions in 1996.

By 1997, legal mobilization had unquestionably become the dominant strategy for human rights defenders because of the difficulty of creating a broad social movement under the Egyptian regime. Gasser Abdel Razeq, director of the Center for Human Rights Legal Aid and later the Hisham Mubarak Center for Legal Aid, firmly contended that "in Egypt, where you have a relatively independent judiciary, the only way to promote reform is to have legal battles all the time. It's the only way that we can act as a force for change." A strong and independent judiciary was so central to the strategy of the human rights movement that activists went beyond simply facing threats to the judiciary and the legal profession on an ad hoc basis; in 1997 activists institutionalized their support for judicial independence by founding the Arab Center for the Independence of the Judiciary and the Legal Profession (ACIJLP).

Under the direction of Nasser Amin, former legal director of the Egyptian Organization for Human Rights (EOHR), the ACIJLP set to work organizing conferences and workshops that brought together legal scholars, opposition party members, human rights activists, and important figures from the Lawyers Syndicate and Judges Association. The ACIJLP began to issue annual reports on the state of the judiciary and legal profession, extensively documenting government harassment of lawyers, critiquing state sequestration of the Lawyers Syndicate, and exposing the regime's interference in the normal functions of judicial institutions. Like other human rights groups, the ACIJLP established ties with international human rights organizations including the Lawyers Committee for Human Rights and attempted to leverage international pressure on the Egyptian government.

But the sophistication of these legal campaigns reached new heights when the leadership of CHRLA began to understand that legal challenges in the SCC were potentially the most effective avenue to challenge the regime because constitutional litigation could induce systemic changes. According to Gasser Abdel Raziq, this change in legal tactics came with the 1997 SCC ruling on Article 195 of the penal code, a major case that CHRLA lawyers had helped prepare.[29] CHRLA attorneys and the human rights movement in general were already following the activism of the SCC with considerable interest. Abdel Raziq recalled that

we were encouraged by [Chief Justice] Awad al-Morr's human rights language in both his formal rulings and in public statements. This encouraged us to have a dialogue with the Supreme Constitutional Court. CHRLA woke up to the idea that litigation in the SCC could allow us to actually change the laws and not just achieve justice in the immediate case at hand.[30]

Beginning in late 1997, CHRLA initiated a campaign to systematically challenge repressive legislation in the SCC. CHRLA's first target was Law 35 of 1976, which governed trade union elections. CHRLA initiated fifty cases in the administrative and civil courts, all with petitions to challenge the constitutionality of Law 35 in the SCC. Ten of the fifty cases were successfully transferred, and within months the SCC issued its first verdict of unconstitutionality against Article 36 of the law.[31] CHRLA also successfully advanced three cases to the SCC that challenged sections of the penal code concerning newspaper publication offenses and three additional cases dealing with the social insurance law.[32] CHRLA was further encouraged by activist judges in the regular judiciary who publicly encouraged groups in civil society to challenge the constitutionality of NDP legislation. Some activist judges went so far as to publicize their opinion of laws in opposition newspapers and vowed that if particular laws were challenged in their court, they would transfer the relevant constitutional question to the SCC without delay.[33]

The ruling of unconstitutionality on Law 35 and the additional fourteen pending decisions in a three-year period represented a tremendous achievement, given the slow speed of litigation in Egyptian courts and the relatively meager resources at the disposal of the human rights movement. Although the results may seem modest, the human rights community came to understand that constitutional litigation was perhaps the most effective way to challenge the regime. Until the CHRLA campaign, activists, opposition parties, and individuals initiated cases in an ad hoc fashion, but CHRLA's coordinated strategy of constitutional litigation was a first.

The SCC had drawn the interest of the Egyptian human rights community for years, but CHRLA's successful constitutional challenges prompted the rest of the human rights community to consider the possibility of constitutional litigation more seriously. A number of conferences and workshops were sponsored to examine the possibilities afforded by constitutional litigation, some of which brought together human rights associations and SCC justices.[34]

Other human rights organizations were eager to emulate CHRLA's approach. The Land Center for Human Rights set their sights on contesting the constitutionality of the regime's land reform program as well as a variety of labor laws. By the close of 2001, the Land Center successfully transferred two cases to the SCC. The first petition challenged the constitutionality of Law 96 of 1992, liberalizing owner-tenant relations in the countryside. The other petition challenged the constitutionality of Law 177 of 1967, which governed the activities of the Principal Bank for Agricultural Development and Credits. Like other human rights activists, lawyers at the Land Center said they were encouraged by the many bold SCC rulings on political issues. However, human rights activists attempting to safeguard the last vestiges of Nasser-era economic rights for the poor were far more pessimistic about the possibility of successfully defending these rights through the SCC, despite the many socialist-oriented provisions in the constitution, because of the free-market orientation of many of the justices on the SCC.

Ironically, as human rights groups used litigation as their primary tool for challenging the regime, they themselves were without solid legal footing due to the restrictions of Law 32/1964 governing civil associations and periodic interference from the Ministry of Social Affairs.[35] Constitutional litigation therefore became the dominant strategy not only for challenging government legislation but also for challenging the Law on Associations to expand the legal foundation of civil society itself. At an NGO workshop convened by the Cairo Institute for Human Rights Studies in December 1996, leading human rights activists began to consider constitutional litigation as the most effective avenue for challenging Law 32 and for liberalizing the legal framework that constrained NGO activities. Discussions revolved around the previous rulings of the SCC, the legal basis for challenging the constitutionality of Law 32/1964, and a strategy for initiating litigation and transferring cases to the SCC. The final position paper of the workshop stated that

The freedom of forming associations is documented in the Egyptian Constitution. The Supreme Constitutional Court has asserted in its rulings that if the constitution authorizes the legislator to organize a constitutional right (like the right to form associations by groups or individuals), this entails that the right is not taken away, undermined or complicated. . . . the participants thus have called for proceeding with legal appeals that cast doubt over the constitutionality of the law.[36]

More than ever, it was apparent that the "constitutional consciousness" of civil society had reached a new plateau. Moreover, the discussion of the legal basis for challenging the constitutionality of the law took on increasing sophistication. In addition to discussing how specific articles of Law 32 violated the constitution, participants in the workshop considered how the law violated the International Covenant on Civil and Political Rights, which had been ratified by the Egyptian government. The discussion of how the law violated Egypt's international treaty commitments was no longer a strictly academic debate because under the leadership of Justice Awad al-Morr, the SCC had demonstrated that international laws signed into force would be used to support the court's interpretations of constitutional provisions. The legal tactics of human rights activists engaged in constitutional litigation began to mirror the language of the court to take advantage of the opportunity that the SCC was providing.

Constitutional litigation was also combined with other tactics. Throughout 1997, a network of sixteen human rights organizations, three leading opposition parties, and a number of prominent academics drafted a new bill on associations. The draft law sought to remove legal restrictions on the establishment of civil associations and to restrict the regime's ability to interfere in the activities of NGOs. By February 1998, the draft law was presented to the People's Assembly by Ali Fateh Bab of the Labor Party, Ayman Nour and Fouad Badrawi of the Wafd Party, and Mohammed Abdel Aziz Shabban of the Tagemmu Party. Opposition parties never expected the legislation to pass through the People's Assembly. Rather, they used the draft law as an opportunity to expose the shortcomings of Law 32 in opposition newspapers and to draw attention to the campaign to challenge the constitutionality of the law in front of the SCC.

Political Retrenchment and the Human Rights Movement

By the mid-1990s, the regime's discomfort with the human rights movement reached new levels. In just over a decade, the movement had grown to over a dozen organizations, many of which had established strong links with the international human rights community and had achieved observer status in a number of international human rights regimes, such as the United Nations Economic and Social Council. The human rights movement increasingly leveraged international pressure on the Egyptian regime through these channels. Domestically, moreover, human rights organizations had begun to cooperate closely with opposition parties and professional syndicates, as demonstrated most effectively in their resistance to Law 95/1995 (a press law) and their campaign in monitoring the 1995 People's Assembly elections. Moreover, the most dynamic human rights organizations increasingly used public interest litigation in the courts as an effective avenue to challenge the regime.

In response, the regime began to turn the screws on the human rights movement as early as 1995 through intimidation, smear campaigns in the state press, and discouraging donor organizations from contributing to local human rights NGOs. Beginning in 1998, however, the regime engaged in a full-fledged campaign to undermine the human rights movement after the EOHR published an extensive report on a particularly shocking episode of sectarian violence in the village of Al-Kosheh in August 1998. The EOHR report uncovered not only the details of one of Egypt's worst bouts of sectarian violence, a politically taboo subject in itself, but also that hundreds of citizens were tortured at the hands of state security forces for weeks following the incident. In response to the report, Hafez Abu Saʿada, secretary-general of the EOHR, was charged by state security prosecutors with "receiving money from a foreign country in order to damage the national interest, spreading rumors which affect the country's interests, and violating the decree against collecting donations without obtaining permission from the appropriate authorities."[37] Abu Saʿada was detained for six days of questioning and then released on bail. The trial was postponed indefinitely but the charges remained on the books.[38] Abu Saʿada's interrogation was a warning to the human rights community that strong dissent and foreign funding would no longer be tolerated by the regime. In the aftermath of Abu Saʿada's interrogation, the EOHR acquiesced to government pressure and stopped accepting foreign funding.

The following year, the regime issued a new law governing NGO activity that tightened the already severe constraints imposed by Law 32/1964. Law 153/1999 first eliminated the loophole that had allowed NGOs to operate as civil companies and forced human rights organizations to submit to Ministry of Social Affairs (MOSA) supervision or face immediate closure. The new law additionally forbade civil associations from engaging in "any political or unionist activity, the exercise of which is restricted to political parties and syndicates." Moreover, MOSA maintained the right to dissolve any association "threatening national unity or violating public order or morals."[39] The new law also struck at the Achilles heel of the human rights movement by further constraining its ability to receive foreign funding without prior government approval.[40] Additionally, Law 153 prevented NGOs from even communicating with foreign associations without first informing the government.[41] These new regulations were clear attempts by the regime to place new constraints on human rights groups that were effectively leveraging international pressure on the Egyptian regime through transnational human rights networks. The greatest asset of the human rights movement now became its greatest vulnerability. Moreover, the vulnerability of the human rights movement went beyond the material support and institutional linkages that were jeopardized by the new law; the moral authority of the human rights movement was increasingly challenged as the regime framed the movement's dependence on foreign support as nothing short of sedition. Law 153 was accompanied by a smear campaign in the state-run press in which human rights groups were portrayed as a treasonous fifth column, supported by foreign powers that only wished to tarnish Egypt's reputation and sow internal discord.

The human rights movement mobilized considerable opposition to the new associations law in a short period of time. Within a week, human rights groups organized a press conference at which they contended that Law 153 violated the constitution and they vowed to fight it in the SCC if it was not repealed. At the same time, human rights groups met with major opposition parties and professional syndicates and secured their support. Days later, a national NGO coalition was convened, bringing together over one hundred associations from across the country. NGOs committed to mobilize domestic and international pressure on the regime through a demonstration in front of the People's Assembly, a weeklong hunger strike, and litigation in the courts. International pressure came quickly with statements from Human Rights Watch, Amnesty International, the International Federation of Human Rights, the Lawyers Committee for Human Rights, and others.

But the regime proved its resolve to rein in human rights NGOs when the state security prosecutor announced in February 2000 that the case against human rights defender Hafez Abu Sa'ada would be reopened and that he would be tried before the Emergency State Security Court under Military Decree 4/1992 for accepting money from foreign donors without governmental approval.[42] The charges carried a maximum sentence of seven years in prison. The announcement came when Abu Sa'ada was in France and for two weeks following the announcement, Abu Sa'ada remained in Paris, allegedly considering political asylum. Zakaria Azmi, chief of the presidential staff, and Kamal el-Shazli, minister of parliamentary affairs, were dispatched to France to negotiate with Abu Sa'ada and defuse the embarrassing political incident. Abu Sa'ada returned to Egypt in March but the trial was not held, possibly because of a deal cut with the authorities. However, just as charges were not dropped following Abu Sa'ada's 1998 interrogation, the new charges against him were not formally withdrawn, once again allowing the authorities to resume the case at any time in the following ten years. The charges cast a shadow not only over Abu Sa'ada and the EOHR but over the entire human rights movement, which depended almost entirely on foreign funding.

The new NGO law, government intimidation, and restrictions on foreign funding threatened to shut down the entire human rights movement. Worse still, rifts within the human rights community emerged over how to deal with the regime's new assault. Some human rights groups, such as the EOHR, declared their intention to fight the new associations law through official avenues but to comply with its requirements by formally registering. Alternately, the Group for Democratic Development decided to suspend its activities in March 2000 to protest the new law, the renewal of emergency law, and the Abu Sa'ada interrogation. The Center for Human Rights Legal Aid (CHRLA), the single most important human rights organization engaged in litigation, faced internal splits when hardliners and softliners disagreed on whether to acquiesce to the new law or to fight it. As a result, CHRLA split into two organizations, with the softliners acquiescing and registering their new Association for Human Rights Legal Aid and the hardliners, forming the majority of CHRLA lawyers, establishing the new Hisham Mubarak Center for Legal Aid under the leadership of Gasser Abdel Razeq.[43] The lack of coordination between human rights organizations and discord within the organizations themselves interfered with their ability to present a united front against the regime.

With the future of the human rights movement looking more bleak each day, a ray of hope emerged in April 2000 when the commissioner's body of the SCC issued its preliminary report on a constitutional challenge to Law 153/1999. The case involved an NGO from Tanta by the name of al-gam'iyya al-shari'yya, which was fighting an order by the MOSA that barred several of the NGO members from running in elections for the group's board of directors. By June 3, 2000, the SCC issued its final ruling in the case, striking down the single most important piece of legislation governing associational life in decades.[44] The SCC crafted and delivered the ruling in a strategic way that maximized the ruling's impact without precipitating a direct confrontation with the regime. First, the SCC issued its ruling only five days before the end of the 2000 People's Assembly session, making it difficult for the regime to issue a new associations law. As a result, NGOs were effectively granted a minimum of a five-month lease on life. More important, this lease on life came at perhaps the most critical time for human rights activists and pro-democracy reformers because national elections for the next People's Assembly were just months away and activists hoped to play a prominent role in monitoring the elections as they had done for the first time in 1995.[45]

The 2000 People's Assembly Elections

In the lead-up to the 2000 People's Assembly elections, the topic of electoral reform emerged once again and the convergence of interests among opposition parties, NGOs, and judicial personnel was never more clear. Khaled Mohieddin, leader of the leftist Tagemmu Party, submitted a bill to the People's Assembly for election reforms on behalf of the main opposition parties. The bill called for elections to be supervised and administered by a "Supreme Election Committee" composed of nine high-ranking judges from the Court of Appeals and Court of Cassation, rather than the Ministry of Interior. The bill also called for a number of procedural changes in the voting process, such as the reform of existing voter lists, safeguards designed to cut electoral fraud, and full judicial supervisions of polling stations. Egyptian judges and NGOs backed opposition reform proposals in a number of public venues. In a "Justice Conference" sponsored by the Judges Association, a resolution was issued with unanimous consent urging the amendment of the law on the exercise of political rights prior to the 2000 People's Assembly elections. The Arab Center for the Independence of the Judiciary and the Legal Profession also held a forum in February 2000 on the topic of judicial supervision for the upcoming elections.[46] The forum brought together prominent judges including the former head of the Judges Association, Justice Yeheya al-Rifa'i, the vice chairman of the Court of Cassation, Justice Ahmed Mekky, and a number of representatives from the various opposition parties and NGOs. Articles circulated in the opposition newspapers highlighting the possibilities for electoral reform and the efforts of the opposition parties, NGOs, and legal professionals themselves to introduce the reforms.

When it became clear that the government would not respond to opposition demands, Saad Eddin Ibrahim and other human rights activists initiated work to build a network of human rights organizations to monitor the 2000 elections, just as they had done with great success with their national commission in 1995. But the regime proved its determination to rein in the human rights movement with or without the associations law that the SCC had struck down just weeks earlier. On June 30, 2000, Ibrahim was arrested on charges of "accepting funds from a foreign party with the purpose of carrying out work harmful to Egypt's national interest and disseminating provocative propaganda that could cause damage to the public interest."[47]

The Egyptian human rights community again mobilized international pressure. Within days, nine international human rights organizations including Amnesty International and Human Rights Watch issued a joint statement condemning Ibrahim's detention and calling for his immediate release. Pressure also came from the U.S. embassy when it reportedly raised concerns at "the highest levels" with the Egyptian government. The international pressure proved effective and Ibrahim was released after two months of detention. As with the detention of Hafiz Abu Sa'ada, however, the charges against Ibrahim were not dismissed. Instead, they were simply suspended and a trial could be initiated at any time.

Just days after Ibrahim and his colleagues were taken into detention, the SCC retaliated once again with another bombshell ruling, this time demanding full judicial supervision of elections for the first time in Egyptian history. The SCC ruling stated unequivocally that Article 24 of Law 73/1956 was unconstitutional because it allowed for public sector employees to supervise polling stations despite the fact that Article 88 of the constitution guaranteed that "the ballot shall be conducted under the supervision of members of the judiciary organ."[48] Once again, what the opposition was unable to achieve through the People's Assembly over the previous three decades they were eventually able to bring about through constitutional litigation. Although opposition activists had been critical of the SCC for stalling on issuing a decision, they celebrated the ruling as a great step forward for democracy in Egypt. The Wafd Party's Ayman Nour went so far as to admit that the SCC had virtually replaced the role of opposition parties in driving the reform agenda when he stated that "this ruling and the previous others will unquestionably affect the future of domestic politics. . . . the judiciary has nearly taken over the role of the political parties in forcing the government to take action in the direction of greater democracy."[49]

Saad Eddin Ibrahim contended that the timing of the ruling, coming a full ten years after the case was transferred to the SCC, was almost surely related to the regime's efforts to stifle the ability of the human rights movement to monitor elections as they had done in 1995. According to Ibrahim, "The timing of the SCC ruling on judicial supervision of elections clearly had to do with this case [the detention of Ibn Khaldun Center staff]. The SCC could have made the ruling a year earlier or a year later. The decision came at this time for a reason."[50]

The focus of state-society contention quickly turned to implementation of the SCC ruling. Within a week, Mubarak issued a presidential decree that amended Law 73/1956 yet again to ensure that there would be continuous judicial monitoring of all voting stations, including auxiliary stations. In order to do this, the elections would be held in three successive stages, covering different regions of the country, and auxiliary voting stations would be combined in order to reduce their number. But it soon became clear that the regime was determined to maintain whatever control it could over the electoral process to minimize the impact of the SCC ruling. Rather than give oversight control to the Judges Association, the Supreme Judicial Council, or an ad hoc committee of judges, oversight remained with the Ministry of the Interior and the Ministry of Justice, both under the direct control of the executive. Interior Minister Habib al-Adli was promptly charged with appointing judges to polling stations and Prosecutor General Abd al-Wahed was appointed to chair a judicial committee within the Ministry of Justice charged with administering judicial supervision. Additionally, many of the judicial personnel selected to cover polling stations were drawn from the prosecutor's office (*niyaba*), an institution under the direct control of the executive branch. Moreover, the government announced that judicial personnel participating in election monitoring would receive a £E 6,600 bonus ($1,700) at the end of the elections. This represented a tremendous sum of money for judges on state salaries, and reformers were immediately concerned that the bonus would be used as a stick and carrot to encourage "cooperation" with the regime's interests.[51]

In addition to subjecting judges and prosecutors to the direct management of the executive authority, it also became clear that the regime would compensate for decreased control inside the voting stations by increasing repression outside the voting stations. As in previous years, the election cycle brought about the predictable repression of the Islamist movement. The Emergency Law gave the regime the legal cover to launch a new campaign of arrests and detentions of Muslim Brotherhood members, and throughout the summer of 2000 as many as 750 suspected Brotherhood members were arrested and 250 more were detained. By the time of the People's Assembly elections, another 1,600 Islamists had been taken into custody.[52] Not surprisingly, most of those arrested were prospective candidates or campaign organizers for the upcoming elections.[53]

Earning his release from detention in August 2000, Ibrahim returned to the work of organizing the monitoring campaign for the People's Assembly elections. Although the government expected that the detention would silence Ibrahim, he promptly returned to the American University in Cairo to deliver a public lecture humorously titled "How I Spent My Summer: Diary of a Prisoner of Conscience." Ibrahim slammed the regime for holding back political reforms and used his speech to call for volunteers to help in monitoring elections. For the next several weeks, Ibrahim and his colleagues worked feverishly to organize the monitoring campaign. Ibrahim was already compiling initial reports focusing on the obstacles that opposition candidates faced when he was taken back into custody. The prosecutor's office announced that Ibrahim and his twenty-seven colleagues would stand trial in the Emergency State Security Court. Ibrahim was formally charged with "disseminating rumors with the purpose of undermining Egypt's reputation" and accepting unauthorized funding from a foreign source in violation of Military Decree 4 of 1992. Despite a campaign by international human rights groups, a vigorous legal defense, and testimony from some of Egypt's most respected figures, including the vice president of the World Bank, Ibrahim was found guilty and sentenced to seven years in prison.

Ibrahim's detention, trial, and sentencing sent a chill through the human rights community. As a respected professor with extensive connections in Egypt and abroad (even the wife of President Mubarak was a former student of Ibrahim) and dual Egyptian-U.S. citizenship, Ibrahim's detention and trial proved the regime's determination to prevent the emergence of a civil society coalition resembling the National Commission for Monitoring the 1995 Parliamentary Elections. The majority of human rights activists decided to play it safe and abandon an extensive campaign to monitor the 2000 elections.

Moreover, because of the suffocation of the human rights movement through restrictions on foreign funding, human rights groups did not have the resources to mount an adequate monitoring campaign as they did in 1995. By the eve of the 2000 elections, the Group for Democratic Development had been dissolved, the entire staff of the Ibn Khaldun Center was on trial, the EOHR was forced to close four of its regional offices and reduce its staff in Cairo by 60 percent, and the remainder of the human rights groups decided not to actively participate in election-monitoring activities for fear of being shut down by the government.[54] Only the EOHR dared to monitor the elections, but due to its precarious financial and legal condition its staff was only able to monitor less than 20 percent of constituencies compared with over 40 percent that the EOHR monitored in the 1995 elections.[55] Moreover, had it not been for the election coming in three stages, human rights groups would have had the capacity to monitor less than 7 percent of constituencies as compared with the nearly 60 percent monitored by the Egyptian National Commission for Monitoring the 1995 Parliamentary Elections. Reduced monitoring during the 2000 elections resulted in less documentation of violations by the regime and fewer lawsuits in the administrative courts.

Despite the weakened capacity of the human rights movement to monitor electoral fraud, the full judicial supervision brought about by the SCC ruling had a clear impact on the ability of opposition candidates to win. By all accounts, the 2000 People's Assembly elections were the cleanest *inside* the polling stations, although the degree of coercion outside polling stations reached unprecedented levels. Perhaps the most surprising outcome in the first two rounds was the strong showing of Muslim Brotherhood candidates. The Brotherhood took fifteen seats in the first two rounds, more than any other opposition trend, and this despite the arrest and detention of thousands of Brotherhood activists.[56] Judicial monitoring was also credited as the likely reason why prominent and longstanding NDP figures suffered early losses, including Ahmed Khayry (head of NDP for Alexandria), Mohamed Abdullah (chair of the foreign relations committee), and Mahmoud Abu el-Nasr (chair of the planning and balancing committee).

By the end of the second stage, Egyptian human rights groups were already celebrating that "judicial supervision has ended the period of filling ballots with fake names, which was prevalent in previous elections."[57] At the same time, however, opposition parties and human rights groups highlighted the fact that what the regime could not produce inside the voting stations, it tried to induce outside the stations.[58] Arrests of hundreds of Brotherhood members continued throughout the three stages and state security forces prevented voters from entering polling stations. According to the EOHR, "In the third stage, security blockades were not limited to a few polling stations, but were extended to block whole roads leading to polling stations, and sometimes up to 2 to 3 kilometers from the stations."[59] Maamoun el-Hodeibi, the leader of the Muslim Brotherhood, lamented that "elections are not about ballot boxes only. Inside the polling stations nobody can tamper with the process, but outside it is like a war."[60]

Increased coercion in the third round contained opposition advances, but the total number of seats won by opposition forces was still greater than they had enjoyed since 1990. By the end of the third round, formal opposition parties had won sixteen seats, independent candidates affiliated with the Muslim Brotherhood won a further seventeen seats, independent Nasserist candidates won five, and unaffiliated independent candidates won fourteen seats. Independent candidates for the Muslim Brotherhood had for the first time won more seats in the People's Assembly than all of the candidates standing for election from the formal opposition parties combined, despite the intense campaign of government repression in the lead-up to the elections.

As with previous rulings on the electoral law, the SCC ruling on judicial monitoring did not dislodge the regime from power, but it did have a significant effect on the means by which the regime maintained its power. Once again, the regime was forced to resort to even more extreme forms of extralegal coercion to ensure that the SCC ruling would not undermine the NDP's grip on power. Yet, despite the increased reliance on extralegal coercion, the regime took every opportunity to capitalize on the SCC ruling. President Mubarak addressed the opening session of the new People's Assembly and hailed both the SCC ruling and full judicial monitoring as a great step forward in the march of democracy. The televised speech was intended to showcase the legitimacy of the voting process in the 2000 People's Assembly elections and to assure the public that the widespread electoral fraud, which had reached unprecedented levels for the 1995 People's Assembly, was a thing of the past. But the continued shift from pseudo-legal to extralegal control increasingly exposed the hypocrisy of the regime; the growing disparity between the regime's constitutionalist rhetoric and its repressive measures was untenable. While Mubarak publicly praised the SCC for its service to democracy, the regime was preparing to deal a blow to SCC independence behind closed doors.

The Supreme Constitutional Court Compromised, a New NGO Law Issued

With the retirement of Chief Justice Asfour in late 2001, the regime would have its opportunity to rein in the SCC. To everyone's surprise, including SCC justices, the government announced that Mubarak's choice for the new chief justice would be none other than Fathi Naguib, the man who held the second most powerful post in the Ministry of Justice. Opposition parties, the human rights community, and legal scholars were stunned by the announcement. Not only had Fathi Naguib proved his loyalty to the regime over the years, but he had drafted the vast majority of the regime's illiberal legislation over the previous decade, including the oppressive law 153/1999 that the SCC had struck down only months earlier. Moreover, by selecting a chief justice from outside the justices sitting on the SCC, Mubarak also broke a strong norm that had developed over the previous two decades. Although the president of the republic always retained the formal ability to appoint whomever he wished for the position of chief justice, constitutional law scholars, political activists, and justices on the court themselves had come to believe that the president would never assert this kind of control over the court and that he would continue to abide by the informal norm of simply appointing the most senior justice on the SCC.[61] Mubarak proved them wrong.

The threat to SCC independence was compounded when Fathi Naguib announced that he would expand the number of justices on the SCC by 50 percent by recruiting five judges, four from the Court of Cassation and another from the Cairo Court of Appeals.[62] Even more troubling were reports that upon reaching the SCC, Naguib proposed that justices on the court be divided into three benches: one would continue to handle petitions of constitutional review; the other two would concentrate on questions of jurisdiction between courts and interpretation of legislation, the other formal roles of the SCC. The prospect of a divided bench coupled with the regime's demonstrated willingness to pack the court raised the possibility that activist judges would be isolated on the benches concerned with jurisdictional disputes and legislative interpretation, leaving the far more important role of constitutional review to the new appointees. Although Naguib's initial attempt to implement this reform was rebuffed by other SCC justices, sources believe that this issue remains unresolved and a renewed attempt to introduce a divided bench may be still be in store.

Several months later, the government issued a new association law (84/2002) to replace Law 153/1999, which had been struck down by the SCC. The new law proved to be just as draconian, giving the Ministry of

Social Affairs the power to reject or dissolve any association threatening "public order or public morality."[63] But this time around, the human rights movement and opposition activists had been so weakened by the government's continuous assaults they could do little to oppose it. The regime proved its intent to apply the full force of the law when it ordered the closing of the New Woman Research Center and the Land Center for Human Rights in June 2003.[64]

Conclusions

In an authoritarian polity, the potential for any given reform movement is perhaps best measured by the way the regime responds to its new opponents. If a regime does little or nothing at all and opponents are left to organize free of interference, the opposition probably does not pose a viable threat to the regime's control. But when the state takes drastic measures to control its opponents, it is a sure sign that the regime believes it faces a credible threat from the opposition, or at least that it faces a potential threat that it would like to confront early on rather than giving it the ability to gain momentum.

The Egyptian regime's aggressive response to both the SCC and its supporters is proof that constitutional litigation and SCC activism increasingly posed a credible threat to the regime's tools for maintaining control. The SCC provided an effective new avenue for activists to challenge the state through one of its own institutions. Success in battling the regime's restrictive NGO law as well as successful litigation forcing full judicial supervision of elections illustrated how human rights groups and opposition parties had become increasingly adept at using judicial institutions to successfully challenge the regime and defend their interests. Moreover, the SCC's willingness to confront the regime with its landmark rulings on NGOs and full judicial monitoring of elections proved once again the commitment of SCC justices to a political reform agenda.

However, just as the SCC and Egypt's civil society coalition built a movement based on the converging interests of the court, opposition parties, and human rights organizations, so, too, was the regime able to incapacitate this cooperative effort by successively undermining each element of the movement through legal and extralegal tactics. Rather than neutralizing the SCC outright in the mid-1990s, the regime instead adopted the subtler strategy of simply moving against the SCC's supporters. The Lawyers Syndicate was neutralized by 1996, human rights associations faced near total collapse by 1999 due to intimidation and restrictions on foreign funding, and opposition parties were progressively weakened throughout the period, despite SCC rulings on political rights. By undercutting each support group, the regime effectively killed two birds with one stone; undermining support groups impaired their ability to monitor the regime's increasingly aggressive violations of civil and human rights while at the same time disabling their capacity to raise litigation and mount an effective defense of the SCC when it came under attack.

The ultimate collapse of the human rights movement, the continued weakness of opposition parties, and the institutional assault on the SCC demonstrate how litigation alone, without support from broad sectors of society, was insufficient to protect the SCC-civil society coalition from collapse. Public interest litigation had become the most effective tool for human rights organizations and opposition activists to challenge the state because it provided an effective strategy for challenging the regime in lieu of a broad social movement. But the continued focus on litigation and the inability of human rights organizations and opposition parties to expand their constituencies ultimately undermined the long-term prospects for the reform movement. If a new, more vigorous human rights movement is to emerge in Egypt, it must effectively address these weaknesses.

Chapter 11
When the Time Is Ripe: The Struggle to Create an Institutional Culture of Human Rights in Morocco

Susan Waltz and Lindsay Benstead

For the three decades that spanned 1960–1990, Morocco's political achievements were stained by a terrible record of human rights violations. Detainees were commonly tortured, sometimes in mobile detention centers. Several hundred prisoners of conscience were incarcerated after patently unfair trials. Deaths in detention went unexplained, and hundreds of individuals disappeared without a trace to secret prisons. The political climate was generally intolerant of dissent, and a quiescent citizenry carefully avoided discourse that questioned God, king, or Morocco's territorial claim to the Western Sahara. King Hassan II was respected and feared by most Moroccans. His minister of interior, Driss Basri, was simply feared.

When King Hassan II died in July 1999, his thirty-six-year-old son was crowned Mohammed VI and ascended the throne amid promises of reform. It is not uncommon for such promises to accompany a political transition, but in this case the new king did not have to initiate the reforms. By the time of Hassan II's death, dramatic changes had already transpired in Morocco. In the early 1990s a series of prison doors had flung open. Hundreds of political prisoners were amnestied, and scores of individuals reappeared as inexplicably as they had disappeared up to fifteen years earlier. More than 150 Saharans, "disappeared" and presumed dead, emerged from secret prisons in the Moroccan South. The notorious prison fortress of Tazmamert was razed, and its surviving inmates gradually reclaimed life.

These developments were not isolated acts of royal clemency. Alongside the political amnesties, King Hassan II inaugurated a series of institutional reforms pertaining to human rights. In 1990 he created a royal advisory council on human rights, known as the Consultative Council on Human Rights (CCDH). In 1992 he personally oversaw the drafting of a new constitution that alludes to international standards of human rights. Late in 1993 he created the Ministry of Human Rights, and in July 1994 he declared his intent to "turn the page" on questions of human rights and political imprisonment.[1] A change of direct consequence was approved in 1996: the penal code was revised to limit *garde à vue* detention to forty-eight hours in standard cases. During Morocco's "dark years" there had been no limit to the period of *garde à vue,* and it was during such incommunicado detention that many prisoners were brutally tortured.

For many years King Hassan had been openly resistant to reform and as late as December 1989, before French television audiences, he dismissed and denied the human rights problems documented by Amnesty International.[2] In assessing measures of clemency and political reform undertaken in the 1990s, few believed that King Hassan's own motives were principled and his commitment to human rights genuine. Nevertheless, the process of change that he initiated developed a life of its own. Constitutional amendments that established a second chamber in the National Assembly allowed the king to ensure parliamentary backing for his rule, but they also prepared the way for elections in 1997 that turned out to be more free and fair than any in decades.[3] Those elections returned a slim majority in Parliament for a loose coalition of left-leaning parties, and in February 1998 Hassan II named opposition leader Abderrahman Youssoufi as prime minister. For the first time in nearly forty years, Morocco had a prime minister from the opposition.[4] Even more dramatic, for the first time in the country's modern history, a Moroccan prime minister (and an opposition one at that) was permitted to select his own cabinet—albeit subject to the king's approval.

Many factors contributed to changes in Morocco at century's end. King Hassan's personal motivations are unknown, but we may speculate about his concern for a stable succession and his awareness of a changing world context. The decade of the 1990s had opened with the dissolution of the Soviet Union, and liberalizing winds that swirled over southern Europe, Eastern Europe, and Latin America also stirred hopes of reform in North Africa. Morocco was under pressure from its European and North American allies to reform, and international support of various kinds was available to pro-democracy forces in Morocco. During the previous decade a vibrant and energetic human rights movement had emerged in Morocco, and the commitment and dedicated work of those in the movement helped place human rights on center stage. The efforts, strategies, and struggles of these local human rights advocates during this period have been documented, though their impact cannot readily be isolated and assessed.[5] Reasoning counterfactually, however, it is difficult to imagine how such far-reaching changes would have occurred without a local constituency to make demands and sustain pressure. Though it was the king who ultimately opened the door to human rights reform, substantial credit belongs to the local human rights movement in Morocco. Its efforts are the focus of this essay.

Over the past fifteen years, Moroccan human rights groups have grown in strength and number. The League of Human Rights (LMDH) was Morocco's first human rights group, founded in 1972 in affiliation with the Istiqlal Party. In 1979—the year that Morocco ratified the International Covenant on Civil and Political Rights—the opposition Socialist Union of Progressive Forces (USFP) created its own group, the Association of Human Rights (AMDH). For two decades, however, both groups were mostly dormant. Things began to change in the 1980s with the demonstrated success of Tunisia's new League of Human Rights. Inspired by their neighbors, activists from the USFP began to shape a deliberately nonpartisan organization and recruited members from Morocco's privileged classes. They succeeded in creating the Moroccan Organization of Human Rights (OMDH) in 1988, and with great energy and a strong sense of mission its members set to work preparing a comprehensive dossier on political imprisonment. The organization's careful attachment to principled argument (enhanced by the social status of its members) afforded protection from political repression.[6] The OMDH's success reinvigorated the AMDH, which is considered by many to be the more proactive of the two organizations today (and no longer tightly linked to the USFP). Both groups regularly organize meetings and issue public statements, and for several years both have published an annual report. Their voices are amplified by several other organizations with a primary interest in human rights, including the Moroccan Section of Amnesty International, the Committee to Defend Human Rights (founded in 1992), the Moroccan Bar Association, the Women's Action Union (UAF), the Democratic Association of Moroccan Women (ADFM), and two new groups founded in 1999, the Forum for Truth and Justice and the Moroccan Prison Observatory.

By the end of the 1990s these human rights groups had secured a presence in Moroccan politics, organizing freely and speaking openly—if somewhat circumspectly. Hassan II retained firm control of the political system through the end of his reign, but by the time of his death many of Morocco's most serious human rights problems had been addressed in some important way. In the late 1990s the political ambiance was charged with cautious optimism and engagement: Moroccans tended to view the king's involvement in politics as a stabilizing force rather than a source of disquiet, and they generally approved of the pace and direction of change. In this sense Mohammed VI's ascent to the throne in July 1999 did not represent political rupture. It came in the midst of political liberalization, and royal succession effectively brought promise for more change in the same direction. Yet the country and the new king faced a number of political and economic challenges in 1999, including the unresolved Saharan conflict, trade with Europe and the world, and continuous susceptibility to drought. Moroccan society was troubled by high levels of unemployment, poor rural health services, a general imbalance between services in rural and urban areas, and an undereducated population with significant pockets of illiteracy.[7] With regard to human rights, in 1999 the main unresolved issues included the redress of past human rights abuses; reform of family law and the legal status of women; and the need to ensure that old patterns of abuse would not re-establish themselves. The extent to which Islamists and Islamist parties should be allowed to participate in Morocco's political life remained an open and thorny question, and there were new indications that the country's large amazigh (Berber) population sought greater recognition within Moroccan society. In 1999, Moroccans waited to see how their new king would address these problems, and few were willing to predict the political future of the Moroccan human rights movement. In the sections that follow, we offer an assessment of the role human rights groups have played in Moroccan politics since 1999, as well as the influence they have had on Morocco's human rights agenda.

Redress and Reconciliation

In 1990 it was unthinkable that hundreds of "disappeared" dissidents, their stories cloaked in secrecy for decades, would ever reappear. It was likewise unthinkable that the Moroccan government, in a newfound commitment to "turn the page on past abuses" whose very existence it had coolly denied only a few years earlier, would initiate a massive indemnity program to offer financial compensation to some four thousand victims and their families.[8] But the unthinkable did come to pass. In 1998 the issue of past injustice was forced to a head. In that year the high drama of the Pinochet case was playing out before courts in Spain and Great Britain, and Moroccans had no trouble drawing parallels between the Latin American "dirty wars" and their own dark "years of lead," *les années de plomb*. Human rights groups campaigned vigorously for a process to bring justice for those who had suffered abuse. Eventually they succeeded in their efforts to secure the monarch's commitment to address, and redress, the human rights crimes committed over the previous thirty years. Six months after Youssoufi was named prime minister, Hassan II ordered the resolution of all human rights cases. That official decree paved the way for a remarkable communiqué from the government's human rights advisory body that was no doubt intended to close the door on further discussions. Instead, it opened the door further. In that groundbreaking statement in April 1998, the CCDH acknowledged that 112 people had been forcibly disappeared while in government custody. While that official toll represented only one-fifth of the victims listed by human rights groups and failed to mention any of the Saharan disappeared at all, it acknowledged government responsibility for the first time.

Beyond this acknowledgment, the matter received little official attention through the final months of Hassan II's reign. For human rights groups, however, justice remained a pressing issue. As the sole human rights group participating as a member of the government's advisory council, the OMDH engaged the question of redress directly and issued two separate statements on the principles that should be followed.[9] Human rights advocates across the country campaigned for justice that included truth-telling as well as compensation.[10] Their frustration and outrage was fueled by the impunity enjoyed by former officials known to have collaborated in grave abuses. They carefully followed news accounts of court proceedings against the Moroccan newspaper *El Bayane* for fingering a former police commissioner, and current Member of Parliament, as a widely recognized torturer. When the court fined *El Bayane* instead of condemning the torturer, they vented with cynicism.[11]

After his father's death, Mohammed VI responded with a new overture. Shortly after taking the throne, he announced that victims of past human rights abuses would be compensated, and he created an independent arbitration commission to oversee the process. The CCDH, as a royal advisory council, was instructed to develop internal procedures for the new commission, which was to begin processing complaints without delay. For human rights advocates the victory was real but incomplete. While the commitment to acknowledge wrongs of the past was a substantial political innovation for Morocco and for the region as a whole, the mechanism developed by the CCDH fell far short of their hopes and expectations.[12] To begin with, the nine-member commission included a representative from the despised Ministry of Interior. Although the commission declared itself ready to receive any legitimate complaints,[13] human rights groups immediately noted that the documents of reference failed to mention some of the most notorious cases. Moreover, the commission's statute completely overlooked the issue of "truth." Effectively, it offered amnesty to those who had perpetrated the abuses.

The arbitration commission set to work immediately but was quickly overwhelmed. Advocates for the victims and their families developed a standard form to facilitate the process of submitting a complaint,[14] and by the cutoff date of December 31, 1999, more than 5,000 complaints had been filed.[15] Human rights activists lost no time organizing themselves to monitor the commission's work and press for a more far-reaching process. A coordinating committee with representatives from six Moroccan organizations convened a planning meeting in October and organized a two-day conference in Casablanca in late November. That meeting gave birth to the Forum for Truth and Justice, with leaders drawn from a wide array of former political prisoners and their families.[16] A former political prisoner was elected the group's president.

Over the next several months, the forum amplified the call for public investigation of past abuses and public rehabilitation of the victims of abuse. Together with the leading national human rights groups, it insisted on a more extensive national process, one that resembled truth and reconciliation processes elsewhere. The forum and its partners sponsored several commemorative days, including a national Day of the Disappeared and a demonstration in front of Parliament. In March 2000 they organized a sit-in at Derb Moulay Cherif, a facility in Casablanca where many political prisoners had been tortured. That political event included an exhibit of commemorative photographs and posters, and more than 1,000 people participated in a human chain intended to convey collective pain and collective memory.[17]

The arbitration commission, meanwhile, moved forward with its work. By June 2001, some 600 separate human rights cases had been settled, more than half of them involving indemnity payments.[18] In this way, abuses suffered by a wide range of detainees held in prisons across the country were formally acknowledged. Contrary to initial expectations, cases as geographically and politically diverse—and as politically evocative—as Tazmamert, Kelaat M'gouna, Laayoune, and Agdez were reviewed by the commission.[19] Yet no accountability was established among those responsible for the misdeeds that were being compensated. Some of the abusive acts were deemed unproven. In other cases, the abuser was excused on the grounds that he was following orders, the statute of limitation had passed, or the governing international instruments were not in force at the time of abuse.[20] As a result of the decision not to press charges against those responsible, Youssef Kaddour—identified as the chief torturer at Derb Moulay Cherif—was permitted to remain a high-level civil servant, and Mahmoud Archane continued to serve in Parliament.[21] In November 1999, Mohammed VI replaced the formidable Driss Basri as minister of interior but allowed him to reclaim his post on the University of Rabat's law faculty rather than banish him in ignominy.

Human rights groups found it difficult to accept such outcomes. They continued to levy both moral and legal criticism and took their arguments to the public. In 2002 a highly visible "Caravan of Truth" to the prison at Kelaat M'gouna, where hundreds of Saharans had been surreptitiously incarcerated for more than a decade, attracted public attention to the event. Through seminars, rallies, and sit-ins—some of them resulting in beatings and arrests[22]—human rights advocates pressed their case for the creation of an independent national commission to "let the truth come forth."[23] Somewhat less openly, they also began to call for prosecution of the perpetrators and an end to the impunity they enjoyed. The AMDH was most outspoken in this regard and went so far as to compile and publicize a list of some forty-five individuals it presumed were implicated in grave human rights violations, five of whom were deceased.[24] The OMDH worked with its international partner, the International Federation of Human Rights (FIDH), to prepare a report for submission to the UN International Committee on Torture and in it reiterated the shared demands for an independent commission to establish the truth on disappearances and human rights abuses.[25]

As the call for truth and accountability grew louder, Mohammed VI issued a new decree ordering a reorganization of the national human rights advisory council. He expanded its powers, authorizing it to initiate investigations on its own. Its composition was also reformed to include a majority of representatives proposed by civil society organizations, with more than one-third of the members to be named by human rights groups.[26] Following the structural reorganization, in December 2002 the king named Omar Azziman as president of the council and Driss Benzekri as secretary-general. Azziman was a law professor who had been a founding member and an early leader of the OMDH. Later he was appointed minister of justice. Benzekri had spent seventeen years in prison for his membership in an outlawed Marxist-Leninist group, and had been named the first president of the Forum for Truth and Justice.

The CCDH's new leaders soon opened discussions on the possibility of expanding the process to settle outstanding issues related to grave human rights abuses of the past. Exercising its new power to make recommendations to the government, in November 2003 the CCDH advised the creation of a "justice and reconciliation body." Shortly thereafter Mohammed VI formally accepted the council's recommendation and confirmed the creation of a new body that would "extend the scope of indemnities offered to victims and their families, try to locate the remains of those who died in detention, and produce a report summarizing the finding of up to a year's research into 'disappearances' and arbitrary detentions."[27] The Justice and Reconciliation Committee was installed in January 2004 and charged with concluding "the process of shelving a thorny issue once and for all."[28] No provisions were included for prosecuting wrongdoers, and both international and domestic critics pointed out the obvious shortcoming.[29] Nevertheless, in what the king called a "bold, comprehensive approach," moral as well as material damages would for the first time be addressed. To lend substance to that rhetoric, in December 2004 the Justice and Reconciliation Committee took the unprecedented step of holding televised hearings in which torture victims were invited to give oral testimony—under condition that the names of perpetrators go unmentioned. The AMDH parried in February with its own open air meetings in Rabat, wherein victims of torture challenged the Justice and Reconciliation Committee's rule of silence about perpetrators and identified those who had abused them in the name of the state.

These recent developments are part of a continuing social and political dialogue, whose conclusion at this point remains unpredictable. Yet the fact that there is any conversation at all is a tribute to human rights groups, who over the previous decade had campaigned vigorously for a process to bring justice to those who suffered abuse. As we have argued, it is difficult to imagine even a limited process of redress and reconciliation without their presence and pressure. They continue to promote public discussion of the need to establish and preserve "the truth" and to bring the perpetrators of abuse to justice. It remains to be seen whether their continued efforts and influence will eventually lead to a full truth and reconciliation process and whether those accused of torture and other crimes will ever meet their accusers in court. Both issues present a political challenge to the royal court, if not the state.

Women's Rights and Family Law

The question of women's rights was a second inescapable human rights issue for the new king. During the early 1990s, in the same political moment that gave rise to the liberalizing reforms we have outlined above, women's rights was placed on the national agenda—due not in small part to the women's rights advocacy groups that were finding new footing in Morocco. Delegates who were preparing for the UN's Beijing Conference on the Status of Women nurtured hopes that Morocco's family law statutes could be addressed along with other constitutional reforms. In 1990 Morocco's family law, also known as the Personal Status Code or Mudawwana, remained as it had been written in 1957. In an age where women—many of them from prominent urban families—held prestigious jobs as doctors, lawyers, accountants, poets, pilots, educators, researchers, government officials, and journalists, the numerous restrictions imposed by the Mudawwana were seen and experienced as both anachronistic and infantilizing.

Despite constitutional promises of gender equality, Morocco's Personal Status Code severely limited the familial, social, economic, and political rights of women and created conditions that contributed to abuse. To begin with, the 1957 family law conferred a lifetime status of legal minor on all women. A male guardian—if necessary, a younger brother—was required to sign all legal documents for a woman, including her marriage contract. Though other provisions of law required a woman's consent for marriage, the fact that a woman's presence was not required at her legal marriage ceremony allowed for considerable abuse. This provision opened the door to forced marriage of young girls, as well as early pregnancies and attendant risks of maternal mortality. It also made it possible to force marriage upon a woman who questioned social norms, if a local court found such questioning to constitute bad conduct.[30]

Once married, a woman was placed under the direction of her husband and had a marital duty to obey him in all matters. The 1957 code also permitted polygamy and gave men an absolute right to divorce through unilateral repudiation. Women were provided the right to divorce, but only under extenuating circumstances. In the case where divorce was sought by a woman due to domestic violence, considerable medical proof was required. Critics of the Mudawwana charged that it implicitly condoned domestic violence in the guise of a husband's duty to discipline, and they held it responsible for the failure to address an epidemic of domestic abuse.[31] Finally, inheritance and filiation laws also discriminated against women. As elsewhere in the Muslim world, inheritance laws embedded in the family law code awarded male heirs twice the inheritance received by their female counterparts, which in many cases contributed to female poverty. And because filiation provisions in the Mudawwana attached children to the agnatic lineage of their father, a Muslim child whose only Moroccan parent was a woman could be denied citizenship, education, or social services.[32]

The 1957 Mudawwana was a product of Moroccan politics in the immediate postcolonial period, and Mounira Charrad has argued that its particular form was designed to strengthen the monarchy in that period by favoring rural kin-based tribal groups over urban interests. During the mid-century struggle for independence, the urban-based nationalist Istiqlal Party had advocated both democratic rule (in the form of a constitutionally limited monarchy) and gender equality in the political, legal, and economic realms as well as the family. That vision was quashed in 1957. By interpreting Islamic law in an ultraconservative manner and enhancing local jurisdiction, the Mudawwana gave kinship groups full ability to control women's choice in marriage and thereby reinforced tribe-based patriarchal authority.[33]

The social contract reflected in the Mudawwana held for several decades. Over the period 1957–1980 a few women's organizations formed, usually as an extension of a political party or trade union, but there was little contestation of the personal status laws. Most opposition parties operated under a cloud of repression during this period, and no national organizations were willing to take up the cause of women's rights—particularly as such a program seemed sure to provoke the ire of conservative religious leaders. Those who sought to improve women's status and condition came increasingly to believe that change could only be achieved through a complete overhaul of the Mudawwana and intervention of the monarch. Given high levels of government repression and opposition among both religious elites and more populist Islamist groups, campaigning for such reform seemed unthinkable.[34]

In 1992, the political context and the dynamics changed. Among the new women's groups born out of the UN Women's Decade was the Union of Feminine Action (UAF). In the late 1980s the UAF had organized a drive for constitutional reform, without much noticeable effect. They attracted both national and international attention, however, with a massive petition drive launched on the eve of International Women's Day in 1992. Their campaign to reform the Mudawwana extended through 1993, a time when all of Morocco was gripped by the horrifying accounts of crimes against some 1,500 women committed and videotaped by Casablanca police chief Mohamed Mustafa Tabet. Fueled by public outrage at the sensational evidence that emerged in Tabet's trial (which resulted in conviction and execution), UAF campaigners succeeded in collecting more than a million signatures backing reform. Their effort tangibly demonstrated support for revising the Mudawwana and it catalyzed the formation of a coordinating council of twenty-three like-minded organizations.[35]

The campaign also provoked the anticipated resistance from conservatives and, more surprisingly, from opposition parties that might have been expected to lend support. Islamists reacted virulently to what they saw as an effort by women (mostly leftists, in their view) to interfere with religion. They claimed that criticism of the Mudawwana was an incitement against Islamic society tantamount to apostasy. Opposition parties, for their part, resisted the women's initiative because they saw it as potentially destabilizing and counterproductive to their larger goals of political reform and class struggle. Out of strategic concerns, some of them not only refused to support the campaign but actively opposed it.[36]

Under the circumstances, reigning King Hassan had few incentives to initiate reform. To placate advocates of change (many of them from

Morocco's ruling classes), he created a reform commission and invited it to propose modifications to the existing code. Though women were invited to participate in consultations, and though the *chargé de mission* from the royal cabinet was a woman, the actual commission was composed of twenty men and included several religious scholars.[37] Not surprisingly, the reforms proposed by this commission were not far-reaching, and they were enacted in 1993 without much fanfare or celebration. The fundamental gender inequities remained, and critics claimed that they would have little practical effect.[38]

For advocates of women's rights, the 1993 modifications were to some extent a political setback. The fundamental questions (and inequities) were not resolved, but political actors could claim they had addressed the issue, which accordingly lost urgency on the political agenda. Through the 1990s, UAF and its partners focused on educational activities, organizing seminars and workshops on a wide range of issues related to domestic violence, the abuse of child maids, and female poverty. Leading human rights groups issued communiqués on International Women's Day, and with assistance from the European Union, the AMDH hosted a summer university program on women's rights in 1998.

With the appointment of an opposition prime minister in 1998, hopes were raised among feminists that a USFP parliamentary plurality could initiate significant reform. By this time opposition parties had warmed to the idea of promoting women's rights, and in early 1999 it appeared that proponents of reform would not be disappointed. In March Prime Minister Youssoufi announced a plan consisting of five development objectives related to the rights of women and female children. The plan targeted access to education, reproductive health, political representation, economic opportunities, and reform of the Mudawwana.[39] It drew fiery rhetoric from Islamists and the *ulama* (religious authorities), who charged it would drive young people away from marriage and destroy values of honor and valor.[40]

At the time of Hassan II's death in July 1999, the issue of Mudawwana reform was simmering on a back burner. Mohammed VI's accession to the throne rekindled hopes among human rights and women's rights advocates. In his first public speeches, the new king gave prominent place to improvement of women's rights and status, as well as democratic reform and human rights. Women's groups began to plan a large demonstration on International Women's Day in favor of the proposed reforms. Some 40,000 people participated in their March 2000 rally in Rabat, a grand success by most measures. To their chagrin, however—and to the chagrin of the monarch as well—an estimated several hundred thousand people heeded a last-minute call from Islamist leaders and took to the streets of Casablanca to reject the reforms outright. Mohammed VI revoked Prime Minister Youssoufi's plan.

Despite the setback, the OMDH and AMDH joined women's groups in a sustained effort to exact reform. In 2001 and 2002 the OMDH issued communiqués that presented detailed proposals for change not only to the Mudawwana but also to the Moroccan constitution and to reservations Morocco had attached to its ratification of certain international treaties. In March 2001, the monarch responded in classic fashion: he created a royal commission and charged it to offer advice on reforming the Mudawwana. This royal commission was composed of Muslim theologians (*ulama*), magistrates, and representatives of civil society, mostly from the field of jurisprudence. Among them were three women.[41] Adopting the strategy Tunisian president Habib Bourguiba had used to develop the most liberal personal code in the Arab-Muslim world some forty-five years earlier, the Moroccan monarch instructed the commission to respect Islamic law and "be fair to women, as prescribed in Islam." The commission worked steadily for more than two years but eventually became mired in a stalemate. By 2003, many despaired of any significant change.

Sometimes openings appear unexpectedly, in unlikely circumstances, and so it was in 2003. In May that year, terrorist attacks rocked Casablanca, implicating homegrown Islamic extremists. Although the attacks appeared to have been launched by radical groups previously unknown in Morocco, the well-known populist Islamist groups (including the legalized Justice and Development Party as well as Sheikh Yassine's unauthorized association, Justice and Charity) braced for a backlash. Municipal elections scheduled for June were immediately postponed to September. The Islamist Justice and Development Party had won the third highest number of seats in Morocco's 2002 parliamentary elections, and they were widely expected to do well in the municipal contests. In the aftermath of the Casablanca attacks, however, they beat a strategic retreat, generally withdrawing from public debate and fielding candidates only in 18 percent of the municipalities.[42]

Mohammed VI took advantage of the Islamist retreat, and at the opening of the fall parliamentary session he stunned the nation with a surprise announcement that he was forwarding legislators a proposal to reform the Mudawwana. In contrast to the outcry at previous junctures, this time there was almost no public opposition. Members of the Justice and Development Party did debate the measure ardently, offering numerous amendments, but in the end the revised code was approved by Parliament in January 2004.[43] The new Personal Status Code abolished the principle of male dominance in the family, giving wives joint responsibility in the family and rescinding the stipulation that wives must obey husbands.[44] Among other changes, the minimum age of marriage for women was raised from fifteen to eighteen (bringing it to parity with that for men), which meant that young women were no longer required by law to accept a marriage arranged by their father. The institution of the guardian—the male family member previously endowed with power of attorney—was abolished. Further restrictions were placed on the practice of polygamy, and divorce by repudiation was replaced by judicial procedure.[45]

It would be misleading to suggest that the 2004 family law reforms eliminated all elements of adverse discrimination against women. In some areas—notably provisions regarding polygamy and inheritance laws—the royal commission considered itself bound by Islamic principles and recommended only modest revisions. In a world in which continuity usually trumps change, however, the developments of 2003/2004 that gave Morocco one of the most progressive family laws in the Arab world were remarkable. The principal credit for this achievement lies with Morocco's young king. Women's groups galvanized support for the initiative more than a decade ago—but their opponents rallied even greater numbers. It seems unlikely that reform efforts would have come to fruition without royal patronage. Women's rights groups, backed by the main human rights organizations, clearly played a role in bringing the issue to the level of national debate, but it was Mohammed VI's decision to take control of the politically sensitive and potentially destabilizing issue that ultimately made the difference. The monarch's choice to bring the issue forward at a moment when Islamist groups were on the defensive was an important strategic move, but it also demonstrated the monarch's personal commitment to advancing this item on the human rights agenda.

Securing a Culture of Human Rights

For Moroccan advocates of human rights, the government's attention to questions of women's rights and progress on the issue of redress represented victories and accomplishments to be celebrated. But they did not remove an uneasiness about the future or the degree to which the infamous "page" had indeed been turned. Securing a *culture* of human rights remained a prominent item on Morocco's human rights agenda.

In the final years of Hassan II's reign, improvements in the human rights situation were reflected in the annual catalog of Amnesty International's concerns, which was much shorter than that of a decade earlier. Nevertheless, there was reason for continuing concern. The aging Islamist leader Sheikh 'Abdessalam Yassine remained under house arrest, without charge or warrant, and his justice and charity organization (al-

'Adl wa'l 'Ihsan) continued to be banned. More than forty political prisoners were serving sentences after unfair trials—including three individuals convicted of "insulting the royal family." Police brutality and
violations of *garde à vue* restrictions were documented, especially in the
Western Sahara or against Saharans living in territorial Morocco. Most
disturbing, reports of torture continued to surface.[46]

Hopes were fed when Mohammed VI ascended the throne and pro-
claimed his attachment to democratic reform and human rights. Moroccan human rights advocates welcomed the institutional changes
announced one after another through 2001. A five-year judicial reform
had already begun at the time of Hassan II's death, and shortly after
Mohammed VI took the throne, prison reforms were announced.[47] An
arbitration commission was created in fall 1999 to settle indemnity issues
related to past abuses, and Driss Basri—the former interior minister who
was practically an institution—was ousted. Almost as surprising, Yassine's
eleven-year house arrest was lifted, in a generous response to the lengthy
letter of advice and criticism sent by the self-styled Islamic sage to the
young monarch.[48]

Over the next several months the king regularly referred to reform
projects in progress, and by the end of 2000 he began to present them
to Parliament. (Several of these have already been mentioned above, but
to appreciate the breadth of reform, a comprehensive review is useful.)
A proposal to reform the 1958 public liberties law went to Parliament in
December, and a plan to incorporate human rights education into the
public school curriculum was announced soon thereafter.[49] In April
2001 the king appointed a royal commission to reform the Mudawwana
and he announced structural changes for the CCDH. The CCDH was
given greater independence and charged with issuing an annual report
on the state of human rights in the nation.[50] Later in the year the monarch issued a decree reviving the *diwan al madhalim* (board of grievances), an Islamic court used in pre-protectorate Morocco to review
complaints against officials. The new office was to serve as a sort of
ombudsman, mediating between citizens and authorities, and using its
authority to uphold the rule of law and principles of fairness.[51] In
another gesture to appease social tensions, the Royal Institute of Amazigh Culture was established. The demand for better recognition of amazigh culture and the tamazighte language had been heightened in the
months leading up to the 2001 World Conference on Racism. Finally,
the 2002 parliamentary elections took place without government interference, in an atmosphere more free and fair than any could remember.
Though Justice and Charity remained banned, the new Justice and
Development Islamic Party had been approved and surprised many

observers when it garnered the third highest number of votes, as well as 42 of 325 seats in the Parliament's lower chamber.

King Mohammed marked the moment with the appointment of a new prime minister, technocrat Driss Jettou. After the flurry of new initiatives floated over the 2000–2002 period, the 2002 session of Parliament opened in October with a full agenda but few new far-reaching proposals. Parliament was still deliberating proposed changes to the 1958 public liberties law when bomb blasts rocked the city of Casablanca in May 2003. The suicide attacks were carried out by the Salafia Jihadia (a previously obscure terrorist group with apparent links to al-Qaida and Ansar al-Islam) and targeted Jewish cultural sites and Western establishments in the city. The attacks claimed forty-four lives and left Moroccans across the country shocked and angry. They also quickly focused parliamentary attention on a second pending bill, an anti-terrorism law that proposed to expand police powers and extend the time in which a detainee could be held in incommunicado detention. The anti-terrorism measure was rapidly passed; the project to liberalize the public liberties law appears to have been shelved. "The moment of truth has sounded," said King Mohammed in late May, "announcing the end of an era of tolerance (*laxisme*) for those who would exploit democracy to attack the authority of the State."[52]

The attacks of May 2003 altered the balance between proponents of security and proponents of liberty, but they did not introduce new factors into the dynamics of Moroccan politics. While human rights advocates had welcomed reforms, they had complained about the slow pace with which they were enacted,[53] and they had also recognized a continuing need for vigilance. There had never been substantial evidence that Moroccan police and security officials intended voluntarily to relinquish either the powers or the techniques used to repress rights in earlier years, and that was reason enough for concern.

Alongside the announced reforms, human rights groups assembled a list of new and recurring concerns. One of the first issues to arise after Mohammed VI's coronation involved the right to assemble. In September 1999 a peaceful demonstration about socioeconomic concerns in the Western Sahara was broken up by security forces, and dozens of Saharans were arrested and/or severely beaten following a subsequent protest march.[54] Over the next three years there were numerous demonstrations and sit-ins, and more than twenty of them were marked by police brutality. Police used force, and often wielded truncheons, to break up demonstrations organized by a wide variety of groups for various purposes. Unemployed university graduates, doctors, engineers, and journalists, for example, as well as the blind and disabled unemployed, called attention to their plight with sit-ins. Students protested transportation problems at their university, and factory workers went on strike. Members of Justice and Charity demonstrated for legal recognition of their organization, and human rights groups marched in front of Parliament on Human Rights Day, demanding that those responsible for abuses be prosecuted.[55] Thirty-six human rights advocates initially charged and convicted of participating in an unauthorized demonstration in December 2000 were eventually acquitted by an appeal court that ruled that the Ministry of the Interior had failed to transmit its rejection of the permit in writing. Meetings and demonstrations planned by amazigh activists were more effectively banned in 2001 and 2002.[56]

Liberties of the press were also tested and trimmed. Morocco's press is among the most liberal in the Arab world, but the topics of God, king, and territorial boundaries (the Western Sahara) have long been taboo. In the mid-1990s Moroccan journalists had cautiously begun to write of Morocco's dark years, and by 1998 the local press was openly referring to the horrors of Tazmamert and other notorious prisons, as well as other social problems of past and present. But in 2000 journalists encountered new limits. During the first months of the Mohammed VI's reign, officials in some localities seemed uncertain about the rules and temporarily seized several publications that risked stirring up trouble. In response to one such seizure, the Moroccan communications minister reportedly declared that censorship was absurd and no longer practiced in Morocco.[57] By mid-summer 2000, however, the government had changed its tune. Through the second half of 2000, both domestic and international publications were seized or banned—for a wide variety of offenses. Sales of a September edition of the *London Economist*, for example, were blocked because the magazine questioned the scale of oil findings recently announced by the government.[58] Other publications were punished for publishing stories about the Western Sahara, criticizing the regime of Hassan II, or threatening to cast new light on historical events deemed best left in the shadows, such as the presumed assassination of political figure Mehdi Ben Barka in 1965. Tensions reached a crisis point at the end of 2000, when three publications were summarily shut down by the prime minister after they published a provocative letter about conspirators in the 1972 attempted military coup against Hassan II. Although the ban was reversed in early 2001, the honeymoon for the press had ended. Over the next two years, foreign papers that carried stories critical of the monarchy or discussed sensitive social issues risked confiscation. The French weekly *Le Courrier International*, for example, was banned for its coverage of amazigh culture and related political tensions.[59] Courts sustained libel charges against several publications that alleged corruption and misdeeds by government officials and ex-officials, and in one prominent case, the government prosecuted newspaper publisher Ali Lamrabet for questioning the "territorial integrity of Morocco" and "insulting sacred institutions."[60] Lamrabet soon became a cause célèbre. His conviction and harsh prison sentence (four years reduced to three on appeal) sparked protests from human rights groups within Morocco and abroad. Reporters without Borders awarded him their annual press freedom award.

By May 16, 2003, the day of the Casablanca bombings, the human rights climate had already deteriorated markedly. In addition to restrictions on public expression, abuses by police and security officials were becoming increasingly frequent. Even the first year of Mohammed VI's reign was marked by three deaths in detention, with autopsies suggesting abuse.[61] In that same year, the AMDH documented 224 cases of alleged torture.[62] Some cases of abuse by low-level officials have been prosecuted, but acquittals are not uncommon and convictions are often overturned on appeal.[63] A number of legal loopholes that either facilitated the practice of torture or impeded prosecution were identified in a joint OMDH-FIDH report submitted to the UN's Committee Against Torture in October 2003. The report makes it clear that the organizations continue to be outraged by "the failure of legislative measures banning torture and by the ongoing impunity for crimes of torture" as well as by the "arbitrary anomalies arising with the fight against terrorism."[64] The AMDH's annual report that year took the concerns a step further, warning about the return of old practices among the state police following the May 2003 terrorist incident in Casablanca. More than fifteen hundred people had been rounded up, and the ensuing judicial proceedings pointed up violations of the *garde à vue* limits, accusations of torture and ill treatment, inhumane conditions of detention, compromised standards of judicial fairness, and application of the death penalty.[65] Adding weight internationally to the concerns expressed by local human rights groups, the UN Committee against Torture recorded its concerns about the upsurge in reports of torture and the erosion of legal protections,[66] and in June 2004 Amnesty International released a report on what it called the systematic practice of torture and ill treatment of suspects held at one of Morocco's main detention centers, near Rabat.[67] Human Rights Watch followed up by urging U.S. officials to raise the human rights issues with King Mohammed during his state visit to Washington in July.[68]

Against this generally somber backdrop, the January 2004 announcement of a royal clemency for some twenty-five political prisoners was welcome news. Among those amnestied were journalist Ali Lamrabet and Ali Salem Tamek, a human rights advocate from Western Sahara who was serving a two-year sentence he received in October 2002.[69] More good news came with the announcement in July—following the Amnesty

International report—that the government was preparing legislation to criminalize torture.[70] These developments can rightfully be viewed as the results of monitoring and pressure from human rights groups, and they are encouraging for advocates of human rights. Nevertheless, it would be naïve to suggest that they represent the advent of an institutional culture of human rights in Morocco. Advances and setbacks illustrate the constant ebb and flow of a human rights situation at the mercy of institutions that are not yet guided by principles of human rights, particularly law enforcement and judicial institutions. The risk of rapid reversal remains real, threatening deterioration of even the most fundamental human rights.

Human rights groups have an important role to play in disseminating values that respect human rights and in ultimately securing a culture of human rights. Moroccan human rights advocates have accepted this role but play it conservatively. Recent repression of the press and harsh responses to peaceful demonstrations point up the need for caution: there are risks attached to actions that cross some threshold difficult to discern. Human rights groups are also aware that they share the stage with many other players, some with considerably more power than they. Reform efforts in recent parliamentary sessions have shown that even the monarch is limited with respect to the change he can impose upon the *makhzen* bureaucrats, and events like the Casablanca bombings effectively shore up the position of those who resist liberalizing reform. It is always easier to plan change at an institutional level than to create a shift in culture.

Moroccan Human Rights Groups as Agents for Norm Change

As many scholars have noted, it is difficult to gauge with confidence the role and impact of human rights groups on human rights practice around the world. In part, the problem is due to the ubiquitous difficulty in "real world" social science of controlling for confounding factors in order to concentrate only on the phenomenon under scrutiny—in this case, variations in strength, character, or activities of human rights groups. The challenge to comparative study is compounded by the fact that groups can reasonably be expected to develop different strategies according to their circumstances, and groups that seek to initiate a process of human rights change may face very different issues than a group seeking to expand a process already in process.[71]

A second aspect of the problem relates to the human rights practices and outcomes themselves—whether amnesties, court verdicts, and patterns of harassment, or norm-violating arrests, detentions, incidences of torture, and disappearances. While human rights groups hope for an immediate end to violations of human rights, in reality, change is rarely observable in the short term. Indeed, the trajectory of norm change is often long because it involves a cultural redirection at the level of public institutions and, in particular, security agencies and other institutions that bolster the state's monopoly on force. If well enforced, legal reform and the imposition of sanctions can speed up a process of cultural change, but even in the best of circumstances lag time should be expected.

Efforts to assess social change and its contributing factors often rely on a counterfactual analysis that speculates about likely outcome in the absence of the phenomenon under study. In the case of Morocco, it would be difficult to imagine either the changes that have come about or the process of change itself absent an influential domestic constituency. For much of the 1990s the palace had little intrinsic interest in reform, and entrenched forces resisted it. In partnership with and alongside international human rights organizations, Morocco-based groups deployed strategies to initiate an observable *process* of norm change. They can claim considerable success, though in no case was their effort sufficient to bring about reform sui generis, and in some cases (notably women's rights), little progress was made before Mohammed VI intervened directly. (And, one might add, both the efforts of these groups and their welfare as individuals might have been in jeopardy without the support of international partners.) Moroccan human rights groups nevertheless made a crucial contribution to reform. Without their sustained pressure and visible presence, international pressures would have been easier to dismiss and human rights might well have slipped from Morocco's political agenda. Instead, when King Hassan's death in 1999 brought change at the palace, domestic groups were in a position to take advantage of new opportunities.

Martha Finnemore and Kathryn Sikkink have developed a model of international norm change that provides heuristic assistance in understanding the *process* by which local human rights groups have affected change in Morocco. Finnemore and Sikkink's model was designed for exclusive application at the international level, and we have added complexity to the model by appending parallel dynamics at the domestic level. The original model portrays the emergence and institutionalization of international norms and identifies three stages: a period when norms emerge (Norm Emergence), a period when they spread (Norm Cascade), and a period when they become politically invested or institutionalized (Internalization).[72] Within the model, norm entrepreneurs— usually acting domestically in a small number of states—advocate new standards of appropriate behavior in the Emergence stage. As states begin to accede to the standard, a tipping point is reached, and Norm Cascade begins. What transpires when a state accedes to new standards is largely dependent on local political context. For some states accession may require a significant reorientation of behavior. Where the behavioral norm is already established, states may participate in its reinforcement internationally with relatively little investment of time or political capital, for example, by ratifying a convention or agreeing to its reference in elaboration of other instruments. In a final stage, the norm acquires a general acceptance.

To this basic model of international dynamics we add a domestic dimension. Once international standards achieve stability, domestic "norm entrepreneurs" can refer to the international regime in their efforts to initiate or advance the process of norm change domestically. They can anticipate success in their efforts to the extent that the government of their state desires association with positive images attached to such norms (e.g., respect for rule of law). Indeed, as Andrew Morasvcik has shown, elites of newly democratized states may recognize that acceding to international instruments can help the new structures lock in the political values for which the ascendant elites have struggled.[73] Far from considering ratification a matter of empty form or lip service to hegemonic powers, new elites may hope that attachment to international human rights standards will help transform their own culture and institutions.

Figure 11.1 represents our understanding of the linkage between processes that contribute to the construction of international norms and the internalization of standards domestically. The successful negotiation of a human rights instrument at the international level—Level I—does not guarantee domestic change for any of the states that participated in the negotiation, but it can be expected to increase the effectiveness of supporters (domestic norm entrepreneurs) in noncompliant states. Once a standard has been established internationally, by treaty, a parallel process must take place domestically (at Level II) if a tipping point is to be reached within the national culture and the norm is to spread throughout society.

Human rights groups in nations that have not accepted international standards of human rights or have not yet developed public cultures of respect for human rights may use international human rights norms achieved at Level I as a reference point and source of legitimacy for their efforts to initiate and advance the process of domestic norm change. The process of institutionalization is furthered when domestic norm entrepreneurs seek to achieve a domestic cascade effect parallel to the international dynamic, edging acceptance beyond the "tipping point."

Domestic human rights groups, operating at Level II, can play impor-

FIGURE 11.1. Two-level model of norm change.

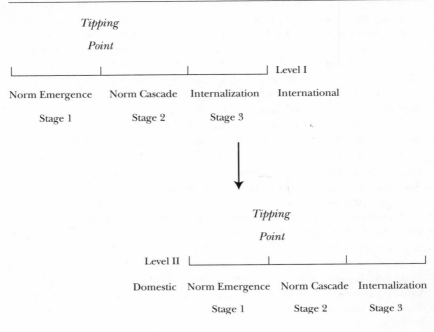

tant roles in two different phases of this process. First, they may be in a position to leverage the international norm and thereby help the norm emerge in an initial domestic phase. An existing international standard may provide a sort of hook or ratchet for local groups working to secure public commitment to new practices. Subsequently, human rights groups as domestic political actors may actively promote the norm at home, helping to reach a tipping point that will allow the norm to root and spread in the domestic context. Both phases are important, though more attention is typically paid to the first phase than the second one. Norms cannot spread and root before they emerge, yet as important as this initial phase is, it should not eclipse the importance of cascading change. Through the dynamic of cascading change, domestic norm entrepreneurs ensure that a culture of human rights takes root in all structures of their society.

Needless to say, such a process of norm internalization takes time. In the Moroccan case, it is not unusual that some problems with human rights practice persist and past abuses have not been fully redressed. That does not diminish the significant impact of local human rights groups, who helped initiate and thereafter participated in a *process* of change that, following Finnemore and Sikkink, might be called "domestic norm cascade." It is a testimony to the success of these groups that they are able to use strategies today that a decade ago would have put them at risk. In an August 2004 article titled "The Slow March to Reform," the *Economist* reported a demonstration by human rights activists before the country's Directorate for the Surveillance of the Territory (DST), the Moroccan secret service agency. Wielding "Torture-Free Zone" banners, protesters demanded parliamentary oversight of the DST in the wake of the Amnesty International report that documented recent incidents of torture. Fifteen years ago, as the article notes, these same "indefatigable" human rights advocates would likely have become the next to endure abuse similar to that which they had come to peacefully protest. On that day in 2004, however, plainclothes officers stood aside, recording only descriptions of individuals who approached the buildings too closely. No arrests were made.

Scenes like these, impossible a decade ago, should not be discounted or minimized in the assessment of Morocco's current human rights situation. Morocco may not yet be able to claim a public culture of full respect for human rights, but neither do practices remain substantially unchanged from a decade ago. Progressive change is not guaranteed, but the government has demonstrated some responsiveness. There is reason to believe, or at least hope, that pressures from Moroccan human rights groups will result in a continued narrowing of the gap between rhetoric and a reality that engages policy reform, legal accountability, institutional transformation, and education.

There are few circumstances under which such political transformation would be easy. Mohammed VI has extended an impressive program of political reform, but these reforms have not been fully consolidated. As the recent legislative decisions regarding terrorism and emergency powers amply demonstrate, even reforms to which the palace is committed could be tested if the power of the monarchy or Morocco's traditional bureaucratic elite (*makhzen*) is challenged or assaulted. Human rights groups have demonstrated that they can make an impact on domestic political processes under favorable circumstances. The greater test of their influence and their resolve may lie ahead as they continue to engage in the painstaking and possibly high-risk task of effectively creating a public culture of human rights.

Conclusion
Normative and Political Dimensions of Contemporary Arab Debates on Human Rights

Amr Hamzawy

Although there is an abundant literature discussing the relevance of human rights to democratization processes in the contemporary Middle East, internal Arab debates on this issue have rarely found their way into Western studies. Moreover, Western-based analyses often assume the stance of an externalized Other to debates on political and social transformations in the region. The major objective of this volume, on the other hand, has been to explore from a variety of perspectives the discursive structures of on-the-ground debates in the Arab world on this topic. This may help shift the nexus of academic discussion on human rights in the Arab world to the actors and forces most intimately involved in these debates.

Since the 1980s, human rights has taken on a central role in the Arab world's political and intellectual discussions for a wide variety of collective and individual actors. In particular, members of moderate Islamist movements, secular organizations, and liberal intellectuals discovered in the concept of human rights, albeit in different ways, a useful instrument to democratically transform their political landscape. As a result, alternative voices informed by human rights developed in opposition to the Arab political status quo. From these voices, three poles emerged as central to debates on rights' relevance, all three of which are reflected in this volume. The first pole centers on multiple interpretations of Western normative and political transformations over the last two centuries and the relevance of liberal democratic traditions. This issue has raised great controversy as to the universality or culturally bound nature of the Western historical experience and the possibility of applying related norms and political concepts to the Arab world, particularly with regard to the question of human rights. Second are debates on conflicting understandings of Arab-Islamic political history and its present impact on state-society relationships. In particular, unsettled issues such as secularism, citizenship, the place of religion in politics, and the challenges of cultural modernization—all repeatedly debated over the last century—have acquired new intellectual and social dimensions in contemporary discussions of human rights. The third pole confronts what have been the obstacles blocking the establishment of democratic civil societies and promotion of human rights in the Arab world.

The contributions to *Human Rights in the Arab World* develop clear accounts of the first and second topics by analyzing both the universality of human rights and the emancipatory potential of Arab-Islamic traditions. When it comes to this third question—the question of "what went wrong" or, put differently, why are democracy and human rights still missing in the contemporary Arab reality—authors in *Human Rights in the Arab World* vary in their answers, as do actors in the Arab world as a whole. One can distinguish four discourses regarding this final question. Arab nationalists blame, ultimately, the colonial and postcolonial West for the Arab world's failure to democratize. Secular intellectuals and activists, after a short phase of criticizing the authoritarian nation-state, now see Islamism as the primary obstacle to the protection of human rights and the modernizing state as a major agent of democracy. Political and intellectual advocates of Islamist discourses blame the nation-state and secular forces for being responsible for the evil of corruption, the loss of state legitimacy over society, and the decline of human rights standards in general. In order to shape and form Arab societies according to Islam—as interpreted by them—Islamists maintain that there must first be a takeover of the state apparatus. The reformist discourse, whose adherents hold the authoritarian state responsible for faltering political democratization, seek to minimize state power through both traditional and modern autonomous organizations led by citizens and, in this way, widen the scope of freedom and human rights.

But where do Arab societies and polities stand in *reality* today? Since September 11 political reform measures have been gaining momentum in the Arab world. In countries like Morocco, Algeria, Jordan, Egypt, Yemen, and Bahrain relative improvements can be witnessed in the realm of human rights and good governance. In others, such as Saudi Arabia, Syria, and Libya—just to mention the most depressing cases—the ruling elites use the notion of human rights as a legitimizing strategy in a way that deprives it of normative and political substance. Although oppositional groups and liberal critics are trying to gain back their discursive control over the notion of human rights, it is virtually impossible to compete with regimes in public spheres they dominate.

In both groups of countries we will have to wait and see what the upcoming years may bring in a region where internal and external destabilizing factors remain largely intact. At the time of this writing, we have been witnessing unusual scenes in an Arab world clearly in flux. Mass demonstrations in Lebanon, joint protest rallies of Egyptian Islamists and liberals against the Mubarak regime, and municipal elections in Saudi Arabia are just as much features of the current situation as violence in Iraq and Palestine. As the debate on democracy and human rights continues, it will be informed by the region's intellectual diversity. This book is a contribution to a developing discourse based in this diversity, and perhaps a small impetus for change in a region where the dream of pluralist polities and open public spheres goes hand in hand with the risk of authoritarian backlash and radical Islamist insurgencies.

Appendix 1
Documents

Following are a few notable documents that flow out of the Arab human rights tradition. These are appended both as a convenient reference and to substantiate two underlying themes of this volume. First, human rights have a significant tradition in the Arab world starting, of course, with the key role played by Charles Malik in the drafting of the Universal Declaration of Human Rights and, as documented by Susan Waltz, the contributions of Arab (and Muslim) states.[1] As in other parts of the world, the language of human rights becomes widespread within decades of the establishment of the modern nation-state structure, to which the human rights regime is a direct response. Second, the specificity of human rights claims has accelerated in the Arab world over recent years. This is particularly notable with the Casablanca Declaration that came out of the 1999 First Arab Human Rights Conference in Casablanca and the increase in the region's human rights activities that followed.

Arab Charter on Human Rights
Cairo Declaration on Human Rights Education and Dissemination
Casablanca Declaration of the Arab Human Rights Movement
Beirut Declaration: Toward an Effective Regional Protection of Human
    Rights
Sana'a Declaration on Democracy, Human Rights and the Role of the
    International Criminal Court

Arab Charter on Human Rights (Council of the League of Arab States, Cairo)

adopted on September 15, 1994 (not yet ratified), full text, translated from Arabic (2)
The Governments of the member States of the League of Arab States

Preamble

Given the Arab nation's belief in human dignity since God honoured it by making the Arab World the cradle of religions and the birthplace of civilizations which confirmed its right to a life of dignity based on freedom, justice and peace,

Pursuant to the eternal principles of brotherhood and equality among all human beings which were firmly established by the Islamic Shari'a and the other divinely revealed religions,

Being proud of the humanitarian values and principles which it firmly established in the course of its long history and which played a major role in disseminating centres of learning between the East and the West, thereby making it an international focal point for seekers of knowledge, culture and wisdom,

Conscious of the fact that the entire Arab World has always worked together to preserve its faith, believing in its unity, struggling to protect its freedom, defending the right of nations to self-determination and to safeguard their resources, believing in the rule of law and that every individual's enjoyment of freedom, justice and equality of opportunity is the yardstick by which the merits of any society are gauged,

Rejecting racism and zionism, which constitute a violation of human rights and pose a threat to world peace,

Acknowledging the close interrelationship between human rights and world peace,
Reaffirming the principles of the Charter of the United Nations and the Universal Declaration of Human Rights, as well as the provisions of the United Nations International Covenants on Civil and Political Rights and Economic, Social and Cultural Rights and the Cairo Declaration on Human Rights in Islam *(4)*

In confirmation of all the above, have agreed as follows:

Part I

Article 1
(a) All peoples have the right of self-determination and control over their natural wealth and resources and, accordingly, have the right to freely determine the form of their political structure and to freely pursue their economic, social and cultural development.

(b) Racism, zionism, occupation and foreign domination pose a challenge to human dignity and constitute a fundamental obstacle to the realization of the basic rights of peoples. There is a need to condemn and endeavour to eliminate all such practices.

Part II

Article 2
Each State Party to the present Charter undertakes to ensure to all individuals within its territory and subject to its Jurisdiction the right to enjoy all the rights and freedoms recognized herein, without any distinction on grounds of race, colour, sex, language, religion, political opinion, national or social origin, property, birth or other status and without any discrimination between men and women.

Article 3
(a) No restriction upon or derogation from any of the fundamental human rights recognized or existing in any State Party to the present Charter in virtue of law, conventions or custom shall be admitted on the pretext that the present Charter does not recognize such rights or that it recognizes them to a lesser extent.

(b) No State Party to the present Charter shall derogate from the fundamental freedoms recognized herein and which are enjoyed by the nationals of another State that shows less respect for those freedoms.

Article 4
(a) No restrictions shall be placed on the rights and freedoms recognized in the present Charter except where such is provided by law and deemed necessary to protect the national security and economy, public order, health or morals or the rights and freedoms of others.

(b) In time of public emergency which threatens the life of the nation, the States Parties may take measures derogating from their obligations under the present Charter to the extent strictly required by the exigencies of the situation.

(c) Such measures or derogations shall under no circumstances affect or apply to the rights and special guarantees concerning the prohibition of torture and degrading treatment, return to one's country, political asylum, trial, the inadmissibility of retrial for the same act, and the legal status of crime and punishment.

Article 5
Every individual has the right to life, liberty and security of person. These rights shall be protected by law.

Article 6
There shall be no crime or punishment except as provided by law and there shall be no punishment in respect of an act preceding the promulgation of that provision. The accused shall benefit from subsequent legislation if it is in his favour.

Article 7
The accused shall be presumed innocent until proved guilty at a lawful trial in which he has enjoyed the guarantees necessary for his defence.

Article 8
Everyone has the right to liberty and security of person and no one shall be arrested, held in custody or detained without a legal warrant and without being brought promptly before a judge.

Article 9
All persons are equal before the law and everyone within the territory of the State has a guaranteed right to legal remedy.

Article 10
The death penalty may be imposed only for the most serious crimes and anyone sentenced to death shall have the right to seek pardon or commutation of the sentence.

Article 11
The death penalty shall under no circumstances be imposed for a political offence.

Article 12
The death penalty shall not be inflicted on a person under 18 years of age, on a pregnant woman prior to her delivery or on a nursing mother within two years from the date on which she gave birth.

Article 13
(a) The States parties shall protect every person in their territory from being subjected to physical or mental torture or cruel, inhuman or degrading treatment. They shall take effective measures to prevent such acts and shall regard the practice thereof, or participation therein, as a punishable offence.

(b) No medical or scientific experimentation shall be carried out on any person without his free consent.

Article 14
No one shall be imprisoned on the ground of his proven inability to meet a debt or fulfil any civil obligation.

Article 15
Persons sentenced to a penalty of deprivation of liberty shall be treated with humanity.

Article 16
No one shall be tried twice for the same offence.
Anyone against whom such proceedings are brought shall have the right to challenge their legality and to demand his release.
Anyone who is the victim of unlawful arrest or detention shall be entitled to compensation.

Article 17
Privacy shall be inviolable and any infringement thereof shall constitute an offence. This privacy includes private family affairs, the inviolability of the home and the confidentiality of correspondence and other private means of communication.

Article 18
Everyone shall have the inherent right to recognition as a person before the law.

Article 19
The people are the source of authority and every citizen of full legal age shall have the right of political participation, which he shall exercise in accordance with the law.

Article 20
Every individual residing within the territory of a State shall have the right to liberty of movement and freedom to choose his place of residence in any part of the said territory, within the limits of the law.

Article 21
No citizen shall be arbitrarily or unlawfully prevented from leaving any Arab country, including his own, nor prohibited from residing, or compelled to reside, in any part of his country.

Article 22
No citizen shall be expelled from his country or prevented from returning thereto.

Article 23
Every citizen shall have the right to seek political asylum in other countries in order to escape persecution. This right shall not be enjoyed by persons facing prosecution for an offence under the ordinary law. Political refugees shall not be extraditable.

Article 24
No citizen shall be arbitrarily deprived of his original nationality, nor shall his right to acquire another nationality be denied without a legally valid reason.

Article 25
Every citizen has a guaranteed right to own private property. No citizen shall under any circumstances be divested of all or any part of his property in an arbitrary or unlawful manner.

Article 26
Everyone has a guaranteed right to freedom of belief, thought and opinion.

Article 27
Adherents of every religion have the right to practise their religious observances and to manifest their views through expression. practice or teaching, without prejudice to the rights of others. No restrictions shall be imposed on the exercise of freedom of belief, thought and opinion except as provided by law.

Article 28
All citizens have the right to freedom of peaceful assembly and association. No restrictions shall be placed on the exercise of this right unless so required by the exigencies of national security, public safety or the need to protect the rights and freedoms of others.

Article 29
The State guarantees the right to form trade unions and the right to strike within the limits laid down by law.

Article 30
The State guarantees every citizen's right to work in order to secure for himself a standard of living that meets the basic requirements of life.

The State also guarantees every citizen's right to comprehensive social security.

Article 31
Free choice of work is guaranteed and forced labour is prohibited. Compelling a person to perform work under the terms of a court judgement shall not be deemed to constitute forced labour.

Article 32
The State shall ensure that its citizens enjoy equality of opportunity in regard to work, as well as a fair wage and equal remuneration for work of equal value.

Article 33
Every citizen shall have the right of access to public office in his country.

Article 34
The eradication of illiteracy is a binding obligation and every citizen has a right to education. Primary education, at the very least, shall be compulsory and free and both secondary and university education shall be made easily accessible to all.

Article 35
Citizens have a right to live in an intellectual and cultural environment in which Arab nationalism is a source of pride, in which human rights are sanctified and in which racial, religious and other forms of discrimination are rejected and international cooperation and the cause of world peace are supported.

Article 36
Everyone has the right to participate in cultural life, as well as the right to enjoy literary and artistic works and to be given opportunities to develop his artistic, intellectual and creative talents.

Article 37
Minorities shall not be deprived of their right to enjoy their culture or to follow the teachings of their religions.

Article 38
(a) The family is the basic unit of society, whose protection it shall enjoy.

(b) The State undertakes to provide outstanding care and special protection for the family, mothers, children and the aged.

Article 39
Young persons have the right to be afforded the most ample opportunities for physical and mental development.

Part III

Article 40
(a) The States members of the League's Council which are parties to the Charter shall elect a Committee of Experts on Human Rights by secret ballot.

(b) The Committee shall consist of seven members nominated by the member States Parties to the Charter. The initial elections to the Committee shall be held six months after the Charter's entry into force. The Committee shall not include more than one person from the same State.

(c) The Secretary-General shall request the member States to submit their candidates two months before the scheduled date of the elections.

(d) The candidates, who must be highly experienced and competent in the Committee's field of work, shall serve in their personal capacity with full impartiality and integrity.

(e) The Committee's members shall be elected for a three-year term which, in the case of three of them, shall be renewable for one further term, their names being selected by lot.
The principle of rotation shall be observed as far as possible.

(f) The Committee shall elect its chairman and shall draw up its rules of procedure specifying its method of operation.

(g) Meetings of the Committee shall be convened by the Secretary-General at the Headquarters of the League's Secretariat. With the Secretary-General's approval, the Committee may also meet in another Arab country if the exigencies of its work so require.

Article 41
1. The States Parties shall submit reports to the Committee of Experts on Human Rights in the following manner:

(a) An initial report one year after the date of the Charter's entry into force.

(b) Periodic reports every three years.

(c) Reports containing the replies of States to the Committee's questions.

2. The Committee shall consider the reports submitted by the member States Parties to the Charter in accordance with the provisions of paragraph 1 of this article.

3. The Committee shall submit a report, together with the views and comments of the States, to the Standing Committee on Human Rights at the Arab League.

Part IV

Article 42
(a) The Secretary-General of the League of Arab States shall submit the present Charter, after its approval by the Council of the League, to the member States for signature and ratification or accession.
(b) The present Charter shall enter into effect two months after the date of deposit of the seventh instrument of ratification or accession with the Secretariat of the League of Arab States.

Article 43
Following its entry into force, the present Charter shall become binding on each State two months after the date of the deposit of Its instrument of ratification or accession with the Secretariat. The Secretary-General shall notify the member States of the deposit of each instrument of ratification or accession.

The Charter was adopted by the Council of the League of Arab States by its resolution 5437 (102nd regular session) on 15 September 1994. The original text may be obtained from the League of Arab States, Permanent Delegation to the United Nations in Geneva, 9 rue du Valais, CH-1202 Geneva. The translation by the United Nations was obtained from the Centre for Human Rights in Geneva. A French translation made by Mohammed Amin Al-Midani has been published in *RUDH* 7 (1995): 212 ff. The 22 member States of the League of Arab States are Jordan, United Arab Emirates, Bahrain, Tunisia, Algeria, Djibouti. Saudi Arabia, Sudan, Syrian Arab Republic. Somalia, Iraq, Oman. Palestine, Qatar, Comoros, Kuwait, Lebanon, Libyan Arab Jamahiriya, Egypt, Morocco, Mauritania, Yemen.
(4) Adopted on 5 August 1990.

The Cairo Declaration on Human Rights Education and Dissemination

Adopted by The Second International Conference of Human Rights Movement in the Arab World, October 13–16, 2000, Cairo

At invitation of the Cairo Institute for Human Rights Studies, in coordination with the Office of the United Nations High Commissioner for Human Rights and the Euro-Mediterranean Human Rights Network, with the participation of around one hundred human rights experts and defenders from forty human rights group from 14 Arab states, as well as experts from Africa, Asia, Latin America and Europe, the Conference on Human Rights Education and Dissemination: A 21st Century Agenda was held in Cairo from the 13th to the 16th of October, 2000.

The Conference,

Having considered the international human rights instruments, as well as documents, declarations and reports adopted by relevant regional and international conferences, especially the UNESCO's International Congress on the Teaching of Human Rights—Vienna, 1978, International Congress on Human Rights Teaching, Information and Documentation—Malta, 1987, the International Congress on Education for Human Rights and Democracy—Montreal, 1993, the UNESCO Regional Conference on Human Rights Education in Africa—Dakar, 1998, the UNESCO Regional Conference on Human Rights Education in Asia and the Pacific—Pune, 1999, the UNESCO Regional Conference on Human Rights Education in the Arab States—Rabat, 1999, and the First International Conference of the Arab Human Rights Movement—Casablanca, 1999,

Having reviewed the United Nations Plan of Action for the Decade for Human Rights Education (1995–2004), and the progress achieved halfway through the Decade,

Having held extensive deliberations throughout its sessions, taking into consideration the close link between the lack of respect for human rights and the prevalence of poverty and corruption as evidenced by the World Human Development Report and the Report on Corruption in the World, and also noting the increasing concern at the adverse effects of globalisation on the economic level, the abuse of human rights considerations in international relations, and the grave injustices they caused against peoples, especially in the Arab World,

Decides to adopt the following Cairo Declaration on Human Rights Education and Dissemination.

Participants reaffirm:

• Human rights principles are universal; civil, political, economic, social, cultural and joint rights are closely interconnected, interdependent and indivisible; women's rights are an integral part of the human rights system.

• Human rights values are the fruit of the interaction and communication between civilizations and cultures throughout history, the product of the struggle by all peoples against all forms of injustice and oppression internal and external. In this sense, such values belong to humanity as a whole.

• Commendable cultural specificity—as a human right—entrenches people's feeling of dignity and equality, promotes their participation in the conduct of public affairs in their countries, and promotes their consciousness and awareness of the common destiny of all humankind. It is not used to justify marginalizing or consolidating the inferior status of women, nor to justify excluding the other on whatever religious, cultural or political grounds, or to waive commitment to international instruments.

• Respect for human rights is a prime interest for every person, group, people, and for humanity as a whole. This is considering that the enjoyment of dignity, freedom and equality by all is a crucial factor in the flourishing of the human person, in advancing nations and developing their material and human wealth, and in promoting the sense of citizenship.

• Human rights education and dissemination is a fundamental human right. This imposes on governments in particular great responsibilities to explicate, propagate and disseminate human rights principles and their protection mechanisms.

First: The Concept of Human Rights Education and Culture

Human rights education is, in essence, a public endeavour to enable people to learn the basic knowledge essential at once for their emancipation from all forms of oppression and suppression and the inculcation of feelings of responsibility and concern as regards the public good.

Human rights culture comprises the host of values, mental and behavioural structures, cultural heritage, norms and traditions commensurate with human rights principles, along with methods of socialization that transmit such culture at home, school, intermediary agencies and the media.

Human rights education and dissemination is a continuous and comprehensive process that covers all the aspects of life, a process that should be brought into all kinds of practices whether personal, professional, cultural, social, political, or civic. It is necessary that all professions adhere to codes of practice committed to values that are inspired by the fundamental human rights.

The fundamental purpose of human rights education is to interweave knowledge and practice. Human rights education, inculcating dignity and responsibility along with social and moral responsibility, inevitably leads people to mutual respect, collective support and adaptation to their respective needs and rights. It leads people to accept working together to reach freely suitable and renewable formulas that would ensure the balance of interests and joint work towards the common good, without the need to resort to the sway violence, arbitrary or organized, which does away with the freedom of everybody.

Second: The Objectives of Human Rights Education and Dissemination

1. Developing and flourishing the human personality in its spiritual, intellectual and social dimensions, and entrenching people's sense of dignity, freedom, equality, social justice and democratic practice.

2. Enhancing men and women's awareness of their rights so as to help enable them to transform human rights principles into social, economic and political reality. It would also enhance their ability to defend, maintain and advance human rights on all levels.

3. Consolidating friendship and solidarity among peoples; promoting respect for the rights of others; cherishing cultural pluralism and diversity and encouraging the flourishing of the national cultures of all groups and peoples; enriching the culture of dialogue, mutual tolerance and renouncing violence; promoting non-violence, fighting bigotry, and immunizing the people against the discourse of hatred.

4. Promoting a culture of peace that is based on justice and respect of human rights, foremost of which are the rights to self-determination and

to resist occupation; in addition to democratising international relations and institutions so as to reflect the common interests of humanity.

Third: Recommendations

Having studied the obstacles to human rights education and dissemination in the Arab World, the **Conference** makes the following recommendations:

1. Calling upon the Arab governments to:

1.1. Ratify all the international human rights instruments; to drop reservations for those states that have ratified with reservations; to monitor their practical application; to respect all human rights indivisibly; and to not use the manipulation of human rights by some parties in the international community or cultural specificity as a pretext to justify waiving their commitments towards their peoples and citizens.

1.2. Eliminate all restrictions to the freedoms of opinion, expression and assembly, and academic freedoms, in conformity with the universally recognized human rights principles, and to the right to own and manage radio and TV stations and print media channels.

1.3. Draw up national plans for human rights education. This would be the greatest contribution to the promotion of the sense of belonging and citizenship, considering that raising people's and societies' awareness of human rights is the first line of defence of human rights and nations' rights.

In this regard, special attention should be given to:

i) Revising educational curricula and media materials to rid them of messages against human rights, and enriching educational curricula with human rights content.
ii) Including courses on human rights in higher and post-graduate education, and encouraging MA and PhD research in human rights.
iii) Including human rights in literacy and informal education programs.
iv) Including human rights courses in programs qualifying teachers, lawyers, judges, physicians, media personnel, religious scholars, police and army officers, civil servants, and those who work in the different fields of art.
v) Establishing national institutions for human rights education and dis-

semination; enhancing the role of those already existing in some Arab countries; and coordinating efforts to realize national plans in cooperation with local, regional and Arab human rights organizations.

vi) Consolidating cooperation with the relevant United Nations bodies and the international human rights education institutions.

vii) Paying special attention to the role the arts and letters may play in human rights education and dissemination, given their special capacity to address and inspire human consciousness. Special attention should also be given to knowledge of living reality as a starting point, in addition to developing non-traditional educational materials (such as films and plays).

2. Urging the League of Arab States to concern itself with the human rights issues of the Arab peoples and citizens. This requires revising the Arab Charter for Human Rights so as to bring it into conformity with human rights values and principles; establishing a special system for the Permanent Arab Committee on Human Rights in order to activate it; and opening channels of cooperation with Arab non-governmental organizations. Also, the League of Arab States is urged to contribute in activating the plans of the United Nations bodies concerned with human rights education and dissemination.

3. Establishing an Arab regional committee for human rights education and dissemination to include Arab governments that are active in this regard and the relevant Arab non-governmental organization, with a view to develop plans and programs in cooperation with the relevant United Nations bodies.

4. Urging education experts to develop human rights education curricula to address the heart and emotions as well as the mind. Such curricula should not be restricted to conveying information and knowledge; they should seek to develop critical thinking and attitudes. Thus they may help create a cultural environment that safeguards individual and collective rights and furthers the establishment of the state of law and right. It is necessary that such curricula be based on the universal human rights principles while drawing upon the respective people's specific culture and historical experience in resisting all forms of political, social, cultural and religious oppression and foreign occupation.

5. Calling upon the political parties in the Arab World to declare their full commitment to the international human rights instruments; to enhance the human rights content in their platforms and practices on the ground; to follow democratic practices internally; and to attach spe-

cial importance to human rights culture in their cadre-training programs for the youth.

6. Urging the radio, TV and the print media to consider seriously promoting human rights values, pluralism and diversity, and to avoid all that may instigate racial or religious hatred, deride the opinions of the other, or degrade human dignity. Also, the Arab Press Union, the different press syndicates and civil society institutions are called upon to monitor the media's adherence to professional codes of ethics in this regard. Moreover, human rights organizations, both governmental and non-governmental, are called upon to adopt special training programs for media personnel.

7. Urging human rights organizations, both governmental and non-governmental, to make the best use of media channels, especially the radio and TV, in disseminating the human rights culture. This may include establishing special platforms, designing special programmes, and making use of modern technology to this end. Human rights organizations are urged to study the components of popular culture that form the consciousness of individuals, with a view to reaching the discourse suitable for the dissemination of human rights.

8. Calling upon the Arab intellectuals, politicians and religious scholars to abstain from entangling religion in a confrontation with human rights, to consider those rights provided by the international human rights law as a minimum to build upon not to be reduced in the name of cultural specificity or any other pretext, and to work towards the entrenchment of human rights values in the Arab cultural traditions.

9. Calling upon academics, researchers and religious scholars to work for highlighting the roots of human rights in the Arab culture, to underscore the contribution of the Islamic and Christian civilizations in establishing human rights values, and to dismantle that artificial contradiction between a number of human rights principles and some obsolete fundamentalist interpretations.

10. Urging the non-governmental human rights institutions in the Arab World to promote local and regional coordination among them, as well as with the relevant local and regional governmental agencies, and with religious institutions concerned with human rights culture. They are also urged to carry out field research to assess the Arab experiences, both governmental and non-governmental, in human rights education,

with a view to identifying the obstacles and making recommendations for improvement.

11. Urging the Secretary-General of the United Nations to take special notice of the issue of human rights education and dissemination, and to designate his yearly address on Human Rights Day, December 10th, this year for calling upon governments to enhance their efforts in this regard, particularly in activating the United Nations Decade for Human Rights Education, including the mobilization of the necessary human and material resources.

12. Urging the United Nations High Commissioner for Human Rights to undertake the necessary doubling of efforts in order to activate the United Nations Decade for Human Rights Education in the best possible way, and to extend better support to the governments and non-governmental organizations active in this field.

13. Urging the United Nations High Commissioner for Human Rights and the UNESCO's Division for Peace, Human Rights, Democracy and Tolerance to consider the translation of all publications related to human rights issues into Arabic and making them widely available for the Arabic reader.

The Casablanca Declaration of the Arab Human Rights Movement

Adopted by the First International Conference of the Arab Human Rights Movement, Casablanca, April 23–25, 1999

At the invitation of the Cairo Institute for Human Rights Studies, and hosted by the Moroccan Organization for Human Rights, the First International Conference of the Arab Human Rights Movement: Prospects for the Future was held in Casablanca from 23 to 25 April, 1999, to examine the human rights conditions in the Arab world, and the responsibilities, tasks and prospects of the Arab human rights movement.

After extensive discussions, the Conference declared that the only source of reference in this respect is international human rights law and the United Nations instruments and declarations. The Conference also emphasized the universality of human rights.

The International Setting

The Conference examined the international setting and conditions affecting the status of human rights specifically in the Arab world and affirmed the following:

• The call for substantial reforms in the United Nations so as to make it more representative of the regions and peoples of the world, and more effective in fulfilling its role and in expressing the common interests and responsibilities of humanity.

• The importance of drawing the attention to the grave consequences of using the principles of human rights for the realization of specific foreign policy objectives of some countries. It affirms that the Arab world is still suffering from the opportunistic, political and propagandist use of human rights by some major powers as evidenced by the double-standards employed by such powers, most notably the United States of America.

• Calling upon the UN Security Council to review the international sanctions system and its application methods. The Conference also urges the UN Security Council to decide to immediately and unconditionally end the economic sanctions on Iraq, considering that their devastating effects on the civilian population could be likened to genocide.

• Rejecting the manipulation by some Arab governments of patriotic sentiments and the principle of sovereignty so as to avoid complying with international human rights standards.

• Rejecting any attempt to use civilizational or religious specificity to contest the universality of human rights. Commendable specificity is that which entrenches the dignity and equality of citizens, enriches their culture and promotes their participation in the administration of public affairs.

Peace and the Rights of Peoples and Minorities in the Arab World

The Conference declares its support for the proposed UN Decade for the Culture of Peace and affirms that acceptable peace is that which is based on respect for fundamental rights, justice and people's inherent dignity. It should also be based upon the provisions of international law, the UN resolutions, and the due respect of human rights—most notably the right to self-determination.

The rights of the Palestinian people are the proper standard to measure the consistency of international positions towards a just peace and human rights. The Arab human rights movement will apply this standard in its relations with the different international organizations and actors.

The Conference declares its full support for the right of the Palestinian people to self-determination and to establish their independent state on their occupied national soil—with Jerusalem as its capital—and the right of return for the refugees and to compensation in accordance with UN resolutions. The Conference demands the dismantling of settlements, the elimination of all forms of racial discrimination and human rights violations against the Arabs of Israel, and the elimination of the racist zionism and the expansionist nature of Israel.

The establishment of a just peace requires the immediate and unconditional withdrawal of Israel from the Golan Heights and South Lebanon in accordance with UN Security Council resolutions.

Meanwhile, the Conference calls upon the contracting parties of the Fourth Geneva Convention on the Protection of Civilian Persons in Times of War to fulfill their legal obligations and to work towards compelling the Israeli occupation forces to apply the provisions of the Convention, considering that these provisions constitute the minimum standards required for the protection and safety of Palestinian civilians. In this regard, the Conference affirms that it is necessary that the High Contracting Parties comply with the UN General Assembly resolution to hold a special conference of the High Contracting Parties on July 15th, 1999, to examine the measures required for the enforcement of the provisions of the Convention in the occupied territories. The Conference also calls upon international and Arab NGOs to join the international campaign to urge the High Contracting Parties of the Fourth Geneva Convention to work towards enforcing its provisions in the occupied territories.

The Conference values the positions of NGOs and states in support of the rights of the Palestinian people and the position of the European Union among them—especially the EU's refusal to recognize the Israeli stance on Jerusalem. The Conference also hails the European Commission's recommendation to embargo the goods produced in the Israeli settlements and calls upon all states to adopt similar positions.

The Conference urges the Palestinian National Authority to respect human rights, to establish the separation of powers, to dissolve State Security Courts, and to release political prisoners.

In discussing the issue of minorities in the Arab world, the Conference affirms its commitment to the right to self-determination and its strong condemnation of all acts of oppression, despotism and war that have been and are still being committed against minorities in the Arab world, especially genocide, displacement and enslavement. The Conference affirms that the Arab human rights movement will treat such actions as crimes against humanity.

In this context, the Conference declares its support for the Kurdish people's right to self-determination and calls upon the United Nations to convene a special international conference with the participation of all the concerned parties to reach an integrated and comprehensive solution to the continued suffering of the Kurdish people.

The Conference also calls for an end to the war in Sudan and urges the establishment of peace within the framework of a formula that ensures the establishment of a democratic system of political plurality, participation in public life, and respect for human rights without discrimination between citizens—including securing the right of the citizens of South Sudan to self-determination.

The General Conditions of Human Rights in the Arab World

Despite the relative relaxation in the human rights situation in a number of Arab countries, the general picture remains gloomy in comparison with the progress realized in other parts of the world. This is exacerbated by the failure of the League of Arab States to provide an effective regional conflict-resolution system and mechanisms for the protection of human rights in the Arab world.

The Conference expresses its alarm at the continued absence of a modern legal structure in a number of Arab countries. This includes the lack of a constitution, a parliament and a modern judicial system, in addition to their persistent rejection of international human rights standards. This applies to Saudi Arabia and a number of Gulf states.

The Conference discussed at length the continuation of acts that completely suppress fundamental rights and freedoms and the persistence of legal systems based upon the codification of cruelty and violence in Iraq, Libya, Syria, Sudan and Bahrain. This is despite their accession to some of the most fundamental international human rights conventions and agreements. The Conference also discussed the prevalence in these countries of grave and flagrant human rights violations that can not be accurately monitored because of the absence of the minimum requirements for fact-finding.

The conference draws attention to the fact that acts of external aggression and military or economic violence against Iraq and Libya further aggravate the human rights situation there.

The Conference affirms that the acts of violence and armed internal conflicts, as in Somalia and Sudan, constitute in themselves a grave violation of the rights to life, physical integrity, life in peace and all other rights.

While expressing its concern at the situation in Algeria since the cancellation of elections in 1992, the Conference strongly condemns the crimes and massacres committed by armed groups and military militias against tens of thousands of citizens. The Conference also condemns the grave human rights violations committed by the state, specifically the enforced disappearance of thousands of people.

The Conference examined the human rights situation in the other Arab countries, which are characterized by defects in the rule of law and in institutional, legislative and other safeguards for the enjoyment of human rights and fundamental freedoms, in addition to infringements of the principle of the independence of the judiciary. These conditions lead to grave and systematic violations of human rights, especially the crime of torture. The Conference regrets the reversal in some countries, which had realized some relative improvement in the condition of human rights, such as Tunisia, Egypt, Yemen and Jordan.

The Conference welcomes the relative progress in the general human rights situation in Morocco in the last decade, due to the efforts of the Moroccan and international human rights organizations.

In this respect, the Conference affirms the following:

1. Generating pressure to reform and upgrade the institutions of the League of Arab States and to achieve the legislative and practical

reforms necessary for safeguarding human rights and for ensuring the participation in and monitoring of these institutions by Arab citizens.

2. Calling upon the League of Arab States to review all its conventions relating to human rights—especially the Arab Agreement on Combating Terrorism—and also to review the Arab Charter of Human Rights of 1994, with a view to drafting a new Arab convention on human rights, in cooperation with Arab human rights NGOs, so as to make it compatible with international standards. The Conference decided to form a working group to prepare a draft proposal for such a convention.

3. Generating pressure to reform the legislations of Arab countries, especially those contravene the freedoms of opinion, expression, and dissemination of information and the right to knowledge. Working towards ending the state's control of all media, and demanding that Arab governments legalize, in the framework of democratic constitutions and laws, the rights of assembly and peaceful association for all intellectual and political groups and forces, including the unarmed political Islamic groups.

4. Calling upon all political Islamic groups to renounce violence and to end its practice, and calling upon the intellectual and political community and forces to abstain from practicing intellectual terrorism through calling others apostates or traitors or defaming their characters.

5. The need to initiate substantial political reforms in Iraq leading to a democratic system and constitution that would bring about the equality of citizens, abolish political confessionalism, allow for diversity as a basis of national unity according to the principle of equality in citizenship, and enshrine fundamental human rights.

6. Calling for an end to the exceptional situation in Sudan and for convening a comprehensive constitutional conference with the participation of all the political and civil forces so as to ensure the restoration of democracy and peace.

7. Calling for the consolidation of the political reforms begun in 1989 in Algeria so as to prepare the ground for ending violence and laying down arms; releasing those detained without trial; retrying those who had been tried under exceptional laws; revealing the fate of the "disappeared"; and bringing those responsible for the crimes of disappearance, torture and killing to justice. The Conference stresses the need for

governments to respond to just and legitimate initiatives for opening a serious dialogue to establish peace and broaden public freedoms.

Responsibilities of the Arab Human Rights Movement

1. Promoting the **struggle for democracy** and basing the general strategy of the movement on such a task. The Conference affirms that the aims of preserving the non-partisan nature of the movement and ensuring its independence from political parties do not exclude working towards a constant dialogue between human rights organizations and all political parties. Such a dialogue should aim at cooperation to consolidate democratic transformation and respect for human rights, and to draft a code of minimum standards for the respect of human rights and democracy that takes into consideration the specific political and social context of every single country.

2. Determining the **common priorities** of the Arab human rights movement in the realms of advocacy and protection. These include the following:

• Putting a final end to the practice of torture, and pursuing its perpetrators and bringing them to justice.

• Annulling martial and emergency laws, and affirming the need to respect freedoms of expression, assembly and association.

• Ending administrative and preventive detention and releasing all prisoners of conscience and those detained without charge or trial.

• Opposing exceptional courts, campaigning for laws and safeguards which guarantee the independence of the judiciary from any administrative manipulation or intervention.

• Introducing necessary reforms to the basic laws, revoking exceptional laws, and putting an end to arbitrary and extra-judicial executions or those resulting from unfair trials.

3. Struggling for the realization of **economic and social rights**, considering that human rights are integrated, indivisible and are not exchangeable. In this respect the Conference affirms:

• Securing citizens' right to participation, including guaranteeing public oversight of the public revenues of the state, is the backbone of the application of the **right to development**.

4. Struggling for entrenching the values of **human rights in the Arab and Islamic culture**. This includes the following:

• Urging those Arab governments that did not ratify international human rights instruments to do so immediately and without reservations, and urging those that ratified them to lift their reservations, and to comply to the provisions of such instruments regarding the mechanisms of protection.

• Urging academics, researchers and religious scholars to shed light on the roots of human rights in the Arab culture, to exhibit the contribution of the Islamic civilization in establishing the values of human rights, and to dismantle the artificial contradictions between some human rights principles and some obsolete fundamentalist interpretations. Calling upon all Arab intellectuals and politicians to refrain from entangling Islam in a confrontation with human rights, and to consider those rights provided by international human rights law as a minimum to build upon and not to seek to reduce or call for their violation in the name of specificity or any other pretext.

5. Struggling for the recognition of **women's rights** as an integral part of the human rights system. This includes the affirmation of the following:

• Women's enjoyment of human rights is an integrated and comprehensive process that should encompass all facets of life within and outside the family.

• Real equality between women and men goes beyond legal equality to encompass changing the conceptions and confronting the stereotypes about women. Thus, it requires not only a comprehensive review of laws, foremost of which are personal status codes, but also the review and upgrading of educational curricula as well as the critical monitoring of the media discourse.

• In this respect, the Conference stresses the necessity of engaging women's and human rights NGOs in the process of reviewing current legislations and in upgrading civil and criminal laws, with a view to resolutely confronting all forms of violence and discrimination against women.

• The Conference also calls upon the Arab governments that did not ratify the Convention on the Elimination of All Forms of Discrimination Against Women to do so expeditiously, and those that ratified it to lift their reservations.

• It also calls upon women and human rights NGOs to work to refute these reservations, to challenge the culture of discrimination, and to adopt courageous stances in exposing the practice of hiding behind religion to legitimize the subordination of women. These NGOs should also give special attention to the continued monitoring of the compliance by Arab governments to their international commitments concerning women's enjoyment of their rights.

• The necessity of considering the possibility of allocating a quota for women in parliaments, representative institutions and public bodies as a temporary measure. This should stand until appropriate frameworks for women's voluntary activity take shape and until the awareness of the necessity of equality and the elimination of all forms of discrimination increases.

6. Confronting the violations of the **rights of the child** in the Arab world, specially those emanating from economic sanctions, the aggravation of armed conflicts in some countries, and the increase in the phenomena of street children and child labor. In this respect the Conference calls for the following:

• Criminalizing the engagement of children in armed conflicts, and supporting efforts aimed at raising the minimum age of military conscription to 18 years.

• Prohibiting the employment of children in occupations that may harm their health, security or morals.

• Prohibiting the implementation of capital punishment in crimes committed by children under 18 years of age; this is until the abolition of capital punishment entirely.

• Prohibiting the confinement of children in the detention places of adults.

7. Disseminating **human rights education** and culture on the basis that the first line of defense of human rights is citizens' awareness of their rights and their readiness to defend them. In this respect, the Conference has decided on the following:

• The need to overcome all obstacles preventing access to the fora provided by the media and the educational institutions to disseminate the message of human rights. It is necessary to try by all means to convince governments to facilitate the work of human rights education institutions, to add the subject of human rights to the educational curricula, and to uproot all that contravenes the values of human rights from the current curricula.

• Consolidating cooperation with the fora of artistic creativity and other non-governmental organizations in the realm of disseminating the culture of human rights, and focusing on some intermediary strata that could be able to play a vital role in this sphere, such as teachers, media personnel, judges and lawyers. In addition, it is necessary to design suitable plans to activate the role of preachers in mosques and churches in this respect.

8. With respect to upgrading and advancing the capabilities of the Arab human rights movement, the Conference draws attention to the signs of substantial developments in **international criminal justice** manifested by the opening for ratification of the Convention on the International Criminal Court, and also the possibility of bringing to justice the torturer Pinochet. The Conference affirms that such developments open the door to the possibility of trying war criminals and perpetrators of crimes against humanity. This necessitates that human rights defenders develop new methodologies and tools to collect and document information that could be used as evidence before such trials.

9. Protecting **human rights defenders** and their rights to receive information, hold meetings, contact all the concerned sides, and make use of local and international law to defend human rights.
In this respect, the Conference

• Absolutely condemns all the reservations made by 13 Arab states to the Declaration on the Right and Responsibility of Individuals, Groups and Organs of Society to Promote and Protect Universally Recognized Human Rights and Fundamental Freedoms;

• Affirms that the conduct of any Arab government toward human rights defenders will be the determinant by which, negatively or positively, the Arab human rights movement will deal with it;

• Stresses that it is necessary for human rights defenders to commit themselves to the professional standards and political neutrality, which require defending the victims of human rights violations regardless of their political or ideological affiliations. It is also necessary that human rights defenders apply the rules of democratic review established in the structures of civil associations and exercise complete transparency regarding their financing sources and expenditures. The Conference considers that the commitment to these principles is consistent with the very essence of the task of defending human rights. This calls for the founding of a body to represent civil society in overseeing the performance of human rights NGOs and their commitment to these standards.

10. **Coordination between the Arab human rights NGOS**. The Conference affirms that the minimum standard required for the fulfillment of these responsibilities and recommendations necessitates the elevation of bilateral and collective cooperation between Arab human rights NGOs to the highest level. Given the lack of national and regional coordination mechanisms and structures on the local and regional levels, the Conference considers these tasks of utmost importance. There is an urgent need for reviewing the present structure of relations between its components on the local, regional and international levels, taking into consideration the quantitative and qualitative developments of the human rights movement in the South. The movement should strive to found a new international mechanism based on continuous and dynamic consultation to promote the relationships of partnership and parity among its components. This is to help further the effectiveness of the movement on the international, regional and local levels.

Toward an Effective Regional Protection of Human Rights: Which Arab Charter on Human Rights? (the Beirut Declaration)

Beirut, Lebanon, June 10–12, 2003

Upon an initiative by the Cairo Institute for Human Rights (CIHRS) and in collaboration with the Association for the Defence of Rights and Freedoms (ADL), a conference titled "Towards An Effective Regional Protection of Human Rights: Which Arab Charter on Human Rights?" was organized between June 10–12th 2003 in Beirut, Lebanon.

The conference was held in the context of the decision by the Arab League to devote a special meeting of its Permanent Human Rights Committee during the period June 18–26th 2003 to revise the Arab Human Rights Charter.

Eighty participants represent 36 NGO's, 11 international NGO's and inter-Governmental Organizations, 15 legal, academic and media experts participated in the conference, in addition to 7 governmental and parliamentarian members as observers. Representatives from the Arab League and the United Nations Commissioner for Human Rights attended the conference. It was supported by the European Union and held in close coordination with the International Federation for Human Rights (IFDH) and the Euro-Mediterranean Human Rights Network (EMHRN).

Whereas, the conference affirms that the Arab Charter on Human Rights lacks a number of the international human rights standards and guarantees adopted by other regions in the world, it is also missing the necessary mechanisms to ensure and monitor its implementation. Thus, the conference expresses reservations on the endeavors that aim at the adoption of the Arab Charter in its present state or introducing superficial or partial modifications. It also emphasizes the importance of ensuring and respecting the universal human rights system as established by the UN. Furthermore, it affirms that the establishment of an integrated and effective protection of human rights in the Arab world requires, particularly, to work according to the following principles and standards:

1. All people in the Arab world are entitled to the right to self-determination. By virtue of that right, they can freely pursue their economic, social, and cultural development, and dispose of their natural wealth and resources. This requires the full enjoyment of freedoms and rights as stipulated in the international human rights instruments.

2. A regional covenant should clearly reflect the ethnic, religious, cultural and linguistic diversity in the region. The Arab world is not solely consistent of Arabs, or Muslims, and its Muslims are not only Sunni. Rather, it is rich in diverse races, sects, beliefs, cultures and languages that should be respected and recognized with equality. This should be emphasized in all the articles of the covenant including its title. Thus, we suggest the following title: "Charter/Convention of Human Rights in the Arab World."

3. Civilization or religious particularities should not be used as a pretext to cast doubt and to question the universality of human rights. The "particularities" that deserve celebration are those which make a citizen have a sense of dignity, equality and enriches his/her culture and life, and promote his/her participation in their own country's public affairs. Assuring the tolerant principles of Islam and religions in general should not be put in a false contradiction to human rights principles. The conference alarms of the adherence of aged interpretations of Islam that

distort Islam and insults Muslims and leads to violations of human rights, particularly when excluding women and not allowing freedom of thought, belief, creative art, literature and scientific research.

4. In reference to the previous statements, the Permanent Commission for Human Rights of AL is urged to base its revision of the Arab Charter on Human Rights in conformity with universal human rights standards that should constitute the minimum of Arab states' obligations in this regard. Fortunately, most Arab states have ratified the major international human rights conventions. Moreover, the Permanent Commission is encouraged to consider that the universality of human rights is the fruit of the interaction of the major civilizations and cultures throughout history including Arab and Muslim cultures.

5. The rule in any legislation related to rights and freedoms is the enjoyment of the fruits of these freedoms, with the exception being prohibition. A regional human rights convention should not allow governments to use the law to breach human rights. It should encourage Arab States to bring their current legislations into conformity with the new convention and should not allow any law that contradicts any of the rights provided in the convention. No restrictions should be made except those, which protect the democratic society and its constitutional institutions as well as others' rights to fully enjoy human rights stipulated in the envisaged convention.

The "charter" should state that no restriction upon or derogation from any of the fundamental human rights recognized or existing in any State Party to the "charter" pursuant to law, conventions, regulations or custom on the pretext that the "charter" does not recognize such rights or that it recognizes them to a lesser extent.

6. It is prohibited to declare a state of emergency except in the time of actual war, or in case of a natural disaster, and should immediately be lifted when the justification of this emergency no longer exists. Furthermore, a state should not use its authority under such emergencies in events, which do not relate to the causes of the emergency imposed. Accordingly, the state has no right to illegally arrest anyone, and everyone has the right to resort to a judge to instantly determine whether or not the arrest is legal.

7. Respecting human rights and fundamental freedoms, above all, the absolute equality in dignity and citizenship. This should be the sound approach to deal with religious, cultural, linguistic, and national groups'

problems in the region. Ignoring this fact for several years has led to wasting human resources and depleting material wealth in extremely harmful and unnecessary civil wars. Such negligence has been very harmful and has nurtured separatist tendencies and opened the door for revenge and foreign intervention.

8. Abandoning the use of violence in politics and all forms of inciting religious and ethnic hatred whether by state or non-state actors. Also, abandoning all forms of racial discrimination against certain national or religious groups in the Arab world and condemning Zionism as a racist ideology.

9. All Arabs have the right to civil representative ruling systems. The people of every Arab nation should be allowed to create their own legislation according to their contemporary conditions. All citizens have the right to participate in the administration of public affairs. They should be allowed to assume public and political office on an equal basis despite their national, religious, and linguistic affiliation.

10. Allowing citizens the freedom of association, assembly, peaceful demonstrations, strikes, disseminating public statements, press and ownership of media entities.

11. The right to form political parties and NGOs simply by notification. Acknowledging of NGOs role and guaranteeing their independence. Human Rights NGO's, should be granted the freedom of work within the context of the 1998 UN Declaration on Human Rights Defenders.

12. Ensuring the freedoms of belief, expression and creative art and literature, and the right to exchange information and ideas. There shouldn't be any punishments that limit the rights of publications.

13. The necessity of acknowledging the independence and impunity of judiciary organs and the right of individuals to a fair trial. Allowing effective measures to appeal and seek remedy against arbitrary measures that violate the convention.

14. No one should be subjected to torture or to cruel or degrading treatment or inhumane punishment. Cases of emergency, such as war or threats of war, or internal political instability, should not be used as a pretext to torture citizens, in addition to orders from high ranking state officials or public authority.

15. Acknowledging the fact that human rights are indivisible, interdependent and interrelated. Accordingly, women's rights should be acknowledged as an inseparable part of human rights. Women have the right to dignity and legal status, which makes them able to control their own destiny and to practice their equal duties and rights as men within the private and public spheres. Women should be protected against family, societal, and institutional violence.

16. Acknowledging child rights related to survival, growth, protection and participation according to the principles of indiscrimination and best interest of the child and according to the Convention on the Rights of the Child—that Arab states have ratified—and the related protocols. Every state party to the regional charter/ convention should ban all forms of slavery and sexual exploitation of women and children.

17. Arab states should guarantee their people enjoyment of economic, social, and cultural rights in the framework of the optimal utilization of the national wealth of the state. A lack of natural resources should not exempt a state from fulfilling the minimum level of these rights especially the vulnerable populations and the areas lacking public services. The convention should guarantee that everyone has the right to health, housing, and social insurance. The Arab Charter on Human Rights doesn't acknowledge these rights.

18. Cooperation between Arab countries for a better utilization of the region's natural wealth ensures development of the entire region, considering the previous commitments that some wealthier Arab countries have taken to help other poorer or occupied ones.

19. Acknowledging the right to form syndicates and to join them. Ensuring syndicates' rights and freedoms including the right to form unions whether according to their type of work, or geographic location on the national, or regional levels while regarding the international conventions of syndicates' freedoms.

20. Ensuring individuals' freedom of movement between Arab countries and within each country.

21. Acknowledging the principle of equal opportunities and non-discrimination in enjoying the right to work and seeking public office regardless of race, gender, religious beliefs, or political affiliation.

22. Protection of emigrant laborers in the Arab world and ensuring the refugees' rights. Arab states should guarantee all Palestinian refugees civil, economic, and social rights until the right to return is achieved.

Measures for protection and guarantee:

23. A committee of independent human rights and international law experts should be elected. This committee should receive complaints and reports on human rights violations either from individuals, Arab and international NGOs, or from any state party. The committee should be allowed to review the reports of the state parties and the progress they achieved, as well as the problems they face implementing human rights. Representatives of NGOs should be allowed to discuss these reports with the committee and should be allowed to submit reports parallel to them. The committee should be allowed to give its reports directly to the League's Assembly, as well as the public.

24. Establishing an Arab Court for Human Rights and appointing a Commissioner for Human Rights in the Arab League. This commissioner should work in collaboration with the national institutions for human rights and the NGOs.

Fundamental Approaches to Develop an Effective Regional Mechanism Based on the above, the conference urges:

1. The Arab League to respond to the previous recommendations of the Arab human rights NGOs Casablanca Declaration, April 1999, which implies the formation of a joint expert committee that joins governmental and non-governmental experts from the Arab world in order to develop a regional document to promote and protect human rights in the region. This document should depart from the minimum international obligations of the Arab governments according to the fact that most of them have ratified the major international human rights instruments. Moreover, the conference emphasizes that any genuine endeavour to launch a regional Arab mechanism to defend human rights should be founded on the principal springboards outlined in this declaration.

2. The UN High Commissioner for Human Rights to provide the necessary advice for the process of establishing a regional mechanism to protect human rights in the Arab World. The Commissioner should work to monitor the extent to which this process is rightly guided by the inter-

national human rights standards and does not bless any deviation of these standards.

Furthermore, the conference proposes for the AL to seek the support of the Technical Assistance Programs at the Office of the UN High Commissioner for Human Rights in the initiation of an effective catalyst for human rights protection in the Arab world.

3. Re-structure the Permanent Commission of Human Rights at the AL to enable it to undertake its role effectively. This requires opening the Commission to the Arab and international human rights NGOs as the established practice in the similar regional and UN bodies. Nevertheless, the conference calls to transform the meetings of the Permanent Commission to a vivid occasions that motivates Arab states that did not ratify the international human rights conventions to promptly ratify them without reservations and to encourage other Arab states that have ratified to drop their previous reservations.

Follow-Up Mechanisms for the Process of Developing a Human Rights Charter in the Arab World

Re-affirming the need to follow-up its recommendations and to reinforce the endeavors aimed at establishing an effective regional mechanism for the protection of human rights, the conference resolves the following:

1. To establish a web site to serve as a focal point for all those interested in the issues of developing a viable human rights protection mechanism in the Arab region.

2. To encourage human rights NGOs in the region, civil society institutions, and all concerned parties to formulate a public opinion that seeks to initiate an effective regional mechanism for the protection of human rights.

3. To work for creating a politically and media lobby that addresses all bodies and institutions that might help to achieve the desired goal including, the Arab Parliament Union, Ministers of Justice, Arab media, UN agencies, and Arab and international civil society institutions.

To organize an annual conference for human rights NGO's in which representatives of governments and national human rights institutions in the Arab world are invited to discuss reports on the current state of human rights. This annual conference should submit its recommendations to the AL and the public, as it will serve as a permanent conscience court for human rights in the Arab world.

Sana'a Declaration on Democracy, Human Rights and the Role of the International Criminal Court

Sana'a Inter-Governmental Regional Conference on Democracy, Human Rights and the Role of the International Criminal Court, January 10–12, 2004

At the conclusion of the Sana'a Inter-Governmental Regional Conference on Democracy, Human Rights and the Role of the International Criminal Court formed by Governmental and Parliamentary Delegations from all the Arab and neighbouring African and Asian countries, organised by the Government of Yemen and the non-governmental organisation No Peace Without Justice, with the participation of 820 participants from 52 countries and representatives from regional and international organisations, as well as representatives of civil society and political parties.

The Conference represented a forum for bringing together representatives of governments, parliaments and legislative bodies to talk about issues related to Democracy and Human Rights issues, the role of civil society, the rule of law and the International Criminal Court, in an open dialogue that is furthering democracy and protecting human rights in the Arab and surrounding countries and underlining achievements in the region in those areas, which is emerging from their social and cultural realities and their heritage and political practice.

During two days of fruitful and profound discussion between participants on those topics, as an inseparable element to reach a consensus of understanding towards questions of the rule of law, democracy and human rights and a common endeavor to reach a common understanding of their dimensions, their interdependency and their repercussions;

Delegations hereby declare they have reached the following principles:

a. Democracy and human rights, which have their origins in faith and culture, are interdependent and inseparable;

b. Cultural and religious diversity is at the core of universally recognised human rights, which should be observed in a spirit of understanding in the application of democratic and human rights principles; this diversity should not be a source of confrontation or clashes but should be a source of dialogue and building bridges of understanding between religions and cultures;

c. Democratic systems protect the rights and interests of everybody without discrimination, especially the rights and interests of disadvantaged and vulnerable groups;

d. Democracy is achieved not only through institutions and laws but also through the actual practice of democratic principles, which should be measured by the degree to which these principles, norms, standards and values are actually implemented and the extent to which they advance the realisation of human rights;

e. The basics of democratic systems is reflected in periodically elected legislatures, representing the citizens in a fair way and ensuring their full participation, in executive bodies that are responsible and committed to principles of good governance and in an independent judiciary that guarantees fair trial rights and protects the rights and freedoms of the people; these principles are the guarantors of good governance, which ensures the protection of human rights;

f. Efforts to ensure a forum for discussion and dialogue must be encouraged in order to exchange ideas, experiences and expertise and to promote participation and political and democratic development among participating countries;

g. The practice of democracy and human rights and enhancing their understanding require overcoming potential threats to the form and substance of democracy, including foreign occupation, imbalances in participation in the international justice system, the concentration and abuse of power, ineffective and unaccountable civil service, poverty, inadequate education, corruption, crimes under international law and discrimination;

h. The effective application of the rule of law is vital to protect democracy and human rights and is the foundation for judicial independence and the application of the separation of powers;

i. A free and independent media is essential for the promotion and protection of democracy and human rights. Pluralism in the media and its privatisation are vital for contributing to the dissemination of human rights information, facilitating informed public participation, promoting tolerance and contributing to governmental accountability. The media should contribute effectively and responsibly towards the strengthening of democracy and human rights knowledge;

j. Proper democratic governance and respect for human rights require a freely functioning, well-organised, vibrant and responsible civil society and a legal framework within which civil society can operate in a spirit of partnership and participation; Civil society should play its role responsibly within the framework of law and the principles of human rights and democracy;

k. The private sector is a vital partner in strengthening the foundations of democracy and human rights; It has a responsibility to work with governments and civil society to enhance progress;

l. The developments in international relations, the increasing international interest in issues of human rights and the rule of law and the serious efforts to stop violations of international law require strong international judicial institutions to prosecute those who commit crimes under international law, in full respect for fundamental fair trial guarantees and the rights of the accused. The participants therefore agree to:

1. Work seriously in order to fulfil the above-stated principles;

2. Strengthen and protect human rights, including people's fundamental rights to express their views and adhere to their religious beliefs and ethnic identity;

3. Occupation is contrary to international law and basic human rights; there should be an end to the occupation of Arab territories and all holy Islamic and Christian sites as well as an end to all violations of human rights, in particular in Palestine, and the civil and political rights of the Palestinian people should be ensured, including their right to self-determination and their right of return according to international resolutions;

4. Empower the role of women and their participation, protecting women from all forms of exploitation and any reduction of women's rights;

5. The establishment of an independent and fair judiciary and the separation of powers;

6. Ensure equality before the law, equal protection under the law and fundamental fair trial guarantees;

7. Support efforts towards sustainable development, which is necessary for the building and strengthening of democracy, including democratic institutions within the State, and for promoting and protecting human rights;

8. Strengthen the role of international judicial institutions, as an important element towards promoting respect for international law and human rights law, including the International Criminal Court;

9. Strengthen democracy and pluralism and the establishment of elected legislative bodies to represent popular will and ensuring the fair representation of all sectors of society;

10. Work towards future modalities of democratic consultation and cooperation among themselves, including civil society, and the establishment of an Arab Democratic Dialogue Forum as an instrument for the promotion of dialogue between diverse actors, for strengthening democracy, human rights and civil liberties, especially freedom of opinion and expression, and strengthening the partnership between public authorities and civil society.

Done in Sana'a, January 12, 2004

Appendix 2
Status of Human Rights Treaty Ratifications, with Notable Reservations, Understandings, and Declarations

Anthony Chase and Kyle M. Ballard

Most human rights activity in the Arab world revolves around individual dissent, persecuted minorities asserting rights claims against the hegemonic state, nongovernmental groups that organize around particular issues and regions, and nascent representatives of civil society that push a broader process of democratization. Part of the Arab world's history with human rights, however, has been a fairly substantial record of formal ratification of international human rights treaties by the region's states. As a general rule, such ratifications have been a cruel joke for anyone who takes human rights seriously, mocking with their hypocrisy those who suffer human rights violations in the region. Nonetheless, these ratifications are worth noting. First, they show that from an early date the region's regimes had some incentive at least to acknowledge the formal validity of international human rights law. Formal consent to human rights treaties mitigates to some degree claims of human rights as a foreign imposition and represents recognition of the legitimacy of human rights. Second, this recognition, however pro forma, is a first step toward the integration of human rights into politics. Even if unintentionally, it validates dialogue around state legal obligations and makes human rights part of a normative debate in the region. This gives a hook for individuals, social groups, and NGOs to assert that the rights regime is not an irrelevant imposition but, to the contrary, responds to political, economic, cultural, social, and civil claims being articulated by Arabs.

In that spirit, this appendix follows gives the state as of 2005 of ratifications of human rights treaties by Arab states. In addition, Kyle Ballard has provided a selection of the reservations, understandings, and declarations (RUDs) that Arab states have taken to these treaty ratifications. This is not meant to be a comprehensive resource for lawyerly research, but rather to give the reader a sense of the common RUDs taken by Arab states as well some of the more particular exceptions that have been claimed.

	CERD[1] *International Convention on the Elimination of All Forms of Racial Discrimination*	*CEDAW Convention on the Elimination of All Forms of Discrimination against Women*	*CESCR International Covenant on Economic, Social and Cultural Rights*	*CCPR International Covenant on Civil and Political Rights*
	Ratified	*Ratified*	*Ratified*	*Ratified*
Algeria	14-Feb-1972	22-May-1996	12-Sep-1989	12-Sep-1989
Bahrain	27-Mar-1990	18-Jun-2002[2]	N/A	N/A
Comoros	22-Sep-2000 (Signed Not Ratified)	31-Oct-1994	N/A	N/A
Djibouti	N/A	2-Dec-1998	5-Nov-2002	5-Nov-2002
Egypt	1-May-1967	18-Sep-1981[3]	14-Jan-1982[4]	14-Jan-1982[5]
Iran	29-Aug-1968	N/A	24-Jun-1975	24-Jun-1975
Iraq	14-Jan-1970	13-Aug-1986[6]	25-Jan-1971	25-Jan-1971
Jordan	30-May-1974	1-Jul-1992	28-May-1975	28-May-1975
Kuwait	15-Oct-1968	2-Sep-1994[7]	21-May-1996	21-May-1996[8]
Lebanon	12-Nov-1971	16-Apr-1997	3-Nov-1972	3-Nov-1972
Libya	3-Jul-1968	16-May-1989[9]	15-May-1970	15-May-1970
Mauritania	13-Dec-1988	10-May-2001[10]	N/A	N/A
Morocco	18-Dec-1970	21-Jun-1993[11]	3-May-1979	3-May-1979
Oman	2-Jan-2003	N/A	N/A	N/A
Qatar	22-Jul-1976	N/A	N/A	N/A
Saudi Arabia	23-Sep-1997[12]	7-Sep-2000[13]	N/A	N/A
Somalia	26-Aug-1975	N/A	24-Jan-1990	24-Jan-1990
Sudan	21-Mar-1977	N/A	18-Mar-1986	18-Mar-1986
Syria	21-Apr-1969	28-May-2003[14]	21-Apr-1969	21-Apr-1969
Tunisia	13-Jan-1967	20-Sep-1985	18-Mar-1969	18-Mar-1969
United Arab Emirates	20-Jun-1974	N/A	N/A	N/A
Yemen	18-Oct-1972	30-May-1984	9-Feb-1987	9-Feb-1987

	CAT *Convention Against Torture and Other Cruel, Inhuman or Degrading Treatment of Punishment*	*CRC* *Convention on the Rights of the Child*	*CPPCG* *Convention on the Prevention and Punishment of the Crime of Genocide*
	Ratified	*Ratified*	*Ratified*
Algeria	12-Sep-1989	16-Apr-1993[15]	31-Oct-63
Bahrain	6-Mar-1998	13-Feb-1992	27-Mar-1990
Comoros	22-Sep-2000 (Signed Not Ratified)	22-Jun-1992	27-Sep-2004
Djibouti	5-Nov-2002	6-Dec-1990[16]	N/A
Egypt	25-Jun-1996	6-Jul-1990	8-Feb-1952
Iran	N/A	13-Jul-1994[17]	14-Aug-1956
Iraq	N/A	15-Jun-1994[18]	20-Jan-1959
Jordan	13-Nov-1991	24-May-1991[19]	3-Apr-1950
Kuwait	8-Mar-1996	21-Oct-1991[20]	7-Mar-1995
Lebanon	5-Oct-2000	14-May-1991	17-Dec-1953
Libya	16-May-1989	15-Apr-1993	16-May-1989
Mauritania	N/A	16-May-1991[21]	N/A
Morocco	21-Jun-1993	21-Jun-1993[22]	24-Jan-1958
Oman	N/A	9-Dec-1996[23]	N/A
Qatar	11-Jan-2000[24]	3-Apr-1995[25]	N/A
Saudi Arabia	23-Sep-1997	26-Jan-1996[26]	13-Jul-1950
Somalia	24-Jan-2000	9-May-2002 (Signed Not Ratified)	N/A
Sudan	4-Jun-1986 (Signed Not Ratified)	3-Aug-1990	13-Oct-2003
Syria	19-Aug-2004	15-Jul-1993[27]	25-Jun-1955
Tunisia	23-Sep-1988	30-Jan-1992	29-Nov-1956
United Arab Emirates	N/A	3-Jan-1997[28]	N/A
Yemen	5-Nov-1991	1-May-1991	9-Feb-1987

	CRC Optional Protocol Armed Conflict	CRC Optional Protocol Sale of Children/Prostitution/ Pornography	CCPR First Optional Protocol	CCPR Second Optional Protocol
	Ratified	Ratified	Ratified	Ratified
Algeria	N/A	N/A	12-Sep-1989	N/A
Bahrain	N/A	N/A	N/A	N/A
Comoros	N/A	N/A	N/A	N/A
Djibouti	N/A	N/A	5-Nov-2002	5-Nov-2002
Egypt	N/A	12-Jul-2002	N/A	N/A
Iran	N/A	N/A	N/A	N/A
Iraq	N/A	N/A	N/A	N/A
Jordan	6-Sep-2000 (Signed Not Ratified)	6-Sep-2000 (Signed Not Ratified)	N/A	N/A
Kuwait	N/A	N/A	N/A	N/A
Lebanon	11-Feb-2002 (Signed Not Ratified)	10-Oct-2001 (Signed Not Ratified)	N/A	N/A
Libya	N/A	18-June-2004	16-May-1989	N/A
Mauritania	N/A	N/A	N/A	N/A
Morocco	22-May-2002	2-Oct-2001	N/A	N/A
Oman	N/A	N/A	N/A	N/A
Qatar	25-Jul-2002	14-Dec-2001[29]	N/A	N/A
Saudi Arabia	N/A	N/A	N/A	N/A
Somalia	N/A	N/A	24-Jan-1990	N/A
Sudan	N/A	N/A	N/A	N/A
Syria	17-Oct-2003	15-May-2003	N/A	N/A
Tunisia	2-Jan-2003	13-Sep-2002	N/A	N/A
United Arab Emirates	N/A	N/A	N/A	N/A
Yemen	N/A	N/A	N/A	N/A

[1]Status current as of 1 October 2004.

[2]**Reservations:** . . . the Kingdom of Bahrain makes reservations with respect to the following provisions of the Convention:
• Article 2, in order to ensure its implementation within the bounds of the provisions of the Islamic Shariʿa;
• Article 16, in so far as it is incompatible with the provisions of the Islamic Shariʿa;

[3]**General reservation on article 2:** The Arab Republic of Egypt is willing to comply with the content of this article, provided that such compliance does not run counter to the Islamic Shariʿa.

In respect of article 16: Reservation to the text of article 16 concerning the equality of men and women in all matters relating to marriage and family relations during the marriage and upon its dissolution, without prejudice to the Islamic Shariʿa's provisions whereby women are accorded rights equivalent to those of their spouses so as to ensure a just balance between them. This is out of respect for the sacrosanct nature of the firm religious beliefs which govern marital relations in Egypt and which may not be called in question and in view of the fact that one of the most important bases of these relations is an equivalency of rights and duties so as to ensure complementary which guarantees true equality between the spouses. The provisions of the Shariʿa lay down that the husband shall pay bridal money to the wife and maintain her fully and shall also make a payment to her upon divorce, whereas the wife retains full rights over her property and is not obliged to spend anything on her keep. The Shariʿa therefore restricts the wife's rights to divorce by making it contingent on a judge's ruling, whereas no such restriction is laid down in the case of the husband.

[4]**Declaration:** . . . Taking into consideration the provisions of the Islamic Shariʿa and the fact that they do not conflict with the text annexed to the instrument, we accept, support and ratify it . . .

[5]**Declaration:** [. . . Taking into consideration the provisions of the Islamic Shariʿa and the fact that they do not conflict with the text annexed to the instrument, we accept, support and ratify it . . .] (Chapter IV.3, Multilateral Treaties Deposited with the Secretary-General)

[6]**Reservations:** Approval of and accession to this Convention shall not mean that the Republic of Iraq is bound by the provisions of article 2, paragraphs (f) and (g), of article 9, paragraphs 1 and 2, nor of article 16 of the Convention. The reservation to this last-mentioned article shall be without prejudice to the provisions of the Islamic Shariʿa according women rights equivalent to the rights of their spouses so as to ensure a just balance between them. Iraq also enters a reservation to article 29, paragraph 1, of this Convention with regard to the principle of international arbitration in connection with the interpretation or application of this Convention.

[7]**Reservations:** Article 16 (f) The Government of the State of Kuwait declares that it does not consider itself bound by the provision contained in article 16 (f) inasmuch as it conflicts with the provisions of the Islamic Shariʿa, Islam being the official religion of the State.

[8]**Interpretative declaration regarding article 23:** The Government of Kuwait declares that the matters addressed by article 23 are governed by personal-status law, which is based on Islamic law. Where the provisions of that article conflict with Kuwaiti law, Kuwait will apply its national law.

[9]**Reservation:** Article 2 of the Convention shall be implemented with due regard for the peremptory norms of the Islamic Shariʿa relating to determination of the inheritance portions of the estate of a deceased person, whether female or male.

Reservation: The implementation of paragraph 16 (c) and (d) of the Convention shall be without prejudice to any of the rights guaranteed to women by the Islamic Shariʿa.

[10]**Reservation:** "Having seen and examined the United Nations Convention on the Elimination of All Forms of Discrimination against Women, adopted by the United Nations General Assembly on 18 December 1979, have approved and do approve it in each and every one of its parts which are not contrary to Islamic Shariʿa and are in accordance with our Constitution.

[11]**Declarations: With regard to article 2:**
The Government of the Kingdom of Morocco express its readiness to apply the provisions of this article provided that:
• They do not conflict with the provisions of the Islamic Shariʿa. It should be noted that certain of the provisions contained in the Moroccan Code of Personal Status according women rights that differ from the rights conferred on men may not be infringed upon or abrogated because they derive primarily from the Islamic Shariʿa, which strives, among its other objectives, to strike a balance between the spouses in order to preserve the coherence of family life.

Reservation: With regard to article 16:
The Government of the Kingdom of Morocco makes a reservation with regard to the provisions of this article, particularly those relating to the equality of men and women, in respect of rights and responsibilities on entry into and at dissolution of marriage. Equality of this kind is considered incompatible with the Islamic Shariʿa, which guarantees to each of the spouses rights and responsibilities within a framework of equilibrium and complementary in order to preserve the sacred bond of matrimony.

The provisions of the Islamic Shariʿa oblige the husband to provide a nuptial gift upon marriage and to support his family, while the wife is not required by law to support the family.

Further, at dissolution of marriage, the husband is obliged to pay maintenance. In contrast, the wife enjoys complete freedom of disposition of her property during the marriage and upon its dissolution without supervision by the husband, the husband having no jurisdiction over his wife's property.

For these reasons, the Islamic Shari'a confers the right of divorce on a woman only by decision of a Shari'a judge.

[12]**Reservations:** [The Government of Saudi Arabia declares that it will] implement the provisions [of the above Convention], providing these do not conflict with the precepts of the Islamic Shari'a.

[13]**Reservations:** "In case of contradiction between any term of the Convention and the norms of Islamic law, the Kingdom is not under obligation to observe the contradictory terms of the Convention.

[14]**Reservation:** . . . subject to reservations to article 2; article 9, paragraph 2, concerning the grant of a woman's nationality to her children; article 15, paragraph 4, concerning freedom of movement and of residence and domicile; article 16, paragraph 1 (c), (d), (f) and (g), concerning equal rights and responsibilities during marriage and at its dissolution with regard to guardianship, the right to choose a family name, maintenance and adoption; article 16, paragraph 2, concerning the legal effect of the betrothal and the marriage of a child, inasmuch as this provision is incompatible with the provisions of the Islamic Shari'a; and article 29, paragraph 1, concerning arbitration between States in the event of a dispute.

[15]**Interpretative declarations: Article 14, paragraphs 1 and 2:**
The provisions of paragraphs 1 and 2 of article 14 shall be interpreted by the Algerian Government in compliance with the basic foundations of the Algerian legal system, in particular:
• With the Constitution, which stipulates in its article 2 that Islam is the State religion and in its article 35 that "there shall be no infringement of the inviolability of the freedom of conviction and the inviolability of the freedom of opinion";
• With Law No. 84–11 of 9 June 1984, comprising the Family Code, which stipulates that a child's education is to take place in accordance with the religion of its father.
• Article 26 of the same Code, which provides that "national and foreign periodicals and specialized publications, whatever their nature or purpose, must not contain any illustration, narrative, information or insertion contrary to Islamic morality, national values or human rights or advocate racism, fanaticism and treason. Further, such publications must contain no publicity or advertising that may promote violence and delinquency."

[16]**Declaration:** [The Government of Djibouti] shall not consider itself bound by any provisions or articles that are incompatible with its religion and its traditional values.

[17]**Reservation upon signature:** "The Islamic Republic of Iran is making reservation to the articles and provisions which may be contrary to the Islamic Shari'a, and preserves the right to make such particular declaration, upon its ratification."

Reservation upon ratification: "The Government of the Islamic Republic of Iran reserves the right not to apply any provisions or articles of the Convention that are incompatible with Islamic Laws and the international legislation in effect."

[18]**Reservation:** The Government of Iraq has seen fit to accept [the Convention] . . . subject to a reservation in respect to article 14, paragraph 1, concerning the child's freedom of religion, as allowing a child to change his or her religion runs counter to the provisions of the Islamic Shari'a.

[19]**Reservation:** The Hashemite Kingdom of Jordan expresses its reservation and does not consider itself bound by articles 14, 20 and 21 of the Convention, which grant the child the right to freedom of choice of religion and concern the question of adoption, since they are at variance with the precepts of the tolerant Islamic Shari'a.

[20]**Declarations: Article 21:** The State of Kuwait, as it adheres to the provisions of the Islamic Shari'a as the main source of legislation, strictly bans abandoning the Islamic religion and does not therefore approve adoption.

Reservation upon signature: "[Kuwait expresses] reservations on all provisions of the Convention that are incompatible with the laws of Islamic Shari'a and the local statutes in effect."

[21]**Reservation:** In signing this important Convention, the Islamic Republic of Mauritania is making reservations to articles or provisions which may be contrary to the beliefs and values of Islam, the religion of the Mauritania People and State.

[22]**Reservation:** The Kingdom of Morocco, whose Constitution guarantees to all the freedom to pursue his religious affairs, makes a reservation to the provisions of article 14, which accords children freedom of religion, in view of the fact that Islam is the State religion

[23] **Reservations:** The Sultanate does not consider itself to be bound by those provisions of article 14 of the Convention that accord a child the right to choose his or her religion or those of its article 30 that allow a child belonging to a religious minority to profess his or her own religion.

[24]**Reservations:** Any interpretation of the provisions of the Convention that is incompatible with the precepts of Islamic law and the Islamic religion;

[25]**Reservation made upon signature and confirmed upon ratification:** [The State of Qatar] enter(s) a general reservation by the State of Qatar concerning provisions incompatible with Islamic Law.

[26]**Reservation:** [The Government of Saudi Arabia enters] reservations with respect to all such articles as are in conflict with the provisions of Islamic law.

[27]**Reservations:** The Syrian Arab Republic has reservations on the Convention's provisions which are not in conformity with the Syrian Arab legislations and with the Islamic Shari'a principles, in particular the content of article (14) related to the Right of the Child to the freedom of religion, and articles 2 and 21 concerning the adoption.

[28]**Reservations: Article 14:** The United Arab Emirates shall be bound by the tenor of this article to the extent that it does not conflict with the principles and provisions of Islamic law.

Reservations: Article 21: Since, given its commitment to the principles of Islamic law, the United Arab Emirates does not permit the system of adoption, it has reservations with respect to this article and does not deem it necessary to be bound by its provisions.

[29]**Reservation:** . . . subject to a general reservation concerning any provisions in the protocol that are in conflict with the Islamic Shari'a.

Reservations, Understandings, and Declarations by Country

Algeria

CAT

Declaration re: Article 21

(Unless otherwise indicated, the declarations were made upon ratification, accession, or succession)

The Algerian Government declares, pursuant to article 21 of the Convention, that it recognizes the competence of the Committee Against Torture to receive and consider communications to the effect that a State Party claims that another State Party is not fulfilling its obligations under this Convention.

Declaration re: Article 22
(Unless otherwise indicated, the declarations were made upon ratification, accession, or succession)

The Algerian Government declares, pursuant to article 22 of the Convention, that it recognizes the competence of the Committee to receive and consider communications from or on behalf of individuals subject to its jurisdiction who claim to be victims of a violation by a State Party of the provisions of the Convention.

CCPR

Reservations and Declarations
(Unless otherwise indicated, the reservations and declarations were made upon ratification, accession, or succession)

Interpretive declarations:

1. The Algerian Government interprets article 1, which is common to the two Covenants, as in no case impairing the inalienable right of all peoples to self-determination and to control over their natural wealth and resources.

It further considers that the maintenance of the State of dependence of certain territories referred to in article 1, paragraph 3, of the two Covenants and in article 14 of the Covenant on Economic, Social and Cultural Rights is contrary to the purposes and principles of the United Nations, to the Charter of the Organization and to the Declaration on the Granting of Independence to Colonial Countries and Peoples [General Assembly resolution 1514 (XV)].

2. The Algerian Government interprets the provisions of article 8 of the Covenant on Economic, Social and Cultural Rights and article 22 of the Covenant on Civil and Political Rights as making the law the framework for action by the State with respect to the organization and exercise of the right to organize.

3. The Algerian Government considers that the provisions of article 13, paragraphs 3 and 4, of the Covenant on Economic, Social and Cultural Rights can in no case impair its right freely to organize its educational system.

4. The Algerian Government interprets the provisions of article 23, paragraph 4, of the Covenant on Civil and Political Rights regarding the

rights and responsibilities of spouses as to marriage, during marriage and at its dissolution as in no way impairing the essential foundations of the Algerian legal system.]

(Chapter IV.3, Multilateral Treaties Deposited with the Secretary-General)

CEDAW

Reservations and Declarations
(Unless otherwise indicated, the reservations and declarations were made upon ratification, accession, or succession)

Reservations:

Article 2:

The Government of the People's Democratic Republic of Algeria declares that it is prepared to apply the provisions of this article on condition that they do not conflict with the provisions of the Algerian Family Code.

Article 9, paragraph 2:

The Government of the People's Democratic Republic of Algeria wishes to express its reservations concerning the provisions of article 9, paragraph 2, which are incompatible with the provisions of the Algerian Nationality code and the Algerian Family Code.

The Algerian Nationality code allows a child to take the nationality of the mother only when:

• the father is either unknown or stateless;

• the child is born in Algeria to an Algerian mother and a foreign father who was born in Algeria;

• moreover, a child born in Algeria to an Algerian mother and a foreign father who was not born on Algerian territory may, under article 26 of the Algerian Nationality Code, acquire the nationality of the mother providing the Ministry of Justice does not object.

Article 41 of the Algerian Family Code states that a child is affiliated to its father through legal marriage.

Article 43 of that Code states that "the child is affiliated to its father if it is born in the 10 months following the date of separation or death."

Article 15, paragraph 4:

The Government of the People's Democratic Republic of Algeria declares that the provisions of article 15, paragraph 4, concerning the right of women to choose their residence and domicile should not be interpreted in such a manner as to contradict the provisions of chapter 4 (art. 37) of the Algerian Family Code.

Article 16:

The Government of the People's Democratic Republic of Algeria declares that the provisions of article 16 concerning equal rights for men and women in all matters relating to marriage, both during marriage and at its dissolution, should not contradict the provisions of the Algerian Family Code.

Article 29:

The Government of the People's Democratic Republic of Algeria does not consider itself bound by article 29, paragraph 1, which states that any dispute between two or more Parties concerning the interpretation or application of the Convention which is not settled by negotiation shall, at the request of one of them, be submitted to arbitration or to the International Court of Justice.

The Government of the People's Democratic Republic of Algeria holds that no such dispute can be submitted to arbitration or to the Court of International Justice except with the consent of all the parties to the dispute.

CERD

Declaration re: Article 14

12 September 1989

The Algerian Government declares, pursuant to article 14 of the Convention, that it recognizes the competence of the Committee to receive and consider communications from individuals or groups of individuals within its jurisdiction claiming to be victims of a violation by it of any of the rights set forth in the Convention.

CESCR

Reservations and Declarations
(Unless otherwise indicated, the reservations and declarations were made upon ratification, accession, or succession)

Interpretative declarations:

1. The Algerian Government interprets article 1, which is common to the two Covenants, as in no case impairing the inalienable right of all peoples to self-determination and to control over their natural wealth and resources.

It further considers that the maintenance of the State of dependence of certain territories referred to in article 1, paragraph 3, of the two Covenants and in article 14 of the Covenant on Economic, Social and Cultural Rights is contrary to the purposes and principles of the United Nations, to the Charter of the Organization and to the Declaration on the Granting of Independence to Colonial Countries and Peoples (General Assembly resolution 1514 (XV)).

2. The Algerian Government interprets the provisions of article 8 of the Covenant on Economic, Social and Cultural Rights and article 22 of the Covenant on Civil and Political Rights as making the law the framework for action by the State with respect to the organization and exercise of the right to organize.

3. The Algerian Government considers that the provisions of article 13, paragraphs 3 and 4, of the Covenant on Economic, Social and Cultural Rights can in no case impair its right freely to organize its educational system.

4. The Algerian Government interprets the provisions of article 23, paragraph 4, of the Covenant on Civil and Political Rights regarding the rights and responsibilities of spouses as to marriage, during marriage and at its dissolution as in no way impairing the essential foundations of the Algerian legal system.

CRC

Reservations and Declarations
(Unless otherwise indicated, the reservations and declarations were made upon ratification, accession, or succession)

Interpretative declarations:

Article 14, paragraphs 1 and 2:

The provisions of paragraphs 1 and 2 of article 14 shall be interpreted by the Algerian Government in compliance with the basic foundations of the Algerian legal system, in particular:

• With the Constitution, which stipulates in its article 2 that Islam is the State religion and in its article 35 that "there shall be no infringement of the inviolability of the freedom of conviction and the inviolability of the freedom of opinion";

• With Law No. 84-11 of 9 June 1984, comprising the Family Code, which stipulates that a child's education is to take place in accordance with the religion of its father.

Articles 13, 16, and 17:

Articles 13, 16, and 17 shall be applied while taking account of the interest of the child and the need to safeguard its physical and mental integrity. In this framework, the Algerian Government shall interpret the provisions of these articles while taking account of:

• The provisions of the Penal Code, in particular those sections relating to breaches of public order, to public decency and to the incitement of minors to immorality and debauchery;

• The provisions of Law No. 90-07 of 3 April 1990, comprising the Information Code, and particularly its article 24 stipulating that "the director of a publication destined for children must be assisted by an educational advisory body";

• Article 26 of the same Code, which provides that "national and foreign periodicals and specialized publications, whatever their nature or purpose, must not contain any illustration, narrative, information or insertion contrary to Islamic morality, national values or human rights or advocate racism, fanaticism and treason. Further, such publications must contain no publicity or advertising that may promote violence and delinquency."

CPPCG

The Democratic and Popular Republic of Algeria does not consider itself bound by article IX of the Convention, which confers on the International Court of Justice jurisdiction in all disputes relating to the said Convention.

The Democratic and Popular Republic of Algeria declares that no provision of article VI of the said Convention shall be interpreted as depriving its tribunals of jurisdiction in cases of genocide or other acts enumerated in article III which have been committed in its territory or as conferring such jurisdiction on foreign tribunals.

International tribunals may, as an exceptional measure, be recognized as having jurisdiction, in cases in which the Algerian Government has given its express approval.

The Democratic and Popular Republic of Algeria declares that it does not accept the terms of article XII of the Convention and considers that all the provisions of the said Convention should apply to Non-Self-Governing Territories, including Trust Territories.

Bahrain

CAT

Reservations and Declarations
(Unless otherwise indicated, the reservations and declarations were made upon ratification, accession, or succession)

Reservations:

. . .

2. The State of Bahrain does not consider itself bound by paragraph 1 of article 30 of the Convention.

CEDAW

Reservations and Declarations

(Unless otherwise indicated, the reservations and declarations were made upon ratification, accession, or succession)

Reservations:

. . . the Kingdom of Bahrain makes reservations with respect to the following provisions of the Convention:

• Article 2, in order to ensure its implementation within the bounds of the provisions of the Islamic Shariʿa;

• Article 9, paragraph 2;

• Article 15, paragraph 4;

• Article 16, in so far as it is incompatible with the provisions of the Islamic Shariʿa;

• Article 29, paragraph 1.

CERD

Reservations and Declarations

(Unless otherwise indicated, the reservations and declarations were made upon ratification, accession, or succession)

Reservations:

With reference to article 22 of the Convention, the Government of the State of Bahrain declares that, for the submission of any dispute in terms of this article to the jurisdiction of the International Court of Justice, the express consent of all the parties to the dispute is required in each case.

Moreover, the accession by the State of Bahrain to the said Convention shall in no way constitute recognition of Israel or be a cause for the establishment of any relations of any kind therewith.

CPPCG

Reservations:

With reference to article IX of the Convention the Government of the State of Bahrain declares that, for the submission of any dispute in terms of this article to the jurisdiction of the International Court of Justice, the express consent of all the parties to the dispute is required in each case.

Moreover, the accession by the State of Bahrain to the said Convention shall in no way constitute recognition of Israel or be a cause for the establishment of any relations of any kind therewith.

Djibouti

CRC

Reservations and Declarations
(Unless otherwise indicated, the reservations and declarations were made upon ratification, accession, or succession)

Declaration:

[The Government of Djibouti] shall not consider itself bound by any provisions or articles that are incompatible with its religion and its traditional values.

Egypt

CCPR

Reservations and Declarations
(Unless otherwise indicated, the reservations and declarations were made upon ratification, accessio,n or succession)

[Declaration:

. . . Taking into consideration the provisions of the Islamic Shari'a and the fact that they do not conflict with the text annexed to the instrument, we accept, support and ratify it . . .]
(Chapter IV.3, Multilateral Treaties Deposited with the Secretary-General)

CEDAW

Reservations and Declarations
(Unless otherwise indicated, the reservations and declarations were made upon ratification, accession, or succession)

Reservation made upon signature and confirmed upon ratification:

In respect of article 9

Reservation to the text of article 9, paragraph 2, concerning the granting to women of equal rights with men with respect to the nationality of their children, without prejudice to the acquisition by a child born of a marriage of the nationality of his father. This is in order to prevent a child's acquisition of two nationalities where his parents are of different nationalities, since this may be prejudicial to his future. It is clear that the child's acquisition of his father's nationality is the procedure most suitable for the child and that this does not infringe upon the principle of equality between men and women, since it is customary for a woman to agree, upon marrying an alien, that her children shall be of the father's nationality.

In respect of article 16

Reservation to the text of article 16 concerning the equality of men and women in all matters relating to marriage and family relations during the marriage and upon its dissolution, without prejudice to the Islamic Shari'a's provisions whereby women are accorded rights equivalent to those of their spouses so as to ensure a just balance between them. This is out of respect for the sacrosanct nature of the firm religious beliefs which govern marital relations in Egypt and which may not be called in question and in view of the fact that one of the most important bases of these relations is an equivalency of rights and duties so as to ensure complementary which guarantees true equality between the spouses. The provisions of the Shari'a lay down that the husband shall pay bridal money to the wife and maintain her fully and shall also make a payment to her upon divorce, whereas the wife retains full rights over her property and is not obliged to spend anything on her keep. The Shari'a therefore restricts the wife's rights to divorce by making it contingent on a judge's ruling, whereas no such restriction is laid down in the case of the husband.

In respect of article 29

The Egyptian delegation also maintains the reservation contained in article 29, paragraph 2, concerning the right of a State signatory to the Convention to declare that it does not consider itself bound by paragraph 1 of that article concerning the submission to an arbitral body of any dispute which may arise between States concerning the interpretation or application of the Convention. This is in order to avoid being bound by the system of arbitration in this field.

Reservation made upon ratification:

General reservation on article 2

The Arab Republic of Egypt is willing to comply with the content of this article, provided that such compliance does not run counter to the Islamic Shari'a.

CERD

Reservations and Declarations
(Unless otherwise indicated, the reservations and declarations were made upon ratification, accession, or succession)

The United Arab Republic does not consider itself bound by the provisions of article 22 of the Convention, under which any dispute between two or more States Parties with respect to the interpretation or application of the Convention is, at the request of any of the parties to the dispute, to be referred to the International Court of Justice for decision, and it states that, in each individual case, the consent of all parties to such a dispute is necessary for referring the dispute to the International Court of Justice.

CESCR

Reservations and Declarations
(Unless otherwise indicated, the reservations and declarations were made upon ratification, accession, or succession)

Declaration:

. . . Taking into consideration the provisions of the Islamic Shari'a and the fact that they do not conflict with the text annexed to the instrument, we accept, support and ratify it . . .

Iran

CRC

Reservations and Declarations
(Unless otherwise indicated, the reservations and declarations were made upon ratification, accession, or succession)

Upon signature:

Reservation:

The Islamic Republic of Iran is making reservation to the articles and provisions which may be contrary to the Islamic Shariʿa, and preserves the right to make such particular declaration, upon its ratification.

Upon ratification:

Reservation:

The Government of the Islamic Republic of Iran reserves the right not to apply any provisions or articles of the Convention that are incompatible with Islamic Laws and the international legislation in effect.

Iraq

CCPR

Reservations and Declarations
(Unless otherwise indicated, the reservations and declarations were made upon ratification, accession, or succession)

[Upon signature and confirmed upon ratification:

The entry of the Republic of Iraq as a party to the International Covenant on Economic, Social and Cultural Rights and the International Covenant on Civil and Political Rights shall in no way signify recognition of Israel nor shall it entail any obligation towards Israel under the said two Covenants.

The entry of the Republic of Iraq as a party to the above two Covenants shall not constitute entry by it as a party to the Optional Protocol to the International Covenant on Civil and Political Rights.

Upon ratification:

Ratification by Iraq . . . shall in no way signify recognition of Israel nor shall it be conducive to entry with her into such dealings as are regulated by the said [Covenant].]
(Chapter IV.3, Multilateral Treaties Deposited with the Secretary-General)

CEDAW

Reservations and Declarations
(Unless otherwise indicated, the reservations and declarations were made upon ratification, accession, or succession)

Reservations:

1. Approval of and accession to this Convention shall not mean that the Republic of Iraq is bound by the provisions of article 2, paragraphs (f) and (g), of article 9, paragraphs 1 and 2, nor of article 16 of the Convention. The reservation to this last-mentioned article shall be without prejudice to the provisions of the Islamic Shari'a according women rights equivalent to the rights of their spouses so as to ensure a just balance between them. Iraq also enters a reservation to article 29, paragraph 1, of this Convention with regard to the principle of international arbitration in connection with the interpretation or application of this Convention.

2. This approval in no way implies recognition of or entry into any relations with Israel.

CERD

Reservations and Declarations
(Unless otherwise indicated, the reservations and declarations were made upon ratification, accession, or succession)

Upon signature:

The Ministry for Foreign Affairs of the Republic of Iraq hereby declares that signature for and on behalf of the Republic of Iraq of the Convention on the Elimination of All Forms of Racial Discrimination, which was adopted by the General Assembly of the United Nations on 21 December 1965, as well as approval by the Arab States of the said Convention and entry into it by their respective governments, shall in no way signify recognition of Israel or lead to entry by the Arab States into such dealings with Israel as may be regulated by the said Convention.

Furthermore, the Government of the Republic of Iraq does not consider itself bound by the provisions of article twenty-two of the Convention afore-mentioned and affirms its reservation that it does not accept the compulsory jurisdiction of the International Court of Justice provided for in the said article.

Upon ratification:

1. The acceptance and ratification of the Convention by Iraq shall in no way signify recognition of Israel or be conducive to entry by Iraq into such dealings with Israel as are regulated by the Convention;

2. Iraq does not accept the provisions of article 22 of the Convention, concerning the compulsory jurisdiction of the International Court of Justice. The Republic of Iraq does not consider itself to be bound by the provisions of article 22 of the Convention and deems it necessary that in all cases the approval of all parties to the dispute be secured before the case is referred to the International Court of Justice.

CESCR

Reservations and Declarations
(Unless otherwise indicated, the reservations and declarations were made upon ratification, accession, or succession)

Upon signature and confirmed upon ratification:

"The entry of the Republic of Iraq as a party to the International Covenant on Economic, Social and Cultural Rights and the International Covenant on Civil and Political Rights shall in no way signify recognition of Israel nor shall it entail any obligation towards Israel under the said two Covenants."

"The entry of the Republic of Iraq as a party to the above two Covenants shall not constitute entry by it as a party to the Optional Protocol to the International Covenant on Civil and Political Rights."

Upon ratification:

"Ratification by Iraq . . . shall in no way signify recognition of Israel nor shall it be conducive to entry with her into such dealings as are regulated by the said [Covenant]."

CRC

Reservations and Declarations
(Unless otherwise indicated, the reservations and declarations were made upon ratification, accession, or succession)

Reservation:

The Government of Iraq has seen fit to accept [the Convention] . . . subject to a reservation in respect to article 14, paragraph 1, concerning the child's freedom of religion, as allowing a child to change his or her religion runs counter to the provisions of the Islamic Shari'a.

Jordan

CEDAW

Reservations and Declarations
(Unless otherwise indicated, the reservations and declarations were made upon ratification, accession, or succession)

Declaration made upon signature and confirmed upon ratification:

Jordan does not consider itself bound by the following provisions:

1. Article 9, paragraph 2;

2. Article 15, paragraph 4 (a wife's residence is with her husband);

3. Article 16, paragraph (1) (c), relating to the rights arising upon the dissolution of marriage with regard to maintenance and compensation;

4. Article 16, paragraph (1) (d) and (g).

CRC

Reservations and Declarations
(Unless otherwise indicated, the reservations and declarations were made upon ratification, accession, or succession)

Reservation:

The Hashemite Kingdom of Jordan expresses its reservation and does not consider itself bound by articles 14, 20, and 21 of the Convention, which grant the child the right to freedom of choice of religion and concern the question of adoption, since they are at variance with the precepts of the tolerant Islamic Shari'a.

Kuwait

CAT

Reservations and Declarations
(Unless otherwise indicated, the reservations and declarations were made upon ratification, accession, or succession)

Reservation:

With reservations as to article (20) and the provision of paragraph (1) from article (30) of the Convention.

CCPR

Reservations and Declarations
(Unless otherwise indicated, the reservations and declarations were made upon ratification, accession, or succession)

Interpretative declaration regarding article 2, paragraph 1, and article 3:

Although the Government of Kuwait endorses the worthy principles embodied in these two articles as consistent with the provisions of the Kuwait Constitution in general and of its article 29 in particular, the rights to which the articles refer must be exercised within the limits set by Kuwaiti law.

Interpretative declaration regarding article 23:

The Government of Kuwait declares that the matters addressed by article 23 are governed by personal-status law, which is based on Islamic law. Where the provisions of that article conflict with Kuwaiti law, Kuwait will apply its national law.

Reservations concerning article 25 (b):

The Government of Kuwait wishes to formulate a reservation with regard to article 25(b). The provisions of this paragraph conflict with the Kuwaiti electoral law, which restricts the right to stand and vote in elections to males.

It further declares that the provisions of the article shall not apply to members of the armed forces or the police.

CEDAW

Reservations and Declarations
(Unless otherwise indicated, the reservations and declarations were made upon ratification, accession, or succession)

Reservations:

1. Article 7 (a)

The Government of Kuwait enters a reservation regarding article 7(a), inasmuch as the provision contained in that paragraph conflicts with the Kuwaiti Electoral Act, under which the right to be eligible for election and to vote is restricted to males.

2. Article 9, paragraph 2

The Government of Kuwait reserves its right not to implement the provision contained in article 9, paragraph 2, of the Convention, inasmuch as it runs counter to the Kuwaiti Nationality Act, which stipulates that a child's nationality shall be determined by that of his father.

3. Article 16(f)

The Government of the State of Kuwait declares that it does not consider itself bound by the provision contained in article 16(f) inasmuch as it conflicts with the provisions of the Islamic Shariʿa , Islam being the official religion of the State.

4. The Government of Kuwait declares that it is not bound by the provision contained in article 29, paragraph 1.

CERD

Reservations and Declarations
(Unless otherwise indicated, the reservations and declarations were made upon ratification, accession, or succession)

In acceding to the said Convention, the Government of the State of Kuwait takes the view that its accession does not in any way imply recognition of Israel, nor does it oblige it to apply the provisions of the Convention in respect of the said country.

The Government of the State of Kuwait does not consider itself bound by the provisions of article 22 of the Convention, under which any dispute between two or more States Parties with respect to the interpretation or application of the Convention is, at the request of any party to the dispute, to be referred to the International Court of Justice for decision, and it states that, in each individual case, the consent of all parties to such a dispute is necessary for referring the dispute to the International Court of Justice.

CESCR

Reservations and Declarations
(Unless otherwise indicated, the reservations and declarations were made upon ratification, accession, or succession)

Interpretative declaration regarding article 2, paragraph 2, and article 3:

Although the Government of Kuwait endorses the worthy principles embodied in article 2, paragraph 2, and article 3 as consistent with the provisions of the Kuwait Constitution in general and of its article 29 in particular, it declares that the rights to which the articles refer must be exercised within the limits set by Kuwaiti law.

Interpretative declaration regarding article 9:

The Government of Kuwait declares that while Kuwaiti legislation safeguards the rights of all Kuwaiti and non-Kuwaiti workers, social security provisions apply only to Kuwaitis.

Reservation concerning article 8, paragraph 1 (d):

The Government of Kuwait reserves the right not to apply the provisions of article 8, paragraph 1 (d).

CRC

Reservations and Declarations
(Unless otherwise indicated, the reservations and declarations were made upon ratification, accession, or succession)

Upon signature:

Reservation:

[Kuwait expresses] reservations on all provisions of the Convention that are incompatible with the laws of Islamic Shariʿa and the local statutes in effect.

Upon ratification:

Declarations:

Article 7:

The State of Kuwait understands the concepts of this article to signify the right of the child who was born in Kuwait and whose parents are unknown (parentless) to be granted the Kuwaiti nationality as stipulated by the Kuwaiti Nationality Laws.

Article 21:

The State of Kuwait, as it adheres to the provisions of the Islamic Shariʿa as the main source of legislation, strictly bans abandoning the Islamic religion and does not therefore approve adoption.

Lebanon

CEDAW

Reservations and Declarations
(Unless otherwise indicated, the reservations and declarations were made upon ratification, accession, or succession)

Reservations:

The Government of the Lebanese Republic enters reservations regarding article 9 (2), and article 16(1)(c) (d) (f) and (g) (regarding the right to choose a family name).

In accordance with paragraph 2 of article 29, the Government of the Lebanese Republic declares that it does not consider itself bound by the provisions of paragraph 1 of that article.

CERD

Reservations and Declarations
(Unless otherwise indicated, the reservations and declarations were made upon ratification, accession, or succession)

The Republic of Lebanon does not consider itself bound by the provisions of article 22 of the Convention, under which any dispute between two or more States Parties with respect to the interpretation or application of the Convention is, at the request of any party to the dispute, to be referred to the International Court of Justice for decision, and it states that, in each individual case, the consent of all States parties to such a dispute is necessary for referring the dispute to the International Court of Justice

Libya

CCPR

Reservations and Declarations
(Unless otherwise indicated, the reservations and declarations were made upon ratification, accession, or succession)

["The acceptance and the accession to this Covenant by the Libyan Arab Republic shall in no way signify a recognition of Israel or be conducive to entry by the Libyan Arab Republic into such dealings with Israel as are regulated by the Covenant."]

(Chapter IV.3, Multilateral Treaties Deposited with the Secretary-General)

CEDAW

Reservations and Declarations
(Unless otherwise indicated, the reservations and declarations were made upon ratification, accession, or succession)

Reservation:

1. Article 2 of the Convention shall be implemented with due regard for the peremptory norms of the Islamic Shari'a relating to determination of the inheritance portions of the estate of a deceased person, whether female or male.

2. The implementation of paragraph 16(c) and (d) of the Convention shall be without prejudice to any of the rights guaranteed to women by the Islamic Shari'a.

CERD

Reservations and Declarations
(Unless otherwise indicated, the reservations and declarations were made upon ratification, accession, or succession)

(a) The Kingdom of Libya does not consider itself bound by the provisions of article 22 of the Convention, under which any dispute between two or more States Parties with respect to the interpretation or application of the Convention is, at the request of any of the parties to the dispute, to be referred to the International Court of Justice for decision, and it states that, in each individual case, the consent of all parties to such a dispute is necessary for referring the dispute to the International Court of Justice.

(b) It is understood that the accession to this Convention does not mean in any way a recognition of Israel by the Government of the Kingdom of Libya. Furthermore, no treaty relations will arise between the Kingdom of Libya and Israel.

CESCR

Reservations and Declarations
(Unless otherwise indicated, the reservations and declarations were made upon ratification, accession, or succession)

The acceptance and the accession to this Covenant by the Libyan Arab Republic shall in no way signify a recognition of Israel or be conducive to entry by the Libyan Arab Republic into such dealings with Israel as are regulated by the Covenant.

Mauretania

CEDAW

Reservations and Declarations
(Unless otherwise indicated, the reservations and declarations were made upon ratification, accession, or succession)

Reservation:

Having seen and examined the United Nations Convention on the Elimination of All Forms of Discrimination against Women, adopted by the

United Nations General Assembly on 18 December 1979, have approved and do approve it in each and every one of its parts which are not contrary to Islamic Shari'a and are in accordance with our Constitution.

CRC

Reservations and Declarations
(Unless otherwise indicated, the reservations and declarations were made upon ratification, accession, or succession)

Upon signature:

Reservation:

In signing this important Convention, the Islamic Republic of Mauritania is making reservations to articles or provisions which may be contrary to the beliefs and values of Islam, the religion of the Mauritania People and State.

Morocco

CAT

Reservations and Declarations
(Unless otherwise indicated, the reservations and declarations were made upon ratification, accession, or succession)

Declaration made upon signature and confirmed upon ratification:

Declaration:

The Government of the Kingdom of Morocco does not recognize the competence of the Committee provided for in article 20.

The Government of the Kingdom of Morocco does not consider itself bound by paragraph 1 of the same article.

CEDAW

Reservations and Declarations
(Unless otherwise indicated, the reservations and declarations were made upon ratification, accession, or succession)

Declarations:

1. With regard to article 2:
The Government of the Kingdom of Morocco express its readiness to apply the provisions of this article provided that:

• They are without prejudice to the constitutional requirement that regulate the rules of succession to the throne of the Kingdom of Morocco;

• They do not conflict with the provisions of the Islamic Shari'a. It should be noted that certain of the provisions contained in the Moroccan Code of Personal Status according women rights that differ from the rights conferred on men may not be infringed upon or abrogated because they derive primarily from the Islamic Shari'a, which strives, among its other objectives, to strike a balance between the spouses in order to preserve the coherence of family life.

2. With regard to article 15, paragraph 4:

The Government of the Kingdom of Morocco declares that it can only be bound by the provisions of this paragraph, in particular those relating to the right of women to choose their residence and domicile, to the extent that they are not incompatible with articles 34 and 36 of the Moroccan Code of Personal Status.

Reservation:

1. With regard to article 9, paragraph 2:

The Government of the Kingdom of Morocco makes a reservation with regard to this article in view of the fact that the Law of Moroccan Nationality permits a child to bear the nationality of its mother only in the cases where it is born to an unknown father, regardless of place of birth, or to a stateless father, when born in Morocco, and it does so in order to guarantee to each child its right to a nationality. Further, a child born in Morocco of a Moroccan mother and a foreign father may acquire the nationality of its mother by declaring, within two years of reaching the age of majority, its desire to acquire that nationality, provided that, on making such declaration, its customary and regular residence is in Morocco.

2. With regard to article 16:

The Government of the Kingdom of Morocco makes a reservation with regard to the provisions of this article, particularly those relating to the equality of men and women, in respect of rights and responsibilities on entry into and at dissolution of marriage. Equality of this kind is considered incompatible with the Islamic Shariʿa, which guarantees to each of the spouses rights and responsibilities within a framework of equilibrium and complementary in order to preserve the sacred bond of matrimony.

The provisions of the Islamic Shariʿa oblige the husband to provide a nuptial gift upon marriage and to support his family, while the wife is not required by law to support the family.

Further, at dissolution of marriage, the husband is obliged to pay maintenance. In contrast, the wife enjoys complete freedom of disposition of her property during the marriage and upon its dissolution without supervision by the husband, the husband having no jurisdiction over his wife's property.

For these reasons, the Islamic Shariʿa confers the right of divorce on a woman only by decision of a Shariʿa judge.

3. With regard to article 29:

The Government of the Kingdom of Morocco does not consider itself bound by the first paragraph of this article, which provides that 'Any dispute between two or more States Parties concerning the interpretation or application of the present Convention which is not settled by negotiation shall, at the request of one of them, be submitted to arbitration.

The Government of the Kingdom of Morocco is of the view that any dispute of this kind can only be referred to arbitration by agreement of all the parties to the dispute.

CERD

Reservations and Declarations
(Unless otherwise indicated, the reservations and declarations were made upon ratification, accession, or succession)

The Kingdom of Morocco does not consider itself bound by the provisions of article 22 of the Convention, under which any dispute between two or more States Parties with respect to the interpretation or application of the Convention is, at the request of any of the parties to the dispute, to be referred to the International Court of Justice for decision. The Kingdom of Morocco states that, in each individual case, the consent of all parties to such a dispute is necessary for referring the dispute to the International Court of Justice.

CRC

Reservations and Declarations
(Unless otherwise indicated, the reservations and declarations were made upon ratification, accession, or succession)

Reservation:

The Kingdom of Morocco, whose Constitution guarantees to all the freedom to pursue his religious affairs, makes a reservation to the provisions of article 14, which accords children freedom of religion, in view of the fact that Islam is the State religion.

CRC OPTIONAL PROTOCOL (ARMED CONFLICT)

Reservations and Declarations
(Unless otherwise indicated, the reservations and declarations were made upon ratification, accession, or succession)

Declaration:

Pursuant to paragraph 2 of the article concerning the involvement of children in armed conflicts, the Kingdom of Morocco declares that the minimum age required by national law for voluntary recruitment in the armed forces is 18 years.

CPPCG

With reference to article VI, the Government of His Majesty the King considers that Moroccan courts and tribunals alone have jurisdiction with respect to acts of genocide committed within the territory of the Kingdom of Morocco.

The competence of international courts may be admitted exceptionally in cases with respect to which the Moroccan Government has given its specific agreement.

With reference to article IX, the Moroccan Government states that no dispute relating to the interpretation, application or fulfillment of the present Convention can be brought before the International Court of Justice, without the prior agreement of the parties to the dispute

Oman

CRC

Reservations and Declarations
(Unless otherwise indicated, the reservations and declarations were made upon ratification, accession, or succession)

Reservations:

1. The words "or to public safety" should be added in article 9 [, paragraph 4,] after the words "unless the provision of the information would be detrimental to the well-being of the child."

2. A reservation is entered to all the provisions of the Convention that do not accord with Islamic law or the legislation in force in the Sultanate and, in particular, to the provisions relating to adoption set forth in its article 21.

3. The provisions of the Convention should be applied within the limits imposed by the material resources available.

4. The Sultanate considers that article 7 of the Convention as it relates to the nationality of a child shall be understood to mean that a child born in the Sultanate of unknown parents shall acquire Oman nationality, as stipulated in the Sultanate's Nationality Law.

5. The Sultanate does not consider itself to be bound by those provisions of article 14 of the Convention that accord a child the right to choose his or her religion or those of its article 30 that allow a child belonging to a religious minority to profess his or her own religion.

Qatar

CAT

Reservations and Declarations
(Unless otherwise indicated, the reservations and declarations were made upon ratification, accession, or succession)

Reservations:

(a) Any interpretation of the provisions of the Convention that is incompatible with the precepts of Islamic law and the Islamic religion;

and

(b) The competence of the Committee as indicated in articles 21 and 22 of the Convention.

CRC

Reservations and Declarations
(Unless otherwise indicated, the reservations and declarations were made upon ratification, accession, or succession)

Reservation made upon signature and confirmed upon ratification:

[The State of Qatar] enter(s) a general reservation by the State of Qatar concerning provisions incompatible with Islamic Law.

CRC OPTIONAL PROTOCOL (ARMED CONFLICT)

Reservations and Declarations
(Unless otherwise indicated, the reservations and declarations were made upon ratification, accession, or succession)

Declaration:

Pursuant to paragraph 2 of article 3 of the Optional Protocol to the Convention on the Rights of the Child on the involvement of children in armed conflict,

The State of Qatar declares that recruitment to its armed forces and other regular forces is voluntary and is for those who have attained the age of 18 years and that it takes account of the safeguards set forth in paragraph 3 of the same article.

In making this declaration, the State of Qatar affirms that its national legislation makes no provision for any form of compulsory or coercive recruitment

CRC OPTIONAL PROTOCOL (SALE OF CHILDREN)

Reservations and Declarations
(Unless otherwise indicated, the reservations and declarations were made upon ratification, accession, or succession)

Reservation:

. . . subject to a general reservation concerning any provisions in the protocol that are in conflict with the Islamic Shari'a.

Saudi Arabia

CAT

Reservations and Declarations
(Unless otherwise indicated, the reservations and declarations were made upon ratification, accession, or succession)

Reservations:

The Kingdom of Saudi Arabia does not recognize the jurisdiction of the Committee as provided for in article 20 of this Convention.

The Kingdom of Saudi Arabia shall not be bound by the provisions of paragraph (1) of article 30 of this Convention.

CEDAW

Reservations and Declarations
(Unless otherwise indicated, the reservations and declarations were made upon ratification, accession, or succession)

Reservations:

1. In case of contradiction between any term of the Convention and the norms of Islamic law, the Kingdom is not under obligation to observe the contradictory terms of the Convention.

2. The Kingdom does not consider itself bound by paragraph 2 of article 9 of the Convention and paragraph 1 of article 29 of the Convention.

CERD

Reservations and Declarations
(Unless otherwise indicated, the reservations and declarations were made upon ratification, accession, or succession)

Reservations:

[The Government of Saudi Arabia declares that it will] implement the provisions [of the above Convention], providing these do not conflict with the precepts of the Islamic Shariʿa.

The Kingdom of Saudi Arabia shall not be bound by the provisions of article (22) of this Convention, since it considers that any dispute should be referred to the International Court of Justice only with the approval of the States Parties to the dispute.

CRC

Reservations and Declarations
(Unless otherwise indicated, the reservations and declarations were made upon ratification, accession, or succession)

Reservation:

[The Government of Saudi Arabia enters] reservations with respect to all such articles as are in conflict with the provisions of Islamic law.

Syria

CEDAW

Reservations and Declarations
(Unless otherwise indicated, the reservations and declarations were made upon ratification, accession, or succession)

Reservation:

. . . subject to reservations to article 2; article 9, paragraph 2, concerning the grant of a woman's nationality to her children; article 15, paragraph 4, concerning freedom of movement and of residence and domicile; article 16, paragraph 1 (c), (d), (f) and (g), concerning equal rights and responsibilities during marriage and at its dissolution with regard to guardianship, the right to choose a family name, maintenance and adoption; article 16, paragraph 2, concerning the legal effect of the betrothal and the marriage of a child, inasmuch as this provision is incompatible with the provisions of the Islamic Shari'a; and article 29, paragraph 1, concerning arbitration between States in the event of a dispute.

The accession of the Syrian Arab Republic to this Convention shall in no way signify recognition of Israel or entail entry into any dealings with Israel in the context of the provisions of the Convention . . .

CCPR

Reservations and Declarations
(Unless otherwise indicated, the reservations and declarations were made upon ratification, accession, or succession)

[1. The accession of the Syrian Arab Republic to these two Covenants shall in no way signify recognition of Israel or entry into a relationship with it regarding any matter regulated by the said two Covenants.

2. The Syrian Arab Republic considers that paragraph 1 of article 26 of the Covenant on Economic, Social and Cultural Rights and paragraph 1 of article 48 of the Covenant on Civil and Political Rights are incompatible with the purposes and objectives of the said Covenants, inasmuch as they do not allow all States, without distinction or discrimination, the opportunity to become parties to the said Covenants.]

(Chapter IV.3, Multilateral Treaties Deposited with the Secretary-General)

CERD

Reservations and Declarations
(Unless otherwise indicated, the reservations and declarations were made upon ratification, accession, or succession)

1. The accession of the Syrian Arab Republic to this Convention shall in no way signify recognition of Israel or entry into a relationship with it regarding any matter regulated by the said Convention.

2. The Syrian Arab Republic does not consider itself bound by the provisions of article 22 of the Convention, under which any dispute between two or more States Parties with respect to the interpretation or applica-

tion of the Convention is, at the request of any of the Parties to the dispute, to be referred to the International Court of Justice for decision. The Syrian Arab Republic states that, in each individual case, the consent of all parties to such a dispute is necessary for referring the dispute to the International Court of Justice.

CESCR

Reservations and Declarations
(Unless otherwise indicated, the reservations and declarations were made upon ratification, accession, or succession)

1. The accession of the Syrian Arab Republic to these two Covenants shall in no way signify recognition of Israel or entry into a relationship with it regarding any matter regulated by the said two Covenants.

2. The Syrian Arab Republic considers that paragraph 1 of article 26 of the Covenant on Economic, Social and Cultural Rights and paragraph 1 of article 48 of the Covenant on Civil and Political Rights are incompatible with the purposes and objectives of the said Covenants, inasmuch as they do not allow all States, without distinction or discrimination, the opportunity to become parties to the said Covenants.

CRC

Reservations and Declarations
(Unless otherwise indicated, the reservations and declarations were made upon ratification, accession, or succession)

Reservations:

The Syrian Arab Republic has reservations on the Convention's provisions which are not in conformity with the Syrian Arab legislations and with the Islamic Shari'a's principles, in particular the content of article (14) related to the Right of the Child to the freedom of religion, and articles 2 and 21 concerning the adoption.

CRC OPTIONAL PROTOCOL (ARMED CONFLICT)

Reservations and Declarations
(Unless otherwise indicated, the reservations and declarations were made upon ratification, accession, or succession)

Declaration:

Ratification of the two Optional Protocols by the Syrian Arab Republic shall not in any event imply recognition of Israel and shall not lead to entry into any dealings with Israel in the matters governed by the provisions of the Protocols.

The Syrian Arab Republic declares that the statutes in force and the legislation applicable to the Ministry of Defence of the Syrian Arab Republic do not permit any person under 18 years of age to join the active armed forces or the reserve bodies or formations and do not permit the enlistment of any person under that age.

CRC OPTIONAL PROTOCOL (SALE OF CHILDREN)

Reservations and Declarations
(Unless otherwise indicated, the reservations and declarations were made upon ratification, accession, or succession)

Reservations:

A reservation is entered to the provisions set forth in article 3, paragraph 5, and article 3, paragraph 1 (a) (ii) of the Optional Protocol on the sale of children, child prostitution and child pornography, which relate to adoption.

Declaration:

Ratification of the two Optional Protocols by the Syrian Arab Republic shall not in any event imply recognition of Israel and shall not lead to entry into any dealings with Israel in the matters governed by the provisions of the Protocols.

Tunisia

CAT

Reservations and Declarations
(Unless otherwise indicated, the reservations and declarations were made upon ratification, accession, or succession)

Upon signature:

The Government of Tunisia reserves the right to make at some later stage any reservation or declaration which it deems necessary, in particular with regard to articles 20 and 21 of the said Convention.

Upon ratification:

[The Government of Tunisia] confirms that the reservations made at the time of signature of the Convention on Tunisia's behalf on 26 August 1987 have been completely withdrawn.

Declarations Re: Articles 21 and 22
(Unless otherwise indicated, the declarations were made upon ratification, accession, or succession)

[The Government of Tunisia] declares that it recognizes the competence of the Committee Against Torture provided for in article 17 of the Convention to receive communications pursuant to articles 21 and 22, thereby withdrawing any reservation made on Tunisia's behalf in this connection.

CCPR

Declaration Re: Article 41

24 June 1993

The Government of the Republic of Tunisia declares that it recognizes the competence of the Human Rights Committee established under article 28 of the [said Covenant] . . . , to receive and consider communications to the effect that a State Party claims that the Republic of Tunisia is not fulfilling its obligations under the Covenant.

The State Party submitting such communications to the Committee must have made a declaration recognizing in regard to itself the competence of the Committee under article 41 of the [said Covenant].

CEDAW

Reservations and Declarations
(Unless otherwise indicated, the reservations and declarations were made upon ratification, accession, or succession)

1. General declaration:

The Tunisian Government declares that it shall not take any organizational or legislative decision in conformity with the requirements of this Convention where such a decision would conflict with the provisions of chapter I of the Tunisian Constitution.

2. Reservation concerning article 9, paragraph 2:
The Tunisian Government expresses its reservation with regard to the provisions in article 9, paragraph 2 of the Convention, which must not conflict with the provisions of chapter VI of the Tunisian Nationality Code.

3. Reservation concerning article 16, paragraphs (c), (d), (f), (g), and (h):

The Tunisian Government considers itself not bound by article 16, paragraphs (c), (d) and (f) of the Convention and declares that paragraphs (g) and (h) of that article must not conflict with the provisions of the Personal Status Code concerning the granting of family names to children and the acquisition of property through inheritance.

4. Reservation concerning article 29, paragraph 1:

The Tunisian Government declares, in conformity with the requirements of article 29, paragraph 2 of the Convention, that it shall not be bound by the provisions of paragraph 1 of that article which specify that any dispute between two or more States Parties concerning the interpretation or application of the present Convention which is not settled by negotiation shall be referred to the International Court of Justice at the request of any one of those parties.

The Tunisian Government considers that such disputes should be submitted for arbitration or consideration by the International Court of Justice only with the consent of all parties to the dispute.

5. Declaration concerning article 15, paragraph 4:

In accordance with the provisions of the Vienna Convention on the Law of Treaties, dated 23 May 1969, the Tunisian Government emphasizes that the requirements of article 15, paragraph 4, of the Convention on the Elimination of All forms of Discrimination against Women, and particularly that part relating to the right of women to choose their residence and domicile, must not be interpreted in a manner which conflicts with the provisions of the Personal Status Code on this subject, as set forth in chapters 23 and 61 of the Code.

CRC

Reservations and Declarations
(Unless otherwise indicated, the reservations and declarations were made upon ratification, accession, or succession)

Declarations:

1. The Government of the Republic of Tunisia declares that it shall not, in implementation of this Convention, adopt any legislative or statutory decision that conflicts with the Tunisian Constitution.

. . .

3. The Government of the Republic of Tunisia declares that the Preamble to and the provisions of the Convention, in particular article 6, shall not be interpreted in such a way as to impede the application of Tunisian legislation concerning voluntary termination of pregnancy.

Reservations:

1. The Government of the Republic of Tunisia enters a reservation with regard to the provisions of article 2 of the convention, which may not impede implementation of the provisions of its national legislation concerning personal status, particularly in relation to marriage and inheritance rights.

. . .

3. The Government of the Republic of Tunisia considers that article 7 of the Convention cannot be interpreted as prohibiting implementation of the provisions of national legislation relating to nationality and, in particular, to cases in which it is forfeited.

CRC (ARMED CONFLICT)

Reservations and Declarations
(Unless otherwise indicated, the reservations and declarations were made upon ratification, accession, or succession)

Declaration:

In accordance with article 3, paragraph 2, of the Optional Protocol to the Convention on the Rights of the Child on the involvement of children in armed conflict, the Republic of Tunisia declares the following:

Under Tunisian law, the minimum age for voluntary recruitment of Tunisian citizens into the armed forces is 18 years.

In accordance with article 1 of Act No. 51-1989 of 14 March 1989 on military service, "all citizens aged 20 shall perform national service in person, except in the case of a medically certified impediment.

However, citizens may, at their request, and with the consent of their legal guardian, perform military service at the age of 18 years, subject to the approval of the Secretary General of the Ministry of Defence."

In accordance with article 27 of Act No. 51-1989 of 14 March 1989 on military service, "any citizen between the ages of 18 and 23 may be admitted into military schools subject to such conditions as may be determined by the Secretary General of the Ministry of Defence.

Young people who have not attained the age of majority must first get the consent of their legal guardian; in such case, the first year of service shall count towards the fulfillment of military service obligations and be considered as enlistment before call-up."

Articles 1 and 27 of the Act of 14 March 1989 provide legal safeguards for citizens under the age of 18 years, since acceptance into national military service or recruitment into the armed forces is on a strictly voluntary basis.

United Arab Emirates

CERD

Reservations and Declarations
(Unless otherwise indicated, the reservations and declarations were made upon ratification, accession, or succession)

The accession of the United Arab Emirates to this Convention shall in no way amount to recognition of nor the establishment of any treaty relations with Israel.

CRC

Reservations and Declarations
(Unless otherwise indicated, the reservations and declarations were made upon ratification, accession, or succession)

Reservations:

Article 7:

The United Arab Emirates is of the view that the acquisition of nationality is an internal matter and one that is regulated and whose terms and conditions are established by national legislation.

Article 14:

The United Arab Emirates shall be bound by the tenor of this article to the extent that it does not conflict with the principles and provisions of Islamic law.

Article 17:

While the United Arab Emirates appreciates and respects the functions assigned to the mass media by the article, it shall be bound by its provisions in the light of the requirements of domestic statues and laws and, in accordance with the recognition accorded them in the preamble to the Convention, such a manner that the country's traditions and cultural values are not violated.

Article 21:

Since, given its commitment to the principles of Islamic law, the United Arab Emirates does not permit the system of adoption, it has reservations with respect to this article and does not deem it necessary to be bound by its provisions.

Yemen

CCPR

Reservations and Declarations
(Unless otherwise indicated, the reservations and declarations were made upon ratification, accession, or succession)

[The accession of the People's Democratic Republic of Yemen to this Covenant shall in no way signify recognition of Israel or serve as grounds for the establishment of relations of any sort with Israel.]

(Chapter IV.3, Multilateral Treaties Deposited with the Secretary-General)

CEDAW

Reservations and Declarations
(Unless otherwise indicated, the reservations and declarations were made upon ratification, accession, or succession)

The Government of the People's Democratic Republic of Yemen declares that it does not consider itself bound by article 29, paragraph 1, of the said Convention, relating to the settlement of disputes which may arise concerning the application or interpretation of the Convention.

CERD

Reservations and Declarations
(Unless otherwise indicated, the reservations and declarations were made upon ratification, accession, or succession)

The accession of the People's Democratic Republic of Yemen to this Convention shall in no way signify recognition of Israel or entry into a relationship with it regarding any matter regulated by the said Convention.

The People's Democratic Republic of Yemen does not consider itself bound by the provisions of Article 22 of the Convention, under which any dispute between two or more States Parties with respect to the interpretation or application of the Convention is, at the request of any of the parties to the dispute, to be referred to the International Court of Justice for decision, and states that, in each individual case, the consent of all parties to such a dispute is necessary for referral of the dispute to the International Court of Justice.

The People's Democratic Republic of Yemen states that the provisions of Article 17, paragraph 1, and Article 18, paragraph 1, of the Convention on the Elimination of All Forms of Racial Discrimination whereby a number of States are deprived of the opportunity to become Parties to the Convention is of a discriminatory nature, and holds that, in accordance with the principle of the sovereign equality of States, the Convention should be opened to participation by all interested States without discrimination or restriction of any kind.

CESCR

Reservations and Declarations
(Unless otherwise indicated, the reservations and declarations were made upon ratification, accession, or succession)

The accession of the People's Democratic Republic of Yemen to this Covenant shall in no way signify recognition of Israel or serve as grounds for the establishment of relations of any sort with Israel.

CPPCG

In acceding to this Convention, the People's Democratic Republic of Yemen does not consider itself bound by article IX of the Convention, which provides that disputes between the Contracting Parties relating to the interpretation, application or fulfillment of the Convention shall be submitted to the International Court of Justice at the request of any of the parties to the dispute. It declares that the competence of the International Court of Justice with respect to disputes concerning the interpretation, application or fulfillment of the Convention shall in each case be subject to the express consent of all parties to the dispute.

Notes

Introduction: Human Rights and Agency in the Arab World

1. Despite jihad's various meanings in Arabic, its usage by Islamists fully conforms to and confirms Western Orientalist stereotypes in a process of mutual reinforcement.

2. And, of course, not just governments but also Islamist groups marginalize dissent, as the Nasr Abu Zeid case makes clear. See Nasr Hamid Abu Zeid, *Voice of an Exile: Reflections on Islam* (Westport, Conn.: Praeger, 2004).

3. There have been, for example, regular columns by authors such as Eyad el-Sarraj in the Palestinian newspaper *al-Quds* and the column al-Haq (a prominent Palestinian human rights NGO) used to run in another Palestinian newspaper, *al-Ayaam*, each specifically dealing with relevant human rights issues on a weekly basis. Journals and publishers from the Arab world's intellectual and academic centers in Beirut and Cairo include a long list of human rights-related books on their lists. Beirut's Dirasat al-Wihda Arabiyya (Center for the Study of Arab Unity) publications on this issue range as far back as the 1983 *al-Dimuqratiyya wa huquq al-insan fi al-watan al-ʿArabi al-muʿasir* (Democracy and Human Rights in the Contemporary Arab Nation) to the present, including a rather interesting roundtable published in 1996, *Haula muʾtamar al-marʾa fi Bikin* (On the Beijing Women's Conference). Think tanks have full publication schedules dealing with human rights issues. The Ibn Khaldun Center—closed by the Egyptian government as part of a campaign against its head Saad Eddin Ibrahim and, more generally, Egyptian NGOs—is worth noting for its extensive publications, which included essential annual volumes on minority rights: *Milal wa-l-nihal wa-l-ʿraq* (Religious and Ethnic Groups in the Arab World) and the magazine *Civil Society*. The Cairo Institute for Human Rights Studies publications include its regular series *Rowaaq al-ʿArabi* and *Mubadarat fikriyya* and the magazine *Sawasiah*. These publications are just the tip of the iceberg.

4. See, for example, Bruce Jentleson, "The Need for Praxis: Bringing Policy Relevance Back In," *International Security* 26, 4 (Spring 2002).

5. *Takhi*, June 3, 2003.

6. This is the common way in the Arab world of referring to the Iran-Iraq War, the Kuwait War, and the 2003 conflict in which the U.S. deposed Saddam Hussein.

7. Cited in Larry Diamond, "Can the Whole World Become Democratic?" Center for the Study of Democracy, University of California, Irvine, 2003, available at http://repositories.cdlib.org/csd/03–05.

8. See Amartya Sen, *Development as Freedom* (New York: Anchor Books, 1999)

and *Integrating Human Rights in Development: What, Why and How* (Geneva: Office of the High Commissioner for Human Rights, 2000).

9. See Nadir Farjani, *The Arab Human Development Report 2002* (New York: UNDP, 2002).

10. For a discussion of the interrelation of human rights and sustainable economic development in the context of Yemen, see Anthony Chase, "The State and Human Rights: Governance and Sustainable Human Development in Yemen," *International Journal of Politics, Culture, and Society* 17, 2 (Winter 2003–4).

11. As a personal aside in this respect, I well remember my first trip to Syria. I was greeted at the airport (and, indeed, throughout the country) with signs announcing a welcome to "al-Assad's Syria" as if the country was a personal medieval fiefdom. In fact, as after the death of Hafez al-Assad power subsequently fell to his son Bashar, it is fair to say that the country is, indeed, properly termed "al-Assad's Syria"—a true *gomalikiyya*.

12. The regimes in power, of course, have not hesitated to exaggerate a so-called Islamist threat as self-justification, neglecting to point out that it is their own repressive apparatuses that make radical, absolutist opposition the most likely alternative to the status quo. It is worth noting that there is little evidence Islamists represent a truly popular alternative.

13. For a complementary view on patrimonialism emphasizing "neopatriarchy," see Hisham Sharabi, *Neopatriarchy: A Theory of Distorted Change in Arab Society* (Oxford: Oxford University Press, 1988).

14. Mohammed M. Hafez, *Why Muslims Rebel: Repression and Resistance in the Islamic World* (Boulder, Colo.: Lynne Rienner, 2003).

15. Abdou Filali-Ansary, "The Sources of Enlightened Muslim Thought," *Journal of Democracy* 14, 2 (April 2003): 22.

16. This point is concisely emphasized in Michael Ignatieff, *Human Rights as Politics and Idolatry* (Princeton, N.J.: Princeton University Press, 2001).

17. Jeffrey C. Isaac, "Hannah Arendt on the Human Rights and the Limits of Exposure, or Why Noam Chomsky Is Wrong About the Meaning of Kosovo," *Social Research* 69, 2 (Summer 2002): 516.

18. Cheryl Rubenberg, "Review of Hisham Nazir, *Power of a Third Kind: The Western Attempt to Colonize the Global Village*," *International Journal of Middle East Studies* 33 (2001): 130.

19. Indeed, without entering too directly into daily politics, it is fair to say that U.S. experiences in Iraq—epitomized by the Abu Ghraib prison torture episodes—have done their part (sadly) in belying a notion of a cultural basis to human rights.

20. For an overview of this subject, see Andrew Cortell and James W. Davis, Jr., "Understanding the Domestic Impact of International Norms: A Research Agenda," *International Studies Review* 2, 1 (Spring 2000).

21. Lisa Anderson, quoted in Eugenie Larson, "Academics as Human Rights Advocates," *Rights News* 23, 1 (Spring 2001): 4.

22. This is not the place for a formal survey of each Middle East textbook on the market, but a check of four textbooks—all editions that are currently in print—shows the only references in them to human rights refer to U.S. policy under Carter toward Iran.

23. Susan Waltz and Sheila Carapico, contributors to this volume, are authors of two of the few academic English language books dealing directly or indirectly with human rights issues in the Arab world. The other major book on human

rights in the Middle East takes an informatively anthropological perspective; see Kevin Dwyer, *Arab Voices: Human Rights and Culture* (Berkeley: University of California Press, 1991).

24. *International Journal of Middle East Studies* and *American Political Science Review* are the leading Middle East and political science journals, and both are notable for their meagerness of attention to human rights issues, though there are a few recent glimmers of change.

25. Cheryl Rubenberg, review, 129.

26. One of the books at the vanguard of integrating human rights into political science and international relations theory includes an excellent chapter dealing with Tunisia and Morocco. See Sieglinde Gränzer, "Changing Discourse: Transnational Advocacy Networks in Tunisia and Morocco," in Thomas Risse, Stephen C. Ropp, and Kathryn Sikkink, eds., *The Power of Human Rights: International Norms and Domestic Change* (Cambridge: Cambridge University Press, 1999).

27. Margaret E. Keck and Kathryn Sikkink, *Activists Beyond Borders: Advocacy Networks in International Politics* (Ithaca, N.Y.: Cornell University Press, 1998), is the most prominent of the now large literature on this topic.

Chapter 1. The Tail and the Dog: Constructing Islam and Human Rights in Political Context

1. See Abdolkarim al-Soroush, *Reason, Freedom and Democracy in Islam* (New York: Oxford University Press, 2000); Anthony Chase, "Islam and Democracy," in David W. Lesch, ed., *The Middle East Since 1945: History in Dispute* (Detroit: St. James Press, 2003).

2. Jean Baudrillard, "Interview with Nathan Gardels," *New Perspectives Quarterly* (Spring 1992).

3. Benjamin Barber, *Jihad vs. McWorld* (New York: Times Books, 1995).

4. Fuad Zakariya, *Middle East Report* (July–August 1993).

5. Samuel P. Huntington, *Foreign Affairs* 72, 3 (Summer 1993).

6. Abdullahi Ahmed An-Na'im, *Toward an Islamic Reformation: Civil Liberties, Human Rights, and International Law* (Syracuse, N.Y.: Syracuse University Press, 1990), 9–10.

7. Ibid., 2.

8. Indeed, An-Na'im's more recent work on secularism in the Muslim world seems to implicitly problematize an overstatement of Islam as the controlling discourse in the Muslim world. Comment based on draft working papers kindly provided by Professor An-Na'im.

9. Abdullahi An-Na'im, "Islam and Human Rights: Beyond the Universality Debate," *ASIL Proceedings* (2000): 95.

10. Nathan Brown, *The Rule of Law in the Arab World* (Cambridge: Cambridge University Press, 1997). Without delving into Islamic legal history, it is important to note that it has a decentralized form and throughout its history it is rare that the state has been its arbiter.

11. Anthony Chase, "Islam and Human Rights, Clashing Normative Orders?" Ph.D. dissertation, Tufts University, 2000.

12. Those claiming to apply the shari'a in its totality—such as the Taliban did in Afghanistan—do so in a politicized, distorted manner, as when women are executed for walking without a male escort. Shari'a-justified acts such as this have more to do with local customary practices or hierarchies of power than

any historically recognized conception of the shariʿa. Regarding human rights violations by the Taliban, see Vincent Iacopino, *The Taliban's War on Women: A Health and Human Rights Crisis in Afghanistan* (Boston: Physicians for Human Rights, 1998).

13. Governments can simply not make controversial elements of constructs of shariʿa law part of top-down, state-enforced policies, leaving it to individual Muslims to decide if, from the bottom up, they will choose to adhere to such provisions by their consent. Freely consented to, such provisions would not be human rights violations—any woman, for example, is free to accept an inheritance arrangement that grants her or her female legatees half of what a man would receive if she feels that is her religious obligation. Imposed by the state, this is a human rights violation.

14. An-Naʿim, "Islam and Human Rights," 100.

15. For one example of the variations in Muslim family law, or Personal Status Law, see Fati Ziai, "Personal Status Codes and Women's Rights in the Maghreb," in Mahnaz Afkhami and Erika Friedl, eds., *Muslim Women and the Politics of Participation: Implementing the Beijing Platform* (Syracuse, N.Y.: Syracuse University Press, 1997).

16. For a full explanation of the fatwa that brought about the original ban, and the political context out of which it emerged, see Ann Elizabeth Mayer, "Islam and Human Rights: Different Issues, Different Contexts. Lessons from Comparisons," in Tore Lindholm and Kari Vogt, eds., *Islamic Law Reform and Human Rights: Challenges and Rejoinders* (Copenhagen: Nordic Human Rights Publications, 1992).

17. Reuters, November 2, 1998. See also Steve Liebman, "Driven to Distraction, Saudi Women May Soon Take the Wheel," *Wall Street Journal*, March 1, 1999, 1.

18. It is worth noting that in the Palestinian Authority—an area with far less severe social structures—there was also a controversy over whether women should be allowed to drive. Despite the religious argument that was made, restrictions were dismissed due to an overarching political-social context that viewed them as absurd.

19. Recent hikes in oil prices may mean the shariʿa can remain sacrosanct for now.

20. Reza Afshari, "An Essay on Islamic Cultural Relativism in the Discourse of Human Rights," *Human Rights Quarterly* 16, 2 (May 1994): 245. Abdallah LaRoui puts this distinction in slightly different terms when he speaks of the "confusion between religious reform and political revolution." LaRoui, "Western Orientalism and Liberal Islam: Mutual Distrust?" *MESA Bulletin* 31, 1 (July 1997): 10. As the transcript of a speech, LaRoui's thoughts in this piece are necessarily elliptical. It is, however, extraordinarily rich and suggestive. Liberalism expressed in religious terms as deism, secularism, individualism, or moralism may well be shallow and weak, and it may lose every battle in the classroom—in the "Madrasa," I should say—and still triumph outside, in the marketplace. This is the distinction, according to LaRoui, between "topical reforms without touching the dogma" and "a situation in which society is set free to operate according to its own rules." Despite the denials of Islamists, Orientalists, and liberal Islamic reformers, underlying sociological realities are ultimately more fundamental than religious norms. If a political society engages in free debate on its own future according to "its own rules" and not distorted by authoritarian governments, these realities will determine political choice more than reactive, defensive, and artificial nationalisms.

21. See, for example, Alison Dundes Renteln, *International Human Rights: Universalism Versus Relativism* (Newbury Park, Calif.: Sage, 1990), and Adamantia Pollis, "Towards a New Universalism: Reconstruction and Dialogue," *Netherlands Quarterly of Human Rights* 16, 1 (March 1998): 5–23, which represent cultural relativist perspectives that also insist that Islam is *the* defining factor in Muslim societies and, therefore, in conflict with the "alternative" norms of human rights.

22. Popularity is, of course, hard to judge in states without elections or some form of popular representation. In Muslim states that have held fair elections, antisecular Islamist parties have usually remained a relatively small minority. In Turkey, the Welfare and Justice and Development parties did win pluralities, but they are not Islamist nationalist parties (more akin to European Christian Democrats) and, in any case, have never won more than 30 percent of the popular vote—in a country whose other major parties have been continuously embroiled in corruption scandals. Algeria is the only case where an Islamic party swept an election, but even then polls showed that among its supporters "barely half approved of the establishment of an 'Islamic state.'" There are no other cases of Islamist electoral victories. As Max Rodenback points out, Islamist parties "have yet to gain an outright majority in national elections in any Muslim country (excepting Iran, where there is no other choice). At internationally monitored polls in Yemen, Pakistan, Turkey, and Jordan, they have not garnered more than 30 percent of votes. In all these cases, too, large parts of their constituencies seem to have been as much repelled by other parties' failings as attracted to Islamist platforms." There is an unfortunately small sample from which to judge electoral support, but polls in other countries show a similarly limited base of support. In the Palestinian Authority, for example, not only did Islamist candidates fare poorly in what are widely considered to have been fair elections, but since then polls have continued to show them with a limited base of support. Max Rodenbeck, "Is Islamism Losing Its Thunder?" *Washington Quarterly* 21, 2 (Spring 1998): 188. See also Asef Bayat, "A Post-Islamist Society?" *Al-Ahram Weekly* 332 (July 9–16, 1997): 10 and Giles Keppel, *Jihad: The Trail of Political Islam* (Cambridge, Mass.: Harvard University Press, 2002).

23. For example, a sampling of Amnesty International reports on three governments in the Arab-Muslim world, spanning the spectrum from secularist Syria, mixed secular-religious Egypt, and Qur'an-as-constitution Saudi Arabia, show similar practices of torture by the security services of each of the three states—just as they occur in many non-Muslim states. See http://www.amnesty.org/. Ann Mayer emphasizes the common political factors at the heart of most human rights abuses, factors with little to do with Islam. For her able comparative analysis, see Mayer, "Islam and Human Rights." Mayer's most interesting comparison is to opposition to granting women the right to drive in the United States. As is so often true, culturalist defenses of rights violations are strikingly cross-cultural.

24. Winin Pereira, *Inhuman Rights: The Western System and Global Human Rights Abuse* (Mapusa: Other India Press, 1997), ii. In the Muslim world, this distrust has led to the charge that those who invoke human rights in the face of state abuses are "anti-Islamic" or beholden to foreign, imperialist values. See, for example, the 1998 arrest of Egyptian Organization of Human Rights Secretary General Hafez Abu Sa'ada in the wake of EOHR's release of a report on Egyptian state human rights abuses in the predominantly Coptic Christian village of Al-Kosheh. Of interest here is not the fact that Sa'ada was arrested but the actual charges brought against him: disseminating information harmful to Egypt's

national interests and "accepting funds from a foreign country for the purpose of carrying out acts harmful to Egypt." This is a classic example of stigmatizing oppositional ideas by ignoring their substance and taking refuge in the rhetoric of embattled cultural purity. Indirect intellectual support of the defensive protests of authoritarian regimes that human rights are a Western construct applicable only in the North American and European cultural-political context is supplied by claims such as those by Pereira. This dodge from internal and international criticism is an obviously cynical ploy. While it may be ludicrous to rationalize, for example, electric shock torture by evoking Islamic versus Western values, this is, in effect, what some governments and their cultural relativist defenders do.

25. Human rights as they have been elaborated in UN General Assembly Declarations and Conference Resolutions and UN-sponsored hard law treaties need to be understood as defined and limited by their state-centric foundation. They arose in response to the development of the modern state system and became a global regime with the post-World War II decolonization process that extended the modern state system around the world. The rights regime is meant as a system of self-regulation by which states—with their explicit consent in all but the most extraordinary circumstances—protect themselves from their own excesses and the destabilizing effects of other states' excesses—as seen most recently in Rwanda and the former Yugoslavia. Human rights are not a panacea for all ills, just as they hardly serve as a front for the leveling ambitions of Western imperialism. They serve state interest in maintaining internal and international stability and can be seized by nonstate actors to advance their own interests.

26. Pereira, *Inhuman Rights.*

27. Mohammed Arkoun, *Rethinking Islam: Common Questions, Uncommon Answers* (Boulder, Colo.: Westview Press, 1994).

Chapter 2. A Question of Human Rights Ethics: Defending the Islamists

1. It is noteworthy that the author did not know of the prison incidents, only learning of them coincidentally while preparing this study.

2. What concerns us about that real series of incidents is only what it denotes in relation to the moral principles tackled by this study. I am not implying that the human rights movement is synonymous with Nasserist groups. The prison incident is merely illustrative and the scenario would have been no different had the Nasserists been Marxists, although perhaps in that case the assault by the Islamists would have been even more brutal, for Islamists see Marxists as true renegades, whereas Nasserists are just believers gone astray.

3. The AOHR had been founded in December 1983 in Limasol, Cyprus, after failing to find a single Arab capital willing to host the founding assembly.

4. It is worth mentioning that Qassem was able later to escape prison and flee the country. There were rumors that he was later extradited by Croatia to Egypt after joining other Islamists in the defense of Bosnia and Herzegovina.

5. At a 1990 meeting of its International Council in Tokyo, the International Secretariat of Amnesty International received a recommendation to monitor, document and report violations by nonstate entities as well governments. However, to date Amnesty International has not been able to implement this recommendation. This issue was the central topic of the meeting that took place in the EOHR offices in the summer of 1993 between the author, Pierre Sane (secretary-general of Amnesty International), and the directors of research on Africa and the Middle East at Amnesty International.

Chapter 3. Globalization and Human Rights: On a Current Debate Among Arab Intellectuals

The author would like to thank his assistants, Jessie Evans and Riad Houry, for their contributions to this piece and their assistance in preparing it for publication.

1. Cf. Munh as-Sulh, "Al-ʿalamiya allati tarfaʿ Amrika liwaʾaha, hal tajni fawaʾidaha wahdaha?" (Does America's Banner of Universality Only Serve Its Own Interests?), *Al-Hayat* 5, 1 (1996): 14.

2. Cf. Ahmad ʿAbdallah, *Nahnu waʾ l-ʿalam al-jadid: muhawala wataniya li-fahm at-tatawwurat al-ʿalamiya* (The New World and Us: A National Attempt at Understanding World Developments) (Cairo: Dar al-mahrusa, 1995), 25–46.

3. Mustafa an-Naschar, *Didda ʾl-ʿaulama* (Against Globalization) (Cairo: Dar qibaʾ, 1999).

4. Cf. Zain al-ʿAbidin ar-Rakkabi, "Ma al-ʿaulama?" (What Is Globalization?), *Asharq al-awsat* 25, 4 (1998): 10; Alfrid Faraj, "Man alladhi yakhaf min al-ʿaulama" (Who Is Afraid of Globalization?), *Al-Ahram* 4, 5 (1998): 13.

5. Jalal Amin, *Al-ʿaulama waʾ t-tanmiya al-ʿarabiya min hamlat Nabilyun ila jaulat al-Urughwai—1798-1998* (Globalization and Development from Napoleon's Campaigns to the Uruguay Rounds—1798–1998) (Beirut: Markaz Dirasat al-Wihda al-ʿArabiya, 1999), 115–22.

6. Cf. Peter Beyer, *Religion and Globalization* (London: Sage, 1994), 45–69.

7. Cf. Muhammad Kamil Zahir, *As-Siraʿ baina ʾt-tayarain ad-dini waʾ l-ʿilmani fi ʾl-fikr al-gharbi al-hadith al-muʿasir* (The Struggle Between Religious and Secular Movements in Contemporary Modern Western Thought) (Beirut: Dar al-bairuni liʾt-tibaʿa waʾn-naschr, 1994), 437–53.

8. Cf. Bumadyan Buzaid, "Al-Fikr al-ʿarabi al-muʿasir wa-ischkaliyat al-hadatha" (Contemporary Arab Thought and the Problematics of Modernity), in Center for Arab Unity Studies, ed., *Qadaya at-tanwir waʾ n-nahda fi ʾl-fikr al-muʿasir* (Issues of Enlightenment and Renaissance in Contemporary Thought) (Beirut: Markaz Dirasat al-Wihda al-ʿArabiya, 1999), 19–30.

9. Hasan Hanafi, *Muqaddima fi ʿilm al-istighrab* (An Introduction in the Science of Wonder) (Cairo: Dar al-fanniya, 1991), 9–15.

10. Sadiq Jalal al-ʿAzm, *Naqd al-fikr ad-dini* (A Critique of Religious Thought), 8th ed. (Beirut: Dar at-taliʿa, 1997), 12–57.

11. ʿAziz al-ʿAzma, *Al-ʿilmaniya min manzur mukhtalif* (Secularism from an Alternate Perspective) (Beirut: Markaz Dirasat al-Wihda al-ʿArabiya, 1992), 197–221; ʿAziz al-ʿAzma, *al-Kitaba at-tarikhiya waʾ l-maʿrifa at-tarikhiya—muqaddima fi usul sinaʿat at-tarikh al-ʿarabi* (Historical Writing and Knowledge—An Introduction in the Principles of the Making of Arab History), 2nd ed. (Beirut: Dar at-taliʿa, 1995), 99–127.

12. Yusuf al-Qaradawi, *Al-Islam waʾ l-ʿilmaniya wajhᵃⁿ li-wajh* (Islam and Secularism Face-to-Face), 4th ed. (Beirut: Muʾassasat ar-risala, 1997), 31–71.

13. Al-Misiri is Professor Emeritus of Literary Criticism (University ʿAin Shams, Cairo) and author in 1999 of the controversial *Encyclopaedia of Zionism*. Cf. ʿAbd al-Wahhab al-Misiri, "Mustalah al-ʿilmaniya" (The Concept of Secularism), in *Hiwarat li-qarn jadid—al-ʿilmaniya tahta ʾl-mijhar* (Dialogues for a New Century—Secularism Under Scrutiny) (Damascus: Dar al-fikr, 2000), 54–55.

14. Ibid., 119–23

15. Cf. Franz-Xaver Kaufmann, *Religion und Modernität* (Tübingen: Sozialwissenschaftliche Perspektiven, J.C.B. Mohr, Paul Siebeck, 1989), 32–69.

16. Al-Misiri, "Mustalah al-'ilmaniya," 227–59.

17. Ibid.

18. cf. Hasan Hanafi, *Min an-naql ila 'l-ibda'* (From Emulation to Creativity), vol. 1, *An-Naql, at-tarikh, al-qira'a, al-intihal* (Emulation, History, Reading, Impersonation) (Cairo: Dar al-qiba', 2000), 7–20.

19. Muhammad 'Abid al-Jabiri, *Al-Din wa'd-daula wa-tatbiq ash-shari'a* (Religion, State, and the Application of Shari'a Law) (Beirut: Markaz Dirasat al-Wihda al-'Arabiya, 1996), 108–114. At this point he explicitly mentions the notion of secularism and evolutionist interpretations of history.

20. Muhammad 'Abid al-Jabiri, *Mas'alat al-huwiya al-'arabiya wa'l-islam . . . wa'l-gharb* (The Question of Arab Identity and Islam . . . and the West), 2nd ed. (Beirut: Markaz Dirasat al-Wihda al-'Arabiya, 1997), 89–95.

21. Muhammad 'Abid al-Jabiri, *at-Turath wa'l-hadatha—dirasat wa-munaqashat,* (Tradition and Modernity—Studies and Discussions) (Beirut: Markaz Dirasat al-Wihda al-'Arabiya, 1991), 45.

22. It is noticeable that Al-Jabiri avoids the concept *umma* and uses instead "the Arab-Islamic civilization," "the Arab world" or "the Arab-Muslim societies."

23. Cf. Al-Jabiri, *At-Turath wa'l-hadatha,* 21–33. The three categories—Islamic world-view, normative views, and philosophical concepts—are not discussed in more detail.

24. Human rights are clearly used by al-Jabiri in a Western-liberal sense.

25. Muhammad 'Abid al-Jabiri, *Al-Dimuqratiya wa-huquq al-insan* (Democracy and Human Rights) (Beirut: Markaz Dirasat al-Wihda al-'Arabiya, 1994), 38–45.

26. Although clearly secular, the Center for Arab Unity Studies has a policy of openness toward the Islamist and reform tendencies and allows moderate representatives to attend its events and contribute to its publications.

27. This justifies considering them first here, as well as their effect on casting the overall shape of the subsequent debate. It is not meant to imply a superiority of the secular approach over the others, but helps in the search to understand and demonstrate the intellectual interactions relating to globalization.

28. Muhammad Salim al-'Awwa, "Al-'aulama min wijhat nazar 'arabiya" (Globalization from an Arab Perspective), in Wahid Taja, ed., *Al-Islam—al-khitab al-'arabi wa-qadaya al-'asr* (Islam: The Arab Discourse and Contemporary Issues) (Aleppo: Fussilat li'd-dirasat wa't-tarjama wa'n-nashr, 2000), 27–35.

29. Muhammad Ibrahim Mabruk, "Al-'aulama al-amrikiya baina 'l-firansiyin wa'l-islamiyin" (American Globalization Between the French and the Islamists), in *Ibn Rushd wa-film al-masir wa-Yusuf Shaheen wa-film al-Akhar wa-'aulamat al-harb didda 'l-islamiyin* (Ibn Rushd and the Film "The Destiny" and Yousef Chahine and the Film "The Other" and the Globalization of the War Against Islamists) (Cairo: Markaz al-Hadara al-'Arabiya, 1999), 63–66.

30. Muhammad Mahfuz was active until 2000 in Saudi Arabia as a cultural scientist.

Chapter 4. Transnational Human Rights Networks and Human Rights in Egypt

1. Thomas Risse, Stephen C. Ropp, and Kathryn Sikkink, eds., *The Power of Human Rights: International Norms and Domestic Change* (Cambridge: Cambridge University Press, 1999).

2. The countries examined were Kenya, Uganda, South Africa, Tunisia,

Morocco, Indonesia, the Philippines, Chile, Guatemala, Poland, and Czechoslovakia.

3. Risse, Ropp, and Sikkink, eds., *The Power of Human Rights*, 258.

4. Ibid., 237.

5. Ibid., 249.

6. Egypt has also ratified the following international human rights treaties: International Convention on the Elimination of All Forms of Racial Discrimination (1967); Convention on the Elimination of All Forms of Discrimination Against Women (1981); Convention Against Torture and Other Cruel, Inhuman or Degrading Treatment or Punishment (1986); Convention on the Rights of the Child (1990); African Charter on Human and Peoples' Rights (1984).

7. See Sieglinde Gränzer, "Changing Discourse: Transnational Advocacy Networks in Tunisia and Morocco," in Risse, Ropp, and Sikkink, eds., *The Power of Human Rights*. See also Neil Hicks, *Promise Unfulfilled: Human Rights in Tunisia Since 1987* (New York: Lawyers Committee for Human Rights, 1993); Susan E. Waltz, *Human Rights and Reform: Changing the Face of North African Politics* (Berkeley: University of California Press, 1995), chapter 4.

8. United Nations World Conference on Human Rights, Vienna Declaration and Program of Action, Article 5: "All human rights are universal, indivisible and interdependent and interrelated."

9. See, e.g., Amnesty International's policy statement on human rights violations by nongovernmental groups.

10. Law 162 of 1958, the Emergency Law, grants far-reaching exceptional powers to the executive branch of government.

11. The emergency legislation also provides the executive branch with powers to override release orders issued by courts charged with reviewing the legality of prolonging the detention of an individual detainee. For details of the emergency legislation, see Amnesty International, *Egypt: Arbitrary Detention Under Emergency Powers* (New York: Amnesty International, 1989).

12. The UN Human Rights Committee identified the anti-terror law as one of its "principal subjects of concern" in its concluding observations on Egypt's second periodic report in July 1993. It commented that "The definition of terrorism contained in that law is so broad that it encompasses a wide range of acts of differing gravity." CCPR/C/79/Add. 23, para. 8.

13. Amnesty International, *Egypt: Military Trials of Civilians: A Catalogue of Human Rights Violations*, AI Index: MDE 12/16/93, October 1993.

14. The laws in question included Law 100 of 1993, Law 26 of 1994, and Law 142 of 1994.

15. The law was abrogated in 1996, but prosecutions of opposition journalists and editors increased in the late 1990s.

16. Amnesty International, *Egypt: Muzzling Civil Society*, AI Index: MDE 12/21/00, September 2000, 7–10.

17. UN doc. E/C.12/1/Add. 44, para.19.

18. Jill Crystal, "The Human Rights Movement in the Arab World," *Human Rights Quarterly* 16 (1994): 435.

19. Interview with Negad al-Borai, Cairo (March 2, 2001).

20. Interview with Amir Salem, Cairo (March 4, 2001).

21. Mustapha Kamel al-Sayyid, "The Third Wave of Democratization in the Arab World," in Dan Tschirgi, ed., *The Arab World Today* (Boulder, Colo.: Lynne Rienner, 1994), 179.

22. Ibrahim Awad, "The External Relations of the Arab Human Rights Move-

ment," in Bahey el-Din Hassan, ed., *Challenges Facing the Arab Human Rights Movement* (Cairo: Cairo Institute for Human Rights Studies, July 1997), 38. The author is referring to the views of the co-founders of the Cairo Institute for Human Rights Studies, Bahey el-Din Hassan and Muhammad al-Sayyed Sa'id.

23. Interview, Negad al-Borai.

24. Interview, Amir Salem.

25. Alaa Qa'oud, "The Egyptian Organization for Human Rights: The Experience and Prospects for the Future," in Hassan, ed., *Challenges*, 88.

26. Muhammad al-Sayyed Sa'id, "The Roots of Turmoil in the Egyptian Organization for Human Rights: Dynamics of Civil Institution Building in Egypt," in Hassan, ed., *Challenges*.

27. "Results of the elections themselves revealed a hidden coalition between Nasserists and Marxists to defeat nominees from other movements, including liberals." Alaa Qa'oud, "The Egyptian Organization," 90.

28. For example, Amir Salem left the EOHR board after the May 1991 assembly to establish his own human rights center, the Legal Research and Resource Center for Human Rights.

29. Muhammad al-Sayyed Sa'id, "The Roots of Turmoil," 78.

30. Ibid., 74.

31. Ibid.

32. Ibid., 75.

33. Eberhard Kienle, "More Than a Response to Islamism: The Political Deliberalization of Egypt in the 1990s," *Middle East Journal* 52, 2 (Spring 1998).

34. James Adams, "Mubarak at Grave Risk of Being Overthrown by March of Islam," *Sunday Times*, London, 20 February 1994, quoted in Cassandra, "The Impending Crisis in Egypt," *Middle East Journal* 49, 1 (Winter 1995).

35. In December 1998 the UN General Assembly passed the Declaration on the Right and Responsibility of Individuals, Groups and Organs of Society to Promote and Protect Universally Recognized Human Rights and Fundamental Freedoms.

36. Interview, Salem.

37. Mustapha Kamel al-Sayyid, "A Clash of Values: U.S. Civil Society Aid and Islam in Egypt," in Marina Ottaway and Thomas Carothers, eds., *Funding Virtue: Civil Society Aid and Democracy Promotion* (Washington, D.C.: Carnegie Endowment for International Peace, 2000), 63.

38. The Cairo Institute for Human Rights Studies has a regional focus and is seeking to negotiate a recognition agreement with the Ministry of Foreign Affairs, similar to that recently obtained by the AOHR.

39. Thomas Risse and Stephen C. Ropp, "Conclusions," in Risse, Ropp, and Sikkink, eds., *The Power of Human Rights*, 276.

40. Ibid.

41. Interview with Bahey el-Din Hassan, Cairo (March 6, 2001).

42. Arab Organization for Human Rights, *The Status of Human Rights in the Arab World in 1999* (Cairo: AOHR, July 2000), 3.

Chapter 5. Women, Citizenship, and Civil Society in the Arab World

1. Valentine M. Moghadam, *Globalizing Women: Transnational Feminist Networks* (Baltimore: Johns Hopkins University Press, 2005). See also Moghadam, "Engendering Citizenship, Feminizing Civil Society: The Case of the Middle East and North Africa," *Women & Politics* 25, 1–2 (2003): 63–87; *Modernizing*

Women: Gender and Social Change in the Middle East, 2nd ed. (Boulder, Colo.: Lynne Rienner, 2003).

2. Ruth Lister, *Citizenship: Feminist Perspectives* (London: Macmillan, 1997); Lyndon Shanley and Uma Narayan, eds., *Reconstructing Political Theory: Feminist Perspectives* (University Park: Pennsyvania State University Press, 1997); Sylvia Walby, "Is Citizenship Gendered?" *Sociology* 28, 2 (May 1994): 379–95; Nira Yuval-Davis, *Gender and Nation* (Thousand Oaks, Calif.: Sage, 1997).

3. Carol Pateman, *The Sexual Contract* (Stanford, Calif.: Stanford University Press, 1988).

4. T. H. Marshall, *Citizenship and Social Class* (Cambridge: Cambridge University Press, 1964). Marshall's historical study was England, but his model has been applied to all of Europe by scholars of social policy and of citizenship.

5. See Kumari Jayawardena, *Feminism and Nationalism in the Third World* (London: Zed Books, 1986); Deniz Kandiyoti, "Beyond Beijing: Obstacles and Prospects for the Middle East," in Mahnaz Afkhami and Erika Friedl, eds., *Muslim Women and the Politics of Participation* (Syracuse, N.Y.: Syracuse University Press: 1997), 3–10; Valentine M. Moghadam, ed., *Identity Politics: Cultural Reassertions and Feminisms in International Perspective* (Boulder, Colo.: Westview Press, 1994).

6. The concept of civil society was revived in the late 1980s by East European dissident intellectuals who were opposed to the strong party-state. Civil society gained currency in the international development community as an alternative site for the delivery of aid, through the participation of NGOs. The concept of civil society spread in the Middle East in the 1990s, mainly in connection with political and economic liberalization. Its impetus is as much global as it is local and regional.

7. Bryan Turner, *Citizenship, Civil Society and Social Cohesion* (Swindon: ESRC, 1991).

8. Gøsta Esping-Anderson, *Three Worlds of Welfare Capitalism* (Princeton, N.J.: Princeton University Press, 1990).

9. Thomas Janoski, *Citizenship and Civil Society: A Framework of Rights and Obligations in Liberal, Traditional and Social Democratic Regimes* (Cambridge: Cambridge University Press, 1998).

10. Michael Walzer, "The Civil Society Argument," in Gershon Shafir, ed., *The Citizenship Debates: A Reader* (Minneapolis: University of Minnesota Press, 1998), 308.

11. Margaret Keck and Katherine Sikkink, *Activists Beyond Borders: Advocacy Networks in International Politics* (Ithaca, N.Y.: Cornell University Press, 1998); Lister, *Citizenship.*

12. Civil society is not synonymous with NGOs; there is also a difference in viewing NGOs in neoliberal economic terms and in viewing them as civil society organizations.

13. Valentine M. Moghadam, *Women, Work, and Economic Reform in the Middle East and North Africa* (Boulder, Colo.: Lynne Rienner, 1998).

14. In the Islamic Republic of Iran, Saudi Arabia, and some other Muslim areas, the penal code is also based on Islamic law. *Qessas* is the tribal-Islamic practice of "retribution" for crimes committed; wrongdoers or their families pay "blood money" to victims or their families (more for a man than for a woman), and physical punishments for theft, adultery, and murder are severe. The Islamic Republic of Iran also has a body of civil laws that discriminate against women. For example, Article 1133 allows for unilateral male divorce; Article 1117 allows a husband to prevent his wife from obtaining a job that he believes

is against the family interest; Article 1158 states that the children of a married couple belong to the husband. Women's rights activists have sought the amendment of these laws.

15. Lamia Shehadeh, "The Legal Status of Married Women in Lebanon," *International Journal of Middle East Studies* 30, 4 (1998): 501–19; Lynne Welchman, *Capacity, Consent and Under-Age Marriage in Muslim Family Law,* International Survey of Family Law (Cambridge: Cambridge University Press, 2001).

16. Valentine M. Moghadam, ed., *Identity Politics and Women: Cultural Reassertions and Feminisims in International Perspective* (Boulder, Colo.: Westview Press, 1993); Hisham Sharabi, *Neopatriarchy: A Theory of Distorted Change in Arab Society* (New York: Oxford University Press, 1988).

17. Selma Botman, *Engendering Citizenship in Egypt* (New York: Columbia University Press: 1999).

18. Mervat Hatem, "Privatization and the Demise of State Feminism in Egypt, 1977–1990," in Pamela Sparr, ed., *Mortgaging Women's Lives: Feminist Critiques of Structural Adjustment* (London: Zed Books, 1994).

19. Nemat Guenena and Nadia Wassef, *Unfulfilled Promises: Women's Rights in Egypt* (Cairo and New York: Population Council, 1999), 1.

20. In the latter part of 1999, Qatari and Kuwaiti women won the right to vote and to participate in elections, with the proviso that they would not be able to exercise political rights for several years. In 2005, Kuwaiti women finally were granted the right to actually exercise the political right to vote.

21. Mounira Fakhro, "Civil Society and Non-Governmental Organizations in the Middle East: Reflections on the Gulf," *Middle East Women's Studies Review* 11, 4 (January 1997): 1–3, 2.

22. Moghadam, *Women, Work, and Economic Reform.*

23. Ibid., 25–26. Article 9 of the Convention on the Elimination of All Forms of Discrimination Against Women requires States Parties to grant women equal rights with respect to their nationality and to the nationality of their children. Many Arab countries that have signed the Convention entered reservations to this article.

24. Egypt, for example, did not have any women judges in the 1990s.

25. *Civil Society* 8, 90 (June 1999): 22–23.

26. *Civil Society* 8, 91 (July 1999): 20–23.

27. Amal Basha, Sisters' Arabic Forum for Human Rights, Sana'a, Yemen, conversation with the author, Chicago, 22 May 2002.

28. Karima Bennoune, "S.O.S. Algeria: Women's Human Rights Under Siege," in Mahnaz Afkhami, ed., *Faith and Freedom: Women's Human Rights* (Syracuse, N.Y.: Syracuse University Press, 1995); Valentine M. Moghadam, "Organizing Women: The New Women's Movement in Algeria," *Cultural Dynamics* 1, 3 (2) (2001): 131–54.

29. Robert Cornwell, "Algeria to Free 5,000 from Jail," *Independent* (UK), 5 July 1999.

30. U.S. Department of State, Bureau of Democracy, Human Rights, and Labor, Country Report on Human Rights Practices, "Algeria," March 4, 2002, www.state.gov/hrrpt/2001. In Morocco and Tunisia, too, women constitute 20–25 percent of judges. In other countries, the religiously based prohibition against women judges persists. Egypt has had women ambassadors and cabinet ministers but no women judges until one was appointed in 2004. In the Islamic Republic of Iran (not part of the Arab region), after a twenty-year post-revolutionary ban on women judges, women were allowed to become judicial deputies and then full judges, but their judgement and verdict remain advisory.

31. Machreq/Maghreb Gender Linking and Information Project, March 2001 Regional Monthly Update, www.macmag-glip.org.

32. E.g., Lister, *Citizenship*.

33. *Pace* Pateman, *The Sexual Contract*.

Chapter 6. Human Rights in the Arab World: Reflections on the Challenges Facing Human Rights Activism

1. Human rights divisions in ministries, presidential advisors on human rights, and government-appointed human rights commissions have existed in Morocco, Algeria, Tunisia, Libya, Egypt, Palestine, Kuwait, and Yemen.

2. In the cases of the Egyptian Organization for Human Rights and the Tunisian League for Human Rights—two unusual examples of organization that have attempted to develop along membership lines—the early days of success and membership growth have not been sustained and have actually declined. In both cases internal political disputes and restrictive government action have not helped.

3. There are many examples of this, but as seen from the region's perspective one can cite recent events such as the international community's responses to the invasion of Kuwait, the Israeli occupation of Palestinian lands, and the civil war in Bosnia.

Chapter 7. Human Rights NGOs and the "Foreign Funding Debate" in Egypt

An earlier version of this chapter was part of the research toward my doctoral dissertation, entitled "Globalization and the Postcolonial State: Human Rights NGOs and the Prospects for Democratic Governance in Egypt," funded by the Economic and Social Research Council, UK, 1998–2001. I would like to thank Dr. Salwa Ismail for her support and constructive criticism throughout my research. I also thank Anthony Chase, Maryam Elahi, and Gasser Abdel-Razek for their useful comments on the first draft of this chapter. However, I, alone, am responsible for the final outcome. Arabic-English translations are my own unless otherwise indicated.

1. I use the term "human rights" in its widest sense to cover civil and political rights, social and economic rights, women's rights, the rights of working people, and child rights. For an outline of the foreign funding debate with particular regard to Egyptian women's rights NGOs, see Nadje Al-Ali, *Secularism, Gender and the State in the Middle East: The Egyptian Women's Movement* (Cambridge: Cambridge University Press, 2000).

2. Current legislation (Law 84/2002) states that any private associations conducting work falling within the remit of the Ministry of Social Affairs (MOSA) must obtain permission before accepting funds from any source (domestic or foreign). Prior to the law change in 2002, most Egyptian human rights organizations were able to bypass this article because they were not registered with MOSA but as civil companies (this loophole has since been closed). Nevertheless, the government resorted to a 1992 military decree (stating that any entity must obtain official permission to accept funds from abroad) in order to harass some human rights activists. In February 2000, the secretary general of EOHR was charged but the case was never pursued. In 2001, the same decree was used to

prosecute and indict Saad el-Din Ibrahim and his colleagues from the Ibn Khaldun Center. They were finally acquitted on appeal and released from prison in 2003.

3. Muhammad al-Sayyed Sa'id, "Phantom of the Foreigner Reigns over Debates Concerning Private Associations," *Sawasiah* (Cairo Institute for Human Rights Studies) 23–24 (1998): 6–9, 23–24.

4. As argued by Edward Said, *Orientalism* (London: Routledge, 1978).

5. See, for example, the writings of Aimé Cesaire and Léopold Senghor of the *négritude* movement. For further development of this argument, see Partha Chatterjee, *The Nation and Its Fragments: Colonial and Postcolonial Histories* (Princeton, N.J.: Princeton University Press, 1993).

6. Muhammad al-Sayyed Sa'id, "The Roots of Turmoil in the Egyptian Organization for Human Rights: Dynamics of Civil Institution-Building in Egypt," in *Human Rights and the Arab World, Proceedings of the Fourth Annual Symposium of the Cairo Papers in Social Science* 17, 3 (1994): 73.

7. El-Sayyed Sa'id, "Phantom of the Foreigner," 7.

8. For example, Andre Gunder Frank, *Capitalism and Underdevelopment in Latin America: Historical Studies of Chile and Brazil* (New York: Monthly Review Press, 1969); Theotonio Dos Santos, "The Structure of Dependence," *American Economic Review* 60 (1970): 231–36; Fernando Henrique Cardoso and Enzo Faletto, *Dependency and Development in Latin America*, trans. Marjory Mattingly Urquidi (1971; Berkeley: University of California Press, 1979).

9. Interview with the author in English, August 2000.

10. Hilmi Sha'rawi, "Mafahim wa haraka huquq al-insan fi-l-watan al-'arabi," in Issa Shivji and Hilmi Sha'rawi, *Huquq al-insan fi afriqiya w-al-watan al-'arabi* (Cairo: Arab Research Center, 1994), 272.

11. Muhammad al-Dumati, *Al-Usbu'a*, November 30, 1998, 18.

12. Mustafa Bakri, *Al-Usbu'a*, November 23, 1998, 1.

13. An example of such harassment includes the charging of the secretary-general of the EOHR in December 1998 and February 2000 with "accepting funds for the purpose of tarnishing Egypt's reputation abroad" following the EOHR's publication of a report condemning police brutality against individuals in the predominantly Coptic Christian village of al-Kosheh in August 1998, and another report on the causes of civil strife in the same village in January 2000.

14. This event was widely reported in both the Egyptian and U.S. media. For a selection of some of the newspaper articles written on the subject, see the "Free Saadeddin Ibrahim" Web site, http://groups.yahoo.com/group/free_saaded din_ibrahim. He was released in March 2003.

15. Interview with the author in Arabic, May 2000.

16. El- Sayyed Sa'id, "Phantom of the Foreigner," 8–9.

17. El- Sayyed Sa'id, "Phantom of the Foreigner," 8. This is the original English translation appearing in the English edition of *Sawasiah*.

18. Ibid., 9.

19. Salama Ahmad Salama, *Al-Ahram*, December 3, 1998, 10.

20. Similar arguments have been put forward by other prominent columnists and writers, namely, the late Lutfi al-Khuli (*Al-Ahram*, December 5, 1998, 10); Husayn 'Abd al-Raziq (*Al-'Arabi*, December 7, 1998, 16); Farida al-Naqqash (*Al-Ahali*, December 2, 1998, 13); and Salah 'Issa (*Al-'Arabi*, December 7, 1998, 6).

21. Salama Ahmad Salama, *Al-Ahram*, December 3, 1998, 10.

22. Ibid. Similar arguments in favor of public monitoring of foreign funding have been put forward by the late Lutfi al-Khuli and Husayn 'Abd al-Raziq.

23. Said, *Orientalism.*

24. Frantz Fanon, *The Wretched of the Earth,* trans. Constance Farrington (London: Penguin, 1990), 31–33.

25. For example, see Fanon, *The Wretched of the Earth,* 170–71; Partha Chatterjee, *Nationalist Thought and the Colonial World: A Derivative Discourse* (London: Zed Books, 1986), 73–78.

26. El-Sayyed Sa'id, "Phantom of the Foreigner," 8.

27. Chatterjee, *Nation and Its Fragments,* 26.

28. Ibid., 120.

29. For a further examination of the ways the actions of Western governments undermine the cause of human rights in Egypt, see Bahey el-Din Hassan, "The Unholy Alliance: The Elite's Discourse as an Obstacle to Democratic Transformation," paper presented to the MESA Annual Meeting, Orlando, Florida, November 16–19, 2000.

30. Frantz Fanon, *Toward the African Revolution,* trans. Haakon Chevalier (New York: Monthly Review and Grove Press, 1967), 105.

31. Husayn 'Abd al-Raziq, in the English language *Al-Ahram Weekly,* January 21–28, 1999, clearly argues against seeing the West as a "single, monolithic entity." Yet, in the Arabic press, he has implicitly represented Egyptian interests as self-evident and monolithic by stressing the contribution of human rights groups to national interests, in addition to proposing public, albeit nongovernmental monitoring of foreign funding.

Chapter 9. Some Yemeni Ideas About Human Rights

An earlier version of this paper was presented to the Conference of the Law and Society Association, Budapest, Hungary, July 4–8, 2001. The author thanks Anna Würth for comments on a subsequent draft.

1. Where Occidentalism is Orientalism in reverse, i.e., a simplified stereotype of promiscuity, violence, and hypocrisy in an undifferentiated "West." See Rhoda Howard, "Occidentalism, Human Rights, and the Obligations of Western Scholars," *Canadian Journal of African Studies* 29, 1 (1995): 110–26.

2. Muhammad 'Abd al-Malik al-Mutawakkil, "Al-islam wa huquq al-insan," *Al-Mustaqbal al-'Arabi* 216 (February 1997): 4–31.

3. See Bernard Haykel, *Revival and Reform in Islam: The Legacy of Muhammad b. 'Ali al-Shawkani* (New York: Cambridge University Press, 2003).

4. Abdillah Hasan Bilfaqih, *Tadhkirat al-bahith al-muhtam fi shu'un wa-ta'rikh al-Ribam* (Matba'at al-Fajjala al-Jadida, n.d.)

5. See Lucine Tumarian, "Persuading the Monarchs: Poetry and Politics in Yemen (1920–1950)," in Remy Leveau, Franck Mermier, and Udo Steinbach, eds., *Le Yemen contemporain* (Paris: Editions Karthala, 1999), 203–19.

6. Brinkley Messick, *The Caligraphic State: Textual Domination and History in a Muslim Society* (Berkeley: University of California Press, 1993), 111.

7. Ahmad Muhammad al-Shami, "Yemeni Literature in Hajjah Prisons 1367/1948–1374/1955," in R. B. Serjeant and R. L. Bidwell, eds., *Arabian Studies II* (London: C. Hurst, 1975), 43–59.

8. R. B. Serjeant, "The Yemeni Poet Al-Zubayri and His Polemic Against the Zaydi Imams," in R. B. Sergeant and R. L. Bidwell, eds., *Arabian Studies V* (London: C. Hurst, 1979).

9. Muhsin al-'Ayni, *Ma'arik wa mu'amarat didda qadiyyat al-Yaman* (1957; Al-Qahirah: Dar al-Shuruq, 1957).

10. J. Leigh Douglas, *The Free Yemeni Movement, 1935–1962* (Beirut: American University in Beirut, 1987).

11. Ibrahim al-Rashid, *Yemen Enters the Modern World* (Chapel Hill, N.C.: Documentary Publications, 1984), 152–58, translated by the American Embassy in Cairo from a version published in the newspaper *Al Akhwan al Muslimun* (February 20, 1948); see also a memorandum from S. Pickney Tuck of the U.S. embassy in Cairo (170–74).

12. Mohamed Anam Ghaleb, "Government Organizations as a Barrier to Economic Development in Yemen," M.A. thesis, University of Texas, 1960, 63, citing a booklet called *The People's Aspirations* (Aden, 1955), Article 3.

13. ʿUmar al-Jawi, *Al-Sihafa al-Niqabiyya fi ʿAdan, 1958–1967* (Aden: Muʾassasat 14 Uktubir, n.d.), 16–18.

14. Fred Halliday, *Arabia Without Sultans* (London: Penguin, 1974), 203–5. See also Michael Crouch, *An Element of Luck: To South Arabia and Beyond* (London: Radcliffe Press, 1993), 193–203.

15. Karl Pieragostini, *Britain, Aden, and South Arabia: Abandoning Empire* (New York: St. Martin's Press, 1991), 146–48, 153–57. Pieragostini describes one such occasion, in 1965, when eight Aden labor leaders were arrested; the next time, police rounded up 760 people, 300 of whom were deported and 80 charged with criminal offenses.

16. Paul Dresch, *Tribes, Government and History in Yemen* (Oxford: Clarendon Press, 1989), 249–50.

17. Salim ʿAbd Allah and Mundʿi Dayan ʿAbd Rabbih, *Jabhat al-Islah al-Yafiʿiyya, (13 Abril 196–31 Yulyu 1967)* and *Nazra fi-l-nizam al-qabali al-ladhi sad qadiman fi-l-mintaqa* (Aden: Muʾassasat 14 Uktubir, 1992).

18. Zayd bin ʿAli al-Wazir, ed., *Muʾtamir Khamir* (Beirut: Federation of Popular Forces, 1965), 44.

19. For these quotations and further detailed analysis, see Helen Lackner, *P.D.R. Yemen: Outpost of Socialist Development in Arabia* (London: Ithaca Press, 1985), 37–42.

20. *Al-Distur al-Daʾim l-al-Jumhuriyya al-ʾArabiyya al-Yamaniyya wʾ al-ʾAlanat al-Disturiyya*, reprinted by Dar al-Masbah l'al-Tabaʾa for the Legal Office of the Republican Leadership and Council of Ministers (1983/84).

21. Ahmad ʿAli al-Wadʾai, "Huquq al-insan fi al-disatir al-Yamaniyya," in Ahmad Jabir ʿAfif et al., eds., *Al-Masuʾa al-Yamaniyya* (Yemen Encyclopedia) (Sanaʾa: Muʾassasat ʿAfif al-Thaqafiyya, 1992), 411–13.

22. On women's rights in the People's Republic, see Maxine Molyneux, "The Law, the State and Socialist Policies with Regard to Women: The Case of the People's Democratic Republic of Yemen, 1967–1990," in Deniz Kandiyoti, ed., *Women, Islam, and the State* (Philadelphia: Temple University Press, 1991), 237–71. Also Suzanne Dalgren, "Islam, the Custom, and Revolution in Aden: Reconsidering the Background to the Changes of the Early 1990s," paper presented at the Conference on Yemen, The Challenge of Social, Economic, and Democratic Development, Center for Arab Gulf Studies, University of Exeter, Exeter, April 1–4, 1998); Najib Shamiri, *Huquq al-marʾa fi tashrīʾat al-Yaman al-dimuqratiyya* (Aden: Dar al-Hamdani, n.d.).

23. Qaʾid Muhammad Tarbush, *Tatawwur al-nizam al-intikhabi fi al-Jumhuriyya al-Yamaniyya 1948–1992* (Manshurat: September 26, 1992), 63–80.

24. Charles Dunbar, "The Unification of Yemen: Process, Politics, and Prospects," *Middle East Journal* 46, 3 (Summer 1992): 465. The PDRY was then still on the U.S. list of terrorist states.

25. *Al-Munazzama al-Yamaniyya li-l-Difa' 'an Huquq al-Insan wa-l-Hurriyat al-Dimuqratiyya al-Munazzama al-Yamaniyya li-l-Difa' 'an Huquq al-Insan wa-l-Hurriyat al-Dimuqratiyya al-Nizam al-Assassi* (Sana'a, 1992)

26. *Al-Burnamij al-Intikhabi l' al-Mu'tamar al-Sha'abi al-'Am* (Sana'a, n.d.), p. 6, number 4.

27. For further details, see Sheila Carapico, "Yemen Between Civility and Civil War," in Augustus Richard Norton, ed., *Civil Society in the Middle East*, vol. 2 (Leiden: E.J. Brill, 1996), 287–316, esp. 307–10.

28. Yemeni Organization for Human Rights, Basic Statute, Article 3, item 1

29. See, for instance, the Yemen report on the Web page of the Committee to Protect Journalists, http://www.cpj.org/attacks99/mideast99/Yemen.html

30. Not all Islamists are political or economic conservatives. See Ludwig Stiftl, "The Yemeni Islamists in the Process of Democratization," in Leveau, Mermier, and Steinbach, eds., *Le Yemen contemporain*, 249–56.

31. See also François Burgat, "Le Yemen islamiste entre universalisme et insularité," in Leveau, Mermier, and Steinbach, eds., *Le Yemen contemporain*, 221–45.

32. On actual practice, see Anna Würth, "A Sana'a Court: The Family and the Ability to Negotiate," *Islamic Law and Society* 2, 3 (1995): 320–40.

33. See, for instance, *Al-ahwah*, August 12, 1993, 1, including an editorial statement that it is not correct that women should stay in the house when there is a role to be played in helping other Muslims.

34. Ahmad Hussayn al-Marwani, "About Human Rights," *Al-Thawrah*, October 13, 1992, 16.

35. On this point, see Gabriele vom Bruck, "Being Zaydi in the Absence of an Imam: Doctrinal Revisions, Religious Instruction, and the (Re-) Invention of Ritual," in Leveau, Mermier, and Steinbach, eds., *Le Yemen contemporain*, 170–92.

36. Ahmad Jabir 'Afif, *Huquq al-Mara' fi al-Yaman.*

37. Ahmad 'Ali al-Wada'i, *Huquq al-Mara' al-Yamaniyya bayn al-Fiqa w' al-Tashri'* (Sana'a: 'Afif Foundation, n.d.).

38. For further analysis, see Renaud Detalle, "Pacte d'Amman: L'espoir déçu des yemenites," *Monde Arabe Maghreb-Mashrek* 145 (July-September 1994): 113–22.

39. See 1994 press accounts in newspapers that previously rarely covered the same events: *Al-Thawrah*, March, 11, 1; *Al-Wahdah*, March, 9, 1, 2; *Al-Shura*, March 6, 1, 2; *Al-Ayyam*, March 9, 1, 2.

40. Jemera Rone and Sheila Carapico for Human Rights Watch, *Yemen: Human Rights in Yemen During and After the 1994 War* (New York: Human Rights Watch, October 1994).

41. I have written about this situation at some length in Carapico, *Civil Society in Yemen: The Political Economy of Activism in Modern Arabia* (Cambridge: Cambridge University Press, 1998), esp. chapter 8.

42. See, for instance, Abu Bakr al-Saqqaf, "Equal Citizenship: The Big Absence," 127–30, and Anis Hassan Yahya, "Toward a Constitution to Establish a Modern State and Take Yemen into the 21st Century," 146–58, both in E. G. H. Joffé, M. J. Hachemi, and E. W. Watkins, eds., *Yemen Today: Crisis and Solutions* (London: Caravel, 1997).

43. Naguib A. R. Shamiry, "The Judicial System in Yemen with Reference to Human Rights," paper presented to the Regional Conference on the Role of the Judiciary in the Protection of Human Rights, Cairo, December 1996, http://www.gpc.org.ye/jud.htm.

44. *Al-Thawrah* editorial, July 9, 1994.

45. *Al-Qistas* (magazine), November 6, 1998, 4.

46. *Yemen Times*, December 6, 1999, 1; on the conference, see 7–8.

47. General People's Congress Web site, http://www.gpc.org.ye/guarante .htm

48. Amnesty International Country Report: "Empty Promises—Government Commitments and the State of Human Rights in Yemen" (MED 31/004/99)

49. See Ahmad al-Wada'i et al., "Al-Qada' . . . w damana al-huquq w'al-huriy-yat fi al-Yaman," *Al-Qistas*, November 6, 1998, 40–45, roundtable discussion.

50. Ibid.

51. Anna Würth, "Yemeni Judicial History as Political History, 1970–1997," paper based on her book *Ash-Shariʿa fi Bab al-Yaman: Recht, Richter und Rechtspraxis an der familienrechtlichen Kammer des Gerichts Süd-Sanaa (Republik Jemen) 1983–1995* (Berlin: Duncker and Homblot, 2000).

52. http://www.yemen-observer.com, accessed 2001.

53. For instance, see Elisabeth Eaves, "The Judge Who Converts Terrorists," *Slate*, May 18, 2004, available at http://slate.msn.com/id/2100581/entry/2100586/#ContinueArticle. A fuller analysis comes from Gregory D. Johnsen, "Reprogramming the Imagination in Yemen: Hamud al-Hitar and the RDC," paper presented at MESA annual meeting, University of Arizona, 2005.

Chapter 10. Got Rights? Public Interest Litigation and the Egyptian Human Rights Movement

1. The full charges against Ibrahim were threefold: receiving foreign funding without prior government approval, propagating false information harmful to state interests, and embezzling money from the Ibn Khaldun Center.

2. These opening observations immediately highlight the need to disaggregate Egypt's various judicial institutions because some (such as the Supreme Constitutional Court) enjoy a relatively high degree of autonomy from regime control and others (such as the emergency state security courts) have almost no independence. For more on the development of the regular and exceptional court system in Egypt, see Nathan Brown, *The Rule of Law in the Arab World: Courts in Egypt and the Gulf* (Cambridge: Cambridge University Press, 1997).

3. The ability to circumvent collective action problems is one of the most significant benefits of legal mobilization even in consolidated democracies where civil liberties are relatively secure, but the possibility of initiating litigation in lieu of a broad social movement is even more crucial for opposition activists in authoritarian systems where the state forcefully interferes with political organizing. Frances Zemans, "Legal Mobilization: The Neglected Role of the Law in the Political System" *American Political Science Review* 77 (1983): 690–703.

4. See Donald Reid, *Lawyers and Politics in the Arab World, 1880–1960* (Chicago: Bibliotheca Islamica, 1981); Farhat Ziadeh, *Lawyers, the Rule of Law and Liberalism in Modern Egypt* (Stanford, Calif.: Hoover Institution, 1968); Raymond William Baker, "Fighting for Freedom and the Rule of Law: The Bar Association," in *Sadat and After: Struggles for Egypt's Political Soul* (Cambridge, Mass.: Harvard University Press); Enid Hill, *Mahkama! Studies in the Egyptian Legal System* (London: Ithaca Press, 1979); Brown, *The Rule of Law*.

5. For more on administrative court reforms, see James Rosberg, "Roads to the Rule of Law: The Emergence of an Independent Judiciary in Contemporary Egypt," Ph.D. dissertation, Massachusetts Institute of Technology, 1995. For more on the establishment of the SCC, see Tamir Moustafa, "Law Versus the

State: The Expansion of Constitutional Power in Egypt," Ph.D. dissertation, University of Washington, 2002, and Bruce Rutherford, "The Struggle for Constitutionalism in Egypt: Understanding the Obstacles to Democratic Transition in the Arab World," Ph.D. dissertation, Yale University, 1999.

6. Due to space limitations, I will explore only a fraction of the most important SCC rulings over the past two decades. For a more comprehensive summary and analysis of many SCC rulings, see Kevin Boyle and Adel Omar Sherif, eds., *Human Rights and Democracy: The Role of the Supreme Constitutional Court of Egypt* (London: Kluwer, 1996); Eugene Cotran and Adel Omar Sherif, eds., *Democracy, the Rule of Law, and Islam* (London: Kluwer Law International, 1999); Rutherford, "The Struggle for Constitutionalism in Egypt"; Moustafa, "Law Versus the State." For a complete listing of all rulings in Arabic, see *Al-Mahkama al-Dusturi-yya al-ʿUlia* (hereafter *Al-Mahkama*), vols. 1–9.

7. SCC, June 26, 1986, *Al-Mahkama*, vol. 3, 353.

8. SCC, May 7, 1988, *Al-Mahkama*, vol. 4, 98.

9. SCC, May 16, 1987, *Al-Mahkama*, vol. 4, 31; SCC, May 19, 1990, *Al-Mahkama*, vol. 4, 256

10. SCC, 15 April 1989, *Al-Mahkama*, vol. 4, 205; SCC, April 15, 1989, *Al-Mahkama*, vol. 4, 191.

11. Prior to the SCC reforms, the regime managed the political field by granting only a handful of opposition parties exclusive representation of opposition to the regime. In a classic corporatist arrangement, the parties themselves were left to exercise *internal* controls on activists who dared to challenge the government outside the bounds that were implicitly negotiated between the regime and opposition parties. After the SCC induced electoral reforms, however, opposition activists were no longer beholden to opposition party leadership, which controlled party platforms, party membership, and the position of candidates on party lists. Moreover, political trends that were not allowed legal party status by the regime, most notably the Islamist trend, were able to compete as independent candidates. These electoral reforms forced the regime to shift its method of maintaining political control from one of *pseudo-legality*, where the regime depended on skewed electoral rules and a corporatist system to dominate the political field, to a method of political control that would become far more *extra-legal* in orientation—depending much more heavily on physical coercion, intimidation, and electoral fraud. For more on the impact of these SCC-mandated electoral reforms, see Moustafa, "Law Versus the State," 98–111.

12. For an excellent account of political retrenchment through the 1990s, see Eberhard Kienle, *A Grand Delusion: Democracy and Economic Reform in Egypt* (London: I.B. Tauris, 2000).

13. SCC, February 6, 1993, *Al-Mahkama*, vol. 5 (2), 183.

14. SCC, July 3, 1995, *Al-Mahkama*, vol. 7, 45. Labor Party chairman Ibrahim Shukri and editor-in-chief of the Labor Party newspaper, Adel Hussein, filed the petition for constitutional review during the proceedings of their criminal trial in March 1994. Shukri and Hussein were standing trial under allegations of libel against a public official for accusations that were published in the Labor Party newspaper, *Al-Shaʿb*. The SCC ruling affirmed the Labor Party petition and struck down the provision of Law 40 that enabled the regime to press vicarious criminal liability charges upon the heads of political parties. The SCC argued that Law 40 violated Articles 41, 66, 67, 69, and 165 of the constitution, which collectively guarantee the presumption of innocence, the right of legal defense, and the right of the courts alone to adjudicate guilt and innocence. This was

also one of the first cases in which the SCC explicitly invoked international human rights frameworks and treaties to lend legal and moral weight to its rulings. The SCC ruled that law 40 contradicted articles 10 and 11 of the Universal Declaration of Human Rights and the principles of justice "shared by all civilized nations." For more on the "internationalization" of SCC legal doctrine, see Boyle and Sherif, *Human Rights and Democracy*, and Moustafa, "Law Versus the State," 204–9.

15. SCC, February 1, 1997, *Al-Mahkama*, vol. 8, 286.

16. The commission was formally established at a workshop on 22 October 1995 organized by the Egyptian Organization for Human Rights, Center for Human Rights Legal Aid, Legal Research and Resource Center for Human Rights, and Ibn Khaldun Center for Development Studies and attended by leaders from the Wafd, Tagemmu', Nasserist, Labor, and Al-Ahrar Parties. The final report of the commission is *Shihadit lil-tarikh, taqrir al-legnet al-watiniyya al-misriyya li-lutabeʾ a al-intikhabat al-barlamaniyya 1995* (Testimony to History: Report of the Egyptian National Commission for Monitoring the 1995 Parliamentary Elections) (Cairo: Ibn Khaldun Center for Development Studies, 1995).

17. For a list of the other major participants in the commission, see *Shihadit lil-tarikh*, 223–28.

18. The commission determined that 5 to 8 percent of the names on the voting lists belonged to dead people and that names were listed more than once (in some cases as many as twenty times) in 50 of the 88 electoral districts examined. *Shihadit lil-tarikh*, 184–85.

19. Egyptian Organization of Human Rights, *Democracy Jeopardized: Nobody "Passed" the Elections* (Cairo: EOHR, 1995), 17.

20. For instance, mosques controlled by the Ministry of Awqaf were used to build support for NDP candidates and public sector factories were used as forums to publicize the programs of pro-NDP candidates. Commission findings are found in *Shihadit lil-tarikh*, 179–222.

21. *Al-Shaʿb*, December 8, 1995.

22. See, for example, *Al-Haqiqa*, December 2, 1995, "Black Wednesday in the History of Democracy"; *Al-Wafd*, December 5, 1995, "Discontent Is Widespread in Egypt"; *Al-Ahrar*, November 30, 1995, "Black Day for Democracy."

23. This gives the NDP yet another tool for controlling its own members in the People's Assembly. Since the majority of the members gained seats through electoral fraud, the NDP, through article 93, can choose to initiate hearings and expel any of these members at virtually any time in the name of defending democracy.

24. The only avenue for legal recourse available to victims of electoral fraud is to return to the courts to seek financial compensation, which generally ranges from £E 25,000 to £E 100,000 ($7,350–29,400). Typically, opposition candidates will use this compensation to pay for their next campaign. Dr. Hossam 'Issa, a law professor and human rights advocate, finds it the ultimate irony that "the citizens pay twice; first for an illegitimate, ineffective government and a second time when the state pays compensation with the people's money" (interview, October 29, 1997).

25. In 1996, CHRLA cases roughly broke down along the following lines: 40 percent economic and social rights, 10 percent freedom of expression, 10 percent women, 8 percent maltreatment and torture, 32 percent juvenile. For specifics on the types of cases initiated by CHRLA, including case studies, see Center for Human Rights Legal Aid Activity Report, 1996.

26. Interview with Mahmoud Gabr, director of the Legal Unit, Land Center for Human Rights, November 11, 2000.

27. Correspondence with Mohamed Zarei, director of the Human Rights Center for the Assistance of Prisoners, January 24, 2002.

28. Interview with Mohamed Goma', vice-chairman of Wafd Committee for Legal Aid, February 2, 2001.

29. Case 59, Judicial Year 18, issued February 1, 1997, *Al-Mahkama*, vol. 8, 286–309.

30. Interview with Gasser Abdel Raziq, director of the Hisham Mubarak Legal Aid Center, formerly Center for Human Rights Legal Aid, April 16, 2000.

31. Case 77, Judicial Year 19, *Al-Mahkama*, vol. 8, 1165–85.

32. Cases 237, Judicial Year 20; 25, Judicial Year 21; 83, Judicial Year 21; 181, Judicial Year 21; 182, Judicial Year 21; 183, Judicial Year 21. As of March 2001 the SCC had still not issued rulings on these cases.

33. For example, see "Vice President of the Court of Cassation Reveals Law of the Professional Syndicates Is Unconstitutional," *Al-Wafd*, November 3, 1997.

34. One of many examples is the conference organized by the newly founded Arab Center for the Independence of the Judiciary and the Legal Profession, The Future Role of the Supreme Constitutional Court in Constitutional Review, June 30 to July 1, 1998.

35. The Ministry of Social Affairs exercised its ability to dissolve NGOs throughout this period. One prominent example is the closure of Nawal el-Sadawi's Arab Women's Solidarity Organization. MOSA charged that the activities of the association violated Islamic law and threatened social peace and security.

36. "Setting Civil Society Free: A Draft Law Concerning Civil Associations and Institutions," 28, Cairo Institute for Human Rights Studies, 1998.

37. A copy of a $25,703 check from the British House of Commons Human Rights Committee to fund EOHR's legal aid project for women was printed on the front page of *Al-Osboa*, November 23, 1998, with the caption "the price of treason."

38. This is a common strategy to intimidate and silence opponents of the regime since they know that the prosecutor can resume the case at any moment.

39. Article 11. As with other laws restricting political rights, Law 153/1999 did not define what constitutes a threat to national unity or a violation of public order, giving the regime maximum leverage to liberally apply the law and to deny activists the ability to seek protection from the law.

40. Article 17 read, "no association shall collect funds from abroad, whether from an Egyptian or foreign person, or a foreign quarter or its representative inland . . . except with the permission of the Minister of Social Affairs." This restriction was not completely new, as Military Decree 4/1992 imposed the same restrictions on foreign funding. The provisions in Law 153 did, however, formalize the regime's decree and built redundancy into the legal framework so that the regime had multiple legal levers to control its opponents.

41. Article 16 reads, "the association may join, participate with or be affiliated to a club, association, authority or organization whose head office is located outside the Arab Republic of Egypt . . . providing it shall notify the administrative authority."

42. Days later, the state of emergency was extended a further three years.

43. The Hisham Mubarak Center was named after the CHRLA founder, who passed away in 1997.

44. Case 163, judicial year 21, issued June 3, 2000.

45. The SCC ruling also strategically declared the law unconstitutional on procedural grounds rather than substantive grounds in order to avoid a confrontation with the regime. The SCC ruled that the law had not been submitted to the Shura Council for debate, a formal requirement of the constitution, and that it violated the jurisdiction of the administrative courts. The court contended that several aspects of Law 153/1999 interfered with the freedom of association, but the SCC did not rule the law unconstitutional on those grounds. By taking this tack, the ruling was less confrontational but simultaneously loaded with the implicit warning that if the next NGO law contained substantive restrictions on the freedom of association, it too could be ruled unconstitutional. For more on the political context and legal reasoning of the SCC, see Moustafa, "Law Versus the State," 226–34.

46. The forum was held February 10, 2000, Judicial Supervision over Elections in Egypt: A Disregarded Guarantee.

47. Aside from Ibrahim's role in organizing the monitoring of People's Assembly elections, Ibrahim had been pushing the envelope with the regime for some time on a number of sensitive political issues. Ibrahim's Ibn Khaldun Center had held conferences and published reports on the status of religious minorities in Egypt and across the Middle East. Following the death of Hafez al-Asad of Syria and the succession of his son Bashar, Ibrahim published a political essay on "the new Arab monarchies" explicitly addressing the apparent grooming of Hosni Mubarak's son, Gamal, for future succession in Egypt.

48. The case had been raised ten years earlier by Kamal Khaled and Gamal al-Nisharti, both candidates who ran for seats in the People's Assembly elections of 1990, in coordination with opposition parties, which recognized the full importance of constitutional litigation as an avenue to challenge the regime after the dissolution of the People's Assembly in 1987 and 1990.

49. Ayman Nour, Al-Ahram Weekly, August 3–9, 2000.

50. Interview with Saad Eddin Ibrahim, September 25, 2000.

51. These shortcomings prompted activist judges and law professors to publish extensive critiques in opposition newspapers. See the many articles reprinted in Yehya al-Rifa'i, Istaqlal al-quda' wa mehna al-intikhabat (The Independence of the Judiciary and the Ordeal of Elections) (Cairo: Al-Maktab al-Misri al-Hadith, 2000).

52. These figures are in addition to the approximately 2,600 Islamists who were already being held on administrative detention under the emergency law.

53. Moreover, the regime's repression of dissent went far beyond the arrest and detention of Islamist activists operating outside the formal political system. The Political Parties Committee had already issued a decision to freeze the activities of the Islamist-oriented Labor Party, including suspension of the only legal Islamist-oriented newspaper, Al-Sha'b.

54. Interviews with Ibrahim; Negad al-Bora'i, October 22, 2000; Hisham Kassem, March 17, 2000; Hafez Abu Sa'ada, February 22, 2001; Gasser Abdel Razeq, February 17, 2001.

55. Interview with Hafez Abu Sa'ada, secretary general of EOHR, February 22, 2001.

56. The Muslim Brotherhood was so weakened by the beginning of the first round of the elections that it was only able to field 77 candidates nationwide.

57. EOHR Statement 3 on Monitoring the Parliamentary Elections for 2000–2005, 1.

58. Interview with Abdel Aziz Mohamed, February 5, 2001; EOHR Statements 1–4.

59. EOHR Statement 4 on the Third Stage of Parliamentary Elections, 4.

60. Maamoun el-Hodeibi, *Al-Ahram Weekly*, November 16, 2000.

61. The only formal restrictions on presidential appointments of Chief Justice concern age, formal legal training, and experience of candidates.

62. The constitutional provisions for the SCC (Articles 174–178) do not specify the number of justices who will sit on the court. Nor does Law 48/1979, governing the functions of the court, prescribe a set number of justices. The explanatory memorandum of Law 48 states "The law does not specify the number of the members of the court to leave ample room for expansion in accordance with the work requirements that unfold as the court proceeds with its tasks." According to Article 5 of Law 49/1979 governing the SCC, new appointments are made by the president from two candidates, one chosen by the General Assembly of the SCC and the other by the Chief Justice of the SCC. It is unclear whether or not there was resistance to Naguib's recruitment efforts from other SCC justices because the deliberations over new appointments are closed to the public.

63. The government tried to improve its human rights image in the same year by establishing a National Council for Human Rights and abolishing state security courts. However hopeful these reforms might appear on the surface, they represent little progress, if any. The National Council for Human Rights has no formal autonomy from the regime, and its main purpose will likely be to coopt the independent human rights movement. Abolition of the state security courts will have little impact on the regime's ability to control opponents because the government still has the ability to try opponents through the *emergency* state security courts for violations of the emergency laws.

64. On the other hand, the EOHR gained a formal license to operate. This recognition can be revoked at any time if MOSA deems the organization a threat to state security.

Chapter 11. When the Time Is Ripe: The Struggle to Create an Institutional Culture of Human Rights in Morocco

1. "King Hassan Gives Birthday, Youth Day Address," Foreign Broadcast News Service, FBIS-NES-94–134, July 13, 1994.

2. Susan Eileen Waltz, *Human Rights and Reform: Changing the Face of North African Politics* (Berkeley: University of California Press, 1995), 207.

3. Henry Munson, "International Election Monitoring: A Critique Based on One Monitor's Experience in Morocco," *Middle East Report* 209 (Winter 1998): 36.

4. Abdullah Ibrahim was named prime minister in December 1958 after a split within the Istiqlal Party provoked the collapse of a government led by Ahmed Balafrej. Heading the new Union Marocaine des Forces Populaires (UNFP), Ibrahim was nevertheless forced to accept a number of ministerial appointments imposed by the palace. Efforts to bring security forces under direct control of the government led to open conflict with the palace, and ultimately brought an end to Ibrahim's administration. In May 1960, Mohammed V dismissed Ibrahim and his cabinet and assumed direct control of the government. At Mohammed V's death in February 1961 he was directly succeeded, as monarch and as prime minister, by his son Hassan II.

5. Sieglinde Gränzer, "Changing Discourse: Transnational Advocacy Networks in Tunisia and Morocco," in Thomas Risse, Stephen C. Ropp, and Kathryn Sikkink, eds., *The Power of Human Rights: International Norms and Domestic Change* (Cambridge: Cambridge University Press, 1999), 109.

6. Susan Waltz, "Making Waves: The Political Impact of Human Rights Groups in North Africa," *Journal of Modern African Studies* 29 (September 1991): 481.

7. Roudi-Fahimi Farzeneh, "Progress Toward the Millennium Development Goals in the Middle East and North Africa," http://www.prb.org/Template .cfm?Section = PRB&template = /ContentManagement/ContentDisplay.cfm& ContentID = 10265 (16 October 2004).

8. "According to the Ministry of Human Rights, the commission had resolved 4677 cases, in which 3657 claimants were awarded $94.5 million (945 million DH). The commission rejected 885 cases because they did not involve disappearances or arbitrary detention and 133 cases because the claimants did not respond to a summons to appear before the commission or did not supply documentation. Two cases were suspended, and a further 450 were considered to be duplicates." U.S. Department of State, Country Reports on Human Rights, 2003, http://www.state.gov/g/drl/rls/hrrpt/2003/27934.htm (October 152004). See also "Morocco: Human Rights at a Crossroads," Human Rights Watch, http://hrw.org/reports/2004/morocco1004/morocco1004.pdf (October 15, 2004).

9. "Disparus: l'OMDH s'interroge," *Libération* (Maroc), February 17, 1999, "Le Conseil national de l'OMDH réaffirme les conditions d'un règlement juste et équitable des dossiers de violations graves des droits humains," OMDH, June 6, 1999, http://www.omdh.org/webfr/index.htm (October 16, 2004).

10. "Open Letter to My Torturer," by former political prisoner Salah El Ouadie, published in three Moroccan papers in April 1999 and summarized in *Le Monde*, April 22, 1999. In June 1999 the Moroccan newspaper *Le Journal* published a statement entitled "Sans la verité, nous refusons toute indemnisation" from the sister of a well-known political prisoner who died in custody.

11. "Affaire archane contre Al Bayane: qui gagne, perd," *Le Journal* (Maroc), June 19, 1999.

12. Charter of Indemnity Committee, http://www.ccdh.org.ma/rubrique .php3?id_rubrique = 13 (October 16, 2004).

13. "La commission d'arbitrage définit ses règles internes," *Libération*, September 17, 1999.

14. Susan Slyomovics, "A Truth Commission for Morocco," *Middle East Report* 218 (Spring 2001).

15. "Total of 609 Human Rights Cases Settled," Maroc Agence Presse via BBC Worldwide Monitoring, June 22, 2001.

16. Slyomovics, "A Truth Commission for Morocco."

17. Ibid.

18. "Total of 609 Human Rights Cases Settled."

19. Ibid.

20. Slyomovics, "A Truth Commission for Morocco."

21. Ibid.

22. For example, a demonstration organized in Rabat on December 9–10, 2000 to "call for the truth to be told" about grave abuses committed during the reign of Hassan II and to prosecute perpetrators was canceled at the last minute by authorities. Three leading members of the AMDH were arrested. "Au Maroc,

islamistes et militants de droits de l'homme se heurtent à la police," *Le Monde,* December 12, 2001, and "Dispersion d'une manifestation de militant des droits de l'homme à Rabat," Agence France Presse, December 9, 2001.

23. "Déclaration finale, symposium national sur les violations graves des droits humains," joint communiqué of AMDH, OMDH, and Forum Marocain de Vérité et Justice, November 11, 2001.

24. "Liste de personnes présumes impliquées dans des violations des droits humains," AMDH, December 15, 2001.

25. FIDH, www.fidh.org/magmoyen/rapport/2003/ma2011a.pdf (October 16, 2004).

26. "Rights Organization's Annual Report Outlines Progress in Morocco," Financial Times Information via BBC, July 19, 2003.

27. Amnesty International, Annual Report, 2004.

28. "King Mohammed Establishes Justice Commission, Delivers Speech," *Financial Times Information,* January 7, 2004.

29. See Human Rights Watch, "A New Moroccan Commission, But How Much Truth?" June 21, 2004. In October several Moroccan human rights groups collaborated with FIDH to sponsor a roundtable on impunity, http://www.fidh .org/article.php3?id_article = 1954.

30. Laurie A. Brand, *Women, the State, and Political Liberalization: Middle Eastern and North African Experiences* (New York: Columbia University Press, 1998).

31. Abdeslam Maghraoui, "Political Authority in Crisis," *Middle East Report* 218 (Spring 2001).

32. Mounira M. Charrad, *States and Women's Rights: The Making of Postcolonial Tunisia, Algeria, and Morocco* (Berkeley: University of California Press, 2001).

33. Ibid.

34. Brand, *Women, the State, and Political Liberalization.*

35. Union de l'Action Féminine, http://www.uaf.mtds.com (October 2004).

36. Ibid., 70.

37. International Women's Rights Action Watch, Country Report, Morocco, http://iwraw.igc.org/publications/countries/morocco.htm (October 16, 2004).

38. Limits were imposed on polygamy, for example, requiring a husband to inform his second and subsequent wives of his intent to marry and to adhere to a nonpolygamous union if his wife had made that stipulation in the marriage contract. In practice, critics argued, women would have little or no recourse if the law were broken since no enforcement procedures were in place and women typically lacked knowledge of their legal rights. Even the more substantive changes, such as those allowing an orphaned woman to sign her own legal documents, seemed unlikely to affect the lives of many women. See Charrad, *States and Women's Rights*; Brand, *Women, the State, and Political Liberalization*; International Women's Rights Action Watch, Country Report, Morocco.

39. Abdeslam Maghraoui, "Political Authority in Crisis," *Middle East Report* 218 (Spring 2001).

40. "Les femmes comptent sur Mohammed VI pour améliorer leur statut," Agence France Presse, August 24, 1999.

41. "Women Wear Armband to Claim Gender Equality," Panafrican News Agency, March 8, 2001.

42. "Elections: Morocco," UNDP, Programme on Governance in the Arab Region, http://www.pogar.org/countries/elections.asp?cid = 12 (October 16, 2004).

43. Stephanie Willman Bordat and Saida Kouzzi, "The Challenge of Imple-

menting Morocco's New Personal Status Law," *Arab Reform Bulletin* (Carnegie Endowment for International Peace), September 2004, http://www.ceip.org/files/Publications/2004–09–09.asp?from = pubdate#morocco. Also see "Morocco's King Takes a Courageous Step," *Qantara: Dialogue with the Islamic World*, February 2, 2004, http://www.qantara.de/webcom/show_article.php/_c-476/_nr-77/i.html.

44. "List of the major improvements introduced in the new Family Law compared to the current provisions," prepared by the Association Démocratique des Femmes du Maroc, http://www.learningpartnership.org/events/newsalerts/moroccofamlaw.pdf (October 16, 2004).

45. Sinikka Tarvainen, "Morocco Establishes near Equality Between Men and Women," Deutsche Presse-Agentur, January 27, 2004.

46. Amnesty International, Annual Report, 2000; Amnesty International, "'Turning the Page': Achievements and Obstacles," June 1999 and addendum, August 1999.

47. U.S. Department of State, Country Reports on Human Rights, 1999, http://www.state.gov/g/drl/rls/hrrpt/1999/422.htm (October 15, 2004).

48. It was just such a letter that provoked royal displeasure in the first place. In 1974 Yassine had sent an epistle to King Hassan, offering criticism and advice to a "frightened and confused king." See Henry Munson, Jr., *Religion and Power in Morocco* (New Haven, Conn.: Yale University Press, 1993).

49. "Les droits de l'homme seront enseignés dans les écoles," Agence France Presse, February 4, 2001.

50. See "Communiqué de l'OMDH concernant la réorganisation du Conseil Consultatif des Droits de l'Homme," 25 April 2001, http://www.omdh.org/webfr/index.htm (October 16, 2004).

51. "'Diwan Al Madhalim': Administration et défense du citoyen," *Matin du Sahara*, December 14, 2001, i.

52. "Terrorisme: retour en force dans le discours sécuritaire au Maroc," Agence France Presse, May 30, 2003, http://www.africatime.com/maroc/nouvelle.asp?no_nouvelle = 66657 (October 16, 2004).

53. U.S. Department of State, Country Reports on Human Rights, 2000, http://www.state.gov/g/drl/rls/hrrpt/2000/nea/804.htm (October 15, 2004).

54. Amnesty International, Annual Report 1999. Also see "Rapport de l'OMDH relatif aux événements de Lâyoune September and October 1999," http://www.omdh.org/webfr/index.htm (October 16, 2004).

55. U.S. Department of State, Country Reports on Human Rights Practices, section 2b of annual entry on Morocco, http://www.state.gov/g/drl/rls/hrrpt (October 16, 2004).

56. U.S. Department of State, Country Reports on Human Rights Practices, section 2b of annual entry on Morocco, 2001 and 2002. The government banned a meeting of Berbers in Fez in April, as well as the Berber national conference originally scheduled for June 22–24 (see Section 5–2001). In April the authorities prevented, for the second time, a demonstration in support of the Berber rights movement in Kabyle, Algeria—2002.

57. U.S. Department of State, Country Reports on Human Rights Practices, 19.

58. Ibid., 20.

59. Ibid., 27.

60. 2003 World Press Freedom Review, http://www.freemedia.at/wpfr/Mena/morocco.htm (October 16, 2004).

61. See OMDH and FIDH, "Observations and Recommendations on the Report by the Moroccan Government in pursuance of the Convention Against Torture and other Cruel, Inhuman and Degrading Treatment or Punishment," www.fidh.org/magmoyen/rapport/2003/ma2011a.pdf, October 2003: U.S. Department of State, Country Reports on Human Rights, Morocco entries, 1999, 2000, 2001. The AMDH report for 2000 lists 4 deaths in detention but details are not supplied (AMDH, Rapport annuel sur les atteintes aux droits humains au Maroc au cours de 2000).

62. AMDH, Rapport annuel sur les atteintes aux droits humains au Maroc au cours de 2000, 6, http://www.amdh.org.ma/html/archives.htm (October 16, 2004).

63. See U.S. Department of State, Country Reports on Human Rights Practices, Morocco entries 2000, 2001, 2002, 2003.

64. OMDH and FIDH, "Observations et recommandations relatives au rapport gouvernemental du Maroc en vertu de la Convention contre la torture et autres peines ou traitements cruels, inhumains ou dégradants," October 2003, http://www.omdh.org/webfr/index.htm (October 16, 2004).

65. AMDH, Annual Report 2004, http://www.amdh.org.ma/html/O_Comm Adminis.htm (October 16, 2004).

66. Amnesty International, Annual Report, 2004.

67. "Torture in the 'anti-terrorism' campaign—the case of Témara detention centre," Amnesty International, 24 June 2004. The report created quite a stir in Morocco, see press review by French Embassy, http://www.ambafrance-ma.org/presse/index.cfm?phebdo = 1&hb = 80 (October 16, 2004).

68. "Morocco: Bush Should Criticize Backsliding on Rights," Human Rights Watch, 8 July 2004, http://hrw.org/english/docs/2004/07/07/morocc9021 .htm (October 15, 2004).

69. "Morocco/Western Sahara: Pardon of Dozens of Political Prisoners Is Positive Step," Amnesty International, January 7, 2004.

70. "Morocco Drafts Bill Against Torture," *Financial Times Information*, July 23, 2004. Also see http://www.ambafrance-ma.org/presse/index.cfm?phebdo = 1&hb = 83 (October 16, 2004).

71. Waltz, *Human Rights and Reform*, 151–72.

72. Martha Finnemore and Kathryn Sikkink, "International Norm Dynamics and Political Change," *International Organization* 52 (Autumn 1998).

73. Andrew Moravcsik, "The Origins of Human Rights Regimes: Democratic Delegation in Postwar Europe," *International Organization* 54 (Spring 2000): 217–52.

Contributors

LINDSAY BENSTEAD is a doctoral candidate in Political Science and Public Policy at the University of Michigan, Ann Arbor. Her dissertation research focuses on legislatures in the Middle East and North Africa region. She is presently conducting fieldwork in Morocco and Algeria on the effects of constituency service and representative role on public opinion toward democracy and the legislature.

SHEILA CARAPICO, Professor of Political Science and International Studies at the University of Richmond, is the author of *Civil Society in Yemen: A Political Economy of Activism in Modern Arabia* and other studies of Yemeni and Arab politics. She has worked with Human Rights Watch and the Committee for Academic Freedom of the Middle East Studies Association, and serves on the editorial committee of the Middle East Report and Information Project (MERIP).

ANTHONY CHASE teaches at Occidental College in Los Angeles. His research focuses on transnational norms, human rights, international relations theory, and the politics of the Middle-East. Recent publications include "Islam and Democracy;" "The State and Human Rights: Governance and Sustainable Human Development in Yemen;" and "Health, Human Rights, and Islam." He has also worked with the World Health Organization, the United Nations Development Programme, and the Office of the High Commissioner for Human Rights on human rights-based economic development programming.

AMR HAMZAWY is Senior Associate for Middle East Politics at the Carnegie Endowment for International Peace. Previously a Fellow at the Free University of Berlin and Professor at the University of Cairo, he is the author of *Kontinuität und Wandel im zeitgenössischen arabischen Denken* (*Continuity and Change in Contemporary Arab Thought*).

BAHEY EL-DIN HASSAN has served as Director of the Cairo Institute for Human Rights since 1994. He is a Founding Member of the Egyptian

Organization for Human Rights and served as its Secretary General from 1988 to 1993. Prior to that, Mr. Hassan was a journalist with the Egyptian daily, *al-Gomhoreya*. Human Rights Watch honored him with its Human Right Monitor award in 1993. He is also the recipient of the 1987 Annual Journalism Award of the Egyptian Press Syndicate for unique coverage of Lebanon war camps. Mr. Hassan is a lecturer and author on human rights issues and serves on the executive and advisory committees of various international human rights organizations.

NEIL HICKS is Director of International Programs at Human Rights First in New York, where he has worked since 1991. He is a graduate of the School of Oriental Studies of the University of Durham and of the Arabic Language Unit of the American University in Cairo. He worked as a researcher on Egypt for Amnesty International in 1985–1991 and was a Senior Fellow at the United States Institute of Peace 2000–2001 when he carried out the bulk of the research reflected in his chapter.

HANNY MEGALLY is Director for Middle East and North Africa at the International Center for Transitional Justice. He has more than twenty-six years of experience in human rights in the Middle East and North Africa. From 1984 to 1994 he headed the Middle East Research department at the International Secretariat of Amnesty International, based in London. In the four ensuing years, he ran the Ford Foundation social justice program in the Middle East from the Foundation's Cairo office, and from 1997 to 2003 he was the Executive Director of the Middle East and North Africa Division of Human Rights Watch.

VALENTINE M. MOGHADAM joined UNESCO in May 2004 as chief of section in the Social and Human Sciences Sector. She is on leave from Illinois State University, where she is Director of Women's Studies and Professor of Sociology. She is author of *Modernizing Women: Gender and Social Change in the Middle East, Women, Work and Economic Reform in the Middle East and North Africa*, and *Globalizing Women: Transnational Feminist Networks*.

TAMIR MOUSTAFA teaches political science at the University of Wisconsin, Madison. He teaches and writes in the areas of judicial politics and religion and politics of the Middle East. His dissertation, "Law Versus the State: The Expansion of Constitutional Power in Egypt," received best dissertation awards from the American Political Science Association and Western Political Science Association, and honorable mention from the Middle East Studies Association.

NICOLA PRATT is Lecturer in the School of Political, Social and International Studies, University of East Anglia. Her interests are in social movements, democratic transitions and gender politics in the Middle East. She has published on democratization in Egypt and is also author of *Democracy and Authoritarianism in the Arab World.*

EYAD EL SARRAJ is a psychiatrist, founder and Director of the Gaza Community Mental Health Programme, and Secretary General of the Palestinian Independent Commission for Citizens' Rights. He was born in Beer Sheva-Palestine, and was forcibly moved to Gaza-Palestine, in 1948. Winner of the Physicians for Human Rights Award in 1997 and the Martin Ennals Award for human rights defenders in 1998, he publishes extensively on issues of peace, civil society, human rights, and the psychology of violence.

SUSAN WALTZ is Professor of Public Policy at the University of Michigan. She is a specialist in human rights and international affairs and author of *Human Rights and Reform: Changing the Face of North African Politics.* She has recently published a series of articles on the historical origins of international human rights instruments and the political processes that produced them.

Index

Acknowledgments

Thanks to Kyle Ballard and Jessie Evans for administrative and research assistance. Particularly appreciative thanks to the manuscript's anonymous reviewers for their extremely productive suggestions and to Maryam Elahi for her key role in this book..

Anthony Chase dedicates this book to participants in the *Alternative Visions of Human Rights in the Arab World* series at the University of Chicago and *Progressive Islam* symposia at Occidental College for the intellectually vibrant contributions that helped frame this book's substance. It is an inspiration to work with those who put principle before purpose and means before ends. And to Sofia, always.

For a very inspiring two years (2002–2004) Amr Hamzawy dedicates this book to the students of Cairo University in the firm belief that they are reshaping Egypt's future. And to Ela and Luay, meinen Lieben.